Distributed
System
Design

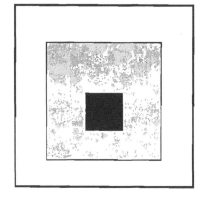

Distributed System Design

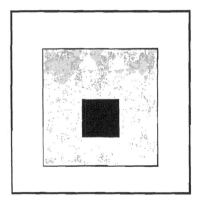

Jie Wu

Department of Computer Science
and Engineering
Florida Atlantic University

CRC Press
Taylor & Francis Group
Boca Raton   London   New York

CRC Press is an imprint of the
Taylor & Francis Group, an informa business

CRC Press
Taylor & Francis Group
6000 Broken Sound Parkway NW, Suite 300
Boca Raton, FL 33487-2742

© 1999 by Taylor & Francis Group, LLC
CRC Press is an imprint of Taylor & Francis Group, an Informa business

First issued in paperback 2019

No claim to original U.S. Government works

ISBN-13: 978-0-367-44777-9 (pbk)
ISBN-13: 978-0-8493-3178-7 (hbk)

Visit the Taylor & Francis Web site at
http://www.taylorandfrancis.com

and the CRC Press Web site at
http://www.crcpress.com

Library of Congress Card Number 98-22214

Library of Congress Cataloging-in-Publication Data

Wu, Jie.
     Distributed system design / Jie Wu.
        p.   cm.
     ISBN 0-8493-3178-1 (alk. paper)
     1. Electronic data processing--Distributed processing. 2. System
design. I. Title.
QA76.9.D5W8 1998
004'.36—dc21
                                                  98-22214
                                                   CIP

To my grandmother

Preface

It is becoming apparent that future requirements for computing speed, system reliability, and cost effectiveness will entail the development of alternative computers to replace the traditional Von Neumann organization. As computing networks come into being, a new dream is now possible – *distributed computing*. Distributed computing brings transparent access to as much computer power and data as the user needs to accomplish any given task, and at the same time, achieves the high performance and reliability objectives. Interest in distributed computing systems has grown rapidly in the last decade. The subject of distributed computing is diverse, and many researchers are investigating various issues concerning the structure of distributed hardware and the design of distributed software so that potential parallelism and fault tolerance can be exploited.

Distributed computing systems (or *distributed systems*) take many forms and cover a variety of system architectures. To some users a distributed system is a collection of multiple processors working closely together to solve a single problem. To other users a distributed system may mean a computer network that is a collection of geographically dispersed, independent processors linked together to allow the sharing of various resources. However, the term distributed systems has been applied to such a wide range of computer systems that its usage has become somewhat devalued. Much of this confusion stems from the lack of distinction between the physical and the logical distribution. By distinguishing the two it is possible to characterize more precisely the properties of a distributed system.

We use the following definition for distributed systems: A distributed system is one that looks to its users like an ordinary system, but runs on a set of autonomous processing elements (PEs) where each PE has a separate physical memory space and the message transmission delay is not negligible. There is close cooperation among these PEs. The system should support an arbitrary number of processes and dynamic extensions of PEs.

Motivation

The main motivations for building a distributed system are

- *Inherently distributed applications.* Distributed systems have come into existence in some very natural ways, e.g., in our society people are distributed and information should also be distributed. In a distributed database system, information is generated at different branch offices (sub-databases) so local access can be done quickly. On the other hand, the system also provides a global view to support various global operations.

- *Performance/cost.* The parallelism of distributed systems reduces processing bottlenecks and provides improved all-around performance, i.e., distributed systems offer a better price-performance ratio.

- *Resource sharing.* Distributed systems can efficiently support information and resource (hardware and software) sharing for users at different locations.

- *Flexibility and extensibility.* Distributed systems are capable of incremental growth and have the added advantage of facilitating modification or extension of a system to adapt to a changing environment without disrupting its operations.

- *Availability and fault tolerance.* With the multiplicity of storage units and processing elements, distributed systems have the potential ability to continue operation in the presence of failures in the system.

- *Scalability.* Distributed systems can be easily scaled to include additional resources (both hardware and software).

Overview and Audience

In this book an attempt is made to present some important issues in the area of distributed systems which address the basic concepts, issues, and some possible solutions. This book is intended as a graduate course in distributed system design. It can also be used for an upper-level undergraduate or graduate course in advanced operating systems. It introduces students to several design aspects that are unique to distributed systems. This book concentrates on the software aspects of design since most of the corresponding hardware aspects are well covered in many textbooks on computer networks and parallel computers.

All the high-level designs and algorithms in this book are expressed using a proposed CSP-like distributed control description language (DCDL). (CSP stands for communicating sequential processes.) Although it is impossible to cover here all the issues related to distributed computing systems, we aim to give basic groundwork on each of the issues covered. Students are encouraged to do more research on these issues through term projects, MS theses, and Ph.D. dissertations. It is assumed that students are familiar with at least one high-level programming language, basic concepts of operating systems and computer architecture and fundamental aspects of discrete mathematics.

Most of the material in the book has been derived from original sources, research papers from contemporary literature, and the author's own research results in this field. The broad scope of distributed processing is reflected in the organization of this book. There are twelve chapters that can be roughly divided into three parts: introduction and foundations (Chapters 1 to 3), various issues in distributed systems (Chapters 4 to 11), and applications (Chapter 12). Some related topics were not included, such as distributed real-time systems and distributed system software. We tried to include just enough material for a one-semester course.

Contents

Chapter 1 introduces some basic concepts, discusses the motivation of distributed computing systems, and presents the scope of distributed computing systems. A brief overview of the book is also provided.

Chapter 2 surveys general distributed programming languages and introduces a CSP-like distributed control description language (DCDL). This language is used to describe several control issues such as expressing parallelism, interprocess communication and synchronization, and fault-tolerant design. A list of commonly used symbols in DCDL appears in the Appendix.

Chapter 3 treats distributed systems in a formal way. Several concepts such as clock, event, and state are introduced as well as two approaches that describe a distributed system: the time-space view and the interleaving view.

Chapter 4 addresses the problem of mutual exclusion which is the key issue for distributed systems design. Mutual exclusion ensures that mutually conflicting concurrent processes can share resources. We also discuss three issues that are related to the mutual exclusion problem: election, bidding, and self-stabilization.

Chapter 5 studies prevention and detection of deadlock in a distributed system. Distributed systems, in general, exhibit a high degree of resource and data sharing; a situation in which deadlocks may happen. This chapter discusses several solutions to deadlock problems that are unique in distributed systems.

Chapter 6 studies efficient interprocessor communication mechanisms that are essential to the performance of distributed systems. Three types of communications: one-to-one (unicast), one-to-many (multicast), and one-to-all (broadcast), as well as their performance, are studied in this chapter.

Chapter 7 covers interprocessor communication mechanisms without specific constraints such as adaptiveness, deadlock-freedom, and fault tolerance. Concepts of virtual channels and virtual networks are introduced to achieve various objectives.

Chapter 8 deals with the reliability issue in distributed systems. An important objective of using distributed systems to achieve high dependability includes reliability, safety, and security. A fundamental issue is to detect and handle faults that might appear in the system. In this chapter we study various methods of handling node, communication, Byzantine, and software faults in a distributed system.

Chapters 9 and 10 include load distribution problems in a distributed system. Load distribution is a resource management component of a distributed system that focuses on judiciously and transparently redistributing the load of the system among the processors such that overall performance of the system is maximized. Chapter 9 studies static load distribution where decisions of load distribution are made by using a priori knowledge of the system and loads cannot be redistributed during the run time. Chapter 10 deals with dynamic load distribution algorithms that use system state information (the loads at nodes), at least in part, to make load distribution decisions.

Chapter 11 describes distributed data management issues. Two specific issues are covered: (1) synchronization of access to shared data while supporting a high degree of concurrency and (2) reliability.

Chapter 12 contains applications of distributed design in operating systems, file systems, shared memory systems, database systems and heterogeneous processing. Possible future research directions are also listed.

The Appendix includes a list of common symbols in DCDL.

Acknowledgments

We consider this book as a continually evolving resource. Readers are encouraged to send suggestions and corrections to the author at his e-mail address: jie@cse.fau.edu.

I am greatly indebted to my mentor Professor Eduardo B. Fernandez for reviewing the early version of this manuscript.

I wish to thank the staff of CRC Press, especially Gerald T. Papke, Suzanne Lassandro, Mimi Williams, and Elena Meyers, for providing professional help at various stages of the book. To Joan Buttery, thanks for proofreading the whole manuscript.

The author is appreciative of the graduate students at the Department of Computer Science and Engineering, Florida Atlantic University who used the manuscript in class in lieu of a finished text.

Finally, I would like to express my appreciation to my wife Ruiguang Zhang, my two daughters, Shela and Stephanie, and my parents, Zengchang Wu and Yeyi Shao for their support and patience during the seemingly endless cycle of writing, typing, drawing, and proofreading this manuscript.

Biography

Jie Wu received a BS degree in computer engineering in 1982, an MS degree in computer science in 1985, both from Shanghai University of Science and Technology, Shanghai, People's Republic of China, and a Ph.D. degree in computer engineering from Florida Atlantic University (FAU), Boca Raton, Florida, in 1989. During 1985-1987 he taught at Shanghai University of Science and Technology. Since August 1989, he has been with the Department of Computer Science and Engineering at FAU where he is a Professor and the director of CSE graduate programs.

Dr. Wu has authored/co-authored over 100 technical papers in various archival journals and conference proceedings including IEEE Transactions on Software Engineering, IEEE Transactions on Computers, IEEE Transactions on Parallel and Distributed Systems, Journal of Parallel and Distributed Computing, The Computer Journal, and Concurrency: Practice and Experience. His research interests are in the area of fault-tolerant computing, parallel/distributed processing, interconnection networks, Petri net applications, and software engineering. He is a recipient of the 1996-97 Researcher of the Year Award at FAU.

Dr. Wu is a member of Upsilon Pi Epsilon and ACM and a senior member of IEEE. He has given lectures and seminars at universities and institutes in Asia, Europe, and North America. Currently, he serves on the editorial board of the International Journal of Computers and Applications. He is also a co-guest-editor of a special issue in IEEE Transactions on Parallel and Distributed Systems on "Challenges in Designing Fault-Tolerant Routing in Networks". Dr. Wu is the conference co-chair of the 12th ISCA International Conference on Parallel and Distributed Computing Systems in 1999. He also served on the program committees of the 1996 and 1998 IEEE International Conference on Distributed Computing Systems.

Contents

Chapter 1

INTRODUCTION

It is becoming apparent that future requirements for computing speed, system reliability, and cost effectiveness will entail the development of alternative computers to replace the traditional Von Neumann organization. As computing networks come into being, a new dream is now possible – *distributed computing*. Distributed computing brings transparent access to as much computer power and data as the user needs to accomplish any given task, and at the same time, achieves high performance and reliability objectives. Interest in distributed computing systems has grown rapidly in the last decade. The subject of distributed computing is diverse and many researchers are investigating various issues concerning the structure of distributed hardware and the design of distributed software so that potential parallelism and fault tolerance can be exploited. We consider in this chapter some basic concepts and issues related to distributed computing and provide a list of the topics covered in this book.

1.1 Motivation

The development of computer technology can be characterized by different approaches to the way computers were used. In the 1950s, computers were serial processors, running one job at a time to completion. These processors were run from a console by an operator and were not accessible to ordinary users. In the 1960s, jobs with similar needs were batched together and run through the computer as a group to reduce the computer idle time. Other techniques were also introduced such as off-line processing by using buffering, spooling and multiprogramming. The 1970s saw the introduction of time-sharing, both as a means of improving utilization, and as a method to bring the user closer to the computer. Time-sharing was the first step toward distributed systems: users could share resources and access them at different locations. The 1980s were the decade of personal computing: people had their own dedicated machine. The 1990s are the decade of distributed systems due to the excellent price/performance ratio offered by microprocessor-based systems and the steady improvements in networking technologies.

Distributed systems can take different physical formations: a group of personal computers (PCs) connected through a communication network, a set of workstations with not only shared file and database systems but also shared CPU cycles (still in most cases a local process has a higher priority than a remote process, where a process is a program in running), a processor pool where terminals are not attached to any processor and all resources are truly shared without distinguishing local and remote processes.

Distributed systems are *seamless*; that is, the interfaces among functional units on the network are for the most part invisible to the user, and the idea of distributed computing has been applied to database systems [16], [38], [49], file systems [4], [24], [33], [43], [54], operating systems [2], [39], [46], and general environments [19], [32], [35].

Another way of expressing the same idea is to say that the user views the system as a *virtual uniprocessor* not as a collection of distinct processors. The main motivations in moving to a distributed system are the following:

- *Inherently distributed applications.* Distributed systems have come into existence in some very natural ways, e.g., in our society people are distributed and information should also be distributed. Distributed database system information is generated at different branch offices (sub-databases), so that a local access can be done quickly. The system also provides a global view to support various global operations.

- *Performance/cost.* The parallelism of distributed systems reduces processing bottlenecks and provides improved all-around performance, i.e., distributed systems offer a better price/performance ratio.

- *Resource sharing.* Distributed systems can efficiently support information and resource (hardware and software) sharing for users at different locations.

- *Flexibility and extensibility.* Distributed systems are capable of incremental growth and have the added advantage of facilitating modification or extension of a system to adapt to a changing environment without disrupting its operations.

- *Availability and fault tolerance.* With the multiplicity of storage units and processing elements, distributed systems have the potential ability to continue operation in the presence of failures in the system.

- *Scalability.* Distributed systems can be easily scaled to include additional resources (both hardware and software).

LeLann [23] discussed aims and objectives of distributed systems and noted some of its distinctive characteristics by distinguishing between the physical and the logical distribution. Extensibility, increased availability and better resource sharing are considered the most important objectives.

There are two main stimuli for the current interest in distributed systems [5], [22]: *technological change* and *user needs.* Technological changes are in two areas: advancements in micro-electronic technology generated fast and inexpensive processors and advancements in communication technology resulted in the availability of highly efficient computer networks.

Long haul, relatively slow communication paths between computers have existed for a long time, but only recently has the technology for fast, inexpensive and reliable *local area networks* (LANs) emerged. These LANs typically run at 10-100 mbps (megabits per second). In response, the *metropolitan area networks* (MANs) and *wide area networks* (WANs) are becoming faster and more reliable. Normally, LANs span areas with diameters not more than a few kilometers, MANs cover areas with diameters up to a few dozen kilometers, and WANs extend with worldwide extent. Recently the *asynchronous transfer mode* (ATM) has been considered as the emerging technology for the future and it can provide data transmission rates up to 1.2 gbps (gigabits per second) for both LANs and WANs.

Among user needs, many enterprises are cooperative in nature, e.g., offices, multinational companies, university computing centers, etc., that require sharing of resources and information.

1.2 Basic Computer Organizations

The Von Neumann organization of a computer consists of CPU, memory unit, and I/O. The CPU is the brain of the computer. It executes programs stored in memory by fetching instructions, examining them, and then executing them one after another. The memory unit stores instruc-

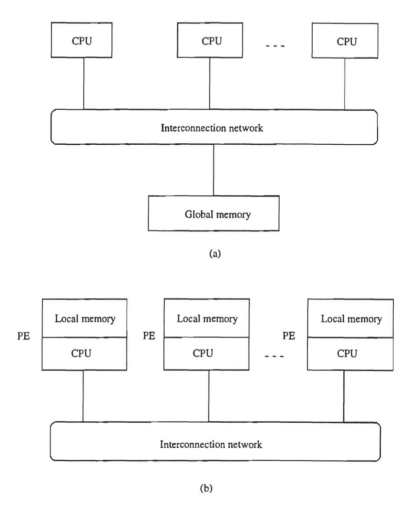

(a)

(b)

FIGURE 1.1
Two basic computer structures: (a) physically shared memory
structure and (b) physically distributed memory structure.

	Logically shared	Logically distributed
Physically shared	Shared memory	Simulated message passing
Physically distributed	Distributed shared memory	Message passing

FIGURE 1.2
Physically versus logically shared/distributed memory.

tions (a sequence of instructions is called a program) and data. I/O gets instructions and data into and out of processors.

If CPU and memory unit can be replicated, two basic computer organizations are:

(a) Physically shared memory structure (Figure 1.1 (a)) has a single memory address space shared by all the CPUs. Such a system is also called a *tightly coupled system.* In a physically shared memory system, communication between CPUs takes place through the shared memory using read and write operations.

(b) Physically distributed memory structure (Figure 1.1 (b)) does not have shared memory and each CPU has its attached local memory. The CPU and local memory pair is called processing element (PE) or simply processor. Such a system is sometimes referred to as a *loosely coupled system.* In a physically distributed memory system, communications between the processors are done by passing messages across the interconnection network through a send command at the sending processor and a receive command at the receiving processor.

In Figure 1.1, the interconnection network is used to connect different units of the system and to support movements of data and instructions. The I/O unit is not shown, but it is by no means less important.

However, the choice of a communication model does not have to be tied to the physical system. A distinction can be made between the *physical sharing* presented by the hardware (Figure 1.1) and the *logical sharing* presented by the programming model. Figure 1.2 shows four possible combinations of sharing.

The box in Figure 1.2 labeled *shared memory* represents uniprocessor concurrent programming and shared memory multiprocessor programming based on the shared-memory model. Synchronization between processes is needed to ensure that shared data are accessed consistently. Programming constructs that provide synchronization between concurrently executing processes include semaphores [12], monitors [17], critical sections [11], and barriers [20]. The box labeled *message passing* represents distributed memory systems in which communication is by message passing. Commands that explicitly send and receive messages are often used. *Simulated message passing* can be used to provide a logically distributed programming model on a physically shared memory architecture. Messages are passed via shared memory buffers. The box in Figure 1.2 labeled *distributed shared memory* (DSM) is also called shared virtual memory or distributed memory system. This model tries to capture the ease of programming shared memory systems in a distributed memory environment by making the distributed memory system appear to the programmers as if it were the shared memory system.

1.3   Definition of a Distributed System

When discussing distributed systems we encounter a number of different types identified by such adjectives as: *distributed, network, parallel, concurrent,* and *decentralized.* Distributed processing is a relatively new field and there is, as yet, no agreed definition. In contrast with sequential computations, parallel, concurrent, and distributed computations involve the coordinated, collective actions of multiple processing elements. These terms overlap in scope and are sometimes used interchangeably. In [44], Seitz gave a definition for each to distinguish differences in meaning:

- *Parallel* means lockstep actions on a data set from a single thread of control. At the parallel computer level a single-instruction, multiple-data (SIMD) computer is an example which uses multiple data-handling elements to perform the same or similar operations on many data items at once.

- *Concurrent* means that certain actions can be performed in any order. For example, partial independence of operations at higher levels and multiple-instruction, multiple-data (MIMD) parallel computers.

- *Distributed* means that the cost or performance of a computation is governed by the communication of data and control.

A system is *centralized* if its components are restricted to one site, *decentralized* if its components are at different sites with no or limited or close coordination. When a decentralized system has no or limited coordination, it is called *networked*; otherwise, it is termed *distributed* indicating a close coordination among components at different sites. Among models that give specific definitions of a distributed system, Enslow [13] proposed that distributed systems can be examined using these three dimensions of hardware, control, and data.

Distributed system = distributed hardware + distributed control + distributed data

Enslow's definition also requires that resource distribution be transparent to the users. A form adapted from the Enslow's model [13] is given in Figure 1.3, where a system can be classified as a distributed system if all three categories (hardware, control, and data) reach a certain degree of decentralization. Several points in the dimension of hardware organization are as follows:

H1. A single CPU with one control unit.

H2. A single CPU with multiple ALUs (arithmetic and logic units). There is only one control unit.

H3. Separate specialized functional units, such as one CPU with one floating-point coprocessor.

H4. Multiprocessors with multiple CPUs but only one single I/O system and one global memory.

H5. Multicomputers with multiple CPUs, multiple I/O systems and local memories.

Similarly, points in the control dimension in order of increasing decentralization are the following:

C1. Single fixed control point. Note that physically the system may or may not have multiple CPUs.

C2. Single dynamic control point. In multiple CPU cases the controller changes from time to time among CPUs.

C3. A fixed master/slave structure. For example, in a system with one CPU and one coprocessor, the CPU is a fixed master and the coprocessor is a fixed slave.

C4. A dynamic master/slave structure. The role of master/slave is modifiable by software.

C5. Multiple homogeneous control points where copies of the same controller are used.

C6. Multiple heterogeneous control points where different controllers are used.

The database has two components that can be distributed: files and a directory that keeps track of these files. Distribution can be done in one of two ways, or a combination of both: *replication* and *partition*. A database is replicated if there are several copies of the database assigned to different locations. A database is partitioned if it is split into sub-databases and then each sub-database is assigned to different sites. The points in this dimension include:

D1. Centralized databases with a single copy of both files and directory.

D2. Distributed files with a single centralized directory and no local directory.

D3. Replicated database with a copy of files and a directory at each site.

D4. Partitioned database with a master that keeps a complete duplicate copy of all files.

D5. Partitioned database with a master that keeps only a complete directory.

D6. Partitioned database with no master file or directory.

Schroeder [34], instead, gave a list of *symptoms* of a distributed system. If a system has all these symptoms listed below, it is probably a distributed system.

1. Multiple processing elements (PEs).

2. Interconnection hardware.

3. PEs fail independently.

4. Shared states.

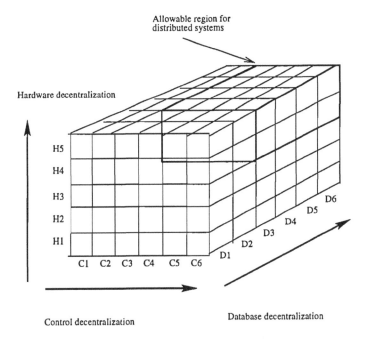

FIGURE 1.3
Enslow's model of distributed systems.

Some researchers also considered computer networks and parallel computers as part of distributed systems [9], [21], [48], [55]. A classification of computer networks and a classification of parallel computers are shown in Figures 1.4 and 1.5, respectively. Among non Von Neumann models, the data flow model is based on *greedy evaluation* where a function (program) is performed as soon as its input data become available. The reduction model is based on *lazy evaluation* where an evaluation is performed only when the result of the function is needed. Most parallel computers are built on the Von Neumann model. Flynn's classification is the most widely used model to classify systems within the Von Neumann model. Flynn's taxonomy is based on the multiplicity of instruction streams and data streams:

- *Single Instruction Single Data* (SISD). This is the classical uniprocessor architecture. It may include parallel mechanisms, e.g., pipelining, overlapped CPU and I/O operations.

- *Single Instruction Multiple Data* (SIMD). Each processor executes the same instruction simultaneously on its own different set of data.

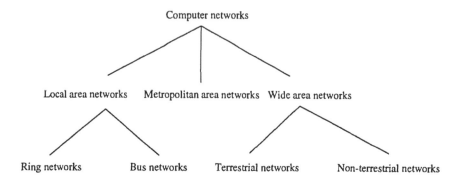

FIGURE 1.4
A classification of computer networks.

Typically, multiple PEs are supervised by a common control unit.

- *Multiple Instruction Single Data* (MISD). This organization involves several processors, each of which is controlled by a separate control unit.

- *Multiple Instruction Multiple Data* (MIMD). Several processors simultaneously execute different instructions on diverse data. Most physical structures of distributed systems belong in this category.

The classifications shown in Figures 1.4 and 1.5 encompass almost all the important types of architectures that have been discussed in the technical literature. The connectivity differentiation category includes different types of interconnection topologies and it will be discussed in detail in the section on interconnection networks. However, several fundamental design choices are not covered in these classifications.

1. Fine-grain vs. coarse-grain parallelism.

2. Shared memory vs. message-passing communications.

3. General-purpose vs. special-purpose systems.

4. Global vs. local memories.

5. Centralized vs. distributed global system control.

6. Uniform vs. nonuniform access.

7. Direct vs. indirect connections.

A *fine-grain parallelism* is a form of parallel execution in which the amount of computational work per process is small compared to the amount of work per process required for communication and overhead. In *coarse-grain parallelism* the amount of computation per process is several times larger than the overhead and communication expended per process.

A *general-purpose system* is the one that is used for general applications; otherwise, it is called a *special-purpose system*. MIMD is a general-purpose system. SIMD is particularly suitable for numerical computation where the same type of operations perform on a large data set.

Global memories are directly accessible from any processor and *local memories* are only visible from associated processors. Typically, global and local memories are combined together with cache memories to form a high-speed memory with low latency.

In a *shared memory system* exchanging information by reading and/or writing shared memory is a natural way to communicate. In a *message-passing system* memory is distributed and sending and receiving message is natural.

In *uniform memory access systems* all memory locations are equally far from all processors; that is, the access time of any memory location from any processor is nearly constant. However, this structure does not scale well. Typically, a shared bus is used to connect processors to shared memory. As the number of processors grows the shared bus becomes a bottleneck. To reduce memory latency and bus contention, the processors can be equipped with a cache. However, the use of caches introduces a new problem: the consistency problem. *Nonuniform memory access systems* solve the scalability problem by providing each processor with local memory and a connection to a scalable interconnection network through which the memory of other processors can be accessed. Memory access times are nonuniform depending on the location of data.

An interconnection network is a set of communication links, buses, or switches that connect together the processors in a parallel/distributed system. In direct connections, processors are directly connected through a set of point-to-point links. In indirect connections, processors are connected through switches. Normally, indirect connection can be dynamically changed by proper switch signals.

For detailed treatment of computer networks and parallel computers the readers may refer to many existing textbooks in these two areas.

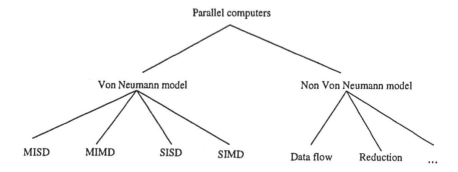

FIGURE 1.5
A classification of parallel computers.

1.4 Our Model

We use the following definition for distributed systems:

A distributed system is one that looks like an ordinary system to its users, but runs on a set of autonomous processing elements (PEs) where each PE has a separate physical memory space and the message transmission delay is not negligible. There is close cooperation among these PEs. The system should support an arbitrary number of processes and dynamic extensions of PEs.

Figure 1.6 shows such a system from the physical and logical point of view. The following are the *attributes* required of a distributed system:

1. *Arbitrary number of processes.* Each process is also called a logical resource.

2. *Arbitrary number of PEs.* Each PE is also called a physical resource.

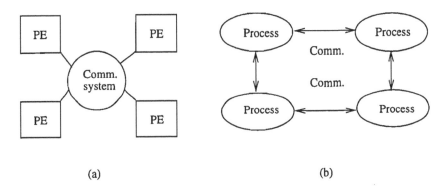

FIGURE 1.6
System structure from the physical (a) or logical point of view (b).

3. *Communication by message passing.* This provides for the transfer of messages in a cooperative rather than the master/slave manner.

4. *Cooperative processes.* The interactions among processes are in a cooperative manner, or processes are used to solve a common application rather than several independent applications.

5. *Communication delay.* The communication delay between two PEs is not negligible.

A distributed system should also have the following properties:

1. *Resource failure independence.* The failure of no single resource either logical or physical should bring the whole system down.

2. *Graceful degradation.* The system should provide means to reconfigure the system topology or resource allocation in the presence of resource failures.

Based on the above definition, computer networks (LANs, MANs and WANs) are not considered distributed systems. This is because processes at different locations (or sites) do not work cooperatively. A physically shared memory multiprocessor is not a distributed system since there is no failure independence. Distributed shared memory (DSM) is a logically shared memory system; however, it has the property of resource failure independence and can support graceful degradation. DSM systems are normally treated as special distributed systems. Tanenbaum [51] showed several major characteristics of three different systems: computer networks, distributed systems, and multiprocessors. These characteristics include support for a virtual uniprocessor, the type and number of copies of operating systems, the number of run queues, and file sharing semantics among others. Normally a network system does not support a virtual uniprocessor while both distributed and multiprocessor systems do. Network systems support multiple operating systems while both distributed and multiprocessor operating systems use one operating system. The difference is that one copy of the operating system is used in a multiprocessor system while multiple copies of the same operating system is used in a distributed system. Both distributed and network systems have multiple run queues while there is a single queue in a multiprocessor system. Usually, file sharing is well-defined in both multiprocessor and distributed systems.

In order to have a better comprehension of the difference between a network and a distributed system, let us consider a system of several PEs (each PE is a CPU with local memory) connected through a communication network. Assume there are terminals that are connected to the PEs. Each terminal may or may not directly connect to a distinct PE. In one configuration each terminal is attached to a PE to form a personal computer (PC). Each PC works independently and the network is used only to exchange certain information such as email. Therefore, this model corresponds to a network system. One variation of this formation is that the PEs have a shared file/database system. However, as long as each PE is doing its independent work and the CPU cycles are not shared, it is still treated as a distributed system. In such a system there is normally a dedicated server to provide various serves, and hence, it is sometimes referred to as the *client/server model*.

In a pure distributed system there is a set of coordinating processes (used to solve one simple problem) executed at different PEs. The users may or may not know the locations of these processes. In the *workstation model* normally the users are aware of the locations of processes by classifying them as local and remote processes. Process migration is supported to share CPU cycles among different PEs. In the *processor-pool model* the users are not aware of the locations of processes. The PEs in the pool have no terminals attached directly to them. The DSM model is a special processor-pool model. We concentrate here on the aspects of distributed control that can be either hardware or software control. Emphasis will be on methods using software control. Note that topics covered here overlap with ones in distributed operating systems.

1.5   Interconnection Networks

Distributed control algorithms can also be divided into network-indepen-dent and network-dependent. *Network-independent algorithms* are general purpose but may not be efficient for specific networks. *Network-dependent algorithms* are designed for specific networks. These algorithms normally are efficient to take advantage of topological properties of the specific net-work.

Figure 1.7 [14] provides a classification of interconnection networks. The topology of an interconnection network can be either static or dynamic. *Static networks* are formed by point-to-point direct connections that are fixed. *Dynamic networks* are implemented with switches which can be dynamically configured to match the communication demand in user pro-grams.

There are three topological classes in the dynamic category: single-stage, multistage, and crossbar (see Figure 1.8). Normally, processors are placed at two sides of a network. A *single-stage network* is composed of a stage of switching elements. Each switching element is a 2×2 switch with two inputs and two outputs, and the input and output connections can be ei-ther *straight* or *crossover* controlled by a Boolean variable. Figure 1.8 (a) shows an example with a perfect-shuffle connection. A *multistage network* consists of more than one stage of switching elements and normally sup-ports connections from an arbitrary input processor to an arbitrary output processor. In some networks simultaneous connections of input and out-put processors may result in conflicts in the use of network communication links. Such networks are called *blocking networks* (see the *baseline* network shown in Figure 1.8 (c)); otherwise, they are called *rearrangeable nonblock-ing networks* (see the *Benes* network shown in Figure 1.8 (d)). In a crossbar switch every input can be connected to a free output without blocking (see Figure 1.8 (b)).

Topologies in the static category can be further classified according to dimensions required for the network layout, e.g., one-dimensional, two-dimensional, and n-dimensional (see Figure 1.9). For a detailed study of interconnection networks see [42] and [56].

Throughout this book we focus on distributed control algorithms de-signed for systems that use static interconnection networks. In general, a static interconnection network is represented by a graph $G = (V, E)$ where V and E are sets of vertices and edges, respectively. Each vertex repre-

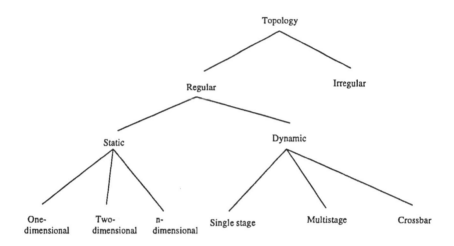

FIGURE 1.7
A classification of interconnection networks.

sents a processor (or node) and each edge a communication link. Recently
some researchers used a vertex to represent a link and a edge to represent
a processor to model an optical network [31], and a *hypergraph* model [57]
is used as a generalization of the traditional graph model. The following
are representative static networks:

- *Completely connected network.* Each processor is directly connected
  to all the other processors in the system (see Figure 1.9 (g)).

- *Linear array and ring.* In a linear array, processors (see Figure 1.9
  (a)) are arranged in a line and adjacent nodes are connected. Interior
  processors thus have two connections and boundary nodes have one.
  If two boundary nodes are connected, then the network forms a ring
  (see Figure 1.9 (b)).

- *Mesh and Torus.* A k-ary n-dimensional (n-d) mesh with $N = k^n$
  nodes has an interior node degree of $2n$ and the network diameter is
  $k(n-1)$. Each node has an address $(u_n, u_{n-1}, ..., u_1)$, where $1 \leq u_i \leq$
  k. Two nodes $(u_n, u_{n-1}, ..., u_1)$ and $(v_n, v_{n-1}, ..., v_1)$ are connected if
  their addresses differ in one and only one element (dimension), say
  dimension i; moreover, $|u_i - v_i| = 1$. Basically, nodes along each
  dimension are connected as a linear array. If the nodes along each
  dimension are connected as a ring, then the network forms an n-
  dimensional torus. 2-d and 3-d meshes are the most popular ones and

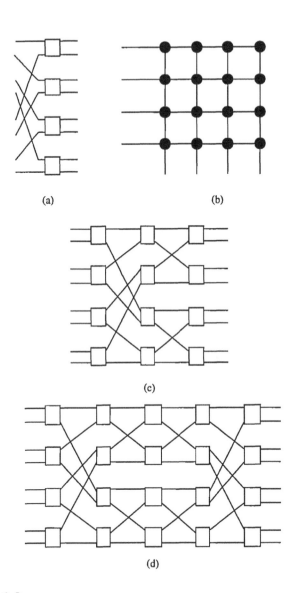

FIGURE 1.8
Examples of dynamic interconnection networks: (a) 8×8 shuffle-exchange, (b) 4×4 crossbar, (c) 8×8 baseline, and (d) 8×8 Benes.

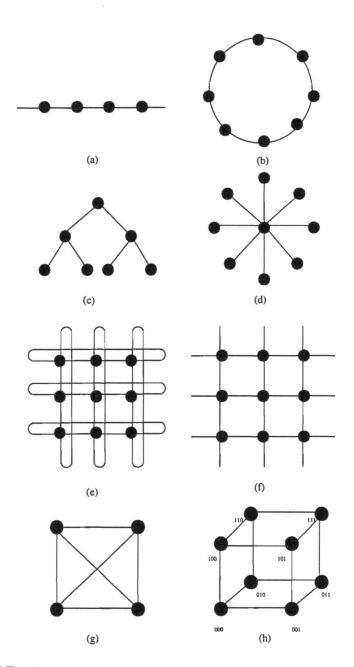

FIGURE 1.9
Examples of static interconnection networks: (a) linear array, (b) ring, (c) binary tree, (d) star, (e) 2-d torus, (f) 2-d mesh, (g) completely connected, and (h) 3-cube.

many parallel computers are built based on them. Tori are meshes with wrap-around connections. Figures 1.9 (e) and (f) show a 2-d torus and a 2-d mesh, respectively.

- *Tree and star.* A graph in which there is a unique path between every pair of vertices is a tree. Nodes in a tree can be arranged in levels. In a binary tree (see Figure 1.9 (c)), interior nodes have degree 3 with two children and one parent, root have degree 2 and leaves have degree 1. A star (see Figure 1.9 (d)) is a two-level tree with a high node degree.

- *Hypercube.* An n-dimensional hypercube (n-cube) consists of $N = 2^n$ nodes with a node degree of n and a diameter of n. Each node has a n-bit binary address. Two nodes are connected if and only if their addresses differ in exactly one bit position. Binary hypercube were very popular both in research and development in the 1980s. The node degree and the network diameter of an n-cube are both n. In fact, the node degree increases linearly with respect to the dimension, making it difficult to consider the hypercube a scalable architecture. With poor scalability and difficulty in packaging higher-dimensional hypercubes, the hypercube architecture is gradually being replaced by other architectures. However, algorithms designed on hypercubes fall in between network-independent and network-dependent algorithms. Research on hypercube algorithms is still important to bridge the gap between the network-independent design using PRAM (parallel random access machine) and the network-dependent design using the network model. Figure 1.9 (h) shows a 3-cube.

To select an interconnection network, the following measurements are normally used.

- *Node degree.* The number of edges incident on a node.

- *Diameter.* The maximum shortest path between any two nodes.

- *Bisection width.* The minimum number of edges along a cut which divides a given network into equal halves.

There are many other measures such as *the number of links* and *narrowness* which measures congestion in a network. So far there is no standard set of criteria. The selection is mainly based on the given application and objective. In [27] a set of network parameters are listed that define and shape

interconnection networks: network use, routing control, switching methodology, hardware implementation, and number of pins per chip. However,
the authors argue that scientifically determining the best topology is as
difficult as saying that one animal is better than another.

1.6   Applications and Standards

Distributed systems are used for many different types of applications.
We list below some applications where the use of a distributed system may
be favored over other architectures such as uniprocessors or shared memory
multiprocessors.

1. *Parallel and high-performance applications.* In principle, parallel applications can be run just as well on shared memory multiprocessors; however, shared memory systems do not scale well to include
   large numbers of processors. HPCC (high performance computing
   and communication) applications [15] normally need a scalable design that depends on distributed processing.

2. *Fault-tolerant applications.* Distributed systems are potentially more
   reliable because the PEs are autonomous; a failure in one unit or
   resource (software or hardware) does not affect the correct functioning
   of other resources.

3. *Inherently distributed applications.* Many applications are inherently
   distributed. These applications are *burst mode* rather than *bulk mode.*
   Examples include transaction processing and Internet *applet.* The
   performance of these applications scales on *throughput* (transaction
   response time or number of transactions per second) instead of elapsed
   execution time as normally used in multiprocessors [25].

One particular use of distributed systems by a group of users is called
computer-supported cooperative working (CSCW) or *groupware*, which supports the users to work cooperatively. Another application is *distributed
conferencing* where electronic meetings take place through a physically distributed network. Also, *multimedia tele-learning* is a similar application.

With a wide variety of applications that are available in different platforms: PCs, workstations, LANs, and WANs, users expect to be able to

reach beyond the limits of their own PC to access a wider range of features, functionality and performance. *Interoperability* among different networks and environments (including distributed system environments) becomes more and more important. To achieve interoperability users need a standard distributed computing environment in which all systems and resources are widely and readily available.

DCE (distributed computing environment) [37] is an OSF (open system foundation) developed industry-standard set of distributed computing technologies. It provides security services to protect and control access to data, name services that make it easy to find distributed resources, and a highly scalable model for organizing widely scattered users, services, and data. DCE runs on all major computing platforms and is designed to support distributed applications in heterogeneous hardware and software environments. DCE consists of a set of technologies, integrated by OSF. These technologies include the following:

1. Threads package.

2. Remote procedure call (RPC).

3. Distributed time service.

4. Name service.

5. Security service.

6. Distributed service.

DCE has been implemented by several vendors, including TRANSVARL, which was a member of the original multi-vendor team whose proposal serves as the basis for the DCE architecture. A guide to developing distributed applications using DCE can be found in [28]. Systems with standard interfaces and protocols are also called *open systems*. In [6], a detailed treatment on distributed open systems is given.

Some other standards are based on a particular model, such as CORBA (common object request broker architecture) [36] which is a standard developed by the OMG (object management group), a consortium of multiple computer vendors. CORBA uses the object-oriented model to implement transparent service requests in a distributed system. Industries have their own standards such as Microsoft's Distributed Component Object Model (DCOM) and Sun Microsystems' JavaBeans.

1.7 Scope

Just as there is no agreed definition for distributed systems, no consensus has been reached among researchers with respect to a set of fundamental problems of distributed systems. Distributed system research issues range from theoretical to practical. Stankovic [48] proposed the following set of important issues:

1. *Theoretical foundations.* Unlike sequential processing systems, distributed systems lack adequate models to address questions of limits of computability and the complexity of computation. This is mainly due to the nondeterministic nature of distributed processing.

2. *Reliability.* Although reliability is one of the main design goals of building a distributed system, it is by no means a easy task. One challenge is that when a message, a remote operation, a file, or a database transaction is committed, we should ensure the message (or file) will arrive at its destination without error and in a timely manner.

3. *Privacy and security.* In a distributed system there is a need to protect data in transit. One simple way to keep privacy and ensure security is to keep data in an exclusive place; however, it violates the objective of information sharing in the distributed system. It is still an open problem to keep a good balance between privacy and access to information. A solution to this may well require both technical and legal means.

4. *Design tools and methodology.* The specification, design, and implementation of a distributed system is a difficult process. There are still insufficient tools. This is mainly because of the complex nature of a distributed system that makes the specification and debugging process extremely difficult. The nondeterministic computation of a distributed process also makes it difficult to predict performance prior to implementation.

5. *Distribution and sharing.* To exploit fully efficient distribution and sharing of resources, we need to study mechanisms for decomposing problems, replicating resources, and distributing workload across the whole system. The challenge is to automate this process. The system built based on replicated resources should generate a good performance result and an enhanced system reliability.

6. *Accessing resources and services.* The simple access of resources in the distributed system is a critical component of the success of the system. With the wide use of the Internet more and more people can access different sites from their home and offices. Currently, the *pull* model is widely used in which information is obtained through a query request by typing certain keywords from a terminal. The *push* model is a promising approach that resembles a broadcasting radio station. Normally, an *intelligent agent* can sort through information on behalf of each user.

7. *User environment.* One design goal is to present the user the abstraction of a *virtual uniprocessor* to hide a complexity of distributed resources. A user friendly, graphics-based, multi-window environment will allow the user to participate in a multi-person interaction. It is still an open problem to provide the right degree of transparency.

8. *Distributed databases.* Distributed databases are special distributed systems that deserve special attention. Many future applications, such as electronic commerce and digital libraries, are based on distributed databases. Some unique research issues include data models, heterogeneous databases, distributed query processing, and multimedia databases.

9. *Network research.* So far, networks have provided transport. Tomorrow's infrastructure will have to provide not only connectivity but also information services as well.

Among other researches, Kleinrock [21] gave several underlying principles of distributed systems behavior. In this book, instead of presenting an overview of the entire field of distributed systems, we treat several areas in depth:

1. *Distributed Programming Languages:*
   Basic structures

2. *Theoretical Foundations:*
   Global state and event ordering
   Logical and physical clocks

3. *Distributed Operating Systems:*
   Mutual exclusion and election
   Detection and resolution of deadlock
   Self-stabilization
   Task scheduling and load balancing

4. *Distributed Communication*:
   One-to-one communication
   Collective communication

5. *Reliability*:
   Agreement
   Error recovery
   Reliable communication

6. *Distributed Data Management:*
   Consistency of duplicated data
   Distributed concurrency control

7. *Applications:*
   Distributed operating systems
   Distributed file systems
   Distributed database systems
   Distributed shared memory
   Heterogeneous processing

The above is not by any means an exhaustive list of the relevant issues of distributed control design; it is just a representative subset of the areas of research today.

1.8   Source of References

There are many journals and conferences related to distributed system design. At least two journals are dedicated to distributed system design: *Distributed Computing* and *Distributed Systems Engineering*. Many articles related to distributed computing can be found in *IEEE Transactions on Parallel and Distributed Systems* and *Journal of Parallel and Distributed Computing*.

Some articles occasionally appear in *ACM SIGOPS Operating Systems Review, ACM Computing Surveys, ACM SIGPLAN Notices, ACM Transactions on Computer Systems, ACM Transactions on Programming Languages and Systems, The Computer Journal, Computer Systems Science and Engineering, IEEE Transactions on Computers, IEEE Transactions on Software Engineering, Information Processing Letters, Parallel Processing Letters, Journal of Computer and System Sciences, International Journal of Parallel Programming, Journal of the ACM, Journal of System Architecture, Parallel Computing, Concurrency: Practice and Experience, Science of Computer Programming, SIAM Journal on Computing, Real-Time Systems, Software: Practice and Experience,* and *Theoretical Computer Science.*

Many general and less theoretical articles appear in *IEEE Concurrency* (formerly *IEEE Parallel & Distributed Technology*) although most articles in this magazine are about parallel technology. Some magazines also publish related articles; they are: *Communications of the ACM* and *IEEE Computers.*

There are four main conferences on distributed computing: *IEEE International Conference on Distributed Computing Systems, Annual ACM Symposium on Principles of Distributed Computing, Annual ACM Symposium on Parallel Algorithms and Architectures,* and *International Workshops on Distributed Algorithms.* There are many other related conferences that carry papers on distributed computing, such as the *Annual Symposium on Theory of Computing* and the *Annual Symposium on Computer Science.*

Most textbooks in this area are related to either distributed operating systems or distributed algorithms. Among books on distributed algorithms, the ones by Barbosa [3], Lynch [29], Raynal [40], Raynal and Helary [41], Tel [52], and Tel [53] cover distributed algorithms for a wide range of problems. There are several excellent textbooks on distributed operating systems, including the ones by Chow and Johnson [8], Singhal and Shivaratri [45], Sinha [47], and Tanenbaum [51]. In [34], edited by Mullender, there is a good collection of articles on various issues of distributed system design. In the book entitled *Readings in Distributed Computing Systems* [7], Casavant and Singhal collected 24 survey type of articles on distributed systems. Some textbooks deal with issues in both distributed systems and network systems, such as the one by Coulouris and Dollimore [10]. There are several tutorial books on distributed systems [1], [26], [30], but most of them are out of date; however, some classical papers in this area are included. There are numerous textbooks and tutorial books on special topics of distributed systems.

A list of pointers to on-line bibliographies on different subjects of distributed system design can be found in [47].

References

[1] Ananda, A. L. and B. Srinivasan, *Distributed Computing Systems: Concepts and Structures*, IEEE Computer Society Press, 1991.

[2] Andrews, G. R., R. D. Schlichting, R. Hayes, and T. D. M. Purdin, "The design of the Saguaro distributed operating system", *IEEE Transactions on Software Engineering*, **13**, 1, Jan. 1987, 104-118.

[3] Barbosa, V. C., *An Introduction to Distributed Algorithms*, The MIT Press, 1996.

[4] Birrell, A. D. and R. M. Needham, "A universal file server", *IEEE Transactions on Software Engineering*, **6**, 9, Sept. 1980, 450-453.

[5] Bowen, J. P. and T. J. Gleeson, "Distributed operating systems", in *Distributed Computer Systems*, H. S. M. Zedan, ed., Butterworths, 1990.

[6] Brazier, F. M. T. and D. Johansen, *Distributed Open Systems*, IEEE Computer Society Press, 1994.

[7] Casavant T. L. and M. Singhal, *Readings in Distributed Computing Systems*, IEEE Computer Society Press, 1994.

[8] Chow, R. and T. Johnson, *Distributed Operating Systems and Algorithms*, Addison-Wesley Publishing Company, 1997.

[9] Conte, G. and D. D. Corso, *Multi-microprocessor Systems for Real-Time Applications*, D. Reidel Publishing Company, 1985.

[10] Coulouris, G. F. and J. Dollimore, *Distributed Systems: Concepts and Design*, Addison-Wesley Publishing Company, 1988.

[11] Dijkstra, E. W., "Solution of a problem in concurrent programming control", *Communications of the ACM*, **8**, 9, Sept. 1965, 569.

[12] Dijkstra, E. W., "Cooperating sequential processes", *Programming languages*, F. Genuys, edited, Academic Press, 1968, 43-112.

[13] Enslow, P. H., "What is a 'distributed' data processing system?", *IEEE Computers*, **22**, 1, Jan. 1978, 13-21.

[14] Feng, T. Y., "A survey of interconnection networks", *IEEE Computers*, Dec. 1981, 12-27.

[15] Feng, T. Y., "From HPCC to new millennium computing", Keynote Address, *The 16th Int'l Conf. on Distributed Computing Systems*, 1996.

[16] Haas, L. M. et al., "R*, a research project on distributed relational DBMS", *Database Engineering*, 5, 4, 1982.

[17] Hoare, C. A. R., "Monitors: An operating system structuring concept", *Communications of the ACM*, 17, 10, Oct. 1974, 549-557.

[18] Hwang, K., *Advanced Computer Architecture: Parallelism, Scalability, Programmability*, McGraw-Hill Publishing Company, 1993.

[19] Johnson, B. C., "A distributed computing environment framework: an OSF perspective", in *Distributed Open System*, F. M. T. Brazier and D. Johansen, eds., IEEE Computer Society Press, 1994.

[20] Jordan, H. F., "A special purpose architecture for finite element analysis", *Proc. of the 1978 Int'l Conf. on Parallel Processing*, 1978, 263-266.

[21] Kleinrock, L., "Distributed systems", *IEEE Computers*, Oct. 1985, 103-110.

[22] LeLann, G., "Synchronization", in *Distributed Systems – Architecture and Implementation*, L. Lampson, et al., eds., LNCS 105, Springer Verlag, 1981.

[23] LeLann, G., "Motivations, objectives, and characterization of distributed systems," in *Distributed Systems – Architecture and Implementation*, Lampson, L., et al., eds., LNCS 105, Springer Verlag, 1981.

[24] Levy, E. and Silberschatz, A., "Distributed file systems: Concepts and examples", *ACM Computing Surveys*, 22, 1990, 321-374.

[25] Lewis, T. G., "The next $10,000_2$ years: Part 1", *IEEE Computers*, 29, 4, April 1996, 64-70.

[26] Libowitz, B. H. and J. H. Carson, *Tutorial: Distributed Processing*, IEEE Computer Society Press, 1989.

[27] Liszka, K. J., J. K. Antonio, and H. J. Siegel, "Is an Alligator better than an Armadillo?" *IEEE Concurrency*, Oct.-Dec. 1997, 18-28.

[28] Lockhart, H. M., *OSF DCE: Guide to Developing Distributed Applications*, IEEE Computer Society Press, 1994.

[29] Lynch, N. A., *Distributed Algorithms*, Morgan Kaufmann Publishing, Inc., 1996.

[30] Mariani, M. P. and D. F. Palmer, *Tutorial: Distributed System Design*, IEEE Computer Society Press, 1979.

[31] Melhem, R., D. Chiarulli, and S. Levitan, "Space multiplexing of waveguides in optically interconnected multiprocessor systems", *The Computer Journal*, **32**, 4, 1989, 362-369.

[32] Morris, J. H. et al., "Andrew, a distributed personal computing environment", *Communications of the ACM*, **29**, 3, 1986.

[33] Mullender, S. J. and A. S. Tanenbaum, "A distributed file service based on optimistic concurrency control", *Proc. of the 10th Symp. on Operating Systems Principles*, 1985, 51-62.

[34] Mullender, S., *Distributed Systems*, ACM Press, Addison-Wesley Publishing Company, 1989.

[35] Needham, R. M. and A. J. Herbert, *The Cambridge Distributed Computing System*, Addison-Wesley Publishing Company, 1982.

[36] OMG, *The Common Object Request Broker – Architecture and Specification*, OMG, 1991.

[37] *Introduction to OSF DCE*, Prentice-Hall, Inc., 1992.

[38] Özsu, M. T. and P. Valduriez, *Principles of Distributed Database Systems*, Prentice-Hall Inc., 1991.

[39] Popek, G. J. and B. J. Walker, *The Locus Distributed System Architecture*, The MIT Press, 1985.

[40] Raynal, M., *Distributed Algorithms and Protocols*, John Wiley & Son, 1988.

[41] Raynal, M. and J. -M. Helary, *Synchronization and Control of Distributed Systems and Programs*, John Wiley & Son, 1990.

[42] Reed, D. A. and R. M. Fujimoto, *Multicomputer Networks: Message-Based Parallel Processing*, The MIT Press, 1987.

[43] Satyanarayanan, M., "A survey of distributed file systems", *Annual Review of Computer Science*, 4, 1990, 73-104.

[44] Seitz, C. L., *Resources in Parallel and Concurrent Systems*, ACM Press, 1990.

[45] Singhal, M. and N. G. Shivaratri, *Advanced Concepts in Operating Systems: Distributed, Database, and Multiprocessor Operating Systems*, McGraw-Hill Publishing Company, 1994.

[46] Sinha, P. K. et al., "The Galaxy distributed operating system", *IEEE Computers*, August 1991, 34-41.

[47] Sinha, P. K., *Distributed Operating Systems: Concepts and Design*, IEEE Computer Society Press, 1997.

[48] Stankovic, J. A., "A perspective on distributed computer systems", *IEEE Transactions on Computers*, **33**, 12, Dec. 1984, 1102-1114.

[49] Stonebraker, M., "Concurrency control and consistency of multiple choices of data in distributed INGRES", *IEEE Transactions on Software Engineering*, **5**, 3, 1979.

[50] Tanenbaum, A. S., *Computer Networks*, Second edition, Prentice-Hall, Inc., 1988.

[51] Tanenbaum, A. S., *Distributed Operating Systems*, Prentice-Hall, Inc., 1995.

[52] Tel, G., *Topics in Distributed Algorithms*, Cambridge University Press, 1991.

[53] Tel, G., *Introduction to Distributed Algorithms*, Cambridge University Press, 1994.

[54] Tichy, W. F. and Ruan, Z., "Towards a distributed file system", *Proc. of the Summer USENIX Conf.*, 1984, 87-97.

[55] Umar, A., *Distributed Computing*, Prentice-Hall, Inc., 1993.

[56] Wu, C. L. and T. Y. Feng, *Tutorial: Interconnection in Networks for Parallel and Distributed Processing*, IEEE Computer Society Press, 1984.

[57] Zheng, S. Q. and J. Wu, "Dual of a complete graph as an interconnection network", *Proc. of the 8th IEEE Symp. on Parallel and Distributed Processing*, 1996, 433-442.

Problems

1. Use your own words to explain the differences between distributed systems, multiprocessors, and network systems.

2. Give several practical examples on the use of distributed systems.

3. Why is a standard like DCE important?

4. What is the advantage of using two different views (physical and logical) of a distributed system?

5. Consider a computer structure with both shared memory and local memory and discuss different ways to construct a logically distributed memory system.

6. Discuss different ways to construct a logically shared memory system on the same physical system structure discussed in Problem 5.

7. Calculate (a) node degree, (b) diameter, (c) bisection width, and (d) the number of links for an $n \times n$ 2-d mesh, an $n \times n$ 2-d torus, and an n-dimensional hypercube.

8. Discuss the relative advantages and disadvantages in using replication and partition in a database system.

Chapter 2

DISTRIBUTED PROGRAMMING LANGUAGES

In this chapter we survey general distributed programming languages and introduce a CSP-like distributed control description language (DCDL). This language is used to describe several control structures such as expressing parallelism, interprocess communication and synchronization, and fault-tolerant design. Control algorithms expressed in DCDL are presented at an abstract level and can be applied at the operating system level, the language run-time system level, or the user level.

2.1 Requirement for Distributed Programming Support

Clearly, classical sequential programming languages, such as Fortran, Pascal, and C, are not suitable for distributed systems. These languages do not address problems such as concurrency, communication, synchronization, and reliability.

There are basically three issues that distinguish distributed programming from sequential programming [7]:

- Use of multiple processing elements (PEs).

- Cooperation among the PEs.

- Potential for survival to partial failure.

The use of multiple PEs is related to the problem of expressing parallelism. Cooperation among the PEs involves two types of interaction:

communication and *synchronization*. A communication typically involves two or more processes to send and receive messages. A synchronization can be due to either *competition* or *condition*. A competition occurs when several processes try to access a limited number of resources in the system. This problem is called *mutual exclusion* and will be treated in detail in a later chapter. Synchronization by condition occurs when a process depends on other processes in the sense that its progression can be held up until a certain condition on the state of the system becomes true. Although distributed systems provide the potential to survive partial failure, users or system designers are still responsible to turn this potential into reality.

Note that the above issues can be achieved at one of the following levels: (a) user level, (b) language run-time level, and (c) operating system level. Instead of considering implementation details of these issues at the different levels, we concentrate here on abstract solutions that are independent of the levels.

The language used to provide abstract solutions is DCDL which is a skeleton control driven language similar to *communicating sequential processes* (CSP) [27] as opposed to pattern driven (PROLOG), data driven (VAL), or demand driven (FP) language. Another classification divides programming languages into *imperative* and *applicative* languages. DCDL is an imperative which is statement- and sequence-oriented. An applicative language expresses programs through function application and binding.

A programming language is defined by its syntax and semantics. The *syntax* of a programming language defines legal strings of symbols used in programs. The *semantics* defines the meaning of each syntactic structure or the type of action to be taken for each structure. DCDL will be used to describe algorithms at any level. A list of common symbols in DCDL is given in the Appendix. Rather than using a formal semantics model such as *operational*, *axiomatic*, and *denotation*, the meaning of each structure in DCDL is described through examples in the subsequent sections.

2.2   An Overview of Parallel/Distributed Programming Language

We distinguish *distributed programming languages* from the *parallel programming languages*. A distributed programming language recognizes the cost of communication while a parallel programming language normally operates on shared storage. In this chapter we focus only on distributed programming languages and we will not cover languages that are mainly intended for parallel computation.

In parallel programming languages, *semaphores* and *monitors* are mainly used to synchronize coordinated multiple access of a shared storage. A semaphore [18] is a non-negative integer variable on which two operations are defined: P (wait) and V (signal). Each access to a shared storage must be proceeded by a P operation followed by a V operation. A monitor [25] defines a resource and the operations that manipulate it. A resource must be accessed only by using the operations defined by the monitor itself.

In distributed programming languages, languages make problem decomposition explicit as well as the details of communication. Among them, CSP (communicating sequential processes) [27] has a strong influence on the design of other programming languages for message passing systems.

Some programming languages are between the above two models. For example, *coordination languages* make decomposition explicit but hide some of the details of communication. The best example is Linda [15] which decouples the send and receive parts of a communication by providing the abstraction of a *tuple space*. A tuple space can be associatively accessed to retrieve values placed in it earlier by other threads. The sending thread does not need to know the receiving thread nor does it even need to know if the receiving thread exists. The above concept has been extended to the WWW (world wide web) framework by introducing a higher abstraction called a *page space* [17].

Skillicorn and Talia [43] gave a classification of parallel models: *arbitrary-computation structures* which allow arbitrary computations to be written, and *restricted-computation structures* which restrict the form of computations so as to restrict communication volume and type. Among restricted-computation structures, *data parallel programming languages* have received much attention due to their extensive uses in numerical computation for high performance computing and communication (HPCC) applications. Most of them are extensions of the popular C (C++) and Fortran. For example, in Europe, the *Europe Consortium* defines a parallel C++ based on an active object. In Japan, the MPC++ program [29] was established to provide powerful mechanisms for user-level extensions to a C++ compiler. In the United States, HPC++ [8] is a C++ library and language extension framework that is being developed by the HPC++ Consortium as a standard model for a portable parallel C++. Among the revisions of Fortran, Fortran 77 and Fortran 90 [1] have become ANSI standards, whereas the High-Performance Fortran Forum (HPF) [38] is developing a de facto standard.

There are several standards for distributing programming such as MPI (message passing interface) [39] and PVM (parallel virtual machine) [24]. PVM is the existing de facto standard for distributed computing and MPI is being considered as the future message passing standard. MPI is expected to be faster within a large system. It has more point-to-point and collective communication options than PVM. This can be important if an algorithm is dependent on the existence of a special communication option. PVM is better when applications are run over heterogeneous networks. It has good interoperability between different hosts. PVM allows the development of fault tolerant applications that can survive host or task failures. Because the PVM model is built around the *virtual machine* concept, it provides a powerful set of dynamic resource manager and process control functions.

Tools for parallel/distributed programming are maturing. These tools include (a) assistants for parallelizing code, (b) GUIs (graphical user interfaces) for constructing programs, and (c) debuggers for tracking the state of any process or thread.

2.3   Expressing Parallelism

Parallelism can be expressed in several ways. An important factor is the *unit of parallelism*. The unit of parallelism can be:

1. A process.

2. An object (in object-oriented programming).

3. A statement.

4. A cause (in logic programming).

Table 2.1 shows four sequential control mechanisms together with their parallel counterparts.

Parallel statements can be represented by a *precedence graph* where nodes are statements and direct edges are precedence relations. A precedence graph is a *directed acyclic graph* (DAG), i.e., it is a directed graph without a cycle. Figure 2.1 shows a precedence graph of eight statements. Note that in a precedence graph there are no redundant links (precedence orders). A precedence order is redundant if it can be derived from other precedence

Statement type \ Control type	Sequential control	Parallel control
Sequential/parallel statement	**begin** S_1, S_2 **end**	**parbegin** S_1, S_2 **parend** **fork/join**
Alternative statement	**goto, case** **if** C **then** S_1 **else** S_2	guarded commands: $G \to C$
Repetitive statement	**for ... do**	**doall, for all**
Subprogram	**procedure** **subroutine**	**procedure** **subroutine**

Table 2.1 Four basic sequential control mechanisms with their parallel counterparts.

orders. For example in Figure 2.1, a link from S_1 to S_4 is redundant since it can be derived from a link from S_1 to S_2 and a link from S_2 to S_4. In other words, the precedence order is *transitive*. A set of precedence orders R is non-redundant if and only if there does not exist a subset of R such that they have the same transitive closure. Intuitively, R is non-redundant if it cannot be further reduced.

In DCDL a *parallel statement* is expressed as:

$$[\ S_1\ \|\ S_2\ \|\ ....\ \|\ S_n\ ]$$

to represent that statements $S_1, S_2, \ldots, S_n$ are performed in parallel. This structure is also used as **parbegin** and **parend** (or **cobegin** and **coend**) in many parallel/distributed languages. S_i $(1 \leq i \leq n)$ can be a command list C or a Dijkstra *guarded command* [19]:

$$G \to C$$

where G is a guard consisting of a list of Boolean expressions, and C is a command list. A guarded command may be executed if the execution of its guard does not fail. In DCDL a sequence of statements $S_1, S_2, \ldots, S_n$ is represented as

$$S_1; S_2; \ldots; S_n$$

In DCDL the precedence graph of Figure 2.1 can be presented by:

$$S_1; [\ [\ S_2; [\ S_3\ \|\ S_4\ ]; S_5; S_6\ ]\ \|\ S_7\ ]; S_8$$

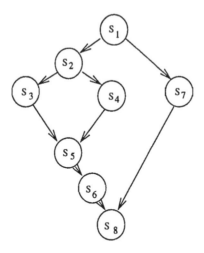

FIGURE 2.1
A precedence graph of eight statements.

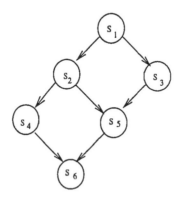

FIGURE 2.2
A precedence graph that cannot be represented by DCDL statements.

Not all the precedence graphs can be represented by a DCDL statement such as the one in Figure 2.2. There are three possible solutions to the above problem. A simple solution is to transform the given precedence graph to a more restrictive precedence graph that can be represented by parallel and sequential statements offered in DCDL. A precedence graph G is said to be more restrictive than G' if all the precedence orders of G' can be derived from the ones in G. In Figure 2.2 if we replace a link from S_3 to S_5 by a link from S_3 to S_2, we can represent the new graph as:

$$S_1; S_3; S_2; [S_4 \| S_5]; S_6$$

Note that a link from S_3 to S_5 can be derived from the link from S_3 to S_2 together with the link from S_2 to S_5. The new graph is a restrictive version of the previous one. Also, the link from S_1 to S_2 becomes redundant. A restrictive graph may lose certain degrees of parallelism.

In the second solution, a more powerful structure, *fork/join*, is used. Actually, any precedence graph can be represented by the fork/join statement. The fork L instruction produces two (or more) concurrent executions in a program. One execution starts at the statement labeled L while the other is the continuation of the current execution thread following the fork instruction. The join instruction has a parameter to specify the number of threads to join. All the threads, except the last one, will quit upon reaching the join statement. The corresponding program for the precedence graph of Figure 2.2 using the fork and join statements is:

```
         s1;
         c1:= 2;
         fork L1;
         s2;
         c2:=2;
         fork L2;
         s4;
         go to L3;
L1:      s3;
L2:      join c1;
         s5;
L3:      join c2;
         s6;
```

Note that in the above solution the initialization of each counter (e.g., c_1 and c_2) can be placed anywhere before the execution of the corresponding join statement. When several threads need to be generated, one may use

$$\textbf{fork } L_1, L_2, ..., L_n$$

to generate m new threads. This structure is equivalent to n sequential statements:

$$\textbf{fork } L_i, \text{ where } 1 \le i \le n$$

In the third solution, parbegin/parend statements plus semaphores are used. Such a combination has the same expressive power as fork/join statements. Recall that a semaphore can be used to administer a set of resources. More formally, a semaphore is an object with two operations P and V. The P operation obtains a copy of the resource associated with the semaphore and the V operation releases a copy of the resource. If the semaphore is busy, i.e., it has run out of the copy of the resource, the requesting process (the one issuing a V operation) is blocked until it is free. When another process executes a V operation on a semaphore, a blocked process is released and is allowed to access the resource. A typical implementation of a semaphore s is to use a nonnegative integer. A $V(s)$ operation increments s and a $P(s)$ operation decrements s. If s is positive, this action succeeds; if it is zero, then the process issuing the P operation is blocked until it becomes positive. A binary semaphore s is a special semaphore where s is either 0 or 1.

To express a precedence graph several binary semaphores are used; one for each link of the given precedence graph. For the two statements S_i and S_j such that S_i directly proceeds S_j, a semaphore s_{ij} is used. Upon completion of S_i, a V operation is issued on s_{ij}. Similarly, before S_j executes, a P operation is issued on s_{ij}. One can consider a semaphore as a lock; a statement can start only when it gets permissions from all of its predecessors through P operations. When a statement is completed, it should grant permission to all its immediate decedents, i.e., pass a key to the lock to each decedent by issuing a V operation on the corresponding semaphore. With the above modification each statement S_i becomes:

$S(i)$: A sequence of P operations; S_i; a sequence of V operations

Then all these $S(i)$ are connected through one parallel statement without any further constraints. Actually, all the precedence constraints are enforced by semaphores defined in each $S(i)$.

Each node in the precedence graph of Figure 2.2 can be presented by:

$$S(1): \quad S_1; V(s_{12}); V(s_{13})$$
$$S(2): \quad P(s_{12}); S_2; V(s_{24}); V(s_{25})$$
$$S(3): \quad P(s_{13}); S_3; V(s_{35})$$
$$S(4): \quad P(s_{24}); S_4; V(s_{46})$$
$$S(5): \quad P(s_{25}); P(s_{35}); S_5'; V(s_{56})$$
$$S(6): \quad P(s_{46}); P(s_{56}); S_6$$

Hence, the program for the precedence graph is:

> all the binary semaphores are initialized zero;
> $\| \ S(i : 1..6)$

$\| \ S(i : 1..6)$ stands for a concurrent statement of six sequential statements $S(i)$, $1 \leq i \leq 6$.

Parallel process execution also can be expressed in a similar way:

$$[\ P_1 \ \| \ P_2 \ \| \ \cdots \ \| \ P_n \ ]$$

where $P_1, P_2 \ldots P_n$ are the names of processes where each process is defined elsewhere. Therefore DCDL can describe parallelism at both the process level and statement level. Assume that each process consists of several sequential statements. A parallel execution of these processes generates a permutation of all the statements in these processes restricted only to keeping the statements of a process in their original order.

For example, if $P_1 : p_1(1)p_1(2)$ and $P_2 : p_2(1)p_2(2)p_2(3)$, then the statement

$$[\ P_1 \ \| \ P_2 \ ]$$

generates one of the following permutations:

$$p_1(1)p_1(2)p_2(1)p_2(2)p_2(3)$$
$$p_1(1)p_2(1)p_1(2)p_2(2)p_2(3)$$
$$p_1(1)p_2(1)p_2(2)p_1(2)p_2(3)$$
$$p_1(1)p_2(1)p_2(2)p_2(3)p_1(2)$$
$$p_2(1)p_1(1)p_1(2)p_2(2)p_2(3)$$
$$p_2(1)p_1(1)p_2(2)p_1(2)p_2(3)$$
$$p_2(1)p_1(1)p_2(2)p_2(3)p_1(2)$$
$$p_2(1)p_2(2)p_1(1)p_1(2)p_2(3)$$
$$p_2(1)p_2(2)p_1(1)p_2(3)p_1(2)$$
$$p_2(1)p_2(2)p_2(3)p_1(1)p_1(2)$$

An *alternative statement* is expressed in the form:

$$[G_1 \rightarrow C_1 \ \square \ G_2 \rightarrow C_2 \ \square ... \square \ G_n \rightarrow C_n \ ].$$

The alternative statement selects the execution of exactly one of the constituent guarded commands. In the case where more than one command list can be selected, the choice is *nondeterministic* [13], [21].

Example 2.1 $[x \geq y \rightarrow m := x \ \square \ y \geq x \rightarrow m := y]$.

If $x \geq y$, assign x to m, if $y \geq x$ assign y to m; if both $x \geq y$ and $y \geq x$, either assignment can be executed.   ∎

A *repetitive statement* specifies a number of interactions of its constituent alternative statements with guards or without guards. It has the form

$*$ [alternative statement with guards]

when all the guards pass the repetitive statement terminates, or

$*$ [alternative statement without guards]

The latter program execution does not terminate. How do we represent traditional programs whose executions do terminate? The approach we use is to distinguish program execution (an infinite sequence of executing statements) from implementation (a finite prefix of the sequence). A state of a program is called a *fixed point* if and only if execution of any statement of the program in this state leaves the state unchanged. The result at a fixed point is the result of the corresponding program.

(n) [alternative statement]

is a special repetitive statement with a maximum number of iterations of n. Note that this statement may still terminate before n rounds of executing the alternative statement when all the guards in the statement (if any) fail.

Example 2.2 *The Meeting Time Problem* [16]: The problem is to schedule a meeting time suitable for three participants: A, B, and C. Initially the proposed meeting time t is zero. If a participant cannot meet at that time, he or she increases the value of the proposed meeting time t to the next possible time through a, b, c, respectively. At the fixed point, r is a common meeting time.

meeting-time-scheduling:: $= t := 0;$
$* [t := a(t) \ \square \ r := b(t) \ \square \ r := c(t)]$ ∎

Notation ::= is used to represent the definition of a function (or procedure). In this program, computation proceeds by executing any one of the assignments selected nondeterministically. The selection should also obey the fairness rule: every assignment is executed infinitely often. For example, assume that the above example is executed for an infinite number of steps, if A is selected at every $6k$, $6k+3$, $6k+4$ steps, B at every $6k+2$ and $6k+5$ steps, and C at every $6k+1$ steps, we say the selection is still fair, although A, B, C have different probabilities of being selected. Fairness is a unique and complex issue in distributed systems. For a detailed treatment of this issue see [22].

The alternative and repetitive statements can be used together to solve more complex problems.

Example 2.3 Given a fixed array of arrays $b[1:m][1:n]$, where $1 < m$ and $1 < n$, search b for a fixed value x.

```
i := 1; j := 1;
* [ i ≤ m ∧ x ≠ b[i, j] →
        [ j := j + 1;
          [ j ≤ n → skip □ j > n → i := i + 1; j := 1 ]
        ]
  ]
```

During the evaluation of the expression $x \wedge y$, if x is false, we can save time by not evaluating y since the expression will evaluate to false no matter what y is. Performing this optimization is known as *short-circuiting*.   ■

Example 2.4 *Rubin's Problem* [20]: Determining whether or not all the elements in one row of an $m \times n$ matrix, $a[1:m][1:n]$, are all zero is a search problem in two dimensions. This problem was presented by Rubin as an example that can be most easily solved using "goto" statements. The difficulty is centered around the issue of how to terminate a nested loop structure. The following solution shows that a simple solution without goto statements is still possible.

```
i := 1; p := m + 1;
* [ i ≠ p →
        [ j := 1; q := n + 1;
          * [ j ≠ q →
                [ a[i, j] = 0 → j := j + 1
                □ a[i, j] ≠ 0 → q := j
                ]
```

$$];$$
$$[\ j = n \rightarrow p := i$$
$$\square\, j \neq n \rightarrow i := i + 1$$
$$]$$

$$]$$

$$]$$
$$found := (i \neq m + 1)$$

The above algorithm generates a Boolean variable $found$. A zero row exists if $found = $ T; otherwise, there does not exist one.

When two statements are executed concurrently, they may not produce the same results obtained by a sequential execution. Let us first define the following notation:

- $R(S_i)$, the *read set* for S_i, is the set of all variables whose values are referenced in S_i.

- $W(S_i)$, the *write set* for S_i, is the set of all variables whose values are changed in S_i.

Bernstein [9] showed that the following three conditions must be satisfied for the two successive statements S_1 and S_2 to be executed concurrently and still produce the same result as when they are executed sequentially in any order.

1. $R(S_1) \cap W(S_2) = \varnothing$

2. $W(S_1) \cap R(S_2) = \varnothing$

3. $W(S_1) \cap W(S_2) = \varnothing$

We use $S_1 \| S_2$ to represent the fact that statements S_1 and S_2 meet the three conditions and can run parallel.

Example 2.5 Suppose $S_1 : a = x + y$, and $S_2 : b = x + z$, then these two statements can be executed concurrently because

$$R(S_1) = \{x, y\}, R(S_2) = \{x, z\}, W(S_1) = \{a\}, W(S_2) = \{b\}$$

However, S_2 cannot be executed concurrently with $S_3 : x = z + 1$, since

$$R(S_2) \cap W(S_3) = \{x\}$$

■

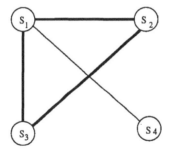

FIGURE 2.3
A graph model for Bernstein's conditions.

The above conditions are also called *Bernstein's conditions*. In general, a set of statements S_i, $1 \leq i \leq n$, can execute in parallel if Bernstein's conditions are satisfied on a pairwise basis, i.e.,

$$S_1\|S_2\|...\|S_n \iff \forall_{i \neq j} S_i\|S_j$$

We can also use Bernstein's conditions to find a largest subset of statements that can run parallel. To do this we define an undirected graph. The node set consists of the set of given statements. Two nodes S_i and S_j are connected if $S_i\|S_j$. A largest subset of statements corresponds to a largest complete subgraph.

Example 2.6 Suppose $S_1 : a := x+y$, $S_2 : b := x \times z$, $S_3 : x := y+z$, and $S_4 : c := y-1$. Using Bernstein's conditions, we have $S_1\|S_2$, $S_1\|S_3$, $S_1\|S_4$, and $S_2\|S_4$. The corresponding graph is shown in Figure 2.3. Clearly, S_1, S_2, and S_3 form a largest complete subgraph. That is, $S_1\|S_2\|S_3$.

2.4   Process Communication and Synchronization

An important issue in the design of distributed systems is how the pieces of a program that are running in parallel on different PEs are going to cooperate. The cooperation involves two types of interaction: *communication* and *synchronization*. Principally there exist two complementary communication schemes in distributed systems:

- *Message passing* which allows processes to exchange messages. An interprocess communication facility basically provides two abstract operations: send (message) and receive (message).

- *Shared data* which shares data for communication in a distributed system with no shared memory. The concept of distributed data structure called tuple space [15], used in Linda, is a method for providing shared data.

The key issue in using shared data is to prevent multiple processes from simultaneously changing the data. Note that the mechanisms in shared memory systems, such as monitors and semaphores, cannot be applied here.

The implementation of a message passing scheme normally requires the following list of decisions:

- *One-to-one or one-to-many.*

- *Synchronous or asynchronous.*

- *One-way or two-way communication.*

- *Direct or indirect communication.*

- *Automatic or explicit buffering.*

- *Implicit or explicit receiving.*

One-to-one is also called point-to-point message passing while one-to-many supports an efficient broadcast or multicast facility [34]. With synchronous message passing, the sender is blocked until the receiver has accepted the message. In asynchronous message passing the sender does not wait for the receiver. One-way communication represents one interaction between the sender and the receiver, while two-way communication indicates many interactions, back and forth, between the sender and the receiver. Direct or indirect communication differentiates whether the sender sends messages to the receiver directly or indirectly through an intermediate object, usually called a mailbox or port.

A *mailbox* supports multiple senders and receivers that share the same storage unit. A *port* is a special example of a mailbox that is normally attached with either a sender or a receiver. When a port is associated with a sender, it supports one sender and multiple receivers. When a port is associated with a receiver, it supports multiple senders and one receiver. Normally a port is a finite first-in-first-out (FIFO) queue maintained by the kernel. In many situations ports and mailboxes are used interchangeably.

A communication scheme is symmetric if both the sender and the receiver name each other. In an asymmetric scheme only the sender names the receiver. Explicit buffering requires the sender to specify the size of the buffer used to hold the message at the receiver to know the source of the message (the sender) while implicit receiving does not care the source of the message.

There are five message-passing models, which are commonly used [7]: synchronous point-to-point, asynchronous point-to-point, rendezvous, remote procedure call, and one-to-many.

The synchronous point-to-point approach has been adopted in the Occam programming language [14] which uses one-way communication between the sender and the receiver. Writing programs using send and receive primitives is relatively difficult because a programmer has to take care of many details, such as the pairing of responses with request messages, data representation, knowing the address of the remote processor or the server, and taking care of communication and system failures. Two commonly used higher level communication structures are *rendezvous* (used in Ada) and *remote procedure call* (RPC) (used in DP [26]). RPC uses two-way communication and is similar to the client/server model where the client requests a service and waits for the results from the server. The difference in these two approaches is that the caller or sender is blocked in RPC and is unblocked in rendezvous. A detailed study of RPC will be discussed in the next section. One-to-many message passing is not frequently used, although some languages such as *broadcasting sequential processes* (BSP) [23] use this scheme.

The issues discussed so far are logical or at the application software level. There are more implementation issues at the underlying hardware and network layers. These issues include [40]:

- How are communication links established?

- Can a communication link be associated with more than two processes?

- How many links should be placed between every pair of processes?

- What is the capacity of a link?

- What is the size of a message? (fixed or variable)

- Is a link unidirectional or bidirectional?

The detailed discussion of these issues is beyond the scope of this book. In the following we focus on commands that are offered in DCDL for process communication and synchronization.

In DCDL asynchronous point-to-point message passing is adopted. Messages are passed to a named receiver process through asynchronous static channels (links). An output command is of the form

send message_list **to** destination

where the destination is a process name (a one-to-one communication) or a keyword **all** representing all the other processes (a one-to-all communication). An input command has the form

receive message_list **from** source

where the source is a process name (optional) and this input command supports both implicit and explicit acceptance of the message. An implicit acceptance of the message is expressed as

receive message_list

An asynchronous static channel (link) is a FIFO queue between two processes. Unless otherwise specified, we assume that there is only one channel between any two processes.

Note that synchronous communication can be simulated by asynchronous communication. At the sending site, we have:

send message_list **to** destination;
receive empty_signal **from** destination

At the receiving site, we have:

receive message_list **from** sender;
send empty_signal **to** sender

The above structure can be extended to implement barrier synchronization. Many iterative algorithms successively compute better approximations to an answer and they terminate when either the final answer has been computed or when the final answer has converged. Each iteration typically depends on the results of the previous iteration. Note that an iteration with a *true* guard corresponds to a periodic process.

$$* [\ true \rightarrow$$
$$[\ \text{code to implement process } P_i;$$

wait for all n processes to complete

    ]

  ]

In the above algorithm *true* is a Boolean constant that always returns a true value, i.e., the condition is always satisfied. This type of synchronization is called *barrier synchronization* [31]. The delay point at the end of each iteration represents a barrier that all processes have to arrive before any are allowed to pass.

In an asymmetric implementation one process is called *coordinator* and the rest are *workers*. The coordinator sends a special signal to all the other processes when it receives a message from each of them.

```
worker(i) ::= * [  true →
                  [ code to implement process Pᵢ
                    send signal to coordinator;
                    receive ack from coordinator
                  ]
              ]
```

```
coordinator ::= * [  true →
                    [ counter := 0;
                      * [ counter ≠ n →
                        [ received signal;
                          counter := counter + 1]
                      ];
                      send ack to all
                    ]
                ]
```

To construct a symmetric barrier (one with the same code in each process), we can use a barrier for two processes as a building block. Suppose $barrier(P_i, P_j)$ is a barrier synchronization between processes P_i and P_j such as the one in the above example. A barrier for eight processes can be:

stage 1:
      $barrier(P_1, P_2)\|barrier(P_3, P_4)\|barrier(P_5, P_6)\|barrier(P_7, P_8)$
stage 2:
      $barrier(P_1, P_3)\|barrier(P_2, P_4)\|barrier(P_5, P_7)\|barrier(P_6, P_8)$
stage 3:
      $barrier(P_1, P_5)\|barrier(P_2, P_6)\|barrier(P_3, P_7)\|barrier(P_4, P_8)$

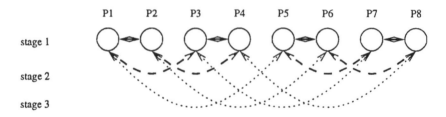

FIGURE 2.4
A three-stage symmetric barrier.

Its graphical representation is shown in Figure 2.4. The following examples show more of the use of send and receive commands in DCDL.

Example 2.7 *Squash* [27]: The squash program replaces every pair of consecutive asterisks "**" by an upward arrow "↑". Assume that the final character input is not an asterisk.

squash::= ∗ [**receive** c **from** input →
                    [$c \neq *$ → **send** c **to** output
                    □[$c = *$ → **receive** c **from** input;
                        [$c \neq *$ → **send** ∗ **to** output;
                        send c **to** output
                        □ $c = *$ → **send** ↑ **to** output
                        ]
                    ]
                ]
            ]

The input process is a repetitive command:

$$\text{input} ::= * [\textbf{send } c \textbf{ to} \text{ squash}]$$

The output process is another repetitive command:

$$\text{output} ::= * [\textbf{receive } c \textbf{ from} \text{ squash}]$$

When a receive command is used as a guard in a repetitive command, the execution of a corresponding guard is delayed until the corresponding send command is executed. A command with a receive command in one of its guards terminates only when the corresponding sender terminates.

Example 2.8 We can have the following recursive solution to compute $f(n) = f(n - 1) \times n^2$, for $n > 1$ and $f(1) = 1$.

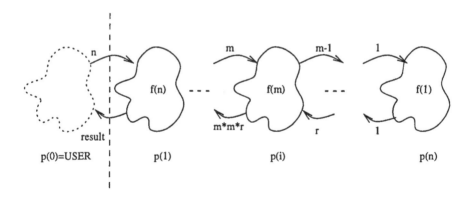

FIGURE 2.5
A recursive solution for Example 2.8.

$$p(i : 1..n) :: = * [\text{ receive } m \text{ from } p(i - 1) \rightarrow$$
$$[\quad [\quad m = 0 \rightarrow \text{send } 1 \text{ to } p(i - 1)$$
$$\square \quad m > 0 \rightarrow \text{send } m - 1 \text{ to } p(i + 1)$$
$$];$$
$$\text{receive } r \text{ from } p(i + 1);$$
$$\text{send } m \times m \times r \text{ to } p(i - 1)$$
$$]$$
$$]$$
$$p(0) :: = \text{send } n \text{ to } p(1);$$
$$\text{receive result from } p(1)$$

The solution to $f(n)$ is a parallel execution of all these $n + 1$ processes:

$$\| \ p(i : 0..n)$$

In the above solution $n + 1$ processes are used to solve the problem (see Figure 2.5). This solution is only used to illustrate the use of interprocess communication and is by no means an efficient one. $p(0)$ is the USER program that sends n to $p(1)$ and receives the result $f(n)$ from $p(1)$. Each $p(i)$ calculates $f(n - i + 1)$ for $1 \leq i \leq n$ and the number of active $p(i)$ depends on n.

One may use only one process to solve the same problem. The definition of $f(n)$ can be easily transformed into a recursive procedure to compute $f(n)$:

$$p(n, ans) ::= ans := 1;$$

$$[\quad n = 0 \rightarrow skip$$
$$\Box \ n > 0 \rightarrow p(n - 1, ans); ans := ans \times n \times n$$
$$]$$

In the above solution the result of $f(n)$ is placed in variable ans. Recursion is useful in deriving a simple solution. At the same time, in theory at least, any recursive program can be written iteratively (and vice versa), and in practice it may make sense to do so. Perhaps problems of space and time efficiency force the use of iteration:

$$f(n) ::= i := n;$$
$$ans := 1;$$
$$* [\, i \neq 1 \rightarrow ans := ans \times i \times i; i := i - 1 \,]$$

■

Example 2.9 DCDL can also be used to implement a *binary semaphore* s:

$$semaphore(s) ::= val := 0;$$
$$* [\ \textbf{receive} \ V() \ \textbf{from} \ proc(i)$$
$$\rightarrow val := val + 1$$
$$\Box \ val > 0 \land \textbf{receive} \ P() \ \textbf{from} \ proc(i)$$
$$\rightarrow val := val - 1$$
$$]$$

where $proc(i)$ is a process requesting a V or P operation to semaphore s.

■

For some other problems, several solutions exist for different interprocess communication structures.

Example 2.10 Fibonacci numbers are a sequence of integers defined by the recurrence $F(i) = F(i - 1) + F(i - 2)$ for $i > 1$, with initial values $F(0) = 0$ and $F(1) = 2$. Provide a DCDL implementation of $F(i)$ with one process for each $F(i)$.

Again we define a set of processes: $f(i)$ which calculates $F(n - i + 1)$. Clearly, if $n - i + 1 > 1$, $f(i)$ depends on values calculated from $f(i + 1)$ and $f(i + 2)$. A natural solution will be $f(i)$ receives $(n - i + 1)$ from $f(i - 1)$ and passes $(n - i)$ to $f(i + 1)$ if $(n - i + 1)$ is larger than 1. Then $f(i)$ waits for results from $f(i + 1)$ and $f(i + 2)$, summarizes the results, and forwards the summation to $f(i - 1)$ and $f(i - 2)$ (see Figure 2.6).

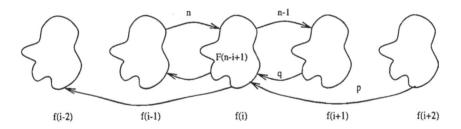

FIGURE 2.6
A solution for $F(n)$.

$$f(0) ::= \text{send } n \text{ to } f(1);$$
$$\quad \text{receive } p \text{ from } f(2);$$
$$\quad \text{receive } q \text{ from } f(1);$$
$$\quad ans := q$$
$$f(i) ::= \text{receive } n \text{ from } f(i-1);$$
$$\quad [\; n > 1 \to [\; \text{send } n-1 \text{ to } f(i+1);$$
$$\quad\quad\quad\quad \text{receive } p \text{ from } f(i+2);$$
$$\quad\quad\quad\quad \text{receive } q \text{ from } f(i+1);$$
$$\quad\quad\quad\quad \text{send } p+q \text{ to } f(i-1);$$
$$\quad\quad\quad\quad \text{send } p+q \text{ to } f(i-2) \;]$$
$$\quad \square\; n = 1 \to [\; \text{send } 1 \text{ to } f(i-1);$$
$$\quad\quad\quad\quad \text{send } 1 \text{ to } f(i-2) \;]$$
$$\quad \square\; n = 0 \to [\; \text{send } 0 \text{ to } f(i-1);$$
$$\quad\quad\quad\quad \text{send } 0 \text{ to } f(i-2) \;]$$
$$\quad]$$
$$f(-1) ::= \text{receive } p \text{ from } f(1)$$

In the above algorithm $f(0)$ is USER and $f(-1)$ is a dummy process. $f(-1)$ can be deleted if we change the statement **send** $p+q$ **to** $f(i-2)$ to $[i \neq 1 \to$ **send** $p+q$ **to** $f(i-2)]$ in $f(i)$.

The second solution restricts communication to neighbors only, i.e., $f(i)$ communicates only with $f(i-1)$ and $f(i+1)$ (see Figure 2.7).

$$f(0) ::= [\; n > 1 \to [\; \text{send } n \text{ to } f(1);$$
$$\quad\quad\quad\quad \text{receive } p \text{ from } f(1);$$
$$\quad\quad\quad\quad \text{receive } q \text{ from } f(1);$$
$$\quad\quad\quad\quad ans := p \;]$$
$$\quad \square\; n = 1 \to ans := 1$$
$$\quad \square\; n = 0 \to ans := 0$$

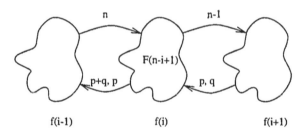

FIGURE 2.7
Another solution for $F(n)$.

$$
\begin{aligned}
f(i)::= \quad &]\\
& \textbf{receive } n \textbf{ from } f(i-1);\\
& [\ n>1 \rightarrow [\ \textbf{send } n-1 \textbf{ to } f(i+1);\\
& \qquad\qquad\qquad \textbf{receive } p \textbf{ from } f(i+1);\\
& \qquad\qquad\qquad \textbf{receive } q \textbf{ from } f(i+1);\\
& \qquad\qquad\qquad \textbf{send } p+q \textbf{ to } f(i-1);\\
& \qquad\qquad\qquad \textbf{send } p \textbf{ to } f(i-1)\ ]\\
& \square\ n=1 \rightarrow [\ \textbf{send } 1 \textbf{ to } f(i-1);\\
& \qquad\qquad\qquad \textbf{send } 0 \textbf{ to } f(i-1)\ ]\\
&]
\end{aligned}
$$

■

2.5   Remote Procedure Calls

The basic communication paradigm for distributed systems is input and output: **send** and **receive** commands as discussed in the last section. However, some programmers prefer the programming style in a centralized system with no explicit communication primitives. *Remote procedure call* (RPC) [12] is introduced to function as send and receive commands but look very much like a local procedure call.

The normal implementation of RPC is the following: When a program needs to read some data from a file, if such a read is a remote procedure, a *client stub* is put into the library. Following the call to read, the client stub packs the parameters into a message and calls a *server stub* at the remote site, blocking itself until the reply comes back. When the message arrives at the server, the server stub unpacks the message and calls the server procedure as though it is called directly by the client. The server performs the requested work and then returns the result to the caller (the server stub). When the server stub gets control back after the call has completed, it packs the result and returns it to the client. When the message gets back to the client, the kernel copies the message to the waiting buffer and the client process is unblocked. The client stub unpacks the result and copies it to its caller. When the caller gets control all it knows is that its requested data are available. It does not know whether the work is done locally or remotely.

However the basic RPC suffers from the following pitfalls:

1. *Communication overhead.* When a client calls several procedures with the same data, this data has to be passed each time with a call because RPC does not support remote objects. In case of nested procedure calls, each intermediate (call) result must be passed back to the client and must be sent to the server again.

2. *Lack of parallelism.* The semantic of RPC is simple but its execution is sequential (the caller is suspended until a result is obtained).

3. *Lack of flexibility.* An RPC client can use only a limited set of services; each new procedure has to be prepared and installed by an experienced programmer.

There are many extensions to the basic RPC. However, many attempts to extend RPC to include parallel features [5] lead to complex semantics losing the main advantage of RPC. The asynchronous RPC proposed by Liskov and Shrira [36] has been successfully implemented in the Mercury communication system at MIT. The lightweight RPC introduced by Bershad [10] aims to improve performance by using the concept of *thread*. A thread is also called a *lightweight process* and many threads can share the same address space. In such a system a (heavyweight) process consists of an address space and one or more threads of control. Each thread has its own program counter, register states, and stack. Each thread can independently make remote procedure calls. Other extensions of RPC to support concurrent access to multiple servers and to serve multiple requests simultaneously can be found in [42].

Another mechanism close to RPC is *remote evaluation* (REV) [44], which allows several procedures (code and data) to be encapsulated in one procedure to be forwarded to a remote site like a procedure call in RPC. The corresponding remote site evaluates the encapsulated procedure. The transmitted data in the encapsulated procedure can be used many times by the procedures in the encapsulated procedure and intermediate results produced (if any) do not need to be passed back to the client, However, if one cannot exploit the above benefit, the communication overhead may even increase due to the frequent transmission of procedures (both code and data). Moreover, relocation can be a problem, especially in a heterogeneous system, because it is not an easy task to move executable code from one machine to another with different instruction sets and data representations.

Recently, a *context driven call* (CDC) [48] model was proposed which extends the well-known RPC and combines merits of both RPC and REV. Like RPC, CDC allows a set of procedures to be disposed on a remote processor and to be called by the same language construct (a procedure call) as local procedures. However, a different implementation mechanism is employed in CDC. In addition CDC supports mechanisms for individually sending data to a remote site and receiving data from a remote site. The programmer does not need to be aware of these data movements.

CDC supports two types of data objects: *local* and *remote*. A local object is a variable allocated to the address space of the current master. A remote object is a variable allocated to a slave's address space. To perform a local or remote evaluation of an expression with remote variables, CDC issues an appropriate combination of sending data to a remote site, remote evaluation, and receiving data from remote sites. Specifically, for a general expression $x = e(x_1, x_2, ..., x_n)$ which contains at least one remote object. If it is evaluated locally, the local site needs to receive input data (if any) from remote sites, perform a local evaluation, and then send (result) data to a remote site if variable x is a remote object. If it is evaluated remotely, local site needs to first send input data to the corresponding remote site. The remote site performs a remote evaluation and the local site receives the result from the remote site if x is a local object. A similar situation applies to a local or remote evaluation of a procedure *void* $f(x_1, x_2, ..., x_n)$ with remote objects. A local evaluation occurs when there are remote objects from different remote sites. In this case the local site receives (remote) data from remote sites and performs a local evaluation. A remote evaluation happens when all remote objects are from the same remote site. In this situation the local site sends (local) data to the remote site and a remote evaluation is performed there.

To support the above actions the following functions that can be requested from a client (a locate site) to a server (a remote site) are introduced:

- *rcreate()* creates a remote object of a certain size at a remote site, names the object with a unique name (handler) and returns the handler to the caller.

- *rremove()* removes a remote object to which a handler is provided as an input.

- *rread()* copies a remote object to a local buffer with both the handler to the object and the address of the buffer being provided as inputs.

- *rwrite()* copies the content of a local buffer to a remote object with both the handler to the object and the address of the buffer being provided as inputs.

- *rfork()* is a nonblocking call which calls a remote stub to generate a new thread and passes the addresses of remote objects as parameters.

The above functions are used to implement various evaluations of expressions and procedures. For example, *rcreate()* and *rwrite()* can be used to create and initialize remote objects, respectively. A call to a remote procedure can be realized by *rfork()*. *rread()* can be used for a client to obtain the value of a remote object, and a client can release the memory for a remote object using *rremove*.

In DCDL none of the above mechanisms is included. We try to keep the simplicity of send and receive commands so the reader can focus on algorithms described in DCDL.

2.6 Robustness

Distributed systems have the potential advantages over centralized systems of higher reliability and availability. However, the responsibility for achieving reliability still relies on the operating system, the language runtime system, and the programmer. Two approaches can be used to achieve the reliability in distributed systems:

- Programming fault tolerance.

- Communication fault tolerance.

These two methods are interrelated. Programming fault tolerance can be achieved by either *forward recovery* or *backward recovery*. Forward recovery tries to identify the error and correct the system state containing the error based on this knowledge [11]. Exception handling in high level languages, such as Ada, PL/1, and CLU, provides a system structure that supports forward recovery. Backward error recovery corrects the system state by restoring the system to a state which occurred prior to the manifestation of the fault. The *recovery block scheme* [28] provides such a system structure. Another programming fault-tolerance technique commonly used is error masking. *N-version programming* [6] uses several independently developed versions of an algorithm. A final voting system is applied to the results of these n versions and a correct result is generated. So far there is no commercially available language which supports a backward recovery scheme although several researchers have proposed some language skeletons [30], [32], as well as some underlying supporting mechanisms such as the *recovery cache* [3] and the *recovery metaprogram* [2].

Communication fault tolerance deals with faults that occur in process communication. Communication fault tolerance depends on both the communication scheme used (message-passing or RPC) and the nature of the faults (fail-stop [41] or Byzantine type of faults [33]).

In general, there are four types of communication faults:

1. A message transmitted from a node does not reach its intended destinations.

2. Messages are not received in the same order as they were sent.

3. A message gets corrupted during its transmission.

4. A message gets replicated during its transmission.

Cases 2, 3, and 4 can be handled by sequence numbers, data encryption, and check-sums. However, it is not easy to identify the cause of an error. For example, if a call terminates abnormally (the time out expires), there are four mutually exclusive possibilities.

1. The receiver did not receive the call message.

2. The reply message did not reach the sender.

3. The receiver crashed during the call execution and either has remained crashed or is not resuming the execution after crash recovery.

4. The receiver is still executing the call in which case the execution can interfere with subsequent activities of the client.

The simplest communication fault tolerance is message passing using the fail-stop model where a PE either works properly or completely stops. Fault tolerance is achieved by fault detection followed by system reconfiguration [4]. The following is a fault detection procedure described in DCDL [47].

```
sender :: = [   setup time (t);
                send diagnostic_signal to receiver;
                [   receive ack from receiver → status:=normal
                □ timeout (t)→ status:=abnormal
                ]
            ]
```

Through the above high level DCDL algorithm a faulty PE can be detected by the sender node by checking the value of the status variable.

Communications based on RPC have side effects so it is important to specify accurately the semantics of a call. Various reliability semantics have been proposed in the context of the RPC: exactly-once, last-one, at-least-once, last-of-many, and at-most-once semantics [45].

In object-based systems [35][1] the partial failure is achieved by using the concept of atomic actions [37]. The failure atomicity property of the atomic actions ensures that a computation can either be terminated normally, producing the intended results, or be aborted, producing no results. A detailed treatment of this topic can be found in Chapter 11.

In general, achieving partial failure in the distributed system is a multidimensional activity that must simultaneously address some or all of the following: fault confinement, fault detection, fault masking, retries, fault diagnosis, reconfiguration, recovery, restart, repair, and re-integration. For a detailed treatment of this topic, see [46] and the Proceedings of the IEEE Symposium on Reliable Distributed Systems of recent years.

Table 2.2 [7] summarizes parallelism, communication, and partial primitives used in different languages.

---

[1]Both object-based and object-oriented systems use the concept of an object. However, an object-based system does not support inheritance.

Primitives	Example Languages
PARALLELISM	
Expressing parallelism	
Processes	Ada, Concurrent C, Linda, NIL
Objects	Emerald, Concurrent Smalltalk
Statements	Occam
Expressions	Par Alfl, FX-87
Clauses	Concurrent PROLOG, PARLOG
Mapping	
Static	Occam, StarMod
Dynamic	Concurrent PROLOG, ParAlfl
Migration	Emerald
COMMUNICATION	
Message passing	
Point-to-point messages	CSP, Occam, NIL
Rendezvous	Ada, Concurrent C
Remote procedure call	DP, Concurrent CLU, LYNX
One-to-many messages	BSP, StarMod
Data sharing	
Distributed data structures	Linda, Orca
Shared logical variables	Concurrent PROLOG, PARLOG
Nondeterminism	
Select statement	CSP, Occam, Ada, Concurrent C, SR
Guarded Horn clauses	Concurrent PROLOG, PARLOG
PARTIAL FAILURES	
Failure detection	Ada, SR
Atomic transactions	Argus, Aeolus, Avalon
NIL	

Table 2.2 Language primitives [7] (©1989 Association for Computing Machinery, Inc.).

References

[1] Adams, J. C., W. S. Brainerd, J. T. Martin, B. T. Smith, and J. L. Wagener, *Fortran 90 Handbook*, Intertext Publications, McGraw-Hill Publishing Company, 1992.

[2] Ancona, M., G. Dodero, V. Gianuzzi, A. Clematis, and E. B. Fernandez, "A system architecture for fault tolerance in concurrent software", *IEEE Computers*, **23**, 10, Oct. 1990, 23-32.

[3] Anderson, T. and R. Kerr, "Recovery blocks in action: A system supporting high reliability", *Proc. of the Int'l Conf. on Software Engineering*, 1976, 562-570.

[4] Anderson, T. and P. A. Lee, *Fault Tolerance – Principles and Practice*, Prentice-Hall, Inc., 1981.

[5] Arbenz, P. et al., " SCIDDLE: A tool for large scale distributed computing", *Concurrency: Practice and Experience*, **7**, 2, Apr. 1995, 121-146.

[6] Avizienis, A., "The n-version approach to fault-tolerant software", *IEEE Transactions on Software Engineering*, **13**, 12, Dec. 1985, 1491-1510.

[7] Bal, H. E., J. G. Steiner, and A. S. Tanenbaum, "Programming languages for distributed computing systems", *ACM Computing Surveys*, **21**, 3, Sept. 1989, 261-322.

[8] Beckman, P., D. Gannon, and E. Johnson, "Portable parallel programming in HPC++", *Proc. of the 1996 Int'l Conf. on Parallel Processing Workshop*, 1996, 132-139.

[9] Bernstein, A. J., "Program analysis for parallel processing", *IEEE Transactions on Electronic Computers*, **15**, 5, Oct. 1966, 757-762.

[10] Bershad, B. N., T. E. Anderson, E. D. Lazowska, and H. M. Levy, "Lightweight remote procedure call", *ACM Transactions on Computer Systems*, **8**, 1, 1990, 37-55.

[11] Best, E. and F. Cristian, "Systematic detection of exception occurrence", *Sci. Comput. Program*, **1**, 1, 1981, 115-144.

[12] Birrell, A. and B. Nelson, "Implementing remote procedure calls", *ACM Transactions on Computer Systems*, **2**, 1, Feb. 1984, 39-59.

[13] Broy, M., "A theory for nondeterminism, parallelism, communication, and concurrency", *Theoretical Computer Science*, **45**, 1986, 1-61.

[14] Burns, A., *Programming in Occam 2*, Addison-Wesley Publishing Company, 1988.

[15] Carriero, N. and D. Gelernter, *How to Write Parallel Programs: A First Course*, MIT Press, 1990.

[16] Chandy, K. M. and J. Misra, *Parallel Program Design: A Foundation*, Addison-Wesley Publishing Company, 1989.

[17] Ciancarini, P., "Coordination models and languages as software integrators", *ACM Computing Surveys*, **28**, 2, 1996, 300-302.

[18] Dijkstra, E. W., "Co-operating sequential processes", in *New Programming Languages*, F. Genuys, ed., Academic Press, 1968, 43-112.

[19] Dijkstra, E. W., *A Discipline of Programming*, Prentice-Hall, Inc., 1976.

[20] Dromey, G., *Program Derivation: The Development of Programs From Specifications*, Addison-Wesley Publishing Company, 1989.

[21] Dymond, P. W., "On nondeterminism in parallel computation," *Theoretical Computer Science*, **47**, 1986, 111-120.

[22] Francez, N., *Fairness*, Springer-Verlag, Inc., 1986.

[23] Gehani, N. H., "Broadcasting sequential processes (BSP)", *IEEE Transactions on Software Engineering*, **10**, 4, July 1984, 343-351.

[24] Geist, A., A. Berguelin, J. Dongarra, W. Jiang, R. Manchek, and V. Sunderam, *PVM: Parallel Virtual Machine*, The MIT Press, 1994.

[25] Hansen, P. B., *Operating System Principles*, Prentice-Hall, Inc., 1973.

[26] Hansen, P. B., "Distributed processes: A concurrent programming concept", *Communications of the ACM*, Nov. 1978, 934-941.

[27] Hoare, C. A. R., "Communicating sequential processes", *Communications of the ACM*, **21**, 8, Aug. 1978, 666-677.

[28] Horning, J. J., H. C. Lauer, P. M. Melliar-Smith, and B. Randall, "A program structure for error detection and recovery", *Proc. of the*

Conf. on Operating Systems: Theoretical and Practical Aspects , 1974, 177-193.

[29] Ishikawa, Y., "The MPC++ programming language V1.0 specification with commentary - document version 0.1", Technical Report TR-94014, Real World Computing Partnership, June 1994.

[30] Jalote, P. and R. H. Campbell, "Atomic actions for fault-tolerance using CSP", *IEEE Transactions on Software Engineering*, **12**, 1, Jan. 1986, 59-68.

[31] Jordan, H. F., "A special purpose architecture for finite element analysis", *Proc. of the 1978 Int'l Conf. on Parallel Processing*, 1978, 263-266.

[32] Kim, K. H., "Approaches to mechanization of the conversation scheme based on monitors", *IEEE Transactions on Software Engineering*, **8**, 3, May 1982, 189-197.

[33] Lamport, L., R. Shostak, and M. Pease, "The Byzantine generals problems", *ACM Transactions on Programming Languages and Systems*, **4**, 2, 1982, 382-401.

[34] Lan, Y., A. Esfahanian, and L. M. Ni, "Multicast in hypercube multiprocessors", *Journal of Parallel and Distributed Computing*, **8**, 1, Jan. 1990, 30-41.

[35] Liskov, B. and R. Scheifler, "Guardians and actions: Linguistic support for robust, distributed program", *Proc. of the 9th Annual Symp. on Principles of Programming Languages*, 1982, 7-19.

[36] Liskov, B. and L. Shrira, "Promises: Linguistic support for efficient asynchronous procedure calls in distributed systems", *Proc. of the ACM SIGPLAN'88 Conf. on Programming Language Design and Implementation*, 1988, 260-267.

[37] Lomet, D. B., "Process structuring, synchronization, and recovery using atomic actions", *Proc. of the ACM Conf. on Language Design for Reliable Software*, SIGPLAN Notice, 1977, 128-137.

[38] Loveman, D. B., "High performance Fortran", *IEEE Parallel & Distributed Technology*, **1**, 1, Feb. 1993, 25-42.

[39] MPI Forum, "MPI: A message-passing interface standard", *International Journal of Supercomputer Application*, **8**, 1994, 165-416.

[40] Peterson, J. L. and A. Silberschatz, *Operating System Concepts*, second edition, Addison-Wesley Publishing Company, 1985.

[41] Schlichting, R. D. and F. B. Schneider, "Fault-stop processor: An approach to designing fault-tolerant computing systems", *ACM Transactions on Computing Systems*, 1, 3, Aug. 1983, 222-238.

[42] Sinha, P. K., *Distributed Operating Systems: Concepts and Design*, IEEE Computer Society Press, 1997.

[43] Skillicorn, D. B. and D. Talia, *Programming Languages for Parallel Processing*, IEEE Computer Society Press, 1995.

[44] Stamos, J. and D. Gifford, "Implementing remote evaluation", *IEEE Transactions on Software Engineering*, 16, 7, July 1990, 710-722.

[45] Stankovic, J. A., K. Ramamritham, and W. H. Kohler, "A review of current research and critical issues in distributed system software", in *Concurrency Control and Reliability in Distributed Systems*, B. K. Bhargava, ed., Von Nostrand Reinhold Company, 1984, 556-601.

[46] Stankovic, J. A., *Reliable Distributed System Software*, IEEE Computer Society Press, 1985.

[47] Wu, J. and E. B. Fernandez, "A fault-tolerant distributed broadcast algorithm for cube-connected-cycles", *Computer Systems and Engineering*, 8, 4, Oct. 1993, 224-233.

[48] Wu, J., V. Rancov, and A. Stoichev, "Parallel computations on LAN-connected workstations", *Proc. of the 1996 Int'l Conf. on Parallel and Distributed Computing and Systems*, 1996, 193-197.

Problems

1. Provide a DCDL implementation of the producer-consumer problem. Three processes (producer, consumer, buffer) are used with n the size of the buffer. Extend your algorithm to the case in which there is more than one consumer (still with one producer) and show that the fairness among consumers is ensured in your extension.

2. Sum the first k elements in an array $a[1 : n]$. Terminate the summation process if the addition of the $(k + 1)$th element will cause

the partial summation $p = \sum_{i=1}^{k+1} a[i]$ to exceed the value of sum $s = \sum_{i=1}^{k} a[i]$.

3. Check whether the array $a[1:n]$ has been partitioned about x such that

$$a[1:i] \leq x \land a[j:n] \geq x \land j = i + 1$$

4. (*The Plateau Problem* by D. Gries) Given is a fixed, ordered array $b[1:n]$, where $n > 1$. A *plateau* of the array is a sequence of equal values. Write a DCDL program to store in variable p the length of the longest plateau of $b[1:n]$.

5. (*The Welfare Crook* by W. Feijen) Suppose we have three long magnetic tapes each containing a list of names in alphabetical order. The first list contains the names of people working at IBM Yorktown, the second the names of students at Columbia University and the third the names of all people on welfare in New York City. All three lists are endless so no upper bounds are given. It is known that at least one person is on all three lists. Write a program to locate the first such person (the one with the alphabetically smallest name). Your solution should use three processes, one for each tape.

6. (*The Dutch National Flag* by E. W. Dijkstra) Given is an array $b[1:n]$ for fixed $n \geq 1$. Each element is colored either red, white, or blue. Write a program to permute the elements so that all the red elements are first and all the blue ones last. The color of an element may be tested with Boolean expressions $red(b[i])$, $white(b[i])$ and $blue(b[i])$ which return the obvious values. The number of tests should be kept to a minimum. The only way to permute array elements is to swap two of them; the program should make at most n swaps. You may just use one process, i.e., no send or receive command is needed.

7. A common problem that occurs when entering text is that words are mistakenly repeated, for example,

"This text contains a repeating repeating word"

Design a program that detects such repetitions.

8. Convert the following DCDL expression to a precedence graph.

$$[\ S_1 \ \|\ [\ [\ S_2 \ \|\ S_3\ ];S_4\ ]\ ]$$

Use **fork** and **join** to express this expression.

9. Convert the following program to a precedence graph:

$$S_1; [[S_2; S_3 \| S_4; S_5 \| S_6] \| S_7]; S_8$$

10. G is a sequence of integers defined by the recurrence $G_i = G_{i-1} + G_{i-3}$ for $i > 1$, with initial values $G_0 = 0$, $G_1 = 1$, and $G_2 = 1$. Provide a DCDL implementation of G_i and use one process for each G_i.

11. Implement the following recursive equation using DCDL:

$$f(n) = \begin{cases} 1 & n = 1 \\ 2 & n = 2 \\ 3 & n = 3 \\ f(n) = f(n - 2 + (-1)^{n+1}) \times f(n - 1) & n > 3 \end{cases}$$

That is, $f(4) = f(1) \times f(3), f(5) = f(4) \times f(4), f(6) = f(3) \times f(5), f(7) = f(6) \times f(6)$, etc. You are required to use one process P_i in computing $f(i)$ and one process (P_0) for the user. It is assumed that each P_i can only communicate with its two neighbors P_{i-1} and P_{i+1}. Demonstrate your algorithm by calculating $f(6)$.

12. You are required to evaluate a polynomial

$$a_0 + a_1 x^1 + ... + a_{n-1} x^{n-1}.$$

Design a DCDL algorithm with n processes. Assume that initially P_i $(0 \le i < n)$ has a_i and x. The final evaluation result should be placed in P_{n-1}. Try to minimize the number of multiplications and number of interprocess communications.

13. Using DCDL to write a program that replaces $a * b$ by $a \uparrow b$ and $a * * b$ by $a \downarrow b$, where a and b are any characters other than $*$. For example, if $a_1 a_2 * a_3 * * a_4 * * * a_5$ is the input string then $a_1 a_2 \uparrow a_3 \downarrow a_4 * * * a_5$ will be the output string.

14. Find all the statement pairs that can be executed concurrently.

$$S_1: a = x + 2$$
$$S_2: b = y + 2$$
$$S_3: y = c + 1$$
$$S_4: c = x + y + b$$

15. Represent the following precedence graph using the concurrent state-
    ment and the sequential statement in DCDL.

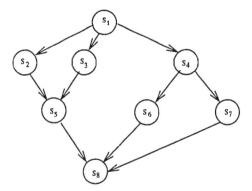

Chapter 3

FORMAL APPROACHES TO DISTRIBUTED SYSTEMS DESIGN

In this chapter we treat distributed systems in a rather formal way. Several concepts such as clock, event, time, and state are introduced as well as two popular approaches that describe a distributed system: the time-space view and the interleaving view.

3.1 Introduction to Models

This section presents an overview of the models commonly used for specifying properties of a distributed system. The purpose of a model is to precisely define specific properties or characteristics of a system to be built or analyzed and to provide the foundation for verifying these properties. Different models are used to specify different properties. The following are three representative models for distributed systems:

- *Mathematical function.* It consists of an input domain, an output domain, and a rule for transforming the inputs into the outputs. In general, a mathematical function is not an algorithm. A mathematical function can be decomposed, i.e., specified by a combination of logic and lower level functions. This feature allows a hierarchy of functions. The benefits arise from its ability to organize a large amount of data and check the consistency of inputs and outputs between a top level function and its decomposition into a number of lower level interconnected functions. One limitation of this approach is no memory: Given an input it produces an output but it does not save data.

- *Finite state machine* (FSM). FSM is a set of inputs, a set of outputs, a set of states, an initial state, and a pair of functions used to specify the outputs and state transitions as results of given inputs. This model appears ideal for the specification of data processing because one can associate the inputs and outputs of the data processor with those of FSM and associate the contents of the data in memory with states and the code with transitions. The limitations are: First, FSM inherently serializes all of the underlying concurrency. Secondly, the model explicitly assumes that all processing on an input is completed before the next input arrives. This model will be discussed in detail in Section 3.1.1.

- *Graph model.* The graph model of computation is a directed graph of vertices (or nodes) and edges (arcs or links) and it is used to specify both control flow and data flow. Each node of the graph represents a processing step that has one or more input arcs and one or more output arcs. The limitation is that it does not incorporate the concept of a "state" which is saved from processing one input data set in order to process subsequent input data. *Petri nets* are a special type of graph model to be discussed later in this chapter.

3.1.1   A state machine model

As defined in Chapter 1 a distributed system is a set of processing elements $PE = \{PE_1, PE_2, \ldots, PE_n\}$ that share no memory and communicate only by message passing. From the logical level a distributed system is a set of cooperating processes $P = \{P_1, P_2, \ldots, P_n\}$. To simplify the discussion we assume that each process is associated with one distinct processing element although, in reality, several processes may execute in the same PE.

A process (or a PE) *view* of the system has only two components: its clock and its local state. A *clock* can be either *physical* or *logical* (to be discussed in later sections). A *local state* is a collection of variables in the process. The local state changes only as a result of *events*. A process executes two types of events: *internal* and *external*. External events include *send* events and *receive* events.

- *Internal events* which change only the local process (or PE) state.

- *Send events* such as **send** message_list to destination which sends the message "message_list" to the process "destination".

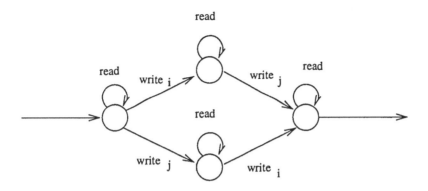

FIGURE 3.1
A deterministic system.

- *Receive events* such as **receive** message_list **from** source, which receives the message "message_list" from the process "source".

A distributed system can also be specified in terms of a finite state machine (FSM) [12] which consists of a set C of possible commands and a set S of possible global states. Each global state is a collection of local states. A refined definition of a global state that includes local states and channel states will be discussed later. A function e (event) is defined as:

$$e : C \times S \to S$$

$s \xrightarrow{c} s'$ represents the result of executing the command c in C at state s that causes the system state to change from s to s'.

A system is *deterministic* iff (if and only if) for any $s \in S$ and $c \in C$ there is at most one s' such that $s \xrightarrow{c} s'$; otherwise, the system is *nondeterministic*. Figure 3.1 shows a deterministic system with $C = \{write, read\}$. $write_i$ and $write_j$ stand for two different writes. However, many distributed systems are nondeterministic. A state s' is *reachable* from a state s iff $s \xrightarrow{*} s'$, where $*$ is the transitive closure of the relation "$\to$". For additional discussion of the state machine formulation for distributed systems the readers may refer to [5].

In this section concepts of clock, event, state (local and global), and time are introduced in a rather informal way. Detailed discussion of these concepts will be given in subsequent sections.

3.1.2   Petri nets

Petri nets [1], [16] are powerful tools to study the behavior of distributed computer systems. As a modeling tool Petri nets can be used to model both the static and dynamic properties of systems and, as a graphically-oriented specification tool, they appear to be one of the best approaches for enhancing interaction among users and specifiers for easy human comprehension.

A Petri net is a five-tuple, $C = (P, T, I, O, u)$, where $P = \{p_1, p_2, \ldots, p_n\}$ is a finite set of *places* with $n > 0$, $T = \{t_1, t_2, \ldots, t_m\}$ is a finite set of *transitions* with $m > 0$. T and P are disjointed $(P \cap T = \phi)$. $I : T \to P^\infty$ is the input function, a mapping from transitions to *bags* (or multi-sets) of places. $O : T \to P^\infty$ is the output function. Vector $u = (u_1, u_2, \ldots, u_n)$ gives for each place the number of *tokens* in that place and is called a *marking*, i.e., place P_i has u_i tokens. An example of a Petri net is given below.

Example 3.1 *University Semester System* [25].

$$C = (P, T, I, O, u)$$
$$P = \{p_1, p_2, p_3, p_4\}$$
where $p_1 = $ fall semester, $p_2 = $ spring semester
$\qquad\qquad p_3 = $ summer semester, $p_4 = $ not summer semester
$$T = \{t_1, t_2, t_3\}$$
where $t_1 = $ start of spring semester
$\qquad\quad t_2 = $ start of summer semester
$\qquad\quad t_3 = $ start of fall semester
$$u = \{1, 0, 0, 1\}$$

$O(t_1) = \{P_2\}$	$I(t_1) = \{P_1\}$
$O(t_2) = \{P_3\}$	$I(t_2) = \{P_2, P_4\}$
$O(t_3) = \{P_1, P_4\}$	$I(t_3) = \{P_3\}$

∎

Petri nets can be represented by graphs where a circle represents a *place* and a *bar* represents a transition. The input and output functions are represented by directed arcs from the places to the transitions and from the transitions to the places, respectively. Each token is represented by a bullet. The Petri net graph for Example 3.1 is shown in Figure 3.2. In this example a university semester system consists of three semesters: fall, spring, and summer; each is represented by a place. Specifically, place P_1 stands for a fall semester, P_2 for a spring semester, P_3 for a summer semester, and P_4 for a semester other than summer. Transition t_1 represents the start of spring semester, t_2 the start of summer semester, and t_3 the

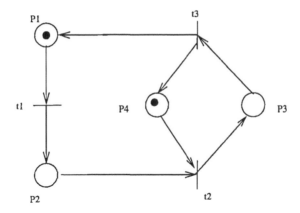

FIGURE 3.2
The Petri net graph for a university semester system.

start of fall semester. The transitions between Petri net execution are represented by the movement of tokens. Tokens move through transition firing. When a transition is validated, i.e., each of its input places has at least one token, the transition can fire which removes one token from each of its input places and deposits one token into each of its output places. The patterns of different token distributions represent different systems states. The example of the university semester system is a repetition of three states shown in Figure 3.3 with the fall semester as the initial state where each state is represented by a 4-tuple (tokens in P_1, tokens in P_2, tokens in P_3, tokens in P_4).

The diagram in Figure 3.3 is also called a *reachability tree*. It consists of a tree whose nodes represent markings of the Petri net and whose arcs represent the possible changes in state resulting from the firing of transitions. Note that when a node (state) repeats itself it becomes a terminating node. Another option is to add an arc pointing to that node generating a cycle. In this case the reachability tree is called a *reachability graph*. In the university semester system the second occurrence of the fall semester is removed and an arc is placed from a summer semester to the first occurrence of a fall semester.

Petri nets can be used to specify precisely concepts of sequence, selection, concurrency, and synchronization. Figure 3.4 shows some of these mechanisms using Petri nets. Figure 3.4 (a) is a sequential statement $S_1; S_2$,

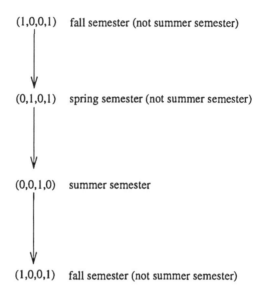

(1,0,0,1)   fall semester (not summer semester)

(0,1,0,1)   spring semester (not summer semester)

(0,0,1,0)   summer semester

(1,0,0,1)   fall semester (not summer semester)

FIGURE 3.3
A state diagram of the university semester system.

Figure 3.4 (b) is a conditional statement:

$$[\, C \rightarrow S_1 \;\square\; \neg\, C \rightarrow S_2 \,]$$

and Figure 3.4 (c) is an iterative statement:

$$*\,[\, C \rightarrow S_1 \,]$$

Note that sequential, conditional, and iterative statements are three basic control structures. Petri nets can also specify ambiguous (nondeterministic) action, i.e., when a place with one token has more than one outgoing fir-able transition. In this case a transition is randomly selected to execute.

Simulations of a distributed system can be automatically generated from Petri nets by defining a Petri net processor. This device examines the status of all transitions, selects one which has met its firing conditions, and moves the tokens according to the rule. This step is repeated until no preconditions are satisfied.

Wu [26], [27] introduced a high-level extended Petri net to model a distributed system with a set of processes. In this model each process is modeled by a subnet. Each internal action of a process can be directly represented by a Petri net. The structure of a distributed system is organized

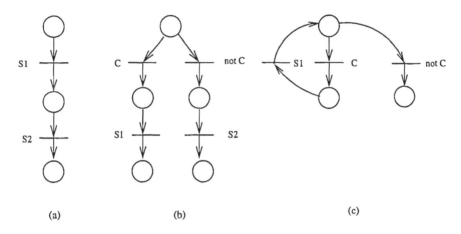

FIGURE 3.4
Petri nets examples: (a) sequential statement, (b) conditional statement, and (c) iterative statement.

hierarchically into several levels. At the highest level only interprocess communication (an external event) is shown. All the internal events are specified at the lower level of specification. The lower level specifications can be represented by replacing each place (transition) in the model with a more detailed Petri net through a *refinement* process by replacing a place (transition) with a subnet starting and ending with a place (transition).

The Petri net model of interprocess communication is shown in Figure 3.5 where local states (places) from different processes are separated by a dashed line. A thick bar is used to represent a transition using different firing rules. Firing rules depend on different implementations and there are three possible implementations of interprocess communication: synchronous (as in CSP), asynchronous (as in DCDL), and buffered. Note that asynchronous communication is a special type buffer communication with an unbounded buffer. The corresponding Petri net refinement of each implementation is shown in Figure 3.6. The number n in a place of Figure 3.6 represents the number of tokens in the place.

Many interesting properties of distributed systems can be defined and validated using the Petri net. For example, a Petri net can be analyzed to determine whether correct termination of a distributed system will always occur or whether the possibility of a deadlock exists, e.g., the Petri net may enter a state where no transitions are possible or whether the possibility of live-lock exists, e.g., the Petri net is cycling through an endless loop.

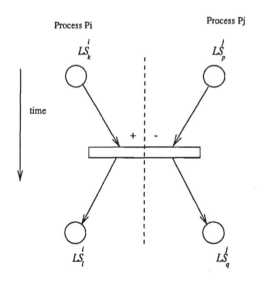

FIGURE 3.5
The Petri net model of interprocess communications, where process P_i is a sender (+ sign) and process P_j is a receiver (− sign).

Petri nets can also be represented by state models. In [27], Wu defined each place in the Petri net specification graph as a state in a process. The state of the complete system, GS_x, at a given time is defined as a vector $(LS_x^1, ..., LS_x^n)$ where LS_x^y is the local state of process P_y in global state x $(1 \leq y \leq n)$ and n is the total number of processes. The local states of the processes along time define a partial order on the Petri net specification graph. For example, the partial order defined by the local states in Figure 3.5 is as follows $LS_k^i < LS_l^i, LS_k^i < LS_q^j, LS_p^j < LS_l^i, LS_p^j < LS_q^j, LS_l^i = LS_q^j$, and $LS_k^i = LS_p^j$ where "=" denotes two local states that have the same order.

With this definition the system can be represented by a sequence of global states:

$$GS_0 \xrightarrow{t_1} GS_1 \xrightarrow{t_2} GS_2... \qquad \text{where } GS_x < GS_{x+1}$$

if

$$GS_x = (LS_x^1, LS_x^2, ..., LS_x^n)$$

and

$$GS_{x+1} = (LS_{x+1}^1, LS_{x+1}^2, ..., LS_{x+1}^n),$$

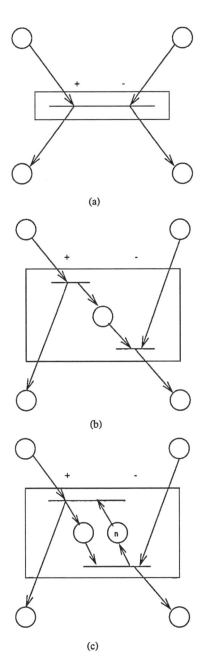

FIGURE 3.6
Petri nets for different types of interprocess communication: (a)
synchronous, (b) asynchronous, and (c) buffered.

then

$$GS_x < GS_{x+1} \longleftrightarrow \forall_y[(LS_x^y < LS_{x+1}^y) \vee (LS_x^y = LS_{x+1}^y)] \wedge$$
$$\exists_y[LS_x^y < LS_{x+1}^y] \ (1 \le y \le n)$$

Each t_i is an interprocess communication transition and GS_x is the global state after interprocess communication t_i. This sequence called an *action ordered tree* is an extended reachability tree for a system with multiple processes. In an action ordered tree a state is derived from its parent state either through a transition or through multiple transitions. For the case of multiple transitions the new states are a summary of the possible states that can occur if only one transition fires at a time.

In spite of its advantages there are two fundamental limitations for using a Petri net to describe a distributed system. First, like the finite state machine model, it is flat, i.e., the Petri net appears in essentially one level. However, several independent approaches have been developed using the concept of subnet (such as the one defined above), thus using the concept of a hierarchy of subnets to handle large complex distributed systems. For example, the Petri net model discussed earlier describes a system at the interprocess level. Each node (cycle) can be refined to describe details at the intraprocess level, i.e., local events within each process. Another significant limitation is that it specifies only control flow not data flow. Although conditions for the transitions can be specified in terms of data values, the semantics for changing values of data is not an inherent part of the Petri net. Some attempts are being made to rectify this problem in [10] and [29], but some details have not been fully worked out.

3.2   Causally Related Events

Causality among events in a distributed system, more formally the causal precedence relation, is a powerful concept for reasoning, analyzing, and drawing inferences about a distributed computation.

3.2.1   The happened-before relation

In a centralized system it is always possible to determine the order two events occurred in two different processes since there is a single common memory and a common clock. In a distributed system, however, there is no common memory and no common clock. Therefore, it is sometimes impossible to say which of the two events occurred first. The *happened-before* relation [12] is a partial ordering defined on the events in a distributed system. The definition is based on the fact that processes are sequential and all the events executed in a single process are totally ordered. Also a message (or message list) can be received only after it has been sent.

The happened-before relation (denoted by $\rightarrow$) is defined as follows:

1. If a and b are events in the same process and a was executed before b, then $a \rightarrow b$.

2. If a is the event of sending a message by one process and b is the event of receiving that message by another process, then $a \rightarrow b$.

3. If $a \rightarrow b$ and $b \rightarrow c$, then $a \rightarrow c$.

Normally $a \nrightarrow a$ holds for any event a. This implies that $\rightarrow$ is an *irreflexive partial ordering*.

3.2.2 The time-space view

The definition of the happened-before relation can best be illustrated by a time-space diagram where the horizontal direction represents space, the vertical direction time, the labeled vertical lines processes, the labeled dots events, and the arrow lines messages.

Example 3.2 Figure 3.7 shows a distributed system with three processes P_1, P_2, and P_3. Each process has four labeled events. Events that are related by the happened-before relation are:

$$a_0 \rightarrow a_1 \rightarrow a_2 \rightarrow a_3$$
$$b_0 \rightarrow b_1 \rightarrow b_2 \rightarrow b_3$$
$$c_0 \rightarrow c_1 \rightarrow c_2 \rightarrow c_3$$
$$a_0 \rightarrow b_3$$
$$b_1 \rightarrow a_3, b_2 \rightarrow c_1, b_0 \rightarrow c_2$$

■

We can also derive $b_1 \rightarrow c_2$ based on $b_1 \rightarrow b_2, b_2 \rightarrow c_1$, and $c_1 \rightarrow c_2$. Two events a and b are *causally related* if $a \rightarrow b$ or $b \rightarrow a$. Two distinct events a and b are said to be *concurrent* if $a \nrightarrow b$ and $b \nrightarrow a$. For the example shown in Figure 3.7, events a_2 and c_0 are concurrent, i.e., $a_2 \| c_0$.

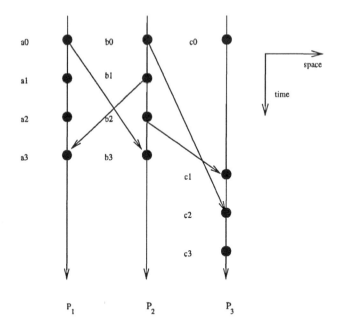

FIGURE 3.7
A time-space view of a distributed system.

3.2.3   The interleaving view

The time-space view is very useful for representing the happened-before relation. However, while our view of the execution of a distributed system may be a set of events, experience has shown that we want to reason about the system in terms of states. The time-space view is biased towards events. To reason about states we need the *interleaving view*. In the interleaving view we assume that the events are totally ordered. If two events do not influence one another, i.e., if they are not related by the happened-before relation, we may pretend that they occurred in either order. The inter-leaving view model is based on the following fact: Since there does exist a notion of global time the events in the system "really do" take place in some definite order. For example, we can order the events by their starting time (or ending time). Without infinitely precise clocks we can never be sure what this total ordering is. However, since it must exist, we can postulate its existence.

We denote a total ordering $\Rightarrow$ on a set of processes and events. The only constraint is that $\Rightarrow$ should be consistent with $\rightarrow$. For example, $a_0 a_1 c_0 b_0 b_1$

$b_2 b_3 c_1 c_2 a_1 a_2 c_3 a_3$ is one of the total orders of the example in Figure 3.7.

Note that there is a unique time-space view corresponding to an interleaving view, but there are many interleaving views corresponding to a time-space view. There are many ways to complete a partial ordering to a total ordering. The total ordering in the interleaving view contains additional information, namely, orderings between events at different processes.

3.3   Global States

A global state consists of a set of local states and a set of states of communication channels. Note that this is a refined definition of global state that was defined early as a set of local states only. Collection of local states alone may result in a partial view of the system. Consider a bank system with two branches A and B. Suppose we transfer $100 from account A (with an initial balance of $500) to account B (with an initial balance of $200). If both accounts record their changes right after each local state change, then when $100 is in transit, i.e., in a channel connecting accounts A and B, account A has a balance of $400 and account B has a balance of $200. Note that the above case results in a partial view but it is still (weak) consistent. However, if we assume that account A records its state before the transfer and account B records its after the transfer is completed, the total amount recorded is $500+$300 = $800. Clearly, this is an inconsistent global state.

In general, the state of a communication channel in a consistent global state should be the sequence of messages sent along that channel before the sender's state was recorded excluding the sequence of messages received along that channel before the receiver's state was recorded. Note that it is difficult to record channel states to ensure the above rule. Another option of recording a global state is without using channel states. The recorded state may or may not be consistent. An algorithm that can capture consistent states without using channel states is discussed in Section 3.3.3.

Based on the delivery assumptions, channels can be classified as: FIFO (first in first out), causally ordered delivery, and random ordered delivery. A channel is said to be FIFO if it keeps the order of the message sent through it. The causally ordered delivery [22] is defined as follows: Suppose P_1 and P_2 send messages m_1 and m_2 to process P_3 in events e_1 and e_2, respectively. If e_1 happens before e_2, then process P_3 receives m_1 before

m_2. There is no constraint on a channel exhibiting random ordered delivery. Without explicitly stating the type of a given channel, we assume it is a FIFO channel. Similarly a set of assumptions are normally made for each process: (1) Normally each process has a unique id and each process knows its own id and ids of other processes. (2) Each process knows its neighbors including their ids.

3.3.1   Global states in the time-space view

In order to define a global state in the time-space view, we define the concept of a *time slice*. Intuitively, a time slice represents the system at some instant of time. However, since we are not assuming any type of clock, we must define this concept in terms of events. The basic idea is to consider a time slice to be a partition of the events: The events that happen "before", denoted as $\rightarrow$, the time slice and those that happen after it. Formally, we define the time slice to be the *before set* E of events: If $b \in E$ and $a \rightarrow b$ then $a \in E$. A time slice E is *earlier* than a time slice E' if $E \subset E'$. Unlike real clock times, time slices are not totally ordered.

Given a time slice E, we define the global state $GS(E)$ associated with this time slice as follows: If there are no events of process P_i in E, the LS_i is the starting state of P_i; otherwise, LS_i is defined to be the final state of the latest event of P_i in E. For each channel c we define the state of c in $GS(E)$ to be the sequence of all messages that are sent by an event in E and received by an event not in E.

Example 3.3 Consider a distributed bank system consisting of a network of three branches A, B, and C connected by unidirectional channels (as shown Figure 3.8).

Figure 3.8 shows a time-space view of the events (transactions) of the bank system. A sequence of global states for the system in Figure 3.8 is shown in Figure 3.9. Note that global states are derived based on the positioning (timing) of events shown in Figure 3.8. In this case the change of a global state is triggered by an external event: send or receive. In the example of Figure 3.8 there are four pairs of send and receive events which correspond to eight external events.

3.3.2   Global state: a formal definition

Let LS_i be the local state of process P_i. Then the global state $GS = (LS_1, LS_2, ..., LS_n)$. Here the global state is defined by local states only,

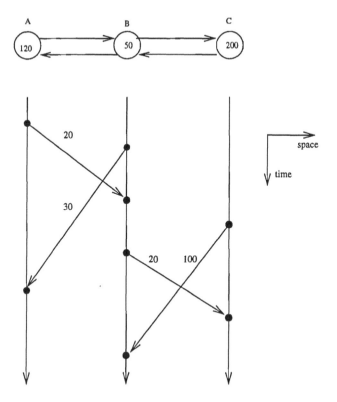

FIGURE 3.8
An example of a network of a bank system.

i.e., the state of each channel is not included. Hence, a state may or may not be consistent. To define a consistent state we need the following two concepts, both represented as a set, where $s(m)$ (and $r(m)$) is a send (and receive) event involving message m.

Transit: $transit(LS_i, LS_j) = \{m|s(m) \in LS_i \wedge r(m) \notin LS_j\}$

Inconsistent: $inconsistent(LS_i, LS_j) = \{m|s(m) \notin LS_i \wedge r(m) \in LS_j\}$

Set $transit$ includes all the messages in channels between P_i and P_j. Set $inconsistent$ contains all the messages whose receive events are recorded at P_j but its send events are not recorded at P_i.

A global state GS is $consistent$ iff

$$\forall i, \forall j, inconsistent(LS_i, LS_j) = \phi$$

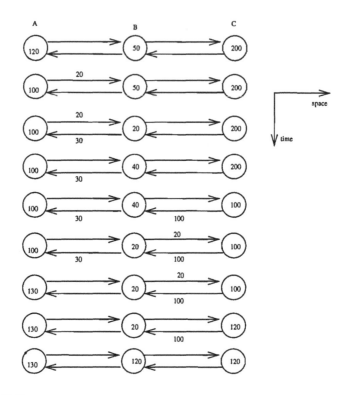

FIGURE 3.9
A sequence of global states for the system in Figure 3.8.

A global state GS is *transitless* iff

$$\forall i, \forall j, transit(LS_i, LS_j) = \phi$$

A global state is *strongly consistent* if it is consistent and transitless. That is, a set of local states is consistent and there is no message in transit.

The concept of a time slice can also be captured by a graphical representation called a *cut*. A cut of a distributed computation is a set $C = \{c_1, c_2, ..., c_n\}$, where c_i is the cut event in process P_i, i.e., a local state that corresponds to the cut. Let e_i be an event in P_i. A cut C is consistent iff

$$\forall P_i, \forall P_j, \nexists e_i, \nexists e_j (e_i \rightarrow e_j) \wedge (e_j \rightarrow c_j) \wedge (e_i \nrightarrow c_i)$$

where c_i and c_j are in C. Symbol $\nexists$ means that "there does not exist".

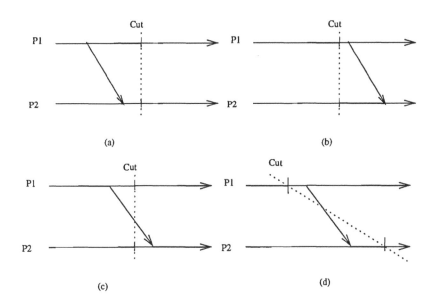

FIGURE 3.10
Four types of cut that cross a message transmission line.

Actually, a cut C is a consistent cut iff no two cut events are causally related. A cut can be graphically represented as a set of cut events connected by a dotted line. A dotted line may or may not "cross" the communication lines as shown in Figure 3.10. In Figures 3.10 (a) and (b) both cut lines do not cross the communication lines; therefore, the corresponding states are consistent. In Figure 3.10 (c) although the cut line goes across the communication line, two cut events are not causally related and it will not cause the inconsistency of the cut. Actually, this situation corresponds to a message in transit – a consistent but not strongly consistent state. In Figure 3.10 (d) two cut events are causally related and they form an inconsistent cut.

3.3.3   The "snapshot" of global states

Chandy and Lamport [6] proposed a simple distributed algorithm to capture a consistent global state also called a snapshot of the global state. It is assumed that all the channels are FIFO and a set of markers are transmitted along these channels. There is one process that runs on each node:

Rule for sender P:

[P records its local state
|| P sends a marker along all the channels
    on which a marker has not been sent.
]

Rule for receiver Q:

/* on receipt of a marker along a channel *chan* */
[Q has not recorded its state $\rightarrow$
    [record the state of *chan* as an empty sequence and
       follow the "Rule for sender"
    ]
□ Q has recorded its state $\rightarrow$
    [record the state of *chan* as the sequence of messages
       received along *chan* after the latest state recording
       but before receiving the marker
    ]
]

The role of markers is to "clean" the corresponding channels, although regular messages along a channel can still be sent after a marker is sent. A process at a node is said to have finished its part of the algorithm when it has executed and received a marker message for each of its incoming channels. It is easy to show that if at least one process initiates the algorithm, i.e., it takes the role of sender P, every process will eventually finish its part of the algorithm. Moreover, it does not matter the number of processes that initiate the snapshot algorithm simultaneously.

Figure 3.11 shows the snapshot algorithm applied to a system with three processes (nodes) P_i, P_j, and P_k. Each process is connected to the other two processes through bidirectional channels. $chan_{ij}$ stands for a channel from process P_i to process P_j. Assume process P_i initiates the snapshot algorithm. It performs three actions simultaneously: (1) calculates local state, (2) sends a marker to $chan_{ij}$ and $chan_{ik}$, and (3) sets up counters to keep track of messages coming from incoming channels, $chan_{ji}$ and $chan_{ki}$. Once process P_j receives the marker from $chan_{ij}$, it also performs three actions: (1) calculates local state and records the state of $chan_{ij}$ as empty, (2) sends a marker to $chan_{ji}$ and $chan_{jk}$, and (3) sets up a counter

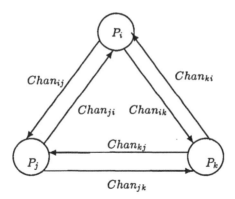

FIGURE 3.11
A system with three processes P_i, P_j, and P_k.

for the message coming from incoming channel $chan_{kj}$. Similarly, process P_k performs three actions. We assume that the marker from process P_i reaches process P_j before the marker from process P_k. Otherwise, the incoming channel at step (3) will be $chan_{ij}$. Once the marker from process P_k reaches process P_j, process P_j will record the channel state of $chan_{kj}$ as the sequence of messages received along this channel since the counter is set. Process P_j then terminates itself since it has received a marker message from every incoming channel and it has performed a local state computation. Similarly, process P_k terminates after receiving the marker sent from both processes P_i and P_j. Process P_i terminates after receiving markers from both processes P_j and P_k.

There are several extensions of Chandy and Lamport's snapshot algorithm. Lai and Yang [11] presented a simple snapshot algorithm over non-FIFO channels. A more elegant algorithm based on the concept of F-channels and flush primitives was proposed by Ahuja [2].

3.3.4   A necessary and sufficient condition for a consistent global state

As mentioned earlier consistent global states are important in many distributed applications. Then, what is the exact condition for an arbitrary checkpoint (a local state), or a set of checkpoints, to belong to a consistent global snapshot? Netzer and Xu [15] determined such a condition by introducing a generalization of Lamport's happened-before relation called a *zigzag path*.

A zigzag path exists from checkpoint A in process P_i to checkpoint B in process P_j. P_i and P_j can refer to the same process iff there are messages $m_1, m_2, ..., m_n$ $(n \geq 1)$ such that

- m_1 is sent by process P_i after A.

- If m_l $(1 \leq l < n)$ is received by process P_k, then m_{l+1} is sent by P_k in the same or a later checkpoint interval. Note that m_{l+1} may be sent before or after m_l is received.

- m_n is received by process P_j before B.

A *checkpoint interval* of a process is all the computation performed between two consecutive checkpoints. Checkpoint C is involved in a *zigzag cycle* iff there is a zigzag path from C to itself.

Note that there is a difference between a zigzag path and a causal path based on Lamport's happened-before relation. Basically, a causal path exists from A to B iff there is a chain of messages starting after A and ending before B with each message sent after the previous one in the chain is received. In a zigzag path, such a chain is allowed; in addition, any message in the chain to be sent before the previous one is received is also allowed as long as the send and receive are in the same checkpoint interval. In Figure 3.12 the path from C_{11} to C_{31} consisting of messages m_1 and m_2 is a zigzag path. The path from C_{11} to C_{32} consisting of messages m_1 and m_3 is a causal path (and a zigzag path). Checkpoint C_{22} forms a zigzag cycle consisting of messages m_4 and m_1.

A consistency theorem provided in [15] is the following: A set of checkpoints S, with each checkpoint coming from a different process, can belong to the same consistent global state iff no checkpoint S has a zigzag path to any other checkpoint (including itself) in S. As direct corollaries we have the following:

- Checkpoint C can belong to a consistent global state iff C does not belong to a zigzag cycle.

- Checkpoints A and B (belonging to different processes) can belong to the same consistent global state iff (1) no zigzag cycle involving A or B exists and (2) no zigzag path exists between A and B.

Normally, two virtual checkpoints are included in each process; one immediately before execution begins and the other immediately after execution ends. In Figure 3.12, checkpoints C_{11} and C_{21} can belong to the same consistent global state as well as checkpoints C_{12} and C_{32}. C_{22} cannot be in any consistent global state.

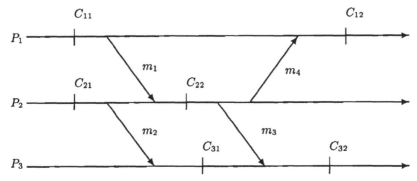

FIGURE 3.12
A distributed system with three processes.

3.4 Logical Clocks

Distributed systems have no built-in physical time and can only approximate it. Even in the Internet's network time protocol that maintains a time accurate to a few tens of milliseconds, it is not adequate for capturing causality in distributed systems. The happened-before relation defined in the previous section can be used to capture causality and can be easily derived from a given time-space view of the system. But how can each process obtain and keep such a relation in a system with no shared global memory? Lamport [12] proposed the principle of *timestamping*, also called the principle of logical clocks.

3.4.1 Scalar logical clock

In this model each process P_i owns a logical clock LC_i (it may be implemented by a counter with no actual timing mechanism). LC_i is initialized to *init* (≥ 0) and it is a nondecreasing sequence of integers. Every message m issued by P_i is stamped with the current value of LC_i and with the process label i, producing the triplet (m, LC_i, i).

The updates on LC_i are based on the following two rules:

- $Rule_1$. Before producing an event (an external send or internal event), we update LC:

$$LC_i = LC_i + d \qquad\qquad (d > 0)$$

(d can have a different value at each application of $Rule_1$)

Events	a_0	a_1	a_2	a_3	b_0	b_1	b_2	b_3	c_0	c_1	c_2
Logical time	1	2	3	4	1	2	3	4	1	4	5

Table 3.1 Events in Example 3.2 with their logical times.

- $Rule_2$. When it receives the timestamped message (m, LC_j, j), P_i executes the update

$$LC_i = \max(LC_i, LC_j) + d \qquad\qquad (d > 0)$$

We assume that each LC_i is initialized to $init$ (≥ 0) which can have a different value for different processes.

The timestamping method can also be implemented in such a way that logical clocks change only when an external event occurs. This can be done by deleting the internal event condition in the above algorithm.

With the timestamping method we can determine the logical time for each event in Figure 3.7, see Table 3.1, assuming that $d = 1$ and $init = 0$.

It is easy to prove that the timestamping method satisfies the following condition: For any events a, b, if $a \rightarrow b$ then $LC(a) < LC(b)$ where $LC(a)$ is the logical time associated with the event a. However, normally the converse condition does not hold, i.e., it is not necessary that $a \rightarrow b$ when $LC(a) < LC(b)$. For example, $LC(c_0) < LC(a_2)$ for events c_0 and a_2 in Figure 3.6. However $c_0 \nrightarrow a_2$.

We can also define the following total ordering $\Rightarrow$, one of many possible orders, on the event set while still satisfying the above condition:

$$a \ (\text{in } P_i\ ) \Rightarrow b\ (\text{in } P_j\ )$$

iff

$$(1)\ LC(a) < LC(b) \text{ or } (2)\ LC(a) = LC(b) \text{ and } P_i < P_j$$

where $<$ is an arbitrary total ordering of the process set, e.g., $<$ can be defined as $P_i < P_j$ iff $i < j$. With this definition the events in Figure 3.2 can be ordered as:

$$a_0\ b_0\ c_0\ a_1\ b_1\ a_2\ b_2\ a_3\ b_3\ c_1\ c_2$$

under the assumption that $P_a < P_b < P_c$.

The total ordering also provides an interleaving view of a distributed system. Although some system information is lost in such a view compared with the time-space view, the interleaving view can be very useful in implementing several types of distributed algorithms [18]; for example, the distributed mutual exclusion algorithm discussed in a later section.

3.4.2   Extensions

The timestamping mechanism discussed uses linear time, i.e., time is represented by an ordinary real number. However, a linear time clock system cannot distinguish between the advancements of clocks due to local events from those due to the exchange of message between processes. Extensions to the timestamping approach include *vector time* and *matrix time*. The vector time approach [14] uses n-dimensional vectors of integers to represent time while the matrix time approach [28] uses $n \times n$ matrices. The objective of using the vector and matrix is the following:

Based on $Rule_2$ (in the previous section) each receiving process receives a message together with the logical global time as perceived by the sender at sending time. This allows the receiver to update its view of the global time. Naturally, when information is included in time the receiver has a better and more accurate view of the global time.

In the vector time approach each P_i is associated with a vector $LC_i[1..n]$, where

- $LC_i[i]$ describes the progress of P_i, i.e., its own process.

- $LC_i[j]$ represents P_i's knowledge of P_j's progress.

- The $LC_i[1..n]$ constitutes P_i's local view of the logical global time.

$Rule_1$ and $Rule_2$ are modified as follows for each P_i:

- $Rule_1$. Before producing an event (an external send or internal event), we update $LC_i[i]$:

$$LC_i[i] := LC_i[i] + d \qquad\qquad (d > 0)$$

- $Rule_2$. Each message piggybacks the vector clock of the sender at sending time. When receiving a message (m, LC_j, j), P_i executes the update.

$$LC_i[k] := \max\ (LC_i[k], LC_j[k]), 1 \le k \le n$$
$$LC_i[i] := LC_i[i] + d$$

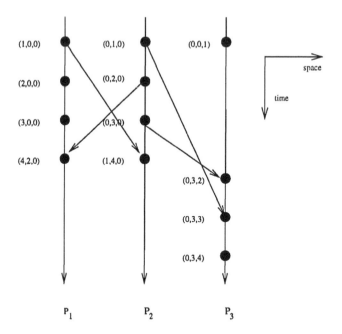

FIGURE 3.13
An example of vector clocks.

Figure 3.13 shows the progress of vector clocks of Example 3.1 with the increment value $d = 1$ and initialization value $init= 0$.

When $d = 1$ and $init = 0$, $LC_i[i]$ counts the number of internal events and $LC_i[j]$ corresponds to the number of events produced by P_j that causally precede the line; LC_i is read at P_i. $\sum_j LC_i(j) - 1$ counts the total number of events, including internal ones, that causally precede the receive event.

Let two events a and b be time stamped respectively by LC_i and LC_j. The timestamp associated with an event is the one that is right after this event but before the next event. We have:

$$a \rightarrow b \iff LC_i < LC_j$$

and

$$a \parallel b \iff LC_i \parallel LC_j$$

where

$$LC_i < LC_j \iff \forall_k(LC_i[k] \leq LC_j[k]) \wedge \exists_l(LC_i[l] < LC_j[l])$$
$$LC_i \parallel LC_j \iff \neg (LC_i < LC_j) \wedge \neg (LC_j < LC_i)$$

In the matrix time approach each P_i is associated with a matrix $LC_i[1..n, 1..n]$ where

- $LC_i[i, i]$ is the local logical clock.

- $LC_i[k, l]$ represents the view (or knowledge) P_i has about P_k's knowledge about the local logical clock of P_l.

In fact, row $LC_i[i, *]$ is a vector clock, and hence, this row inherits the properties of the vector clock system. In addition, we have the following fact. If

$$\min(LC_i[k, i]) \geq t$$

then P_i knows that every other process knows its progress until its local time t.

The update of matrix time can be done similarly using $Rule_1$ and $Rule_2$. See [21] and [28] for a detailed treatment of this topic. An application of logical time in systems where processes are dynamically generated or deleted can be found in [8]. Basically the dynamic approach considers both process creation and process termination. A computation consists of one or more possibly nested process instances.

- *Process creation.* If event a and process instance Q occur in process instance P, event b occurs in Q, and Q begins after a, then $a \rightarrow b$.

- *Process termination.* If event a and process instance Q occur in process instance P, event b occurs in Q and a occurs after Q terminates, then $b \rightarrow a$.

3.4.3 Efficient implementations

When there are a large number of processes in a given distributed system and there is heavy communication between processes, the vector and matrix clocks must piggyback a large amount of information to update the logical clocks. In [23] Singhal and Kshemkalyani proposed a differential method to reduce the amount of information sent at each communication. This approach is based on the fact that, between successive events, only a few entries of the vector clock are likely to change. When a process P_i sends a message to a process P_j, P_i piggybacks only those entries of its vector clocks that have changed since the last message it sent to P_j. However, each process needs to maintain additional vectors to store information regarding the clock value at the time of the last interaction with other processes. A

survey of other efficient implementations of vector clocks is discussed in
[20]. An efficient implementation in mobile computing environments can
be found in [17].

Logical clocks have been used in a number of practical and theoretical areas: (1) languages, (2) debugging distributed systems, and (3) concurrency
measures. A detailed discussion on their applications is in [9].

3.4.4   Physical clocks

A physical clock runs continuously rather than in discrete "ticks" as
a logical clock. In order for a clock PE_i to be a true physical one and
two clocks at different sites to be synchronized, Lamport [12] defined the
following two conditions:

- Correct rate condition:
  $\forall_i |dPC_i(t)/dt - 1| < \alpha \ \ (\alpha << 1)$

- Clock synchronization condition:
  $\forall_i \forall_j |PC_i(t) - PC_j(t)| < \beta \ \ (\beta << 1)$

Lamport also proposed a clock synchronization method as follows:

1. For each i, if P_i does not receive a message at physical time t, then
   PC_i is differentiable at t and $dPC(t)/dt > 0$.

2. If P_i sends a message m at physical time t, then m contains $PC_i(t)$.

3. Upon receiving a message (m, PC_j) at time t, process P_i sets PC_i to
   maximum $(PC_i(t-0), PC_j + \mu_m)$ where μ_m is a predetermined minimum delay to send message m from one process to another process.

In the above algorithm $t-0$ represents the time just before t. $dPC(t)/dt >$
0 means that PC is always set forward.

3.5   Applications

In this section we will consider two applications of formal models: One
is the application of a total ordering on a distributed mutual exclusion and
the other is the application of logical vector clocks on ordering of messages.

3.5.1 A total ordering application: distributed mutual exclusion

Mutual exclusion is an important issue for both distributed system and operating system design [7]. Assume that a distributed system is composed of a fixed collection of processes which share a single resource. Only one process can use the resource at a time so the processes must synchronize themselves to avoid conflict.

A mutual exclusion algorithm that grants the resource to a process should satisfy the following conditions [12]:

1. The resource must first be released before granted.

2. Requests must be granted in the order in which they are made.

3. If every process that is granted the resource eventually releases it, then every request is eventually granted.

To simplify the discussion, we assume that the messages are received in the same order as they are sent and messages sent will eventually be received. The LC_i associated with P_i is a linear time and each process maintains a request queue. The algorithm is designed based on the following rules [12].

1. To request the resource process P_i sends its timestamped message to all the processes (including itself).

2. When a process receives the request resource message, it places it on its local request queue and sends back a timestamped acknowledgment.

3. To release the resource, P_i sends a timestamped release resource message to all the processes (including itself).

4. When a process receives a release resource message from P_i, it removes any requests from P_i from its local request queue. A process P_j is granted the resource when (1) its request r is at the top of its request queue and (2) it has received messages with timestamps larger than the timestamp of r from all the other processes.

3.5.2 A logical vector clock application: ordering of messages

In many applications, such as the database management system, it is important that messages are received in the same order as they are sent. For example, if each message is an update, every process in charge of updating a replica receives the updates in the same order to maintain the consistency of the database. The above requirement is also called the (causal) *ordering of messages*.

Let $s(m)$ $(r(m))$ denote the send (receive) event of a message m from process P_i to process P_j. $C(e)$ denotes the time at which event e is recorded by either a logical clock (LC) or a physical clock (PC). Then messages are ordered if the following condition is true:

$$C(s(m)) > C(s(n)) \Rightarrow C(r(m)) > C(r(n))$$

Figure 3.14 shows two situations when out-of-order messages occur. In Figure 3.14 (a) two messages from the same process (P_1) are out of order at the receiving site (P_2). This can be easily handled using a logical clock since its value corresponds to the number of events in the process by assigning $d = 0$ and all initial values 0. When a receiver receives an out-of-order message, it will wait until all messages proceed it arrive.

In Figure 3.14 (b) two causally related messages from different processes are out of order at the receiving site. In this case message m_1 from P_1 happens before message m_2 from P_2. A logical vector clock can be used in this case. Recall that $LC_2[1]$ represents P_2's knowledge of P_1's progress. Since $LC_2[1]$ is piggybacked with message m_2 forwarded to process P_3, P_3 knows the situation of P_1 when it receives message m_2 from P_2. P_3 will wait for message m_1 from P_1 before accepting m_2 from P_2.

Therefore, in order to enforce the ordering of messages in a distributed system, the basic idea is to accept a message only if the message immediately preceding it has been delivered. The following protocol proposed by Birman et al. [4] requires processes to communicate only by broadcasting messages.

/* vector clocks (LCs) are used at all the processes in the system */

1. Before broadcasting a message, P_i updates its LC_i.

2. When P_j receives message m with LC_i from P_i, it delays its delivery until:

    (a) $LC_j[i] = LC_i[i] - 1$
    (b) $LC_j[k] \geq LC_i[k], \forall k \neq i$.

Condition (a) ensures that process P_j has received all the messages from P_i that proceed m while (b) ensures that P_j has received all those messages received by P_i before sending m. The above causal ordering protocol

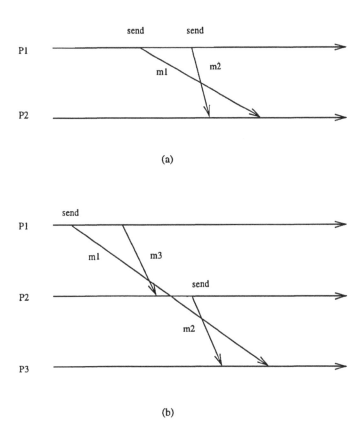

FIGURE 3.14
Two out-of-order messages.

requires that the processes communicate through a broadcast message. A protocol [22] that does not require processes to communicate only by broadcast message exists; however, it is very involved and complex.

3.6   Classification of Distributed Control Algorithms

In general, a rigid classification of distributed algorithms is dangerous. However, an assessment of the quality (especially resiliency to failures) of a distributed algorithm can be useful. There are many different types of distributed algorithms. They differ by some of the attributes listed below:

- *Process structure.* A distributed algorithm consists of a set of processes. These algorithms differ by the text structure of each process.

- *Interprocess communication method.* Some commonly used approaches include accessing shared memory, sending and receiving point-to-point messages, collective communication such as broadcasting and executing remote procedure calls.

- *Knowledge of timing and propagation delay.* Different assumptions can be made about the timing of events and the knowledge of propagation delays.

- *Fault model.* The system, upon which a distributed algorithm runs, may not be reliable. Such a system may exhibit different behaviors when a processor fails: processors may just stop (the fail-stop model), may fail transiently (the transient-fault model), or can behave arbitrarily (the Byzantine-fault model).

- *Types of applications.* Distributed algorithms differ in the problems that they solve.

The interprocess communication method was discussed in length in Chapter 2 and the fault model will be addressed in Chapter 8. For the process structure, Raynal [18] provided an assessment based on the level of symmetry:

- *Asymmetry.* Every process executes a different program text, e.g., a client and server algorithm.

- *Textual symmetry.* The texts by all processes are identical apart from a reference in each text to the name of the process that executes it. The processes behave differently according to the different messages received.

- *Strong symmetry.* The texts are identical and there is no reference to process names. Identical or different behaviors are again possible according to the messages received.

- *Total symmetry.* The texts are identical and all processes behave in the same way.

The knowledge of the timing and propagation delays can be treated separately. In a distributed system the message transmission delay is not negligible in comparison with the time events in a single process. The knowledge of the propagation delays plays an important role in deciding the nature of a distributed system. LeLann [13] proposed a distributed system classification based on their propagation delays:

- *Type-one distributed system.* For any pair of processes propagation delays for interprocess communication are fixed, finite and known with absolute accuracy; they may be different for each process pair.

- *Type-two distributed system.* Propagation delays are variable, finite and their values are not known with absolute accuracy.

- *Type-three distributed system.* Propagation delays are variable, finite and known *a posteriori* with absolute accuracy.

- *Type-four distributed system.* Propagation delays are variable, but their values are upper bounded.

In the above classification LeLann assumed that, for each distributed system, there are several time-space references and each process will be observed at least once within a time period $(t - \delta, t)$ where δ is a finite value and t is a local time. Unless specified otherwise the distributed system considered in this book belongs to type-two, type-three, or type-four, i.e., the system under consideration does not have the knowledge of the propagation delays.

There are several different assumptions about the knowledge of the timing of events that may be used in a distributed algorithm. At one extreme processors are completely *synchronous* performing communication and computation in a lock-step synchrony. At another extreme processors can be totally *asynchronous* taking steps at arbitrary speeds and orders. Everything in between these extremes is called *partially synchronous.* In such a model, processors have partial knowledge of timing of events. Although for most cases the synchronous model is unrealistic, it is often a useful intermediate step toward solving a complex problem in a more realistic model (such as the asynchronous model). Sometimes it is possible to run a synchronous algorithm in a real system (that is asynchronous) through "simulation"; while for other cases it is impossible to directly implement a synchronous algorithm in a real system. A *synchronizer* [3] is a distributed asynchronous algorithm that allows any synchronous algorithm to be executed on an asynchronous system. For a detailed discussion on this concept see [19].

There are many different types of problems, A list of typical problems in the area of distributed algorithms is as follows [24]: (1) Fault tolerance related; (2) communication related; (3) synchronization related; (4) control related.

3.7 The Complexity of Distributed Algorithms

In sequential algorithms time complexity and space complexity are two commonly used measures. However, distributed systems normally do not contain a notion of time especially in an asynchronous system. A more popular measure in distributed systems is *message complexity* which is the total number of messages exchanged by the algorithm. A more refined measure is *bit complexity* which measures the actual amount of messages (in bits) exchanged. In most cases, message complexity is used unless the system under consideration involves many long and short messages.

Many distributed algorithms are nondeterministic. Performance measures may vary from different runs. In many systems (especially asynchronous ones) the number of active processes differ in each run; for example, the problem of selecting a leader where one or more process can initiate the selection process. Therefore, a distinction between best-case, worst-case, and average-case complexity is normally needed.

References

[1] Agerwala, T., "Putting Petri nets to work," *IEEE Computers*, **12**, 12, Dec. 1979, 85-94.

[2] Ahuja, M., "Flush primitives for asynchronous distributed systems", *Information Processing Letters*, **34**, 1990, 5-12.

[3] Awerbuch, B., "Complexity of network synchronization", *Journal of the ACM*, **32**, 1985, 804-823.

[4] Birman, K. P. et al., "Lightweight causal and atomic group multicast", *ACM Transactions on Computer Systems*, **9**, 3, 1991, 272-314.

[5] Bochmann, G. V., *Concepts for Distributed System Design*, Springer-Verlag, 1983.

[6] Chandy, K. M. and L. Lamport, "Distributed snapshots: determining global states of distributed systems", *ACM Transactions on Computer Systems*, **3**, 1, Feb. 1985, 63-75.

[7] Deitel, H. M., *An Introduction to Operating Systems*, Second Edition, Addison-Wesley Publishing Company, 1990.

[8] Fidge, C., "Logical time in distributed computing systems," *IEEE Computers*, **24**, 8, August 1991, 28-31.

[9] Fidge, C., "Logical time in distributed computing systems", in *Readings in Distributed Computing Systems*, T. L. Casavant and M. Singhal, eds., IEEE Computer Society Press, 1994, 73-82.

[10] France, R., J. Wu, M. M. Larrondo-Petrie, and J. M. Bruel, "A tale of two case studies: Using integrated methods to support rigorous requirements specification", *Proc. of the Int'l Workshop on Formal Methods Integration*, 1996.

[11] Lai, T. and T. Yang, "On distributed snapshots", *Information Processing Letters*, **25**, 1987, 153-158.

[12] Lamport, L., "Time, clock, and the order of events in a distributed system", *Communications of the ACM*, **21**, 7, July 1978, 558-568.

[13] LeLann, G., "Distributed systems – towards a formal approach", *Proc. of the IFIP Congress*, 1977, 155-160.

[14] Mattern, F., "Virtual time and global states of distributed systems", *Proc. of Parallel and Distributed Algorithms Conf.*, 1988, 215-226.

[15] Netzer, R. H. and J. Xu, "Necessary and sufficient conditions for consistent global snapshots", *IEEE Transactions on Parallel and Distributed Systems*, **6**, 2, Feb. 1995, 165-109.

[16] Peterson, J. L., *Petri Net Theory and the Modeling of Systems*, Prentice Hall, Inc., 1981.

[17] Prakash, R., M. Raynal, and M. Singhal, "An efficient causal ordering algorithm for mobile computing environments", *Proc. of the 16th Int'l Conf. on Distributed Computing Systems*, 1996, 744-751.

[18] Raynal, M., *Distributed Algorithms and Protocols*, John Wiley & Sons, 1988.

[19] Raynal, M. and J. M. Helary, *Synchronization and Control of Distributed Systems and Programs*, John Wiley & Sons, 1990.

[20] Raynal, M. and M. Singhal, "Capturing causality in distributed systems", *IEEE Computers*, **29**, 2, Feb. 1996, 49-56.

[21] Sarin, S. K. and L. Lynch, "Discarding obsolete information in a replicated database system", *IEEE Transactions on Software Engineering*, **13**, 1, Jan. 1987, 39-46.

[22] Schiper, A. J. et al., "A new algorithm to implement causal ordering", *Proc. of the Int'l Workshop on Distributed Algorithms*, 1989, 219-232.

[23] Singhal, M. and A. Kshemkalyani, " An efficient implementation of vector clocks", *Information Processing Letters*, **43**, Aug. 1992, 47-52.

[24] Tel, G., *Topics in Distributed Algorithms*, Cambridge University Press, 1991.

[25] Wu, J. and E. B. Fernandez, "Petri nets modeling techniques and application", in *Modeling and Simulation*, W. G. Vogt and M. H. Mickle, eds., **21**, 3, 1989, 1311-1317.

[26] Wu, J. and E. B. Fernandez, "A simplification of a conversation design scheme using Petri nets", *IEEE Transactions on Software Engineering*, **15**, 5, May 1989, 658-660.

[27] Wu, J. and E. B. Fernandez, "Using Petri nets for determining conversation boundaries in fault-tolerant software", *IEEE Transactions on Parallel and Distributed Systems*, **5**, 10, Oct. 1994, 1106-1112.

[28] Wuu, G. T. J. and A. J. Bernstein, "Efficient solutions to the replicated log and dictionary problems", *Proc. of the 3rd ACM Symp. in PODC*, 1984, 233-242.

[29] Yau, S. S. and M. U. Caglayan, " Distributed software system design representation using modified Petri nets", *IEEE Transactions on Software Engineering*, **9**, 6, Nov. 1983, 733-744.

Problems

1. Consider a system where processes can be dynamically created or terminated. A process can generate a new process. For example, P_1

generates both P_2 and P_3. Modify the happened-before relation and the linear logical clock scheme for events in such a dynamic set of processes.

2. For the distributed system shown in the figure below.

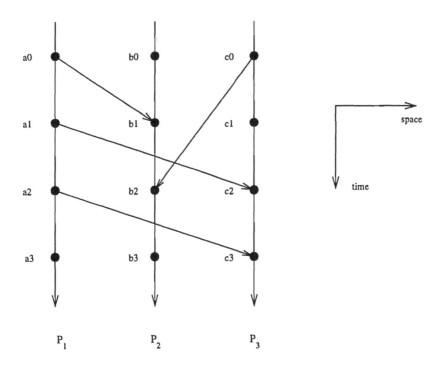

(a) Provide all the pairs of events that are related.

(b) Provide logical time for all the events using
   (i) linear time, and
   (ii) vector time
   Assume that each LC_i is initialized zero and $d = 1$.

3. Define a total order ($\Rightarrow$) of events in a distributed system based on the vector logical clock associated with each event. Note that for two events a and b: if $a \rightarrow b$, then $a \Rightarrow b$.

4. Provide linear logical clocks for all the events in the system given in Problem 2. Assume that all LC's are initialized zero and the d's for

P_a, P_b, and P_c are 1, 2, 3, respectively. Does condition $a \rightarrow b \Rightarrow$ $LC(a) < LC(b)$ still hold? For any other set of d's? and why?

5. Express Lamport's mutual exclusion algorithm using DCDL.

6. Extend Lamport's mutual exclusion algorithm for the cases where messages received at each process may not be in the same order as they are sent. We assume that the message transmission delay is bounded by time δ.

7. Use the extended Petri net to model the system in Figure 3.7.

8. Use a four-process example to illustrate the snapshot of global states. It is assumed that four processes (nodes) are fully connected by bi-directional links and only one process initiates the snapshot process.

Chapter 4

MUTUAL EXCLUSION AND ELECTION ALGORITHMS

Mutual exclusion is the key issue for distributed systems design. Mutual exclusion ensures that mutually conflicting concurrent processes can share resources. We also discuss three issues that are related to the mutual exclusion problem: election, bidding, and self-stabilization.

4.1 Mutual Exclusion

The problem of mutual exclusion, or of defining fundamental operations such that it is possible to resolve conflicts resulting from several concurrent processes sharing resources, has emerged as a prime example of the difficulties associated with distributed systems.

The mutual exclusion problem was originally considered for centralized computer systems for the synchronization of exclusive control. The first software solution to this problem was provided by Dekker [13]. Dijkstra offered an elaboration of Dekker's solution and introduced semaphores. Hardware solutions are normally based on special atomic instructions such as Test-and-Set, Compare-and-Swap (in IBM 370 series), and Fetch-and-Add [24]. For a detailed discussion of centralized solutions to the mutual exclusion problem see [3], [31], and [38].

A simple solution to distributed mutual exclusion uses one coordinator. For each process requesting the *critical section* (CS), it sends its request to the coordinator who queues all the requests and grants them permission based on a certain rule, e.g., based on their timestamps. Clearly, this coordinator is a bottleneck. General solutions to the distributed mutual exclusion problem are classified as *non-token-based* and *token-based*.

In token-based algorithms a unique token is shared among different processes. A process is allowed to enter the CS if it possesses the token. Therefore, the mutual exclusion is automatically enforced. In non-token-based algorithms one or more successive rounds of message exchanges among the processes are required to obtain the permission for the CS. A mutual exclusion algorithm can be *static* when its action is independent of the system state or *dynamic* when its action is dependent on the system state.

The primary objective of mutual exclusion is to guarantee that only one process can access the CS at a time. Some extended mutual exclusion problems have also been studied. The *k-exclusion* problem ([1], [37]) is an extension of the traditional mutual exclusion problem which guarantees that the system does not enter a state where more than k processes are executing the critical section. A regular mutual exclusion algorithm should satisfy:

1. *Freedom from deadlock.* When the CS is available, processes should not wait endlessly and no one can enter.

2. *Freedom from starvation.* Each request to the CS should eventually be granted.

3. *Fairness.* Requests should be granted based on certain fairness rules. Typically, it is based on the request time determined by logical clocks. Starvation and fairness are related with the latter being a stronger condition.

The performance of mutual exclusion algorithms is measured by:

1. Number of messages per request.

2. Synchronization delay, measured by the time between the time when a process exits the CS and the time when the next process enters the CS.

3. Response time, measured by the interval a process issues a request and the process exits the CS.

Note that both (1) and (2) are measures of the performance of a given mutual exclusion algorithm. (3) depends more on system load and/or the length of each CS execution. A system can be either *heavily loaded* (with many pending requests) or *lightly loaded* (without many pending requests). In many cases the performance of an algorithm depends on the system load.

The following assumptions are made about the system for a distributed mutual exclusion problem. Processes communicate through message passing. The network is logically completely connected. The transmission is error-free. By default, communication is asynchronous, i.e., message propagation delay is finite but unpredictable. Messages may be delivered in the order sent unless otherwise stated.

4.2   Non-token-based Solutions

In non-token-based algorithms all processes communicate with each other to determine which should execute the CS next. Most algorithms in this category are truly distributed, i.e., decisions are made in a decentralized manner.

4.2.1   A simple extension to Lamport's algorithm

In a distributed system, control mechanisms using message exchange are employed for decentralized resource management and synchronization. Using timestamping, Lamport's algorithm discussed in the last chapter needs $3(n-1)$ messages to ensure mutual exclusion for a set of n processes. In the example of Figure 4.1 there are three processes P_1, P_2, and P_3 with P_1 and P_2 requesting a CS (assume that P_1 requests before P_2 does). Three types of message are shown in the figure: A solid line represents a request signal, a dashed line an acknowledge signal, and a dotted line a release signal. The bar line corresponds to a process in the CS. In Lamport's algorithm, when a process receives a request resource message, it places the request on its local request queue and sends back a timestamped acknowledgment. A process can enter the CS only after it has received acknowledgments from all the processes. To release the resource, P_i sends a timestamped release resource message to all the processes.

We can easily improve Lamport's algorithm in the following way: Suppose process P_j receives a request from process P_i after it has sent its own request with a timestamp larger than the one of P_i's request. In this case there is no need to send an acknowledgment. This is because when process P_i receives P_j's request with a timestamp larger than its own, it can conclude that P_j does not have any pending request that has a smaller timestamp. Note that the acknowledgment used in Lamport's algorithm

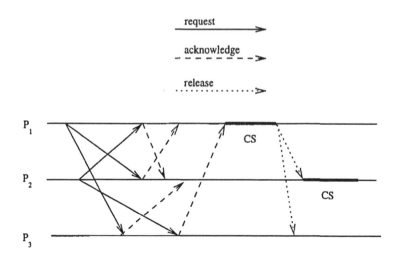

FIGURE 4.1
An example using Lamport's algorithm.

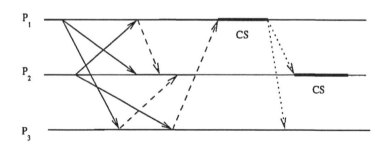

FIGURE 4.2
An example using the enhanced Lamport's algorithm.

is not for reliability purposes. However, the above improvement may still require $3(n-1)$ messages in the worst case.

Figure 4.2 shows the result of applying the enhanced approach to the example of Figure 4.1. Since P_2 receives a request from P_1 after it has sent its own request with a timestamp larger than P_1's, there is no need for P_2 to send an acknowledgment.

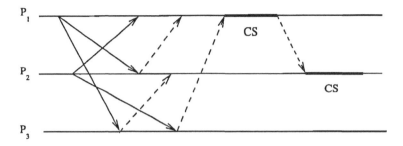

FIGURE 4.3
An example using Ricart and Agrawala's algorithm.

4.2.2   Ricart and Agrawala's first algorithm

In Ricart and Agrawala's algorithm [40] $2(n-1)$ message exchanges are required: $n-1$ for a process P_i to inform all the other processes of its request, and another $n-1$ for conveying the agreements. That is, it merges acknowledge and release messages into one message *reply*. Reply is a permission. A process can access the CS only after it receives a permission from all the other processes. There is no need to perform any logical operation on the reply messages to decide its eligibility in contrast to Lamport's approach. The algorithm is as follows: When process P_j receives a request from P_i, it sends a reply back if it is neither requesting nor executing the CS or it is requesting and the timestamp of P_j's request is larger than the timestamp of P_i's request. Upon releasing the CS the process sends a reply message to all the deferred requests. Basically a process holds all of its requests that have lower priorities even when the process cannot collect all the replies, i.e., it cannot access the CS.

Figure 4.3 shows the result of applying Ricart and Agrawala's algorithm to the example of Figure 4.1. When P_1 receives a request from P_2, it will hold the acknowledgment since P_1 has the highest priority. Process P_3 does not have any request; it sends acknowledgment to both requesting processes.

In Ricart and Agrawala's algorithm a process can grant permission to many processes simultaneously. A process grants permission to a requesting process if it is not using the CS or its own request has a lower priority. In other words, the decision is made at the requesting process but the receiver exercises a certain degree of control by sending or holding its grant signal. Once a process acquires grant signals from all the other processes, it can enter the CS. Note that a process can potentially send many grant signals to different requests. It is easy to see that only one process can collect all grant signals at a time.

To allow a receiver to exercise more control over the decision process, a process can grant permission only to one requesting process at a time based on a priority rule. A requesting process can access the CS only after it receives grant signals from all the other processes. The condition for grant signals from all the other processes can also be relaxed: A requesting process can access the CS after it receives signals from a predefined subset of processes (such a subset is called *request subset*). To avoid the situation when two processes enter the CS at the same time, the intersection of request subsets of any two processes must be non-empty. A common process (of two request subsets) acts as an arbiter. Since this process has only one grant signal, it will be granted to only one requester. Maekawa's algorithm discussed in the next subsection is such an example.

4.2.3 Maekawa's algorithm

In Maekawa's algorithm [30] a process does not request permission from every other process but only from a subset of processes. Assume that R_i and R_j are the request sets for processes P_i and P_j, respectively. It is required that $R_i \cap R_j \neq \phi$. Since each process grants one signal to a requesting process, mutual exclusion is automatically enforced. When a process P_i requests the CS, it sends the request message only to processes in R_i. When a process P_j receives a request message, it sends a reply message (grant signal) if it has not sent a reply message to a process since the last release. Otherwise, the request message is placed in the queue. Note that the granting procedure is not based on timestamp, i.e., a strong fairness based on timestamp is not enforced here. Rather, it is based on the arrival time of each request. However, if the communication delay of each channel is bounded, no starvation will occur. A process P_i can access the CS only after receiving reply messages from all the processes in R_i. Upon releasing the critical section, P_i sends release messages only to processes in R_i.

Consider an example with seven processes and the request set for each process is listed as follows:

$$R_1 : \{P_1, P_3, P_4\}$$

$$R_2 : \{P_2, P_4, P_5\}$$

$$R_3 : \{P_3, P_5, P_6\}$$

$$R_4 : \{P_4, P_6, P_7\}$$

$$R_5 : \{P_5, P_7, P_1\}$$

$$R_6 : \{P_6, P_1, P_2\}$$

$$R_7 : \{P_7, P_2, P_3\}$$

In the above request set assignment any two request sets have exactly one common process. Mutual exclusion is guaranteed since each process can have only one outstanding reply message. If the size of a subset is k and it is same for each request set, and n is the number of processes, then the minimum value of n should be $n = k(k - 1) + 1$. Obviously, for each access, the number of requests is $k = O(\sqrt{n})$.

Let us consider two other selections of R_i. In the centralized mutual exclusion with P_c as the sole arbiter, we have

$$R_i : \{P_c\}, 1 \le i \le n.$$

Another extreme is the fully distributed mutual exclusion algorithm where a requesting process requests permission from all other processes:

$$R_i : \{P_1, P_2, ..., P_n\}, 1 \le i \le n.$$

Maekawa's algorithm is prone to deadlocks because a process can be exclusively locked by other processes. For example, consider the first solution of the seven-process example, where three processes P_1, P_6, and P_7 request the CS at the same time. Because of different communication delay, P_3 may grant its reply to P_1, P_4 to P_6, and P_2 to P_7. None of the three processes can obtain three reply messages at the same time and a deadlock occurs.

One solution to the deadlock problem is to require a process to yield a lock if the timestamp of its request is larger than the timestamp of some other requests waiting for the same lock. Another conservative approach ensures that a process grants its reply to a requesting process only when there are no other requests with a smaller timestamp, an approach similar to Lamport's. However, a significant amount of message exchanges are needed in this case.

One can further generalize Maekawa's algorithm by introducing an *inform set* which includes a set of processes to which a release signal is sent. Note that in Maekawa's algorithm request set and inform set are the same. A detailed discussion of this generalized approach can be found in [43].

4.3 Token-based Solutions

In token-based algorithms the notion of token is introduced. The token represents a control point and it is passed around among all the processes. A process is allowed to enter the CS if it possesses the token.

4.3.1 Ricart and Agrawala's second algorithm

As an improvement to Ricart and Agrawala's algorithm another algorithm was proposed by Carvalho and Roucairol [11]. This algorithm requires a number of messages between zero and $2(n-1)$ by using a different definition of symmetry by introducing a *token*, i.e., a dynamic single point control. In this algorithm after process P_i has received a reply message from process P_j, P_i can enter the CS (assuming it gets reply messages from all the other processes) any number of times without requesting permission from process P_j. Because one process P_i has received a reply message from P_j, the authorization implicit in this message remains valid until after the reception of a request message from P_j.

A further improvement by Ricart and Agrawala [41] is as follows (see Figure 4.4): A process that enters the critical section holds a token. Initially the token is assigned arbitrarily to one of the processes. A process P_j that wishes to use the critical section will not know which process is holding the token and will request it by issuing a message that is timestamped and broadcast to all other processes. When process P_i currently holding the token no longer needs to use the critical section, it searches other processes in the order $i+1, i+2, \ldots, n, 1, 2, \ldots, i-1$ for the first j such that the timestamp of P_j's last request for the token is larger than the value recorded in the token for the timestamp of P_j's last holding of the token, that is, P_j has a pending request. P_i then transfers the token to P_j. Note that the priority is not strictly based on the timestamp of each request. However, since the token is circulated around one direction, no starvation will occur.

Ricart and Agrawala's second algorithm:

$$P(i) ::= * [\text{ request-resource}$$
$$\square \text{ consume}$$
$$\square \text{ release-resource}$$
$$\square \text{ treat-request-message}$$
$$\square \text{ others}$$

]

distributed-mutual-exclusion ::= || $P(i : 1..n)$

The following variables are used in each P_i:

clock: $0, 1, \ldots$, (initialized 0)
token_present: **Boolean** (*F* for all except one process)
token_held: **Boolean** (*F*)
token: **array** $(1..n)$ **of** *clock* (initialized 0)
request: **array** $(1..n)$ **of** *clock* (initialized 0)

Note that each process has a copy of a local *clock* (which is updated following Lamport's rules), *token_present* and *token_held*, but there is only one copy of the *token* array in the system (see Figure 4.4). The functions in each P_i are defined as follows:

others::= all the other actions that do not request
            to enter the critical section.

consume::= consumes the resource after entering the critical section
request-resource::=
              [*token_present* = T
                 → [**send** (*request_signal, clock, i*) **to all**;
                      receive (*access_signal, token*);
                      token_present:= T;
                      token_held:= T
                    ]
              ]
release-resource::=
              [*token* (i):=*clock*;
                token_held:=F;
                min j in the order $[i + 1, \ldots n, 1, 2, \ldots, i - 2, i - 1]$
                      $\wedge$ (*request*(j) >*token*(j))
                      → [*token_present*:= F;
                           send (*access_signal, token*) **to** P_j
                         ]
              ]
treat-request-message::=
              [**receive** (*request_signal, k, j*)
                   → [*request*(j) := max (*request*(j), k);

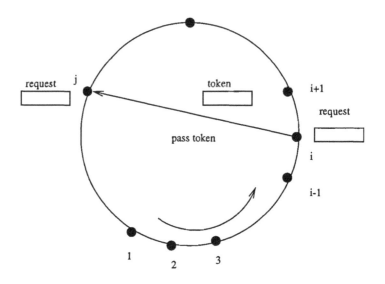

FIGURE 4.4
Carvalho and Roucairol's algorithm.

$$token\_present \wedge \neg \ token\_held \rightarrow \text{release-resource}$$
$$]$$
$$]$$

The above algorithm requires either n messages ($n - 1$ to broadcast the request and 1 to transfer the token) when the requesting process does not hold the token or 0 when it does. Note that in the above algorithm a request-resource can potentially be interrupted after $token_present := $ T but before $token_held := $ T by a treat-request-message. In this case a request will have to release the token that is just received. One way to solve this problem is to make these two statements atomic. That is, these two statements as a whole are treated as a statement. Another solution is to place $token_held := $ T before $token_present := $ T.

It is easy to prove that the above algorithm ensures mutual exclusion by the fact that only one $token\_present$ is true among all the processes. Its fairness follows from the fact that the token is transferred in a circular order. By assuming that the holding and transmission time is finite (no loss of the token), all the processes that make a request will eventually get the token and therefore enter the critical section. Note that a stronger fairness can be ensured if the priority is made based on the timestamp of each request. However, the decision process is rather complex like the one in Lamport's algorithm. A trade-off can be made if the decision is made based on the timestamps of all the requests currently available in the request queue. There may be requests with smaller timestamps still in transit.

4.3.2 A simple token-ring-based algorithm

There exists a simple algorithm [39] for mutual exclusion if the processes, P_i, $0 \le i \le n - 1$, are connected as a ring and this ring can be embedded in the underlying network. Again, one token is used to represent a dynamic single point of control (see Figure 4.5 (a)) and it is circulated around the ring:

$$P(i : 0..n - 1) ::= [\; \textbf{receive } token \textbf{ from } P((i - 1) \bmod n);$$
$$\text{consume the resource if needed;}$$
$$\textbf{send } token \textbf{ to } P((i + 1) \bmod n)$$
$$]$$

$$\text{distributed-mutual-exclusion} ::= \; \| \; P(i : 0..n - 1)$$

The above algorithm is extremely simple and is easy to follow. This algorithm works well in heavily loaded situations where the probability that the process with token needs to enter the CS is high. However, it works poorly in lightly loaded cases where only few processes request the CS. This algorithm wastes CPU time in circulating the token.

4.3.3 A fault-tolerant token-ring-based algorithm

Dynamic single control point algorithms suffer from the possibility of loss of control point (or token). Several fault-tolerant algorithms [28] have been proposed involving the use of timeouts. The algorithm in [32] requires no knowledge of delays or process identities. It uses two tokens (*ping* and *pong*) (see Figure 4.5 (b)), each of which serves to detect the possible loss of the other. The loss of a token is detected by the process which is visited by the same token two consecutive times. Both tokens are associated with a number (*nbping*, *nbpong*) and these two numbers satisfy the following invariant condition.

$$nbping + nbpong = 0$$

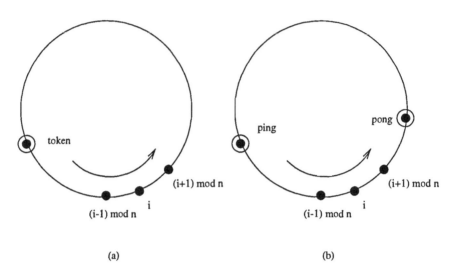

FIGURE 4.5
The simple token-ring-based algorithm (a) and the fault-tolerant token-ring-based algorithm (b).

In the fault-tolerant token-ring-based algorithm the control process associated with each process is as follows:

$P(i : 0..n - 1) ::=$
 [**receive** $(ping, nbping)$ **from** $P((i - 1) \bmod n)$
  $\rightarrow$ [$m_i = nbping$
    $\rightarrow$ [$nbping := (nbping + 1) \bmod n;$
      $nbpong := -\ nbping;$
      send $(ping, nbping)$ **to** $P((i + 1) \bmod n)$
      send $(pong, nbpong)$ **to** $P((i + 1) \bmod n)$
      ]
     /* loss of token *pong* */
   □ $m_i \neq nbping$
     $\rightarrow$ [$m_i := nbping;$
      send $(ping, nbping)$ **to** $P((i + 1) \bmod n)$
      ]
     /* normal situation */
   ]
  □ **receive** $(pong, nbpong)$ **from** $P((n - 1) \bmod n)$
    $\rightarrow$ (same as above interchanging the role of *ping* and *pong*)
  □ **meet** $(ping, pong)$ **at** P_i

$\rightarrow$ [$nbping:=(nbping+1)$ mod n;
$nbpong:=(nbpong-1)$ mod n;
send $(ping, nbping)$ **to** $P((i+1)$ mod $n)$;
send $(pong, nbpong)$ **to** $P((i+1)$ mod $n)$
]
/* *ping* meets *pong* */
]

The following main program initializes all the parameters and calls all the processes P_i.

main-program ::= [$nbping:= 1$; $nbpong:= -1$;
$m_i := 0, 0 \leq i \leq n-1$;
|| $P(i : 0..n-1)$
]

Variable m_i stores the number associated with the token that most recently visited P_i. Therefore, a match between m_i and the number of the current token indicates the loss of a token. Each token will not be updated more than n times in one cycle, and hence, it is sufficient to increment tokens by modulo n.

4.3.4 Token-based mutual exclusion using other logical structures

Other than ring structures for token-based mutual exclusion, graph and tree structures are also frequently used. In graph-based algorithms [34] processes are arranged as a directed graph with a sink node holding the token. A request for token and token propagation are handled in a similar way as in tree-based algorithms shown below.

In tree-based approaches [36] processes are arranged as a directed tree with the root node holding the token. A request for token propagates serially along a path from the requester to the root. The token is passed serially from the root to the requester and the token traverses the edges in the path from the root to the requester; meanwhile, the direction of the edges along the path is reversed so that the requester becomes the new root of the tree. Figure 4.6 (a) shows a request from a leave node to the root node. Figure 4.6 (b) shows the corresponding result after the root passes its token to the leave (new root). As shown in Figure 4.6 (b) each node in the new tree can still send its request along a directed path that leads to the node holding the token.

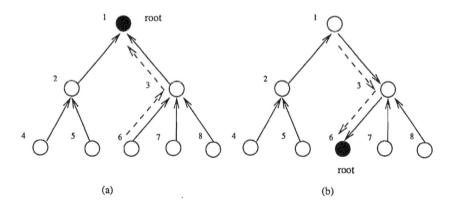

FIGURE 4.6
A tree-based mutual exclusion algorithm.

A general scheme for token- and tree-based mutual exclusion algorithms was proposed in [22]. A survey on distributed mutual exclusion can be found in [46].

4.3.4.1 Other related issues

Most of the algorithms discussed strive to minimize message complexity. Some researchers argue that time complexity, in terms of synchronization delay, is also important. For example, Lamport's algorithm needs $3(n-1)$ messages and two time units delay. Maekawa's algorithm requires only $O(\sqrt{n})$ messages and two time units delay to enter the CS; however, it needs one more time delay to release the locked site before it can send a reply message to one of the requesting processes. Chang [10] studied the problem of minimizing both messages and time complexity at the same time. The approach used is a hybrid distributed mutual exclusion algorithm that combines several algorithms. Goscinski [19] proposed two mutual exclusion algorithms which are suitable for an environment requiring priorities such as a real-time system. Algorithms together with rigorous proofs can be found in [7] and [23].

Distributed mutual exclusion can be also achieved by *bidding* [8], [47], *election* [17], and *self-stabilization* [14], all of which will be discussed in the subsequent sections.

4.4   Election

Election [17] is a general style of computation in distributed systems in which one process from the process set is selected to perform a particular task. For example, after a failure occurs in a distributed system, it is often necessary to reorganize the active nodes so that they can continue to perform a useful task. The first step in such a reorganization or reconfiguration is to elect a coordinator to manage the operation. The detection of a failure is normally based on a time-out. A process that gets no response from the leader for a period of time suspects a failure of the coordinator and initiates an election process.

Applications of elections can be found in the following areas [25]: (1) group server, (2) load balancing, (3) replicated data updating, (4) crash recovery, (5) joining group, and (6) mutual exclusion.

Different distributed election algorithms have been proposed based on the type of topology used: complete graph, ring, and tree. These algorithms can also be classified based on the type of network used: (1) Store-and-forward networks, including unidirectional rings [9], [15], [35]; bidirectional rings [16]; complete graphs [6], [26]; trees [12], [36]; and chordal rings [33]. (2) Broadcast networks [25].

Normally two phases are used in an election process: (1) Select a leader with the highest priority and (2) inform other processes the leader (winner). In both phases process ids need to be distributed in the system and can be done either through point-to-point communication or through broadcasting. Broadcasting can be easily done in a completely connected network. Otherwise, a spanning subgraph is constructed statically or dynamically. For example, if a unidirectional ring is used as a spanning subgraph, messages are passed around the ring in both phases. Another commonly used spanning subgraph is a tree that can be statically selected or dynamically created.

If a spanning tree is known *a priori*, all leave nodes start the election process and push their ids upwards to their ancestors with only the highest priority one surviving along each path to the root. The first phase is completed when the highest priority id reaches the root node. The second phase starts by broadcasting the winner's id along the spanning tree from the root to all the leave nodes. If a spanning tree is dynamically created, one process (the root) initiates the process of generating a spanning tree. This process terminates at each leave node. Then, each leave node starts an election process following the same procedure used for the static spanning tree case.

Most election algorithms are based on a global priority where each process (processor) is given a priority *a priori*. These algorithms are also called *extrema-finding algorithms*. The main argument against the extrema-finding algorithm is that when a leader is to be elected, that leader should ideally represent a good choice, e.g., from a performance or reliability standpoint. Recently, more work has been done on *preference-based algorithms* [45] where voting is more generally based on a personal preference, e.g., locality, reliability estimation, etc. Also, priority may not be linearly ordered as in preference-based algorithms.

We consider here three types of extrema-finding algorithms. Chang and Roberts' algorithm is based on the ring topology and each process is not aware of the priority of other processes. Garcia-Molina's bully algorithm [17] is based on the completely connected topology and each process is aware of the priority of other processes. Both algorithms are *comparison-based* in which the leader is selected by comparing ids of all the processes and by sending and receiving ids in messages. The third type is *non-comparison-based* in which the messages are "coded" in time in terms of rounds (this type of algorithm only works in a synchronous system).

The similarity of election and mutual exclusion is rather obvious. Using election, all processes that intend to enter the critical section will compete through an election to decide which process should enter the critical section. The difference is that a mutual exclusion algorithm should ensure no starvation while an election algorithm is more concerned with a quick election process. Also, participating processes should be informed of the winner of an election. In a mutual exclusion algorithm the participating processes do not care who is currently in the critical section.

4.4.1   Chang and Roberts' algorithm

The following is an election algorithm for processes interconnected as a unidirectional ring proposed by Chang and Roberts [9] which uses the principle of *selective extinction* and requires only $O(n \log n)$ messages with n as the number of processes. It is a generalization of an algorithm proposed by LeLann [28].

In the algorithm n processes are arranged in any order around the ring. We assume that all the process ids are distinct and the smallest one has the highest priority. Whenever P_i receives an election message (an identifier of a process), it compares this message with its own identifier $id(i)$ and transmits the smaller one to its neighbor along the counter-clockwise direction or the clockwise direction. When P_i receives its own identifier, it becomes the coordinator and informs all the others by sending out the id of the elected process.

Parameters in each process P_i:

$id(i)$: **cons**;
participant: **var Boolean** (F);
coordinator: **var integer**;

Chang and Roberts' algorithm:

$P(i : 0..n - 1) ::=$
      $*$ [initiate election $\rightarrow$
           [*participant*:= T;
               send (*election*, i, $id(i)$) **to** $P((i + 1) \bmod\ n)$
           ]
      $\Box$ **receive** (*election*, j, $id(j)$) $\rightarrow$
           [$id(j) < id(i) \rightarrow$
               [**send** (*election*, j, $id(j)$) **to** $P((j + 1) \bmod\ n)$
               $\|$ *participant* $:=$ T
               ]
           $\Box\, id(j) > id(i) \wedge$ *participant* $\rightarrow \phi$
           $\Box\, id(j) > id(i)\ \wedge \neg$ *participant* $\rightarrow$
               [**send** (*election*, i, $id(i)$) **to** $P((i + 1) \bmod n)$
               $\|$ *participant* $:=$ T
               ]
           $\Box$ $id(j) = id(i) \rightarrow$
               send (*elected*, i) **to** $P((i + 1) \bmod n)$
           ]
      $\Box$ **receive** (*elected*, j) $\rightarrow$
           [*coordinate* $:= j$
           $\|$ *participant* $:=$ F
           $\|$ $j \neq i \rightarrow$ **send** (*elected*, j) **to** $P((j + 1) \bmod n)$
           ]
      ]

election-algorithm $::= \| P(i : 0..n - 1)$

It is obvious that the algorithm picks one and only one number – the smallest identifier of all the processes. The time required to select a coordinator is between two and three turnaround times on the ring. It is clear that the number of transmissions of the message with type *elected* is n. To calculate the number of transmissions of the message with type *election*, we first consider two extreme cases. One case is that election is initiated by a process with a maximum value. The election message travels exactly one round and it terminates at the initiator. The number of message transfers is $O(n)$. The other case (the least favorable) corresponds to the situation where the processes are arranged in decreasing order and each process initiates an election simultaneously. The message then issued by P_i undergoes $i + 1$ transfers so that the total number of messages is

$$\sum_{i=0}^{n-1} i + 1 = \frac{1}{2}n \cdot (n+1)$$

or $O(n^2)$

In general, let $P(i, k)$ be the probability that the message i is transferred k times (or $k - 1$ neighbors of P_i have identifiers that are less than i, but the kth neighbor's identifier is greater than i). Clearly,

$$P(i, k) = \frac{\binom{i-1}{k-1} \times (n-i)}{\binom{n-1}{k-1} \times (n-k)}$$

The message carrying the number n is transferred n times; the mean number of transfers from that of number i is

$$E_i = \sum_{k=1}^{n-1} k P(i, k)$$

and, therefore, the mean total number is

$$E = n + \sum_{i=1}^{n-1} E_i$$

which can be shown [9] to be $O(n \log n)$. Note that the above complexity is in the average case not in the worst case.

Franklin [16] proposed an algorithm with a complexity of $O(n \log n)$ in the worst case. However, it is assumed that the ring network is bidirectional. Initially each process is *active* and it compares its id with ids from two neighboring *active* processes in both directions. If it is a local minimum of three ids, it remains *active*; otherwise, it becomes *passive*. After each round only half of the participating processes will survive. Therefore, a total of $\log n$ rounds is needed. Note that when a process becomes *passive*, it will not participate in the subsequent comparison but it will still forward incoming ids. This algorithm has been extended in [15] and [35] to a unidirectional ring network with the same message complexity.

It has been shown that $O(n \log n)$ is a lower bound for comparison-based algorithms. We will show later that this bound can be improved using non-comparison-based algorithms.

4.4.1.1 Garcia-Molina's bully algorithm

The *bully* algorithm [17] is a reliable election algorithm for a system where each process knows the priority of all other processes. Again, the process with the highest priority level is elected. It is assumed that a process can fail and recover at any time. The recovered process forces all processes with lower priorities to let it become the coordinator if there is no other active process with a higher priority.

Whenever a process P detects a failure of a coordinator through a time-out, it broadcasts an election message to all processes with a higher priority and waits for a reply from one of the higher priority processes. If no response is received within a time limit, it is assumed that all these processes fail, and P declares itself the new coordinator and broadcasts its id to all processes with a lower priority. If a response is received within the time limit, process P sets up another timeout to receive the id of the new coordinator. Either the id of the new coordinator is received within the new time limit or nothing is received and process P resends the election message.

For a process with a higher priority number than P receiving the request it responds to P and begins its own election algorithm by sending an election message to all processes with a higher priority. If this process itself has the highest priority, it can declare itself the winner immediately.

In general, election is usually performed only if there is a system failure; therefore, failure detection and handling is normally an integral part of the election algorithm. The bully algorithm can be easily extended to include a reliable failure detector under a synchronous system, i.e., the time for a message delivery and the time for a node to respond are known a priori. A more realistic algorithm, called *invitation algorithm* [17], is based on the asynchronous model but it is much more complex than the bully algorithm.

There are many other reliable (or resilient) mutual exclusion and election algorithms. One reliable mutual exclusion algorithm uses a token and it checks whether the token is lost during network failure and regenerates it if necessary. Three types of network failures: PE failure, communication controller failure, and communication link failure can be tolerated by using a timeout mechanism. In [25] King et al. provided a reliable election algorithm which can tolerate both fail-stop and Byzantine type faults (a malicious type of fault to be discussed in Chapter 8).

4.4.2 Non-comparison-based algorithms

In non-comparison-based algorithms the leader is not selected by comparing its id with others; instead, it is selected through other means and usually its id is tied to time in terms of rounds. Therefore, these algorithms are intended for synchronous systems where all processes coordinate their activities in terms of rounds. In each round a process performs local updates and exchanges messages with other processes.

The following procedure can be used to code a process id in time, i.e., the receiver can obtain the sender's message without this message being physically sent from the sender:

- If the id of sender P_i is $id(i)$ at round x, P_i sends $(start, i)$ to receiver P_j.

- At round $x + id(i)$, P_i sends (end, i) to P_j.

- If P_j receives $(start, i)$ in round x and (end, i) in round $x + id(i)$, it accepts the id from P_i as $[x + id(i)] - x = id(i)$.

Note that although the above approach reduces message complexity especially bit complexity of a long message, it increases time complexity – it takes $id(i)$ rounds for receiver P_j to accept a message from sender P_i.

The following two non-comparison-based election algorithms are credited to Lynch [29]. Both algorithms are for synchronous systems:

Time-slice algorithm:

Assume that n is the total number of processes. Process P_i (with its $id(i)$) sends its id in round $id(i) \cdot 2n$, i.e., at most one process sends its id in every $2n$ consecutive rounds. Once an id returns to its original sender, that sender is elected. It sends a signal around the ring to inform other processes of its winning status.

The $2n$ rounds are enough for the leader (the process with minimum id) to circulate its id and inform its winning status to other processes before any other can start its circulation. Obviously the message complexity of the above algorithm is $O(n)$. However, its time complexity is $\min\{id(i)\}\cdot n$, which is an unbounded number. Another restriction is that each process should know the number of processes n *a priori*. The following algorithm works for the case when n is unknown.

Variable-speed algorithm:

When a process P_i sends its id $(id(i))$, this id travels at the rate of one transmission for every $2^{id(i)}$ rounds. If an id returns to its original sender, that sender is elected.

The message complexity can be easily calculated by the following observation: When the smallest id circulates around once, the second smallest id can only get at most halfway around. Therefore, the total message exchanges are at most:

$$n + \frac{n}{2} + \frac{n}{2^2} + \ldots + \frac{n}{2^{n-1}} < 2n$$

That is, $O(n)$. However, its time complexity is $2^{\min\{id(i)\}}n$.

4.5 Bidding

A special implementation of the election process is *bidding* [8], where every competitor selects a bid value out of a given set and sends its bid to every other competitor in the system. Every competitor recognizes the same winner. Most bidding schemes are probabilistic in nature. A competitor who participates in such a probabilistic algorithm first selects a value out of a given set either by flipping a coin or by going through a random number generation. It then compares its value with the values selected by the other competitors.

Chang [8] gave a bidding scheme that satisfies the principle of *protection against competitors*. If a process selects its bid from set B, with $|B| = n$, equally likely, then its probability of winning is $1/n$ regardless of the bid values selected by the other processes. The scheme is based on four assumptions:

1. Competitors communicate with each other only by exchanging messages.

2. Communication is error-free.

3. Every competitor will send out its bid before a given deadline.

4. Competitors cannot send conflicting information to different competitors.

Chang also provided the following variations and extensions to the bidding scheme.

- Bidding with unequal weights.

- Bidding with more than one winner.

- Bidding with an unknown number of competitors.

With the objective of reducing the communication costs in terms of total messages exchanged, Wu and Fernandez proposed a solution based on the concept of a *gang* [47]. A gang is a group of competitors who work together trying to control the outcome of the bid. It is possible that there exists more than one gang in a system. Let a *gang-free subset* be defined as a group of competitors that includes at least one competitor who does not participate in any gang. Let m be a minimum integer such that all the subsets with size greater than or equal to m are gang-free[1]. We call those subsets with size m *minimum gang-free subsets* (denoted as MGFS). In our solution the size of a MGFS is known *a priori* and a subset with size m is arbitrarily selected to participate in the bidding. The result of the bidding is then distributed among the competitors not in the selected subset.

The following notation is used in the bidding process:

n	Number of competitors in the system.
i	Index for competitors.
P_i	The ith competitor.
b_i	The bid value selected by the ith competitor ranging from 1 to n.

---

[1]If we assume that the members from different gangs will never reach an agreement to control the outcome of the result, a *gang-free subset* can be defined as a group of competitors that has no gang or has more than one gang because the net effect is the same as having no gangs. In this case if M is the maximum size of any gang in the system, any sets with size $m = M + 1$ are gang free.

k Index for the winner (a competitor) ranging from 1 to n.

m The size of the minimum gang-free subset (MGFS).

f Decision algorithm.

In Chang's approach:

$$f(b_1, b_2, \ldots, b_n) = P_k$$

and

$$k = \sum_{i=1}^{n} b_i \bmod n + 1$$

In the extended bidding scheme, without loss of generality, we select a minimum gang-free subset of m elements where competitors have indexes from 1 to m. It is easy to see that the scheme still works if these elements in the MCFS have indices that are scattered around. The bidding problem solution can be expressed as:

$$f(b_1, b_2, \ldots, b_m) = P_k$$

and

$$k = \sum_{i=1}^{m} b_i \bmod n + 1$$

Clearly the index for the winner still ranges from 1 to n and is dependent on all the bidding values selected by the competitors in the MGFS. Since Chang's solution uses only one MGFS which is a collection of all the n competitors, his solution can be considered as a special case.

The performance of these two schemes can be evaluated using some specific network topologies. We consider here two types of network: completely connected networks and hypercubes. We assume that each process representing a competitor is assigned to a distinct processor (or node). In a completely connected network each pair of nodes can exchange messages directly and we assume that each node can exchange messages with the rest of the other nodes at the same time. Under this assumption Chang's algorithm requires $n(n-1)$ message exchanges and one round of exchanges. The proposed algorithm requires $m(m-1)$ message exchanges in the phase for selecting a winner (phase 1) and $n-m$ message exchanges in the phase of distribution of the result (phase 2). It is clear that Chang's solution needs $(n-m)(n+m-2)$ more message exchanges than the proposed solution. This difference of message exchanges reaches its maximum value when $m = 1$ [2].

Completely connected networks, although having several desirable features, are rarely used in distributed systems, especially in massively parallel systems. Among other networks the hypercube [42] has been one of the dominating topologies because of its regularity and symmetry. In an l-dimensional hypercube each node is addressed distinctively by l-bit binary numbers, $a_l a_{l-1}...a_1$, from 0 to $2^l - 1$. Two nodes are directly connected via a link (and hence are neighbors) if and only if their binary addresses differ in exactly one bit position. In order to reduce the total amount of message exchanges in the process of selecting a winner, each node calculates the partial sum of all the bidding values collected so far. The result of the partial sum is transmitted to one of the neighboring nodes.

The following algorithm implements Chang's scheme in an l-dimensional hypercube Q_l where $2^l = n$. Each competitor c selects a bid value which is used as the initial accumulated value (v) for each c. We denote by $c^{(d)}$ (with value v^d) the neighboring node along the dth dimension.

$$P(c)::= * [\ [\ \textbf{send} \ v \ \textbf{to} \ c^{(d)} \ \| \ \textbf{receive} \ v^d \ \textbf{from} \ c^{(d)}];$$
$$v := (v + v^d) \ \text{mod} \ n$$
$$]$$

hypercube-bidding $::= \forall_{c \in Q_l} P(c)$

In the proposed scheme, we assume $m = 2^s$ and $n = 2^l$ with $s < l$ and competitors with address codes $00...0a_s...a_1$ are selected as a MGFS. The implementation of the two phases in the solution is as follows:

1. Selection of the winner: The algorithm hypercube-bidding is applied to the selected MGFS; that is, subcube $00...0a_s...a_1$.

2. Distribution of the result: Each P in the MGFS sends its accumulated value to 2^{l-s} competitors who have the same s least significant bits (LSBs) as those of P in their address codes.

Figures 4.7 and 4.8 show the above two algorithms applied to a four-dimensional hypercube where subcube $0a_3a_2a_1$ is selected as the MGFS.

---

[2] Let $f(m) = (n - m)(n + m - 2)$, with m ranging from 1 to n. Since $f(m)' = -2m + 2$ is less than zero, $f(m)$ monotonically decreases and reaches its minimum value 0 when $m = n$ and its maximum value $(n - 1)(n - 3)$ when $m = 1$.

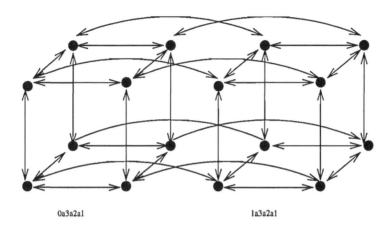

0a3a2a1   1a3a2a1

FIGURE 4.7
**Chang's algorithm implemented on a four-dimensional hyper-
cube.**

64 and 32 message exchanges are required in Figures 4.7 and 4.8, respectively. Four rounds are required for both cases and the number associated
with each link indicates the round in which message exchanges take place
bidirectionally on that link.

In the implementation of Chang's algorithm on a hypercube $l2^l = n \log n$
messages are required which is twice the total links in the hypercube as well
as l rounds of messages[3]. In the implementation of the proposed method, as
shown in Figure 4.8, where nodes that do not participate in the election process are represented by white nodes, the first phase of the implementation
involves $m \log m$ messages and the second phase involves $n - m$ messages.
The total messages are $m \log n + (n - m)$. Again l rounds are needed:
s of them are used in the first step and the remaining $l - s$ rounds are
used for result distribution. In summary, when the proposed solution is
applied to a non-completely connected network such as a hypercube network, the number of messages is reduced while the number of rounds of
messages remains the same. Therefore, the proposed solution appears to
be particularly suitable for non-completely connected networks.

When the number of competitors are unknown, a practical and efficient
method that needs two rounds of synchronization can be defined as follows:

---

[3]The complexity of the numerical calculation, that is, the decision algorithm f at each
node is neglected.

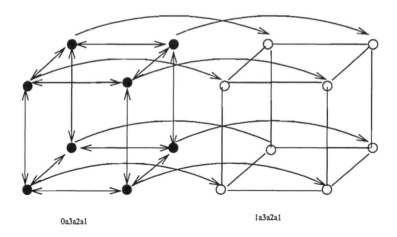

0a3a2a1   1a3a2a1

FIGURE 4.8
The proposed algorithm implemented on a four-dimensional hypercube.

1. In the first round, process P_i sends a signal together with its *id* to the other processes.

2. After P_i has received all the signals, it counts the number of processes that actually participated in the bidding (let it be n). In the second round, the solution for the normal bidding problem is used.

The concept of MGFS can also be used in this solution if the size of the MGFS is known *a priori*.

In a bidding with unequal weights each process has a different probability of winning. Assume that each process P_i is associated with a weight w_i which is an integer. The higher w_i is the higher the probability for P_i to be the winner. For example, if $w_2 = 2$ and $w_1 = 1$, then process P_2 has the double chance of winning. One simple solution is as follows: Suppose there are n processes P_i, $1 \le i \le n$, with weight w_i. Assume $m = \sum_{i=1}^{n} w_i$. The decision algorithm is

$$f(b_1, b_2, ..., b_n) = k$$

and

$$k = \sum_{i=1}^{n} b_i \bmod m + 1,$$

where w_i different elements in $[1..m]$ are *a priori* mapped to P_i. Therefore, if k is mapped to P_c, then P_c is the winner. For example, consider a system with three processes. Assume w_1, w_2, and w_3 are 2, 1, 3, respectively. $m = 2 + 1 + 3 = 6$ and value $\{1,2\}$, $\{3\}$, and $\{4,5,6\}$ will be mapped to P_1, P_2, and P_3, respectively. The decision algorithm will be

$$k = \sum_{i=1}^{3} b_i \bmod 6 + 1$$

4.6   Self-Stabilization

Let us consider a system with n processes. A system is self-stabilizing if, regardless of its initial state, it is guaranteed to arrive at a legitimate state (depicted by a predicate P) in a finite number of steps. Each step is a state transition defined by a privilege. Privileges associated with processes are Boolean functions of its local process state and the states of its neighbors. A system is in a legitimate state if and only if one process has a privilege; otherwise, it is in an illegitimate state. A conflict can happen when two privileges are "present" (i.e., Boolean functions are true) at two neighboring processes. It is assumed that there is a central demon that can "select" one of the privileges present.

More formally, a system S is self-stabilizing with respect to predicate P if it satisfies the following two properties [44].

1. *Closure.* P is closed under the execution of S; that is, once P is established in S it cannot be falsified.

2. *Convergence.* Starting from an arbitrary global state, S is guaranteed to reach a global state satisfying P within a finite number of state transitions.

An example of a self-stabilizing system is given by Dijkstra in [14] where the system is a ring of finite-state machines. In such a system there is one "distinguished" process that uses a distinct privilege for state transition and the other processes use another privilege. Given n k-state processes with $k > n$ which are labeled P_0 through P_{n-1}, where P_0 is distinguished, and P_i, $0 < i \leq n-1$, are identical. The state transition for P_i is as follows:

$$P_i \neq P_{i-1} \rightarrow P_i := P_{i-1}, 0 < i \leq n - 1$$

and for P_0 we have,

$$P_0 = P_{n-1} \rightarrow P_0 := (P_0 + 1) \bmod k$$

P_0	P_1	P_2	privileged processes	process to make move
2	1	2	P_0, P_1, P_2	P_0
3	1	2	P_1, P_2	P_1
3	3	2	P_2	P_2
3	3	3	P_0	P_0
0	3	3	P_1	P_1
0	0	3	P_2	P_2
0	0	0	P_0	P_0
1	0	0	P_1	P_1
1	1	0	P_2	P_2
1	1	1	P_0	P_0
2	1	1	P_1	P_1
2	2	1	P_2	P_2
2	2	2	P_0	P_0
3	2	2	P_1	P_1
3	3	2	P_2	P_2
3	3	3	P_0	P_0

Table 4.1   Dijkstra's self-stabilization algorithm.

Table 4.1 shows an example of a system with three processes and $k = 4$. Initially each process has a privilege and the selection of a move is random. After two steps (moves) the system reaches a legitimate state – a state in which there is exactly one process that has privilege. The state remains in a legitimate state thereafter.

The above algorithm uses k-state processes where k depends on the number of processes. Another algorithm uses only three states:

The state transition for P_0 is as follow:

$$(P_0 + 1) \bmod 3 = P_1 \rightarrow P_0 := (P_0 - 1) \bmod 3$$

The state transition for P_{n-1} is as follow:

$$P_{n-2} = P_0 \wedge (P_{n-2} + 1) \bmod 3 \neq P_{n-1} \rightarrow P_{n-1} := (P_{n-2} + 1) \bmod 3$$

For all the other processes:

$$[\ (P_i + 1) \bmod 3 = P_{i+1} \rightarrow P_i := P_{i+1}$$
$$\square \ (P_i + 1) \bmod 3 = P_{i-1} \rightarrow P_i := P_{i-1}$$
$$]$$

In order to associate the self-stabilization problem with the mutual exclusion problem, we may consider each privilege as a token corresponding to the right to access the CS. That is, if a process has one of these tokens, it is allowed to enter its critical section. At first there may be more than one token in the system but after a finite amount of time only one token exists in the system that is circulated among the processes.

Numerous work has been done to extend the above simple self-establishing algorithm. Extensions can be classified as follows:

- The role of demon.
  The role of the demon is to select a privilege that can be implemented in a decentralized way. Another approach [4] defines state transitions that are non-interfering.

- The role of asymmetry.
  It is easy to see that if the processes are identical, in general, the self-stabilization problem is unsolvable. Two possible forms of asymmetry are possible: One may choose to make all of the processes different or to make one "distinguished" and the others identical. However, symmetry is not always unattainable. Burns and Pachl [5] showed a symmetric self-stabilizing ring with a prime number of processes.

- The role of topology.
  The original solution for the self-stabilization problem is on a unidirectional ring. A limited amount of work has been done to solve the self-stabilization problem on other topologies such as bidirectional rings and trees [27].

- The role of the number of states.
  In the original solution the number of states k is unbounded. In general, it is desirable to have a solution that uses the minimum number of states. It is shown that the minimum k is three for a ring although there exists a special network that needs only binary-state machines [18].

The concept of self-stabilization has been applied to many areas including self-stabilizing communication protocols [21] such as the sliding window protocol, the two-way handshake protocol, fault-tolerant clock synchronization [20], and distributed process control [2].

One of the most important application areas is fault tolerance design to cover transient failures. Traditionally fault tolerance design is done by countering the effects of their individual causes. By doing this many design approaches were developed without their commonality. Self-stabilization provides a unified approach to transient failures by formally incorporating them into the design model. At least the following transient faults can be tolerated in a self-stabilization system:

- Inconsistent initialization which results in a local state inconsistent with others.

- Transmission errors which cause inconsistency between the states of the sender and receiver.

- Process failure and recovery which cause its local state inconsistent with the rest.

- Memory crash will cause a loss of local states.

One weakness in most self-stabilization systems is that they do not provide information on how fast an illegitimate state can be converged into a legitimate one. In some situation it is not fast enough. For example, Dijkstra's k-state algorithm requires an order of $n^{1.5}$ local state changes for each node and the message complexity is n^2. In many cases tradeoffs are needed between how fast a system stabilizes and how fast it executes.

References

[1] Agrawal, D., Ö. Eğecioğlu, and A. El Abbadi, "Analysis of quorum-based protocols for distributed (k+1)-exclusion", *IEEE Transactions on Parallel and Distributed Systems,* **8**, 5, May 1997, 533-737.

[2] Bastani, F. and M. Kam, "A self-stabilizing ring protocol for load balancing in distributed real-time process control systems", Tech. Report No. UH-CS-87-8, Dept. of Computer Science, Univ. of Houston, Texas, Nov. 1987.

[3] Brinch Hanson, P., *Operating System Principles*, Prentice-Hall, Inc., 1973.

[4] Burns, J. E., "Self-stabilizing rings without demons", Tech. Rep. GIT-ICS-87/36, Georgia Inst. of Technology, 1987.

[5] Burns, J. E. and J. Pachl, "Uniform self-stabilizing rings", *ACM Transactions on Programming Languages and Systems*, **11**, 2, 1989, 330-344.

[6] Chan, M. Y. and F. Y. L. Chin, "Distributed election in complete networks", *Distributed Computing*, **3**, 1988, 19-22.

[7] Chandy, K. M. and J. Misra, *Parallel Program Design: A Foundation*, Addison-Wesley Publishing Company, 1989.

[8] Chang, C. K., "Bidding against competitors", *IEEE Transactions on Software Engineering*, **16**, 1, 1990, 100-104.

[9] Chang, E. G. and R. Roberts, "An improved algorithm for decentralized extrema-finding in circular configurations of processors", *Communications of the ACM*, **22**, 5, May 1979, 281-283.

[10] Chang, Y. I., "A hybrid distributed mutual exclusion algorithm", *Microprocessing and microprogramming*, **41**, 1996, 715-731.

[11] Carvalho, O. and G. Roucairol, "On mutual exclusion in computer networks", *Communications of the ACM*, **26**, 2, Feb. 1983, 146-147.

[12] Chow, R., K. Luo, and R. Newman-Wolfe, " An optimal distributed algorithm for failure-driven leader election in bounded-degree networks", *Proc. of IEEE Workshop on Future Trends of Distributed Computing Systems*, 1992, 136-153.

[13] Dijkstra, E. W., "Cooperating sequential processes", in *Programming Languages*, F. Genuys, ed., Academic Press, 1968, 43-112.

[14] Dijkstra, E. W., "Self-stabilizing systems in spite of distributed control", *Communications of the ACM*, **17**, 1974, 643-644.

[15] Dolev, D., M. Klawe, and M. Roth, "An $O(n \log n)$ unidirectional distributed algorithm for extrema finding in a circle", *Journal of Algorithms*, **3**, 1982, 245-260.

[16] Franklin, W. R., "On an improved algorithm for decentralized extrema-finding in circular configurations of processors", *Communications of the ACM*, **25**, 5, May 1982, 336-337.

[17] Garcia-Molina, H. "Elections in a distributed computing system", *IEEE Transactions on Computers*, **51**, 1, Jan 1982, 48-59.

[18] Ghosh, H., "Self-stabilizing distributed systems with binary machines", *Proc. of 28th Allerton Conf. on Communication, Control, and Computing*, 1990.

[19] Goscinski, A., "Two algorithms for mutual exclusion in real-time distributed computer systems", *Journal of Parallel and Distributed Computing*, 1990, 77-85.

[20] Gouda, M. and T. Herman, "Stabilizing unison", *Information Processing Letters*, **35**, 1990, 171-175.

[21] Gouda, M. and N. Multari, "Self-stabilizing communication protocols", *IEEE Transactions on Computers* , **40**, 4, Apr. 1991, 448-458.

[22] Helary, J. -M, A. Mostefaoui, and M. Raynal, " A general scheme for token- and tree-based distributed mutual exclusion algorithms", *IEEE Transactions on Parallel and Distributed Systems*, **5**, 11, Nov. 1994, 1185-1196.

[23] Hofri, M., "Proof of a mutual exclusion algorithm – a classic example", *Operating Systems Review*, **24**, 1, Jan 1990, 18-22.

[24] Hwang, K. and F. A. Briggs, *Computer Architecture and Parallel Processing*, McGraw-Hill Publishing Company, 1984.

[25] King, G. T., T. B. Gendreau, and L. M. Ni, "Reliable election in broadcast networks", *Journal of Parallel and Distributed Computing*, **1**, 1989, 521-546.

[26] Korach, E., S. Moran, and S. Zabs, "The lower and upper bounds for some distributed algorithms for a complete network of processors", *Proc. of TAP ACM Conf.*, 1984, 199-205.

[27] Kruijer, H., "Self-stabilization (in spite of distributed control) in tree structure systems", *Information Processing Letters*, **8**, 2, 1979, 91-95.

[28] LeLann, G., "Distributed systems: towards a formal approach", *Proc. of IFIP Congress*, 1977, 155-160.

[29] Lynch, N. A., *Distributed Algorithms*, Morgan Kaufmann Publishing, Inc., 1996.

[30] Maekawa, M., "A square-root(N) algorithm for mutual exclusion in decentralized systems", *ACM Transactions on Computer Systems*, **2**, 4, May 1985, 145-159.

[31] Milenkovic, M., *Operating Systems: Concepts and Design*, McGraw-Hill Publishing Company, 1987.

[32] Misra, J., "Detecting termination of distributed computations using markers", *Proc. of 2nd ACM Conf. on Principles of Distributed Computing*, 1983, 290-294.

[33] Mans, B. and N. Santoro, "Optimal elections in faulty loop networks and applications", *IEEE Transactions on Computers*, **47**, 3, Mar. 1998, 286-297.

[34] Nishio, S., K. F. Li, and E. G. Manning, "A resilient mutual exclusion algorithm for computer networks", *IEEE Transactions on Parallel and Distributed Systems*, **1**, 3, July 1990, 344-355.

[35] Peterson, G. L., "An $O(n \log n)$ unidirectional algorithm for the circular extrema problem", *ACM TOPLAS*, **4**, 4, Oct. 1982, 758-762.

[36] Raymond, K., "A tree-based algorithm for distributed mutual exclusion", *ACM Transactions on Computer Systems*, **7**, 1, Feb. 1989, 61-77.

[37] Raymond, K., "A distributed algorithm for multiple entries to a critical section", *Information Processing Letters*, **30**, 4, Feb. 1989, 189-193.

[38] Raynal, M., *Algorithms for Mutual Exclusion*, The MIT Press, 1986.

[39] Raynal, M., *Distributed Algorithms and Protocols*, John Wiley & Sons, 1988.

[40] Ricart, G. and A. K. Agrawala, "An optimal algorithm for mutual exclusion in computer networks", *Communications of the ACM*, **24**, 1, Jan. 1981, 9-17.

[41] Ricart, G. and A. K. Agrawala, "Author's response to 'on mutual exclusion in computer networks' by Carvalho and Roucairol", *Communications of the ACM*, **26**, 2, Feb. 1983, 147-148.

[42] Saad, Y. and M. H. Schultz, " Topological properties of hypercubes", *IEEE Transactions on Computers*, **37**, 7, July 1988, 867-872.

[43] Sanders, B., "The information structure of distributed mutual exclusion algorithms", *ACM Transactions on Computer Systems*, **5**, Aug. 1987, 284-299.

[44] Schneider, M., "Self-stabilization", *ACM Computing Surveys*, **25**, 1, Mar. 1993, 45-67.

[45] Singh, S. and J. Kurose, "Electing 'good' leaders", *Journal of Parallel and Distributed Computing*, **21**, 2, 1994, 184-201.

[46] Singhal, M., "A taxonomy of distributed Mutual exclusion", *Journal of Parallel and Distributed Computing*, **18**, 1, 1993, 94-101.

[47] Wu, J. and E. B. Fernandez, "An extended bidding scheme for the distributed consensus problem", Technical Report, TR-CSE-92-38, Florida Atlantic University, 1992.

Problems

1. Modify or enhance Lamport's mutual exclusive algorithm for the following system: Each pair of PE has only one communication path (consisting of a sequence of FIFO channels) with a fixed propagation delay. Different paths may have different delays and the delay of each path is not known when the system starts. Only physical clocks are used and all of them are accurate and are synchronized initially. Consider various modifications and enhancements and discuss their pros and cons.

2. Show that in Ricart and Agrawala's algorithm the CS is granted according to the increasing order of timestamps associated with requests. Explain why timestamps are not used in Maekawa's algorithm and then modify Maekawa's algorithm such that the grant signal is sent based on timestamps of requests.

3. Assume that up to two processes can enter a critical section simultaneously. Provide possible extensions to Lamport's algorithm and the simple token-ring-based algorithm.

4. Suppose the request sets of a six-process system are the following:

$$R_1 : \{P_1, P_2, P_3, P_4, P_5, P_6\}$$

$$R_2 : \{P_1, P_3\}$$

$$R_3 : \{P_2, P_3\}$$

$$R_4 : \{P_1, P_2\}$$

$$R_5 : \{P_2, P_3\}$$

$$R_6 : \{P_1, P_3\}$$

What is the potential problem for the above arrangement?

5. To apply Chang and Roberts' election algorithm to a hypercube one can first generate a spanning ring in the given hypercube (see the figure below for a 3-dimensional hypercube example.)

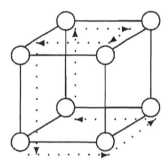

A spanning ring in a 3-dimensional hypercube

Assume that one process initiates an election process at a time. In the worst case, almost 2 rounds are needed to elect a winner. Enhance Chang and Roberts' algorithm to obtain a faster election process for the hypercube topology by using multiple paths provided by the hypercube. Assume that each node can send a message to multiple neighbors simultaneously. Only a high-level description of your algorithm is needed. Use the 3-dimensional hypercube example to illustrate your approach.

6. Provide a revised Misra and Chandy's ping-pong algorithm in which the ping and the pong are circulated in opposite directions. Compare the performance and other related issues of these two algorithms.

7. Design a modified ping-pong type of resilient algorithm where three tokens (t_1, t_2 and t_3) are used on a logical ring consisting of n process. Your algorithm should tolerate a loss of up to 2 tokens. State explicitly how your algorithm detects three different situations: (1) no token is lost, (2) one token is lost, and (3) two tokens are lost. Your algorithm should also include a recovery process.

8. Show the state transition sequence for the following system with $n = 3$ and $k = 5$ using Dijkstra's self-stabilizing algorithm. Assume that $P_0 = 3$, $P_1 = 1$, and $P_2 = 4$.

9. For any given n-dimensional hypercube where $n > 3$ find a path in which each (ordered) pair of nodes in the cube appears at least once. That is, this path consists of two consecutive Hamiltonian paths.

Extend Dijkstra's k-state self-stabilization algorithm on a ring from one privilege to two privileges. That is, within the finite number of state transitions there are two privileges among nodes in the ring.

10. In the bidding algorithm, is it possible to define the decision function as

$$k = \prod_{i=1}^{n} b_i \bmod n + 1?$$

(Hint: Ensure that each process has the same chance of winning.)

11. In the Lynch's time-slice algorithm suppose we change the algorithm such that process P_i sends its id in round

    (a) n

    (b) $\frac{n}{2}$

Change the rest of the algorithm accordingly to ensure it can still select a leader correctly. In addition the time complexity should remain the same.

12. If the range of process id is given, i.e., $id(i) \in [a..b]$ where a and b are integers, improve Lynch's variable-speed algorithm by reducing its time complexity.

Chapter 5

PREVENTION, AVOIDANCE, AND DETECTION OF DEADLOCK

Distributed systems, in general, exhibit a high degree of resource and data sharing, a situation in which deadlocks may happen. Deadlocks arise when members of a group of processes which hold resources are blocked indefinitely from access to resources held by other processes within the group. In this chapter methods for prevention, avoidance, and detection of deadlock in distributed systems are discussed.

5.1 The Deadlock Problem

In a computer system deadlocks arise when members of a group of processes which hold resources are blocked indefinitely from access to resources held by other processes within the group. For example, consider a system with two I/O controllers. The system will immediately allocate an I/O controller to a requesting process upon each request. Suppose two processes P_i and P_j have the following requests:

- P_i requests one I/0 controller and the system allocates one.

- P_j requests one I/O controller and again the system allocates one.

- P_i wants another I/O controller but has to wait since the system ran out of I/O controllers.

- P_j wants another I/O controller and waits.

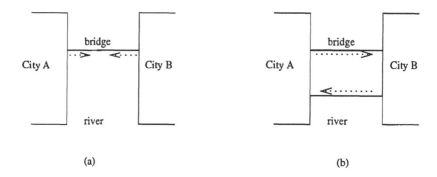

(a)   (b)

FIGURE 5.1
Two cities connected by (a) one bridge and by (b) two bridges.

In the above example both processes are in the state of permanent blocking and a deadlock involving these two processes occurs.

5.1.1   Conditions for deadlocks

Formally, a deadlock can arise if and only if the following four conditions hold simultaneously [14]:

- *Mutual exclusion.* No resource can be shared by more than one process at a time.

- *Hold and wait.* There must exist a process that is holding at least one resource and is waiting to acquire additional resources that are currently being held by other processes.

- *No preemption.* A resource cannot be preempted.

- *Circular wait.* There is a cycle in the wait-for graph.

Figure 5.1 shows a deadlock example where there are two cities A and B separated by a river. The two cities are connected by a bridge (Figure 5.1 (a)). Assume that the bridge is so narrow that only one person can walk through at a time. There will be no problem if several persons walk towards the same direction. Deadlock occurs when two persons heading in different directions – one from city A to city B and the other one from city B to city A – meet in the middle of the bridge.

5.1.2 Graph-theoretic models

A *wait-for* graph consists of a set of processes $\{P_0, P_1, \ldots, P_n\}$ as the node set, and an edge (P_i, P_j) exists in the graph if and only if P_i is waiting for a resource which is held by P_j. A variation of the wait-for graph is the *resource allocation graph* where nodes are partitioned into process nodes and resource nodes. Each edge is an ordered pair (P_i, r_j) or (r_j, P_i) where P is a process and r a resource type. An edge (P_i, r_j) implies that P_i requested an instance of resource type r_j (type r_j may have several instances) and is currently waiting for that resource. An edge (r_j, P_i) implies that an instance of resource type r_j has been allocated to process P_i. The resource allocation graph is a more powerful model than the wait-for graph since in the wait-for graph it is assumed that there is only one instance of each resource.

Based on the conditions mentioned above, a directed cycle in a wait-for graph corresponds to a deadlock situation, assuming that a process needs to acquire all the resources before it can proceed. However, if there is a directed cycle in the resource allocation graph, the system *may* or *may not* be in a deadlock state. Figures 5.2 (a) and (b) show two resource allocation graphs, where a rectangle represents a resource node with several tokens within representing the number of instances and a circle represents a process node. There are cycles in both Figure 5.2 (a) and Figure 5.2 (b). The processes in Figure 5.2 (b) are in a deadlock state. However, there is no deadlock in the graph of Figure 5.2 (a) because process P_4 may release its instance of resource type r_2 and that resource can then be allocated to P_3 to break the cycle.

To simplify the discussion we only consider cases where there is only one resource of each resource type and use the wait-for graph. Any resource allocation graph with a single copy of resources can be transferred to a wait-for graph. The transformation procedure is as follows:

1. Examine a resource r that has not been checked before in the given resource allocation graph. If all resources have been checked, go to step 3.

2. Add a directed edge from each input process node to each output process node. An input process node is the one that waits for r and an output process node is the one that has an instance of r. Go to step 1.

3. Remove all the resource nodes together with the associated edges.

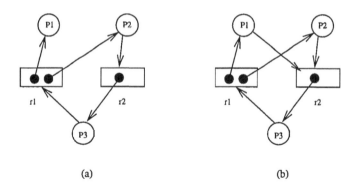

(a)   (b)

FIGURE 5.2
Two resource allocation graphs: (a) without deadlock and (b) with deadlock.

Let us consider the *dining philosophers problem* where five philosophers spend their lives thinking and eating on a round table. When a philosopher gets hungry, he tries to pick up two forks closest to him: one that lies in between him and his left-hand side neighbor and another that lies in between him and his right-hand side neighbor. When a philosopher has both forks, he starts eating. When he finishes eating, he puts down both of his forks. A deadlock situation occurs when each of the five philosophers (P_i) has his right-hand side fork (F_i) and wants to access his left-hand side fork (F_{i+1} or F_5 if $i = 1$) as shown in the resource allocation graph in Figure 5.3 (a). Following the transformation procedure we can derive the corresponding wait-for graph as shown in Figure 5.3 (b).

5.1.3 Strategies for handling deadlocks

There are three strategies for handling deadlocks:

- *Deadlock prevention.* Prevents deadlocks by restraining requests made to ensure that at least one of the four deadlock conditions cannot occur.

- *Deadlock avoidance.* Dynamically grants a resource to a process if the resulting state is *safe*. A state is safe if there is at least one execution sequence that allows all processes to run to completion.

- *Deadlock detection and recovery.* Allows deadlocks to form; then finds and breaks them.

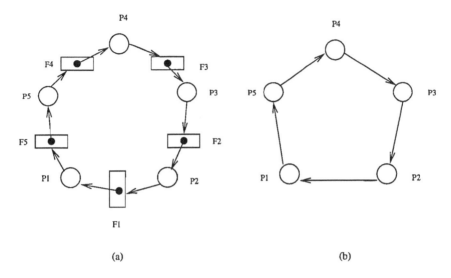

(a)   (b)

FIGURE 5.3
The dining philosophers problem: (a) A deadlock situation shown in a resource allocation graph. (b) The corresponding wait-for graph.

Both deadlock prevention and avoidance use a pessimistic approach: Assume that deadlock will occur and try to prevent or avoid it. One commonly used deadlock prevention is done by having a process acquire all the needed resources simultaneously before it starts (it may not be a trivial task) or by preempting a process that holds the needed resource(s). The former method is inefficient because it decreases system concurrency. The latter approach is also inefficient because irrelevant processes may be aborted.

Although deadlock avoidance strategies are often used in centralized systems and many algorithms have been proposed (e.g., Dijkstra's banker's algorithm [4]), they are rarely used in a distributed system. This is because checking for safe states is computationally expensive due to the large number of processes and resources in distributed systems without a global clock.

Deadlock detection and recovery uses an optimistic approach. However, it may not be efficient for applications where deadlocks occur frequently. Some distributed detection algorithms can be easily implemented and will be discussed later in this chapter.

We use the bridge crossing example to illustrate these three approaches. A typical deadlock prevention will place constraints on the direction people are allowed to move from one city to another. One naive approach is to allow people to move only from city A to city B. However, this is not a feasible approach since no one can move from city B to city A. One solution is to build another bridge (see Figure 5.1 (b)) that allows people to move from city B to city A. This approach is feasible, but resources (bridges) may not be fully utilized. For example, when there is heavy traffic from city A to city B and at the same time almost no traffic from city B to city A, only one bridge can be utilized – a utilization of close to fifty percent of resources.

In deadlock avoidance, the concept of a safe state is introduced which is dependent on the application. In the bridge crossing example, there is no need to place any constraints on moving directions in deadlock avoidance. However, whenever a person is about to step onto the bridge, he or she needs to check if there are other people coming from the other direction and have already been on the bridge (a safety check). However, the safety concept cannot be easily defined or captured for some applications. In this example the avoidance approach fails when either the bridge is too long or the weather is too foggy for people to see the other end of the bridge.

In deadlock detection and recovery, neither constraints nor safety checks are necessary. A detection mechanism is needed to detect a possible deadlock situation. In the bridge crossing example, when two persons coming from different directions meet on the bridge and no one is willing to back off a deadlock occurs. However, in reality the detection process is much more complex especially in distributed systems. There are several ways to perform a recovery: Either one process is aborted (one person is thrown into the river in the river crossing example) or one process is forced to release the occupied resources (at least one person backs off in the river crossing example). The selection of the victim is also important: Logically a person who is close to the destination should have a higher priority than the one who just stepped onto the bridge.

5.1.4 Models of request

There are in general two types of deadlock:

- Resource deadlock

- Communication deadlock

In communication deadlocks, messages are the resources for which processes wait. The real difference between resource deadlock and communication deadlock is that the former usually uses the AND condition while the latter uses the OR condition defined as follows:

- *AND condition.* A process that requires resources for execution can proceed when it has acquired all those resources.

- *OR condition.* A process that requires resources for execution can proceed when it has acquired at least one of those resources.

The reason the OR condition is used for communication deadlocks is that most distributed control structures are nondeterministic; a process may be waiting for a message from more than one process. Another condition is called P-out-of-Q which means that a process simultaneously requests Q resources and remains blocked until it is granted any P of those resources. The AND-OR model is another generalization of the AND and OR models. AND-OR requests may specify any combination of AND and OR requests. For example, it is possible to request a AND (b OR c). Since it is hard to analyze the deadlock situation under this model, we consider here the AND and OR conditions separately.

5.1.5 Models of process and resource

Normally a process may use a resource following the steps below: (1) *Request.* If the request is not immediately granted, the requesting process has to wait until it acquires the resource. (2) *Use.* The process uses the resource. (3) *Release.* The process releases the resource.

A resource is any object that processes can request and wait for. In general, a resource is either *reusable* or *consumable*. A reusable resource does not disappear as a result of its use and it can be used over and over again. Examples of reusable resource are CPU, memory, and I/O. A consumable resource vanishes as a result of its use. Examples of consumable resource are message, signal, etc.

5.1.6 Deadlock conditions

The condition for deadlock in a system using the AND condition is the existence of a *cycle*. However, in a system using the OR condition a cycle may or may not cause a deadlock. The condition for deadlock in a system using the OR condition is the existence of a *knot*. A knot (K) consists of a set of nodes such that for every node a in K, all nodes in K and only the nodes in K are reachable from node a. For example, in Figure 5.4 (a)

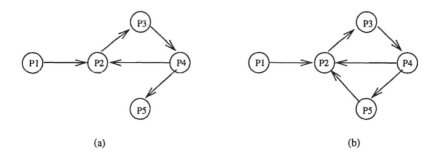

(a)   (b)

FIGURE 5.4
Two systems under the OR condition with (a) no deadlock and without (b) deadlock.

there is a cycle, $P_4 \to P_2 \to P_3 \to P_4$; therefore, $S = \{P_2, P_3, P_4\}$ forms a cycle. However, the successor of P_4 is $P_5 \notin S$. Therefore, S is not a knot. Actually, there is no knot in Figure 5.4 (a). In this example P_4 is waiting for a message from either P_2 or P_5. A message received by P_4 from P_5 will break the cycle. It is easy to see that set $\{P_2, P_3, P_4, P_5\}$ in Figure 5.4 (b) forms a knot; therefore, the wait-for graph in Figure 5.4 (b) has a deadlock. In this chapter we focus on resource deadlocks only; for a more detailed discussion on communication deadlocks see [2] and [7].

In the subsequent discussion the deadlock handling methods are general to both types of deadlock unless otherwise specified.

5.2   Deadlock Prevention

Deadlock prevention algorithms prevent deadlocks by restraining how process requests can be made. Deadlock prevention is commonly achieved by one of the following approaches; all of which are based on breaking one of the four deadlock conditions:

1. A process acquires all the needed resources simultaneously before it begins its execution, therefore breaking the hold and wait condition. In the dining philosophers' problem, each philosopher is required to pick up both forks at the same time. If he fails, he has to release the fork(s) (if any) that he has acquired.

2. All resources are assigned unique numbers. A process may request a resource with a unique number i (also called an id) only if it is not holding a resource with a number less than or equal to i and therefore breaking the circular wait condition. In the dining philosophers problem, each philosopher is required to pick a fork that has a larger id than the one he currently holds. That is, philosopher P_5 needs to pick up fork F_5 and then F_1; the other philosopher P_i should pick up fork F_i followed by F_{i-1}.

3. Each process is assigned a unique priority number. The priority numbers decide whether process P_i should wait for process P_j and therefore break the non-preemption condition. Assume that the philosophers' priorities are based on their ids, i.e., P_i has a higher priority than P_j if $i < j$. In this case P_i is allowed to wait for P_{i+1} for $i = 1, 2, 3, 4$. P_5 is not allowed to wait for P_1. If this case happens, P_5 has to abort by releasing its acquired fork(s) (if any).

Another way to break the hold and wait condition is to allow a process to request resources during its execution as long as it holds no other resource. If a process is holding some resources, it can first release all of them and then re-request these resources.

Practically it is impossible to provide a method based on breaking the mutual exclusion condition since most resources are intrinsically non-sharable, e.g., two philosophers cannot use the same fork at the same time. Alternative ways may exist as has been done for a printer by spooling printer outputs.

Both approaches 1 and 2 are conservative, overly cautious strategies. The problem with approach 3 is the possibility of starvation. Processes with low priorities may always be rolled back. This problem can be handled by raising the priority of a process every time it is victimized.

The example in the following section shows an application of deadlock prevention in a transaction system where the priority of each process is based on a fixed timestamp.

5.3   A Deadlock Prevention Example: Distributed Database Systems

We use deadlock prevention in distributed database systems as an example. In a distributed database system, the user accesses *data objects* of the database by executing transactions. Each data object can be treated as a resource and each transaction a process. A *transaction* is a sequence of *read* and *write* operations on a set of data objects. A transaction should acquire (by locking) all the objects before updating them and release (by unlocking) them before completion. Locking is the strategy of reserving access rights (locks) to prevent other transactions from obtaining certain other (conflicting) locks. For example, a transaction T_1 involving two accounts A and B may look like this:

T_1:
>   lock A;
>   lock B;
>   transaction starts;
>   unlock A;
>   unlock B;

If there is another transaction T_2 involving accounts A and B, a deadlock occurs when T_1 and T_2 each acquires one lock and waits for the other. The deadlock problem in distributed databases is part of the area of concurrency control. *Concurrency control* deals with the problem of coordinating the actions of processes that operate in parallel, access shared data, and therefore potentially interfere with each other. A detailed treatment of this topic (other than deadlock) will be discussed in Chapter 11.

Rosenkrantz [15] proposed a dynamic priority scheme using timestamps. Two complementary deadlock prevention schemes using timestamps have been proposed.

The *wait-die* scheme is based on the non-preemptive method. When process P_i requests a resource currently held by P_j, P_i is allowed to wait only if it has a smaller timestamp than P_j; that is, P_i is older than P_j. Otherwise, P_i is rolled back (dies). More specifically:

$$[\quad LC_i < LC_j \rightarrow \textbf{halt } P_i \text{ (wait)}$$
$$\square \quad LC_i \geq LC_j \rightarrow \textbf{kill } P_i \text{ (die)}$$
$$]$$

When a process dies it releases all the locks obtained. We assume that a dead process will come back with the same timestamp. Freedom from deadlock is obvious since only processes with smaller timestamps wait for ones with larger timestamps. When a process waits for a particular resource, no lock will be released. Once a process releases a resource, one of the waiting processes on the queue associated with this resource is activated.

Going back to the previous example with two transactions operated on two common accounts, we assume $LC_1 < LC_2$, i.e., T_1 has a higher priority than T_2. Let us look at the following three situations:

- If T_1 gets both locks A and B and then T_2 requests lock B, T_2 is killed. When T_2 comes back later with the same timestamp it will have a higher priority than any newly created transactions.

- If T_2 first gets both locks B and A (T_2 requests locks in reverse order) and then T_1 requests for lock A, T_1 will be blocked at lock A. Note that there may be other transactions blocked at lock A. The blocked processes on the queue are arranged based on either FIFO (first in first out) or timestamps. Once T_2 has completed, it unlocks A and B, and the first blocked transaction, say T_1, is activated.

- If each transaction gets one lock, i.e., T_1 has lock A and needs lock B, and T_2 gets lock B and needs lock A. Suppose T_1 requests lock B before T_2 requests lock A, T_1 is blocked and queued at B. T_2 dies when it requests lock A and releases all its locks (lock B) which in turn activates T_1 at B. If T_2 requests lock A before T_1 requests lock B, T_2 is killed releasing lock B and T_1 will never be blocked.

The *wound-wait* scheme is based on the preemptive method. When process P_i requests a resource currently held by P_j, process P_i is allowed to wait only if it has a larger timestamp than P_j; that is, P_i is younger than P_j. Otherwise, P_j is rolled back (P_j is wounded by P_i). More specifically,

$$[\quad LC_i < LC_j \rightarrow \textbf{kill } P_j \text{ (wound)}$$
$$\square \quad LC_i \geq LC_j \rightarrow \textbf{halt } P_i \text{ (wait)}$$
$$]$$

Both schemes avoid starvation (or livelock) provided that when a process is rolled back it is not assigned a new timestamp. Since timestamps always increase, a process which is rolled back will eventually have the smallest timestamp. Thus it will not be rolled back again. Also, if a process never

process id	priority	1st request time	length	retry interval
P_1	2	1	1	1
P_2	1	1.5	2	1
P_3	4	2.1	2	2
P_4	5	3.3	1	1
P_5	3	4.0	2	3

Table 5.1   A system consisting of five processes.

receives a grant message for which it is waiting, it is permanently blocked. While a process is blocked it may not send any request or grant messages. The main problem with these two schemes is that some unnecessary roll-backs may occur especially in the wait-die scheme. This may affect the performance of the system.

Table 5.1 describes a system consisting of five processes. Priority represents timestamp of each process. 1st request time indicates the time when a process requests a resource for the first time. We assume that each dead process is activated periodically with a fixed retry interval. The execution time of each process at the CS is represented by length.

Using the wait-die scheme, we have the following result on process assignment along the time axis.

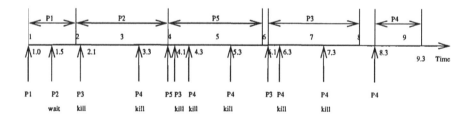

Using the wound-wait scheme and assuming when a process is killed it must start over, we have the following result:

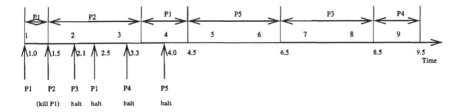

In the above example, we assume that each wounded process retries and starts from the beginning. Another approach is that a dead process retries and continues execution where it was stopped; that is, local states were saved.

5.4 Deadlock Avoidance

In deadlock prevention it normally prevents one of the four necessary conditions; therefore, no deadlock will occur. The negative impacts are low resource utilization and reduced system throughput.

Another approach for avoiding deadlocks is to require additional information on how resources are requested. Such an approach is called *deadlock avoidance* which dynamically examines the resource-allocation state to ensure that there can never be a circular-wait condition. A state is *safe* if the system can allocate resources to each process in some order and still avoid a deadlock. *Banker's algorithm* [4] is a classical approach with its name chosen for a banking system to ensure that the bank never allocates its available cash such that it can no longer satisfy the needs of all its customers.

For example, consider a bank system with three account holders A, B, and C with their initial balances (in million) 6, 4, 5, respectively. Assume the bank has a total sum of 8 million and holders A, B, and C have already withdrawn 3, 2, 1, respectively. The current state is still *safe* since the account holder can still withdraw all his or her funds following some order of requests, assuming once a holder has withdrawn the full amount he or she will release funds by re-depositing the whole amount. This can be done by first meeting the need of B with the remaining 2 million, then C (after B re-deposits 4 million), and finally A. However, if the account holder A withdraws 1 more million, that leaves only 1 million left in the bank. The corresponding state is *unsafe* because any future transactions will lead to a deadlock state, assuming that each holder will not re-deposit funds until he or she gets to hold the whole amount.

Normally the safe state definition varies from application to application. The example in the following subsection shows an approach that derives safe states from the given reachability graph of a Petri net and illustrates the approach with an example of multi-robot flexible assembly cells.

5.4.1   An avoidance approach using Petri nets

There is no uniform definition of a safe state that can be applied to any system. The approach in [19] is based on Petri nets and it follows the steps below:

1. Provides the specification of a given system and derives a Petri net model of the system [1].

2. Derives the corresponding reachability graph (or tree) of the Petri net [13].

3. Determines the deadlock states from the reachability graph.

4. Finds out all the critical states together with their inhibited transitions based on deadlock states.

In general, the specification of a system can be either model-oriented or property-oriented. A *model-oriented* specification is an explicit system model constructed of abstract or concrete primitives. A *property-oriented* specification is given in terms of axioms which define the relationships between operations: No value or explicit construction are defined in this type of specification. Normally the model-oriented specification is used and is similar to a Petri net specification in terms of their semantics.

Wu and Fernandez [18] proposed three models of Petri nets that describe a given system: *event-condition model*, *token-object association model*, and *place-object association model*. Among these methods, the event-condition model is most convenient where the notation of "condition" and "event" is used. A condition is considered as a passive component in the system while an event is considered as an active component. For each event a precondition and a postcondition are attached. Normally events are presented as transitions and conditions as places in a Petri net.

There are standard techniques for deriving the reachability graph of a given Petri net and there are several reduction methods which transform an infinite reachability graph to a finite one without losing important information. A deadlock state is identified by pinpointing dead transitions.

States in a Petri net are classified into safe and unsafe states. *Safe states* are deadlock-free while *unsafe states* are either deadlock states or deadlock-bound states. Safe states are further classified into *critical* and *non-critical*. A state (place) is critical if it is the closest state to a deadlock state but can still reach other states that do not lead to a deadlock state. More formally, we have the following definition of a critical state where a reachable path of state s is a path from s to an end-state (where no transition is possible) in the given reachability graph. Note that an end-state may or may not be the deadlock state.

State s is *safe* in a given reachability graph if one of its reachable paths has an infinite length or has a finite length with a non-deadlock end-state. A safe state s is *critical* if one of its child states is not safe; otherwise, it is called *noncritical*. A state is unsafe if it is not a safe state. An unsafe state is a *deadlock state* if it is a deadlock state; otherwise, it is called a *deadlock-bound state*.

It is easy to see that all the paths of a deadlock-bound state have finite lengths and all of them lead to deadlock end-states. Figure 5.5 shows a reachability graph with nine states. State 9 is a deadlock state. States 1 to 6 are safe states; among them states 1 and 5 are critical because their child nodes 7 and 8 are not safe. States 7 to 9 are unsafe states; among them 7 and 8 are deadlock-bound states because all the paths from either 7 or 8 lead to the deadlock state.

The following algorithm identifies the status of each state: deadlock, deadlock-bound, critical, and non-critical:

1. Find all the deadlock states and label them deadlock states.

2. Construct an inverted reachability graph from a given reachability graph. This can be easily done by reversing each edge of the given graph.

3. Find all the child nodes of each deadlock state in the inverted reachability graph and put them in an evaluation queue.

4. Select a node a from the evaluation queue, and find all the reachable paths from node a in the original reachability graph. Label node a critical if one of its reachable paths in the original reachability graph has infinite length or one finite length leads to a non-deadlock end-state; otherwise, label node a deadlock-bound.

5. If node a is deadlock-bound, find all the child nodes of node a and place them in the evaluation queue. Nodes that have been in the queue will not be placed again.

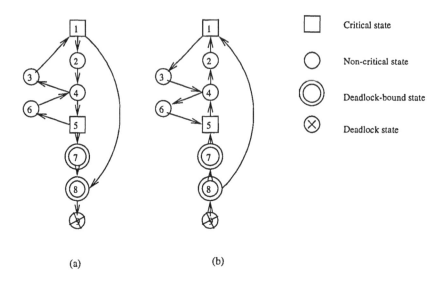

(a)   (b)

FIGURE 5.5
(a) A reachability graph and (b) the corresponding reverse reachability graph.

6. Go to step 3 if the evaluation queue is not empty.

7. Label all the remaining nodes non-critical.

Figure 5.5 (b) shows the inverted reachability graph of Figure 5.5 (a). Using the proposed algorithm we have node 9 as the only deadlock state. In the next step, node 8 (the child node of node 9) is placed in the evaluation queue and is labeled deadlock-bound since the only finite-length path 89 (meaning a path from node 8 to node 9) leads to the deadlock state. Then the child nodes of 8, nodes 7 and 1 are placed in the evaluation queue. These two nodes can be evaluated in any order. Assuming that node 1 is evaluated first, the five paths from node 1 are: $(1243)^*12(456)^*45789$, $12(456)^*45789$, $(1243)^*1245789$, $(1243)^*189$, 189, where a represents a sequence of nodes and $*$ means any number of repetitions. These paths can be easily determined from the given reachability graph as shown in Figure 5.5 (a). Clearly, all of the first four paths have infinite lengths. Therefore, node 1 is labeled critical. The next round of evaluation selects the only node in the queue that is 7. Clearly, node 7 is labeled deadlock-bound and its child node 5 is labeled critical since one of the two paths $(564) * 5789$, 5789 has an infinite length. Because the evaluation queue is empty, the algorithm executes step 7 and assigns a non-critical status to all the remaining nodes 2, 3, 4, and 6.

Note that the concept of a critical state is similar to that of a safe state used in normal deadlock avoidance algorithms. Recall that a state is safe if the system can allocate resources to each process, up to its maximum, in some order and still avoid a deadlock. Any other states are called unsafe states. The difference between a critical state and a non-critical state is that the next state of a critical state is either in a non-critical state, a critical state, or in a state that leads to a deadlock while the next state of a non-critical state is either non-critical or critical. Therefore, the critical state is a special safe state that has a neighboring unsafe state. In general, a critical state is a safe state while a safe state may or may not be a critical state.

5.5 A Deadlock Prevention Example: Multi-Robot Flexible Assembly Cells

The following example of multi-robot flexible assembly cells [19] shows how the method discussed in Section 5.4 works. The system (Figure 5.6) consists of two robots performing various pick-and-place operations accessing common space at times to obtain and transfer parts. It is assumed that each robot always holds a resource-square in Figure 5.6 representing a discrete region in space. The current resource cannot be relinquished until the next resource in the production sequence becomes available.

The two paths defined in the workspace of Figure 5.7 correspond to the production sequences of these two robots. When both robots enter the shadow regions (sr) a collision will occur. Robot 1 follows the order sr_1, sr_2, sr_3, and Robot 2 follows the order sr_3, sr_2, sr_1. A deadlock situation involves two types of entities: active entities called processes which are the robots in the flexible assembly cell example and passive entities called resources which are the discrete regions in the same example.

The collision and deadlock situation can be modeled by the Petri net of Figure 5.7. The places and transitions in this figure have the following interpretations:

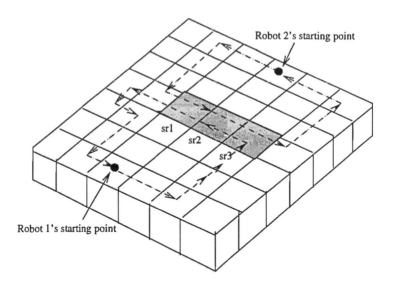

FIGURE 5.6
The flexible assembly cell example with two robots.

Places:

$p_{i1}(i = 1, 2)$:	Robot i's initial state.
$p_{i2}(i = 1, 2)$:	Robot i's state before entering the first shadow region, i.e., outside the shadow region.
$p_{i3}(i = 1, 2)$:	Robot i's state after entering the first shadow region but before entering the second shadow region.
$p_{i4}(i = 1, 2)$:	Robot i's state after entering the second shadow region but before entering the third shadow region.
$p_{i5}(i = 1, 2)$:	Robot i's state after leaving shadow regions.
sr_1, sr_2, sr_3 :	Shadow regions.

Transitions:

$t_{i1}\,(i = 1, 2)$:	Robot i's production sequence before entering the shadow regions.
$t_{i5}\,(i = 1, 2)$:	Robot i's production sequence after leaving the shadow regions.
t_{12}, t_{24} :	Requests for shadow region sr_1.
t_{13}, t_{23} :	Requests for shadow region sr_2.
t_{14}, t_{22} :	Requests for shadow region sr_3.

The approach to analyze Petri nets is to use the reachability graph. The nodes (or states) of the reachability graph of a Petri net represent the reachable markings of the net which is a 5-tuple of local states: Robots 1 and 2, shadow regions sr_1, sr_2, and sr_3. Since each shadow region has either one token or no token, its local state can be represented by 0 (no token) or 1 (one token). Figure 5.8 shows the reachability graph of the flexible assembly cell example.

In general, deadlock avoidance is a stronger requirement than collision avoidance. In the flexible assembly cell example the deadlock avoidance problem includes the collision avoidance problem. Critical states are $p_{13}p_{22}$ 011, $p_{12}p_{23}$110, $p_{14}p_{22}$001, and $p_{12}p_{24}$100 where the first two elements represent states of the two robots and the next three elements represent states of the three shadow regions. The corresponding inhibited transitions are t_{22}, t_{12}, t_{22}, and t_{12}. That is, by disabling these transitions in the corresponding critical states, the system will never enter a deadlock or deadlock-bound state. State $p_{13}p_{23}$010 is a deadlock-bound state where the firable transitions may lead to two deadlock states $p_{14}p_{23}$000 and $p_{13}p_{24}$000.

A deadlock situation is equivalent to a state in the reachability graph which has no firable transition. To avoid deadlock (including collision) we only need to prohibit certain transitions at critical states. The way to implement restrictions on certain transitions depends largely on applications. The problem can become complicated when autonomous robots are used in which each robot is required to keep a global state in the reachability graph in order to avoid the occurrence of deadlocks.

Note that one potential problem of implementing the above avoidance algorithm is the gathering of a consistent global state in a timely manner. In general, deadlock avoidance is rarely used in distributed systems because of its strict requirement for knowledge of requesting processes and the amount of resources available.

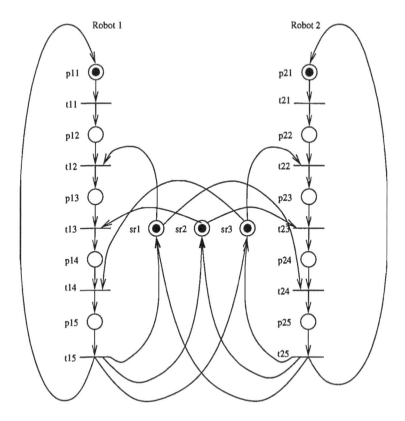

FIGURE 5.7
The Petri net representation of the flexible assembly cell example.

5.6   Deadlock Detection and Recovery

Deadlock detection involves two basic operations: Maintenance of a wait-for graph and search in the graph for the presence of cycles. Centralized, distributed, and hierarchical are three approaches to handle deadlock in distributed systems. They are different in the way of storing the wait-for graph.

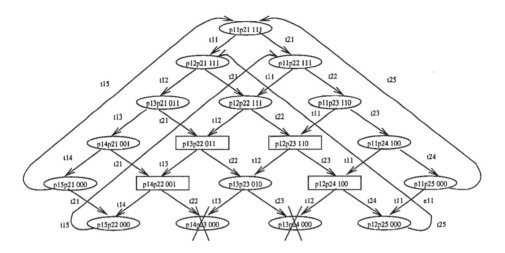

FIGURE 5.8
The reachability graph of the flexible assembly cell example.

5.6.1 Centralized approaches

In the centralized approach a global wait-for graph is constructed as the union of all of the local wait-for graphs. There is only one coordinator for deadlock detection. The global wait-for graph may be constructed at different points in time [14]:

1. Whenever a new edge is inserted or removed in one of the local wait-for graphs.

2. Periodically when a number of changes have occurred in a local wait-for graph.

3. Whenever the coordinator needs to invoke the cycle detection algorithm.

When the deadlock detection starts, the coordinator searches the global graph. If a cycle is found, a victim is selected to be rolled back. The coordinator then notifies all the sites about the selected victim. The sites, in turn, rollback the victim process. This scheme may result in unnecessary rollbacks because of possible false cycles (or knots) in the global wait-for graph. In Figure 5.9 assume that the OR model is used. Suppose that P_1 releases the resource it is holding which results in the deletion of edge (P_2, P_1) in P_1 (and edge (P_2, P_3) in P_1), and then P_1 requests a resource

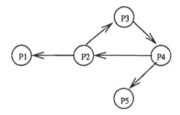

FIGURE 5.9
A false deadlock example.

hold by P_4 which triggers an addition of edge (P_1, P_4). Process P_5 requests a resource held by P_2. If the insert (P_5, P_2) signal from P_5 and the insert (P_1, P_4) from P_1 signal arrive before the delete (P_2, P_1) signal from P_1 at the node where the coordinator resides, the coordinator may discover a false knot $\{P_1, P_2, P_3, P_4, P_5\}$.

An algorithm proposed by Stuart et al. [17] can avoid the report of false deadlocks where each request is associated with a unique identifier (time-stamp). Other problems with the centralized approach are the single point of failure and communication congestion near the control site where the co-ordinator resides. However, centralized algorithms are conceptually simple and easy to implement.

5.6.2 Distributed approach

In distributed deadlock detection algorithms each separate site retains its autonomy and a local failure is not fatal to the algorithm. There are, in general, two types of algorithms. In the first type [8] a copy of the global wait-for graph is kept at each site with the result that each site has a global view of the system. In the second type the global wait-for graph is divided and distributed to different sites. Information about the wait-for graph can be maintained and circulated in various forms such as: table, list, string, etc. The problems with this approach are undetected deadlocks and false deadlocks. Algorithms with no such problems are normally too expensive to be practical.

Knapp [10] classified distributed deadlock detection algorithms into the following four types:

- *Path-pushing algorithms.* Build some simplified form of global wait-for graph at each site. Each site sends its copy to a number of neigh-bors every time a deadlock detection is performed. Update local copy that is then passed along. This process is repeated until some site has a sufficiently complete picture of the wait-for graph to make a decision (deadlock or no deadlock). Unfortunately, many algorithms of this type are incorrect mainly because the portions of the wait-for graph that are transmitted may not represent a consistent view of the global wait-for graph since each site takes its snapshot asynchronously.

- *Edge-chasing algorithms.* The presence of a cycle in a distributed graph structure can be verified by propagating special messages called *probes* along the edges of the graph. When an initiator (there may be several) receives a matching probe, it knows that it is on a cycle in the graph.

- *Diffusing computation.* When a deadlock is suspected, a transaction manager initiates a diffusing process by sending *queries* to its dependent processes. The actual global wait-for graph is never built. The diffusing computation grows by sending query messages and shrinks by receiving replies. A deadlock is detected at the initiator based on the reply information. Typically the diffusing process dynamically generates a subtree of the wait-for graph.

- *Global state detection.* This is based on Chandy and Lamport's global snapshot approach. A consistent global wait-for graph can be constructed by building a consistent global state that is determined without temporarily suspending the underlying computation.

5.6.3 Hierarchical approaches

In hierarchical deadlock detection algorithms, sites are arranged hierarchically in a tree [11]. A site detects deadlocks involving only its descendant sites. For example, let A, B, and C be controllers such that C is the lowest common ancestor of A and B. Suppose that node P_i appears in the local wait-for graph of controllers A and B. Then P_i must also appear in the local wait-for graph as:

- Controller of C.

- Every controller in the path from C to A.

- Every controller in the path from C to B.

In addition, if P_i and P_j appear in the wait-for graph of controller D and there exists a path from P_i to P_j in the wait-for graph of one of the children of D, then an edge (P_i, P_j) must be in the wait-for graph of D.

In Ho and Ramamoorthy's algorithm [6] sites are grouped into several disjoint clusters. Periodically a new site is chosen as the central site which, in turn, dynamically chooses a control site for each cluster.

The deadlock resolution process usually follows the deadlock detection. The speed of its resolution depends on the information available which, in turn, depends on the information passed around during the deadlock detection phase. For most cases a "good" deadlock detection algorithm, e.g., the one in [3], usually provides little information needed for deadlock resolution. In general, deadlock resolution involves the following nontrivial steps [16]:

- Select a victim.

- Abort a victim.

- Delete all the deadlock information.

Topics that have not been explained are algorithm correctness and algorithm selection. The correctness of a detection and recovery algorithm, in most cases, is shown using informal, intuitive ways. Since most algorithms are very sensitive to the timing of requests, time-dependent proof techniques such as temporal logic are particularly necessary. The selection of deadlock handling approach is dependent on both deadlock frequency and the type of application. Also, the information available on a deadlock when it is detected is also important. For example, in Chandy et al.'s algorithm in the next section, a process that detects a deadlock does not know all the other processes involved in the deadlock. Therefore, the recovery process is difficult. Singhal [16] pointed out the following five areas of research direction for deadlock detection and recovery:

- *Algorithm corrections.* A formal proof of the correctness of deadlock detection algorithms is difficult because of the lack of the global state of unpredictable message delay.

- *Algorithm performance.* A trade-off is needed between message traffic (complexity of the detection and recovery algorithm) and deadlock persistence time (the speed of detection and recovery).

- *Deadlock resolution.* A good and fast detection algorithm may not provide sufficient information for recovery.

- *False deadlock.* A detection program should not only meet the progress property, i.e., a deadlock must be detected in a finite amount of time, but also satisfy the safety property. If a deadlock is detected, it must indeed exist.

- *Deadlock probability.* The design of a detection and recovery algorithm depends on the frequency of deadlocks in a given system.

For a detailed discussion of deadlock handling see [14]. For surveys on distributed deadlock handling the readers may refer to [5], [9], and [16].

5.7 Deadlock Detection and Recovery Examples

In this section, we show several deadlock detection and recovery algorithms under either the AND or the OR model.

5.7.1 Chandy, Misra, and Hass's algorithm for the AND model

This is an example of edge-chasing algorithms where the distributed deadlock detection algorithm uses a special *probe signal* that is forwarded on the wait-for graph from process to process (site to site). A deadlock is detected if the signal comes back to the initiator. In [3], Chandy et al. uses a signal called a *probe* which is a triplet (i, j, k) denoting that it belongs to a deadlock detection initiated from process P_i and is sent by the home site of P_j (the site where P_j locates) to the home site of P_k. Figure 5.10 shows such an application. If process P_1 initiates deadlock detection, the controller of the home site of P_1 sends probe $(1, 2, 3)$ to the controller at the home site of P_3. A deadlock is detected if a process receives a signal that was initiated from itself. In Figure 5.10 process P_1 detects a deadlock when it receives signal $(1, 6, 1)$ from process P_6.

In the above algorithm two or more processes may independently detect the same deadlock. If every process that detects a deadlock resolves it, it will be inefficient because several processes will be aborted to resolve a deadlock. Another problem is that although a process detects a deadlock, it does not have information on which processes are involved. For example, in Figure 5.10 processes $P_1, P_2, P_3, P_4, P_5, P_6$ form a cycle. Process P_1 detects this deadlock but does not have information about the involved processes.

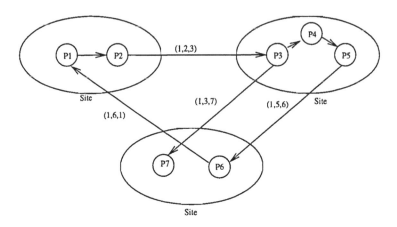

FIGURE 5.10
An example of Chandy et al.'s algorithm.

5.7.2   Mitchell and Merritt's algorithm for the AND model

Mitchell and Merritt [12] proposed an edge-chasing scheme that ensures only one detector in the system. This is a fully distributed deadlock detection algorithm that has a very simple implementation. The constraint is that each process only requests one resource at a time. The idea is similar to Chandy's algorithm except that each process has a distinct id. A signal is passed in a backward direction in the wait-for graph (such a graph is called a *reversed wait-for graph*) together with an id. Whenever a process receives a signal, it compares its id with the one associated with the signal and keeps the larger one in the outgoing signal. A process detects a deadlock when it receives its own id. Note that, when several processes initiate the detection process at the same time, only one process will receive its id and become the detector unless there is another disconnected cycle in the wait-for graph (see Figure 5.11 for an example).

This algorithm will not work correctly if messages are transmitted in the same direction in the wait-for graph. If a deadlocked process that is not part of a cycle has the largest id among the deadlocked processes, this label may enter the cycle and circulate once without any process in the cycle detecting the deadlock. The constraint for single-resource is also necessary. If multiple-resource requests are allowed, as shown in Figure 5.11 (b), then Figure 5.11 (a) becomes the corresponding reversed wait-for graph and the above problem again occurs.

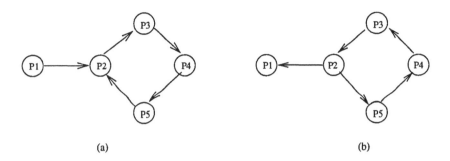

(a) (b)

FIGURE 5.11
(a) A signal-resource wait-for graph and (b) its reversed graph.

5.7.3 Chandy, Misra, and Hass' algorithm for the OR model

This is an example of diffusing computations which normally run faster by diffusing special signals to multiple neighbors in the wait-for graph. The Chandy, Misra, and Hass' algorithm for the OR model is an application of this technique. Two types of messages are used: $(query, i, j, k)$ and $(reply, i, j, k)$, denoting that these messages belong to the diffusing computation initiated by process P_i and are being sent from P_j to P_k. Normally a blocked process starts a deadlock computation by sending queries to processes in its dependent set. A *dependent set* of a process includes all the processes from which it is waiting to receive a message. If the receiving process P_k is active, it ignores all query (and reply) messages. If it is blocked, the receiving process sends query to processes in its dependent set. Once reply messages are collected, the receiving process sends a reply message to the initiator. A counter is used at the initiator (also at each intermediate process) to keep track of the number of queries and the number of replies. If these two numbers match, i.e., the initiator receives replies to all the queries sent, then the initiator is in a state of deadlock. When the receiving process P_k is blocked, there are several possibilities: If it is the first message initiated from P_i and sent from P_j (the sender of this message P_j is called the *engager* of P_k with respect to P_i), it propagates the query to all processes in its dependent set and sets the number of queries sent in a local variable $num(i)$. Let the local variable $wait(i)$ denote the fact that this process has been continuously blocked since it received its first query initiated from P_i. If a query is not the first one, P_k replies back immediately if $wait(i)$ still holds. If it has been executing since then, i.e.,

$wait(i)$ is false, it discards the query.

Initially, $wait(k)$=F for all k and assume S is the dependence set for P_k. For each blocked process P_k, we have the following algorithm:

```
*[ initiate a diffusing computation →
      [ send (query, k, k, j) to all Pⱼ's in S;
        num(k) := |S|; wait(k):=T
      ]
 □ receive (query, i, j, k) →
      [ the first query for initiator Pᵢ (i.e., wait(i)=F) and |S| ≠ φ →
        [ send (query, i, k, m) to all Pₘ's in S;
          num(i) := |S|; wait(i):=T;
          record Pⱼ as the engager with respect to Pᵢ
        ]
      □ the subsequent query for initiator Pᵢ (i.e., wait(i)=T) →
          send (reply, i, k, j) to Pⱼ
      ]
 □ receive (reply, i, j, k) →
      [ wait(i) →
      [ num(i) ≠ 0 → num(i) := num(i) − 1
      □ num(i) = 0 →
          [ i = k → declare deadlock for Pₖ
          □ i ≠ k → send (reply, i, k, n) to Pₙ
                    where Pₙ is the engager with respect to Pᵢ
          ]
      ]
      ]
 ]
]
```

In order to ensure that no messages will stay in communication links, each active process should receive commands to clean up channels although no other actions are needed. Results regarding the above algorithms are:

- If the initiator is deadlocked when it initiates the above algorithm, it will declare itself deadlocked.

- If the initiator declares itself deadlocked, then it belongs to a deadlocked set.

- At least one process in every deadlocked set will report deadlock if every process initiates a new diffusing computation whenever it becomes blocked.

References

[1] Agerwala, T., "Putting Petri nets to work", *IEEE Computers*, **12**, 12, Dec. 1979, 85-94.

[2] Barbosa, V. C., "Strategies for the prevention of communication deadlocks in distributed parallel programs", *IEEE Transactions on Software Engineering*, **16**, 11, Nov. 1990, 1311-1316.

[3] Chandy, K. M., J. Misra, and L. M. Hass, "Distributed deadlock detection", *ACM Computer Systems*, May 1983, 144-156.

[4] Dijkstra, E. W., "Solution of a problem in concurrent programming control", *Communications of the ACM*, **8**, 9, Sept. 1965, 569.

[5] Elmagarmid, A. K., "A survey of distributed deadlock detection algorithms", *ACM SIGMOD*, **15**, 3, Sept. 1986, 37-45.

[6] Ho, G. S. and C. V. Ramamoorthy, "Protocols for deadlock detection in distributed database systems", *IEEE Transactions on Software Engineering*, **8**, 6, Nov. 1982, 554-557.

[7] Huang, S. T., "A distributed deadlock detection algorithm for CSP-like communication", *ACM Trans. on Programming Languages and Systems*, **12**, 1, Jan. 1990, 102-122.

[8] Isloor, S. S. and T. A. Marsland, "An effective on-line deadlock detection technique for distributed database management systems", *Proc. of COMPASC'78*, 1978, 283-288.

[9] Isloor, S. S. and T. A. Marsland, "The deadlock problem: an overview", *IEEE Computers*, **13**, 9, Sept. 1980, 58-77.

[10] Knapp, E., "Deadlock detection in distributed database", *ACM Computing Surveys*, **19**, 4, Dec. 1987, 303-328.

[11] Menasce, D. and R. Muntz, "Locking and deadlock detection in distributed database", *IEEE Transactions on Software Engineering*, **5**, 3, May 1979.

[12] Mitchell, D. P. and T. A. Merritt, "A distributed algorithm for deadlock detection and resolution", *Proc. of the ACM Conf. on Principles Distributed Computing*, 1984, 282-288.

[13] Peterson, J. L., *Petri Net Theory and the Modeling of Systems*, Prentice-Hall, Inc., 1981.

[14] Peterson, J. L. and A. Silberschatz, *Operating System Concepts*, Second Edition, Addison-Wesley Publishing Company, 1985.

[15] Rosenkrantz, D. J., R. E. Stearns, and P. M. Lewis, "System level concurrency control in distributed databases", *ACM Transactions on Database Systems*, **3**, 2, June 1978, 178-198.

[16] Singhal, M., "Deadlock detection in distributed systems", in *Readings in Distributed Computing Systems*, T. L. Casavant and M. Singhal, ed., IEEE Computer Society Press, 1994, 52-71.

[17] Stuart, D., G. Buckley, and A. Silberschatz, "A centralized deadlock detection algorithm," Technical Report, University of Texas at Austin, 1984.

[18] Wu, J. and E. B. Fernandez, "Petri net modeling techniques," *Proc. of the 21st Annual Pittsburgh Conf. on Modeling and Simulation*, 1990, 1311-1317.

[19] Wu, J. and H. Zhuang, "A Petri-net-based collision and deadlock avoidance scheme for FMS", *Proc. of 1995 INRIA/IEEE Conf. on Emerging Technologies and Factory Automation*, 1995, II 511-II 520.

Problems

1. In your own words define a deadlock situation and illustrate this concept using an example.

2. Give suitable examples to show that if one of the four necessary conditions for a deadlock is absent, there will be no deadlock.

3. Show the resource allocation time for each of the five processes in the table below

process id	priority	retry interval	request time	length
P_1	1	4	1	1
P_2	2	1	1.5	2
P_3	3	2	2.1	1
P_4	4	1	3.3	1
P_5	5	2	4.0	2

when

(a) the wait-die scheme is used, and

(b) the wound-wait scheme is used.

We assume that priorities among the processes are based on their request time.

4. Determine if there is a deadlock in each of the following resource allocation graphs.

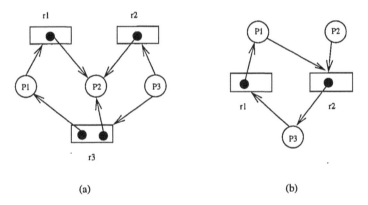

(a)   (b)

5. Determine if there is a deadlock in each of the following wait-for graphs assuming the OR model is used.

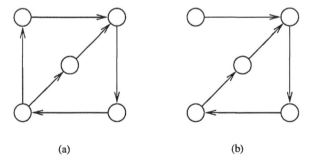

(a)   (b)

6. Suppose that each process is assigned a unique priority number. Provide a detailed design for a deadlock prevention mechanism that can support dynamic priority of each process.

7. Convert the following resource allocation graph into a wait-for graph.

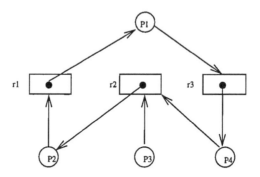

8. For the following reachability graph of a Petri net, find the status of each state. Status can be deadlock, deadlock-bound, safe, unsafe, critical, etc.

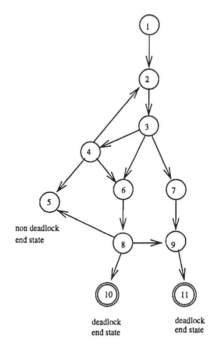

9. Prove in Mitchell and Merritt's algorithm that the id of a process that is outside a cycle will never be circulated inside a cycle.

10. Describe Chandy, Misra, and Hass's algortihm for the OR model using an example.

Chapter 6

DISTRIBUTED ROUTING ALGORITHMS

Efficient interprocessor communication mechanisms are essential to the performance of distributed systems. Depending on the number of destinations, many different types of interprocessor communication are possible. In this chapter, we consider one-to-one (unicast), one-to-many (multicast), and one-to-all (broadcast) communication.

Routing algorithms can be classified as general purpose and special purpose depending on the use of these algorithms. Some algorithms are designed based on selected objectives such as adaptivity, fault tolerance, and freedom from deadlock. Also, they depend on switching techniques, network topology, and system port models. We focus on algorithms for the above three types of communications and their performance with the objectives of reaching destinations with minimal communication delay. In the next chapter we concentrate on the use of virtual channels and virtual networks to achieve adaptivity, fault tolerance, and/or freedom from deadlock.

6.1 Introduction

In a message passing distributed system, message passing is the only means of interprocessor communication. Non-neighboring PEs have to communicate indirectly via other PEs. Thus, in general, a message may have to go through one or more intermediate nodes before reaching its destination(s).

Communication latency in a distributed system depends on the following factors [21]:

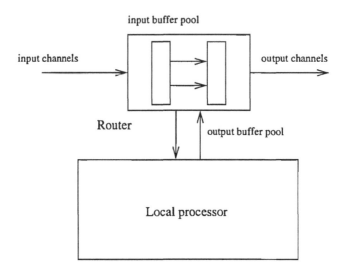

FIGURE 6.1
A general PE with a separate router.

- *Topology.* The topology of a network, typically modeled as a graph, defines how PEs are connected.

- *Routing.* Routing determines the path selected to forward a message to its destination(s).

- *Flow control.* A network consists of channels and buffers. Flow control decides the allocation of these resources as a message travels along a path.

- *Switching.* Switching is the actual mechanism that decides how a message travels from an input channel to an output channel.

Figure 6.1 shows a general PE structure with a separate router. In order to avoid being too involved in low level design, we focus here on routing only with a brief introduction of topology and switching techniques.

6.1.1   Topology

Network topology, also called interconnection networks, can be classified as *general purpose* and *special purpose*. A general purpose network does not have a uniform and structured formation while a special purpose network follows a predefined structure. Special purpose networks can be further divided into *static* and *dynamic* networks as discussed in Chapter 1. Here we use k-ary n-cubes to illustrate routing algorithms for special purpose networks.

Consider a distributed system with N PEs. Let a distinct factorization of N be:

$$N = n_d \times n_{d-1} \times n_{d-2} ... \times n_1$$

Each PE can be addressed in a mixed radix number system with a d-digit address: $(u_d, u_{d-1}, u_{d-2}, ..., u_1)$. In a k-ary n-cube with $k = n_i$ for all i and $n = d$, each PE is connected to every other processor whose address differs in exactly one digit by $\pm 1 \bmod k$. For example, a node $(2,1)$ in a 4-ary 2-cube is connected to nodes $(1,1)$, $(0,1)$, $(3,1)$, $(2,0)$, $(2,2)$, $(2,3)$. When $n = 1$ the network becomes a ring. When $k = 2$ the network reduces to a binary cube. When $n = 2$ ($n = 3$) the network is called a 2-d torus (3-d torus). If the connection is defined by ± 1 instead of $\pm 1 \bmod k$ when $n = 2$ ($n = 3$), the network is called a 2-d mesh (3-d mesh) which is a torus without wraparound connections.

6.1.2 Switching

There are two switching techniques: *store-and-forward* that includes packet switching and *cut-through* that includes *circuit switching, virtual cut-through*, and *wormhole routing*. In store-and-forward switching a message is divided into packets that can be sent to a destination via different paths. When a packet reaches an intermediate node, the entire packet is then forwarded to the next node. In circuit switching a physical circuit is constructed before the transmission. After the packet reaches the destination, the path is destroyed. In virtual cut-through the packet is stored at the intermediate node only if the required channel is busy; otherwise, it is forwarded immediately without buffering.

Wormhole routing differs from virtual cut-through in two aspects: (1) Each packet is further divided into a number of flits. (2) When the required channel is busy, instead of buffering the remaining flits by removing them from the network channels, the flow control blocks the trailing flits and they stay in flit buffers along the established route.

At the system level the main difference between store-and-forward and cut-through is that the former is sensitive to the length of the selected path while the latter, especially in wormhole routing with pipelined flits, is almost insensitive to path length in the absence of network congestion. Therefore, for store-and-forward based routing, *time steps* and *traffic steps* [14] are the main criteria to measure the performance of routing at the system level. The maximum number of links the message traverses to reach one of the destinations is defined as time steps and the total number of distinct links the message traverses to reach all destinations is measured in traffic steps. Note that if the routing is one-to-one (one source and one destination), traffic and time steps are the same. As we will discuss later the objective for using this model is to minimize the path length. Using the cut-through model the objective is to reduce network congestion. Note that although path length does not have a direct impact on the network latency, a longer path increases network traffic and, hence, the probability of network congestion. To simplify the discussion the number of steps is counted as one for any one-to-one routing. When network congestion occurs, it is time-multiplexed, i.e., if k messages try to pass the same channel, it will take k steps to complete the transmission.

6.1.3   Type of communication

Depending on the number of sources and destinations, various types of communication can be uniformly represented as i-to-j, where i $(1 \leq i \leq n)$ is the number of sources and j $(1 \leq j \leq n)$ is the number of destinations. We can use words "one", "many", "all" to represent 1, k $(\neq 1$ and $\neq n)$, and n, respectively. For example, if $i = 1$ and $j = n$, an i-to-j communication is called a one-to-all communication. If we define the dual of a communication as the opposite of the original operation and it can be performed by reversing the direction and sequence of messages in the original communication, we can reduce the types of communication by half: one-to-one, one-to-many, one-to-all, many-to-many, many-to-all, and all-to-all. Normally, by default we assume that each source sends the same message to multiple destinations.

Another type of communication is called *personalized* in which a source sends different messages to different destinations. The major difference between personalized and regular communication is the way the traffic is calculated. In regular communication only one copy of the message needs to be forwarded along the network; it is replicated as needed and a path is forked into several paths. In personalized communication one copy of a different message has to be sent for each destination even when the shared path is used for different destinations.

To simplify the discussion we consider only three types of communication: one-to-one (unicast), one-to-many (multicast), and one-to-all (broadcast). Another classification was provided in [19] and [23] where communication operations can be either *point-to-point* with one source and one destination or *collective* with more than two participating processes.

6.1.4 Routing

Routing algorithms can be classified as:

- *Special purpose* vs. *general purpose.*

- *Minimal* vs. *nonminimal.*

- *Deterministic* vs. *adaptive.*

- *Source routing* vs. *destination routing.*

- *Fault-tolerant* vs. *non fault-tolerant.*

- *Redundant* vs. *non redundant.*

- *Deadlock-free* vs. *non deadlock-free.*

General purpose algorithms are suitable for all types of networks but may not be efficient for a particular network. Special-purpose algorithms only fit specific types of networks such as hypercubes, meshes, etc. These algorithms are usually efficient by taking advantage of the topological properties of specific networks.

Most algorithms belong to the class of *minimal-path algorithms* which provide a least cost path between a given source-destination pair. The cost of the path is defined to be the linear sum of the cost of each hop (link). This scheme can lead to congestion in parts of a network. A nonminimal routing scheme, in contrast, may route the message along a longer path to avoid network congestion. In some cases random routing [30] can be effective.

In a deterministic algorithm the routing path changes only in response to topological changes in the underlying network and does not use any information regarding the state of the network. In a dynamic algorithm the routing path changes based on the traffic in the network.

In a source routing algorithm the routing path is centrally established while it is set up in a decentralized manner in a decentralized algorithm.

In a fault-tolerant routing a routing message is guaranteed to be delivered in the presence of faults. A set of objectives similar to the regular ones may be required such as minimal paths, etc. In a non fault-tolerant routing it is assumed that no fault may occur, and hence, there is no need for the routing algorithm to dynamically adjust its activities.

A typical routing algorithm is nonredundant, i.e., for each destination one copy of the message is forwarded. In certain cases a shared path is used to forward the routing message to several destinations. For the purpose of fault tolerance, multiple copies are sent to a destination via multiple edge- (or node-)disjoint paths. As long as one of these paths remains healthy at least one copy will successfully reach its destination. Clearly, an extra step is needed at each destination to ensure that one and only one copy of the message is accepted. In some other cases multiple paths are used to forward part of the message (the message is partitioned first into multiple pieces) instead of multiple copies of the message. The objective of this approach is to reduce overall communication delay, especially for long messages. However, an assembly process is needed at each receiver to piece together different parts of the message.

A deadlock-free routing ensures freedom from deadlock through carefully designed routing algorithms. In a non deadlock-free routing no special provision is given to prevent or avoid the occurrence of a deadlock. Therefore, a deadlock may or may not occur for a set of routing depending on the locations of the source and destination nodes. Note that the deadlock detection and recovery approach can also be applied for routing algorithms ([13], [31]).

A general survey of routing strategies can be found in [24], adaptive routing for hypercubes in [9], wormhole routing in [21], and collective routing in wormhole-routed systems in [19].

6.1.5   Routing functions

The *routing function* defines how a message is routed from the source node to the destination node. Each processor, upon receiving a message, decides whether the message should be delivered to local memory or forwarded to a neighboring node. There exists a number of different definitions of a routing function. The following are several representative ones:

- *Destination-dependent.* This routing function depends on the current and destination nodes only.

- *Input-dependent.* This routing function depends on the current and destination nodes and the adjacent link (or node) from which a message is received.

- *Source-dependent.* This routing function depends on the source, current, and destination nodes.

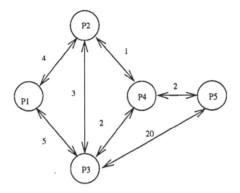

FIGURE 6.2
An example network [26] (ⓒ1990 IEEE).

- *Path-dependent*. This routing function depends on the destination node and the routing path from the source node to the current node. Normally, such a path is encoded in the routing message.

In general, when more information is used in a routing function, better results can be derived, especially for fault-tolerant and/or deadlock-free routing. Throughout this chapter and the next one, we use only the destination-dependent routing function. For a detailed discussion on different routing functions see [7].

6.2   General-Purpose Shortest Path Routing

Most packet-switched networks, such as Transpac in France or ARPAnet in the US, use some form of shortest-path routing. More recently switch-based interconnections such as Myrinet [4] have been built to support networks with irregular topologies. Multicast communication in irregular topologies is studied in [16], [12]. In general, a distributed system can be represented as a graph with nodes as PEs and edges as communication links (see Figure 6.2). The number associated with each link represents link costs. Two types of shortest path routing algorithms are considered in this section. Both of them use the table look-up approach where each node has a routing table attached.

round	N	D(1)	D(2)	D(3)	D(4)
Initial	$\{P_5\}$	∞	∞	20	2
1	$\{P_5, P_4\}$	∞	3	4	2
2	$\{P_5, P_4, P_2\}$	7	3	4	2
3	$\{P_5, P_4, P_2, P_3\}$	7	3	4	2
3	$\{P_5, P_4, P_2, P_3, P_1\}$	7	3	4	2

Table 6.1   Dijkstra's algorithm applied to the network of Figure 6.2 with P_5 being the destination node.

6.2.1   Dijkstra's centralized algorithm

The first type of routing algorithm [6] performs the routing in a centralized fashion. This algorithm finds the shortest paths from a source to all other nodes. To do this, this algorithm requires global topological knowledge of a given network, i.e., a list of all the remaining nodes in the network and their interconnections as well as costs for each link.

Let $D(v)$ be the distance (sum of link weights along a given path) from source s to node v. Let $l(v, w)$ be the given cost between nodes v and w. There are two parts to the algorithm: An initialization step and a step to be repeated until the algorithm terminates:

1. *Initialization.* Set $N = \{s\}$. For each node v not in N, set $D(v) = l(s, v)$. We use ∞ for nodes not connected to s. Any number larger than the maximum cost or distance in the network will suffice.

2. *At each subsequent step.* Find a node w not in N for which $D(w)$ is a minimum and add w to N. Then update $D(v)$ for all nodes remaining that are not in N by computing:

$$D(v) := \min[D(v), D(w) + l(w, v)]$$

Step 2 is repeated until all nodes are in N. The application of the above algorithm to the network of Figure 6.2 is demonstrated by successive steps in Table 6.1 where P_5 is the source.

6.2.2   Ford's distributed algorithm

The second type of routing algorithms [8] carries out the routing in a decentralized fashion. Each node exchanges cost and routing information

round	P_1	P_2	P_3	P_4
Initial	$(.,\infty)$	$(.,\infty)$	$(.,\infty)$	$(.,\infty)$
1	$(.,\infty)$	$(.,\infty)$	$(P_3, 20)$	$(P_5, 2)$
2	$(P_3, 25)$	$(P_4, 3)$	$(P_4, 4)$	$(P_5, 2)$
3	$(P_2, 7)$	$(P_4, 3)$	$(P_4, 4)$	$(P_5, 2)$

Table 6.2   Ford's algorithm applied to the network of Figure 6.2 with node P_5 being the destination.

with its neighbors on an interactive basis until routing tables at the nodes converge to the appropriate shortest-path entries.

The algorithm considered below also has two parts: An initialization step and a shortest-distance calculation part that is repeated until the algorithm has been completed. Here the shortest distance represents the distance between a given node and the destination node. It ends with all nodes labeled with their distance from the destination node and a *label* as the next node to the destination node along the shortest path.

Each node v has the label $(n, D(v))$ where $D(v)$ represents the *current* value of the shortest distance from the node to the destination and n is the next node along with the currently computed shortest path.

1. *Initialization.* With node d being the destination node, set $D(d) = 0$ and label all other nodes $(., \infty)$.

2. *Shortest-distance labeling of all nodes.* For each node $v \neq d$ do the following: Update $D(v)$ using the current value $D(w)$ for each neighboring node w to calculate $D(w) + l(w, v)$ and perform the following update:

$$D(v) := \min\{D(v), D(w) + l(w, v)\}$$

Update the label of v by replacing n with the adjacent node that minimizes the expression just given and by replacing $D(v)$ with the new value found. Repeat for each node until no further changes occur.

The application of the above algorithm to the network of Figure 6.2 is shown in Table 6.2, where N_5 is the destination node. In Table 6.2 all the actions in each node are synchronized through the rounds. Ford's algorithm also works in an asynchronized system where each node updates its $D(v)$ value at a random rate. The use of the synchronized approach is solely for ease of demonstration.

6.2.3   ARPAnet's Routing Strategy (APRS)

In this section we consider a practical distributed and reliable routing algorithm that was used previously by ARPAnet's Routing Strategy (APRS), a predecessor of the popular Internet today. This algorithm is similar to the Ford's algorithm; however, every node in this algorithm maintains a generalized routing table to record the shortest path via different neighboring nodes. This table contains the delays of the optimal paths from that node to all other nodes. This table is also passed to all of its adjacent nodes at fixed time intervals until the minimal delay table remains stable at a fixed point (defined in Chapter 3).

Table 6.3 shows generalized routing tables for P_1, P_2, P_3, and P_4 in Figure 6.1 under APRS where P_5 is the destination node (parts for other destination nodes are not shown in this figure). Each table includes the shortest distance to P_5 through each neighbor. For example, P_1 has two neighbors P_2 and P_3, and hence, there are two rows in the generalized routing table associated with P_1 (see Table 6.3 (a)). Assume that a fixed point is reached before time 0 and there is a link failure between P_4 and P_5 at time 0. When P_4 detects the fault it updates its cost and the minimal delay is then transmitted to all the neighbors of P_4 and causes the changes of minimal delay tables in all these nodes. This process is continued until a new fixed point is reached. Notice that in this case it requires 20, 19, 17, and 20 time intervals respectively for P_1, P_2, P_3, and P_4 to obtain their optimal paths to P_5.

Under APRS each node sends the same routing message to all its neighbors without making any distinction between receiving nodes. This forces some nodes to receive useless routing messages which results in undesirable *looping* in the case of link/node failures (such as the above case). For example, in Figure 6.1 where the link between P_4 and P_5 fails, node P_4 may get a short distance from P_2 which is 3 to node P_5. So the shortest path will be $3 + 1 = 4$. That is, the path is $P_4 \rightarrow P_2 \rightarrow P_4 \rightarrow P_5$. The problem is that the information at P_2 is not updated when it is used by P_4. One obvious way to eliminate looping is to include all nodes in each path in routing messages and send these messages to neighboring nodes. However, this approach is very inefficient due to its excessive overhead. Shin and Chou [26] proposed an efficient loop-free routing algorithm in which only the most recent l nodes in the path are kept in routing messages where l is related to the maximum size of a loop in the underlying network.

time / next node	0	1	2	3	$k,$ $4 < k < 15$	16	17	18	19	$(20, \infty)$
P_2	7	7	9	9	$\lfloor \frac{n}{2} \rfloor 2 + 7$	23	23	25	25	27
P_3	9	9	11	11	$\lfloor \frac{n}{2} \rfloor 2 + 9$	25	25	25	25	25*

(a) Network delay table of P_1.

time / next node	0	1	2	3	$k,$ $4 < k < 15$	16	17	18	19	$(20, \infty)$
P_1	11	11	11	13	$\lceil \frac{n}{2} \rceil 2 + 9$	25	27	27	29	29
P_3	7	7	9	9	$\lfloor \frac{n}{2} \rfloor 2 + 7$	23	23	23	23	23
P_4	3	5	5	7	$\lfloor \frac{n}{2} \rfloor 2 + 3$	19	21	21	23*	23

(b) Network delay table of P_2.

time / next node	0	1	2	3	$k,$ $4 < k < 15$	16	17	18	19	$(20, \infty)$
P_1	12	12	12	14	$\lceil \frac{n}{2} \rceil 2 + 10$	26	28	28	30	30
P_2	6	6	8	8	$\lfloor \frac{n}{2} \rfloor 2 + 5$	22	22	24	24	26
P_4	4	6	6	8	$\lfloor \frac{n}{2} \rfloor 2 + 4$	20	22	22	24	24
P_5	20	20	20	20	20	20	20*	20	20	20

(c) Network delay table of P_3.

time / next node	0	1	2	3	$k,$ $4 < k < 15$	16	17	18	19	$(20, \infty)$
P_2	4	4	6	6	$\lfloor \frac{n}{2} \rfloor 2 + 4$	20	20	22	22	24
P_3	6	6	8	8	$\lfloor \frac{n}{2} \rfloor 2 + 5$	22	22	22	22	22*
P_5	∞	∞	∞	∞	∞	∞	∞	∞	∞	∞

(d) Network delay table of P_4.

Table 6.3 Generalized routing tables [26] with destination node P_5 of Figure 6.2 (©1990 IEEE).

6.3 Unicasting in Special-Purpose Networks

The routing algorithms in the previous section are general and are suitable for all types of network topologies. However, they may not be efficient for special-purpose networks such as rings, meshes, and hypercubes. A major source of overhead in general-purpose routing algorithms is that each node needs to keep a routing delay table. By taking advantage of topological properties of specific networks, we can have a shortest path routing algorithm without routing delay tables. To simplify our discussion we assume that link costs for all types of topologies are one for all the links.

In this section we discuss minimal routing on rings, meshes (and tori), and n-cubes. For each case we consider both deterministic and adaptive routing. Switching techniques used can be either store-and-forward or cut-through because in unicasting the switching method does not affect the routing algorithm. Multiple-path unicasting is also considered as well as system port models.

6.3.1 Bidirectional rings

Deterministic unicasting on a bidirectional ring is rather simple; a message is forwarded along one direction (clockwise or counterclockwise). Since a message can potentially be forwarded in two directions, the source determines a direction depending on the location of the destination: The clockwise direction is selected if the destination is closer to that direction; otherwise, the counterclockwise direction is the choice. A message is passed clockwise or counterclockwise through several intermediate nodes until the destination is reached. The node address increases along the clockwise direction.

$$P(i) ::= * [\text{ start-a-routing}$$
$$\square \text{ receive-a-data-clockwise}$$
$$\square \text{ receive-a-data-counterclockwise}$$
$$]$$
$$\text{start-a-routing::=}$$
$$[\text{ destination is closer along clockwise direction}$$
$$\rightarrow \textbf{send } (m, des) \textbf{ to } P((i + 1) \bmod n)$$
$$\square \text{ destination is closer along counterclockwise direction}$$
$$\rightarrow \textbf{send } (m, des) \textbf{ to } P((i - 1) \bmod n)$$
$$]$$

receive-a-data-clockwise::=
> **receive** (m, des) **from** $P((i-1) \bmod n) \rightarrow$
> [$des \neq i \rightarrow$ **send** (m, des) **to** $P((i+1) \bmod n)$
> □ $des = i \rightarrow$ save m
>]

receive-a-data-counterclockwise::=
> **receive** (m, des) **from** $P((i+1) \bmod n) \rightarrow$
> [$des \neq i \rightarrow$ **send** (m, des) **to** $P((i-1) \bmod n)$
> □ $des = i \rightarrow$ save m
>]

routing-on-bidirectional-ring ::= $[P(0) \parallel P(1) \parallel \ldots \parallel P(n-1)]$

In the above algorithm, *des* stands for the address of the destination nodes. The condition "destination is closer along the clockwise direction" can be expressed as

$$(0 < \ des \ -i \leq \lfloor \tfrac{n}{2} \rfloor) \vee (des \ -i < -\lfloor \tfrac{n}{2} \rfloor),$$

where n is the number of nodes in the system. The condition "destination is closer along the counterclockwise direction" is

$$(\text{des} \ -i > \lfloor \tfrac{n}{2} \rfloor) \vee (-\lfloor \tfrac{n}{2} \rfloor \leq \text{des} \ -i < 0)$$

In multiple-path routing two paths can be used: One is along the clockwise direction and the other the counterclockwise direction. Two copies of the routing message are sent, one to each direction; or the message is halved and each half is forwarded to a different direction.

Bidirectional rings are k-ary 1-cubes, i.e., there is only one dimension. If the dimension is more than 1 $(n > 1)$ such as meshes and hypercubes, *dimension-ordered routing* is used for deterministic routing: Each message is routed in one dimension at a time. Note that nodes within a dimension are connected as a ring with wraparound connections as in a torus or a linear array without wraparound connections as in a mesh. The above ring routing approach can be used to route the message within a dimension. The routing along a linear array is straightforward. After the message arrives at a proper coordinate in each dimension, the next dimension is used. By enforcing a strict monotonic order on the dimensions traversed, freedom from deadlock is guaranteed; however, there is no adaptivity. The general deadlock-free routing will be treated in detail in the next chapter.

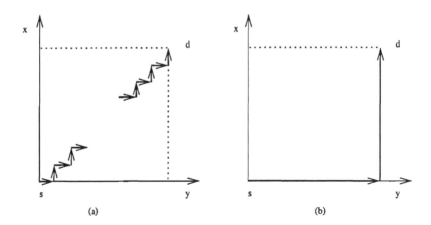

FIGURE 6.3
(a) Adaptive routing and (b) XY routing in 2-d mesh.

6.3.2   Meshes and Tori

2-d meshes and tori are k-ary 2-cubes with wraparound connections in tori and without wraparound connections in meshes. Similarly, 3-d meshes and tori correspond to k-ary 3-cubes. We use 2-d meshes as examples where each node is addressed as (x, y). In 2-d meshes the dimension-ordered routing is called *XY-routing*. The message is first forwarded along the X dimension and is then routed along the Y dimension. Specifically, if (s_x, s_y) and (d_x, d_y) are source and destination, respectively, the routing message will be sent along the X dimension in $|d_x - s_x|$ steps followed by $|d_y - s_y|$ steps along the Y dimension.

In a minimal and fully adaptive routing, each intermediate node, including the source, should make use of all the feasible minimal paths. In 2-d meshes when $d_x - s_x \neq 0$ and $d_y - s_y \neq 0$, there are always two choices of neighboring nodes at each node. A good adaptive routing should be able to choose either neighbor and try to maintain conditions $d_x - s_x \neq 0$ and $d_y - d_x \neq 0$ as long as possible. Obviously XY-routing is the least flexible one. Figure 6.3 (a) shows an adaptive routing and Figure 6.3 (b) shows the XY-routing between nodes s and d.

If each link (channel) has the same probability of getting congested, then what is the best routing approach under constraints of minimal routing? By best we mean that under this routing approach the message has the maximum chance of reaching the destination without delay. Badr and Podar [1]

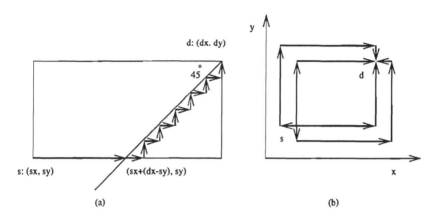

FIGURE 6.4
(a) Zig-zag routing and (b) four node-disjoint paths in 2-d meshes.

proposed a zig-zag (Z^2) routing for 2-d meshes: First build a rectangle that contains source $s = (s_x, s_y)$ and destination $d = (d_x, d_y)$ at two opposite corners. A line L is derived that crosses end point $d = (d_x, d_y)$ and equally divides the angle between two boundary lines of the rectangle that both cross the end point d (see Figure 6.4). The message should be routed first towards line L but still within the rectangle, i.e., each intermediate node is selected based on its distance to L – the closest one is always selected among eligible ones.

Figure 6.4 (a) shows such a routing example. Assume that $d_x \geq s_x \geq 0$ and $d_y \geq s_y \geq 0$. Clearly if $d_x - s_x \geq d_y - s_y$, L is a line that crosses points of node $d = (d_x, d_y)$ and node $(s_x + (d_y - s_y), s_y)$. The zig-zag routing for this case will go along line L connecting node $s = (s_x, s_y)$ and node $(s_x + (d_y - s_y), s_y)$ until reaching node $(s_x + (d_y - s_y), s_y)$, and then follow the line connecting node $(s_x + (d_y - s_y), s_y)$ and node $d = (d_x, d_y)$.

Note that the zig-zag routing may not be optimal in 2-d tori because an intermediate node may have more than two eligible neighbors. Specifically, for an $n \times n$ torus where n is even, there is one node that has four eligible neighbors. Also, there are $2(n - 2)$ nodes that are $n/2$ rows or columns away from the source (but not both) for which three directions lie on the shortest path.

Searching for an optimal solution for the above case, Wu [32] proposed a new routing policy, *maximum shortest paths* (MP) routing, within the class of shortest-path routing policies for k-ary n-cubes. In this policy the routing message is always forwarded to a neighbor from which there exists a maximum number of shortest paths, not necessary node-disjoint, to the destination. A routing based on maximum shortest paths was presented which is optimal for both 2-d meshes and n-cubes. However, it is still an open problem whether the maximum shortest path is optimal in 2-d tori.

It is easy to construct four edge- (or node-) disjoint paths between a source and destination node if both have four neighbors. In general, there exist k (≤ 4) edge- (or node-) disjoint paths between source and destination nodes where k is the minimum number of neighbors for the source and destination nodes (see Figure 6.4 (b)).

6.3.3   Hypercubes

Routing in hypercubes can also be done in a relatively simple way without keeping a routing delay table at each node. An n-dimensional hypercube (or n-cube) can be defined as: (1) Q_0: a trivial graph with one node. (2) $Q_n = K_2 \times Q_{n-1}$ where K_2 is the complete graph with two nodes and $\times$ is the Cartesian product operation of two graphs. The address of a node in Q_n is represented as $u = u_n u_{n-1} \ldots u_1$ with $u_i = 0$ or $1, 1 \leq i \leq n$. The length of the shortest path between two nodes $u = u_n u_{n-1} \ldots u_1$ and $w = w_n w_{n-1} \ldots w_1$ is the Hamming distance between u and w denoted as $H(u, w)$. More specifically, $H(u, w)$ is defined as:

$$H(u, w) = \sum_{i=1}^{n} h(u_i, w_i), \text{ where } h(u_i, w_i) = \begin{cases} 1 \text{ if } u_i \neq w_i \\ 0 \text{ if } u_i = w_i \end{cases}$$

The exclusive-OR operation of two nodes u and w denoted by $u \oplus w = r_n r_{n-1} \ldots r_1$ is defined as $r_i = 0$ if $u_i = w_i$ and $r_i = 1$ if $u_i \neq w_i$ for $1 \leq i \leq n$. It is obvious that $H(u, w)$ is equal to the number of 1s in $u \oplus w$. $u^{(i)}$ changes the ith bit (also called dimension) of u, e.g., $1101^{(3)} = 1001$.

In hypercube routing the relative address (ra), $u \oplus w$, of the current node u and the destination node w is sent along with the message to be sent to the next node (also called forward node). The relative distance is updated at each hop by replacing one of the 1s in $u \oplus w$. In the following algorithm node u is the current node (it can be the source node) and node w is the destination node.

$$P(u) ::= * [\text{ start-a-routing}$$
$$\square \text{ receive-a-data}$$
$$]$$

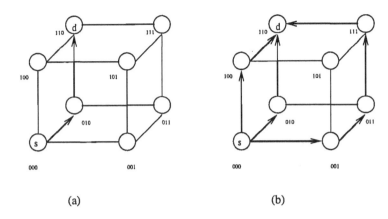

(a)   (b)

FIGURE 6.5
A routing in a 3-cube with source 000 and destination 110: (a) Single path. (b) Three node-disjoint paths.

start-a-routing::= [select i such that $u \oplus w(i) = 1$;
               send $(m, (u \oplus w)^{(i)})$ **to** $u^{(i)}$
             ]
receive-a-data::= [**receive** $(m, ra) \rightarrow$
                    [$ra = 0 \rightarrow$ save m
                    $\Box ra \neq 0 \rightarrow$ [select i such that $ra(i) = 1$;
                                    send $(m, ra^{(i)})$ **to** $u^{(i)}$
                              ]
                    ]
            ]
routing-on-hypercube::= $\forall_{u \in Q_n} \parallel P(u)$

In the above algorithm the selection of i is random which means that there is more than one shortest path. Actually, the number of shortest node-disjoint paths equals the Hamming distance between the source and destination nodes. If the selection follows a predefined order, the routing is deterministic and is called *e-cube* routing. For example, the order of dimensions follows the ascending order: dimension one is first, followed by dimension two, and so on. Dimension n is the last. Figure 6.5 (a) shows a routing example in Q_3 with source $n = 000$ and destination $w = 110$.

The multiple-path routing in hypercubes is based on the following property: If two nodes u and w are separated by k-Hamming-distance in an n-cube, there are n node-disjoint paths between nodes s and d. Out of these n paths k have a length of k and the remaining $n - k$ have a length of $k + 2$.

Figure 6.5 (b) shows a routing in 3-cubes with three node-disjoint paths between 000 and 110:

Path 1: $000 \to 100 \to 110$
Path 2: $000 \to 010 \to 110$
Path 3: $000 \to 001 \to 011 \to 111 \to 110$

Note that the distance between 000 and 110 is $|000 \oplus 110| = 2$. Therefore, out of these three paths two have a length of two and the other one has a length of four. Similarly, three node-disjoint paths between 000 and 100 are:

Path 1: $000 \to 100$
Path 2: $000 \to 001 \to 101 \to 100$
Path 3: $000 \to 010 \to 110 \to 100$

6.4 Broadcasting in Special-Purpose Networks

In distributed applications it often requires a single process to send an identical message to all the other processes. It is a one-to-all type of communication (also called *broadcasting* [11]) which is an important means of communication. This operation is extremely important in the areas of distributed fault diagnosis, distributed agreement, distributed election and for the execution of some parallel algorithms such as compute, aggregate, and broadcast [20]. We classify broadcasting algorithms based on network topologies, switching techniques, and system port models.

6.4.1 Rings

Broadcasting in rings is straightforward: Two copies of a message are sent from both directions and they terminate at the two furthermost nodes, respectively. The total number of steps is half of the number of nodes.

In cut-through routing the communication delay is insensitive to the distance provided there is no congestion. That is, one unicasting to any destination is considered one step. The best strategy is the following: The

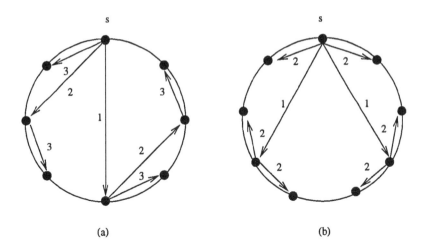

(a)   (b)

FIGURE 6.6
Contention-free broadcasting in a wormhole-routed ring: (a) One-port. (b) All-port.

source s sends the message to the furthermost node in the first step (see Figure 6.6 (a)). Partition the ring into two equal halves with one node that has a copy of the message in each half. The above process is repeated until all the nodes have a copy. This procedure is also called *recursive doubling* with the number of nodes that has a copy of the message doubled after each step. Clearly, a total of $\log n$ steps are needed in a system with n nodes (see Figure 6.6 (a)).

The above approach is based on the one-port model. In the all-port model each node can forward a copy of the message to all its neighbors in one step. Using the store-and-forward model the source sends the message to both neighbors in one step. However, overall time steps are reduced by only one step when n is odd. If the cut-through model is used, the source can send the message to two nodes that are $\frac{n}{3}$ distance away (see Figure 6.6 (b)) where n is the total number of nodes. In the next step each of three nodes sends the message to two nodes that are $\frac{n}{6}$ distance away. In general, after k steps 3^k nodes have a copy and each sends the message to two nodes that are $\frac{n}{3(k+1)}$ distance away. Basically, this approach cuts a path (initially a ring is treated as a path) into three subpaths of equal length with the center node of each subpath as the only node with a copy of the routing message.

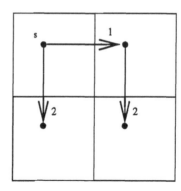

FIGURE 6.7
An example of broadcasting in a wormhole-routed mesh under
the one-port model.

6.4.2   2-d meshes and tori

Broadcast algorithms for 2-d meshes and tori are similar to the ones for
rings. For example, the basic ring broadcast under the one-port and store-
and-forward model can be used in tori once in one row (the row where the
source locates) and each element in this row performs a broadcast along
the corresponding column.

Under the one-port and cut-through model, the recursive doubling technique is applied to the row where the source is located and then the same
technique is used on each column. The total number of steps is $2 \log n$ in
an $n \times n$ torus or mesh. Figure 6.7 shows an example of broadcasting in an
$n \times n$ mesh. This mesh is partitioned into four $\frac{n}{2} \times \frac{n}{2}$ meshes. After two
steps exactly one node in each of the four submeshes has a copy of message.
This approach is then recursively applied to each of the four $\frac{n}{2} \times \frac{n}{2}$ meshes.
In general, the location of each of the three receivers (at steps 1 and 2) in
submeshes can be randomly selected. In [5] Cang and Wu defined special
nodes called *eyes* in each submesh such that the total distance that the
broadcast message traverses is the shortest if the eye node is selected as the
receiver of the corresponding submesh.

The all-port and store-and-forward model is rarely used because it is
rather difficult to take advantage of all ports while at the same time keep
the routing algorithm simple. Optimal all-port and cut-through routing
is also difficult. It is hard to manage an approach that can increase the
number of nodes (that have a copy of the message) five times at each step
while at the same time maintain contention free. Tasy and Wang [29]

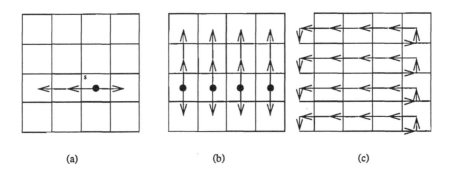

(a)   (b)   (c)

FIGURE 6.8
**A broadcast with message-partition: (a) personalized broadcast
of 1/4 message in one row, (b) broadcast of 1/4 message in
columns, and (c) collecting four 1/4 messages in each row.**

proposed a nearly optimal broadcast algorithm for tori based on the all-port and cut-through model. However, it is relatively easy to partition a square into four small squares at each step. Note that the result is not optimal because the number of nodes that have a copy of the message will be increased only four times at each step. The *extended dominating node* model [28] uses this approach.

The message-partition approach can be used to further reduce communication delay. For example, consider a broadcast in an $n \times n$ mesh. The message can be first partitioned into n pieces in which each is sent to a distinct node in the row (a personalized broadcasting within a row). Then a regular broadcast is performed in each column. In the last step a circular shift of pieces is performed on each row and each node collects the other $n - 1$ pieces. Figure 6.8 shows a broadcast with message-partitioning in a 4×4 mesh. An extension is that in the second step each piece is further divided into n pieces and a personalized broadcast is performed at each column. In this case two rounds of collecting processes are needed, one at each row and the other at each column.

Path-based routing in rings can also be used for broadcasting in 2-D meshes and tori. One simple approach is to construct a Hamiltonian path initiated at the source in a torus or mesh of $n_1 \times n_2$ where n_1 or n_2 is even. In order to take advantage of multiple neighbors, a better approach is to construct four paths all initiated from the same source. The mesh (torus) is partitioned into four rectangles (excluding the source) and each path is a spanning path in a distinct rectangle.

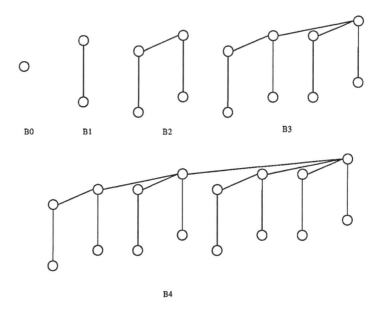

FIGURE 6.9
The construction of binomial trees.

6.4.3 Hypercubes

An approach that makes better use of the dense hypercube topology is
the *spanning binomial tree* approach. An n-level spanning binomial tree B_n
is recursively defined as follows:

1. Any tree consisting of a single node is a B_0 tree.

2. Suppose that T and T' are disjoint B_{n-1} trees for $n \geq 1$. Then the
   tree obtained by adding an edge to make the root of T become the
   left most offspring of the root of T' is a B_n tree.

Figure 6.9 shows the construction of a B_n out of two B_{n-1}'s. Note that
a B_n has 2^n nodes. Binomial trees are usually used in the one-port and
store-and-forward model.

Broadcasting using binomial trees follows the same recursive doubling
process in which the source node sends the message to the neighbor whose
address differs in the lowest bit position. In the second step these two nodes
send the message to their respective neighbors in the next dimension. This
process continues until it reaches the nth step where half of the nodes in
the hypercube forward the message to the other half through the highest

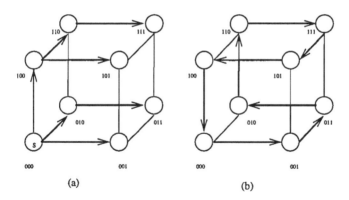

FIGURE 6.10
(a) A broadcasting initiated from 000. (b) A Hamiltonian cycle in a 3-cube.

dimension. For example, in a 3-cube with source 000 (node 0), in the first step, a copy is forwarded to node 100 (node 4). In the second step, nodes 000 and 100 send a copy to nodes 010 and 110, respectively. In the third step, nodes 000, 100, 010,. and 110 send a copy to nodes 001, 101, 011, and 111, respectively. The way each dimension is resolved forms a *coordinate sequence (cs)*. In the above example this sequence is $\{3, 2, 1\}$, i.e., dimension 3 is resolved first, followed by dimension 2, and dimension 1 is the last (see Figure 6.10 (a)).

The detailed broadcasting algorithm [27] on an n-cube, presented based on the all-port model, is as follows:

$$P(k) ::= [\quad \text{generate a message } m \rightarrow$$
$$\forall_{1 \leq i \leq n} \parallel \textbf{ send } (m, i) \textbf{ to } b(k)^{(i)}$$
$$\square \textbf{ receive } (m, i) \rightarrow$$
$$[\text{ save } m;$$
$$\forall_{1 \leq j < i} \parallel \textbf{ send } (m, j) \textbf{ to } b(k)^{(i)}$$
$$]$$
$$]$$

$$\text{broadcasting-on-hypercube} ::= [P(0) \parallel P(1) \parallel \ldots \parallel P(2^n - 1)]$$

In the above algorithm $b(k)$ is an n-bit binary representation of k, e.g., $b(5) = 0101$ in a 4-cube. The above algorithm can be easily modified to the one-port model. The parallel send command is replaced by a sequence of sequential send commands and the sending order is based on the coordinate sequence.

The path-based approach can be easily used in hypercubes. A spanning ring of a hypercube can be constructed using Gray code. For example, $000 \rightarrow 001 \rightarrow 011 \rightarrow 010 \rightarrow 110 \rightarrow 111 \rightarrow 101 \rightarrow 000$ is a Hamiltonian cycle in a 3-cube. A Hamiltonian path from any source can be constructed by breaking the cycle at the source (see Figure 6.10).

If communication delay is considered as part of overall performance, the *postal model* [2] can be used based on a parameter $\lambda = s/l$ where s is the time it takes for a node to send the next message and l is the communication latency. Under the one-port model the binomial tree is optimal when $\lambda = 1$. An optimal tree for a specific λ is constructed based on:

$$N_\lambda(t) = \begin{cases} N_\lambda(t-1) + N_\lambda(t-\lambda), & \text{if } t \geq \lambda \\ 1, & \text{otherwise} \end{cases}$$

where $N_\lambda(t)$ represents the maximum number of nodes that can be reached in time t on a one-port model exhibiting λ. It is easy to derive the corresponding optimal tree structure as: $T(n)$ is constructed out of $T(n-1)$ and $T(n-\lambda)$ with the root node of $T(n-\lambda)$ as the son of the root node of $T(n-1)$. As initial conditions $T(1)$ consists of one node and $T(i)$ $(1 \leq i < \lambda)$ consists of i nodes in a two-level tree. Under the one-port and store-and-forward model, the binomial tree structure is optimal when $\lambda = 1$. Figure 6.11 shows two different broadcast trees in a 3-cube for $\lambda = 6$. Two members associated with each edge are sending time and receiving time. Clearly, the binomial tree implementation is no longer optimal. The optimal tree needs only 12 time units to complete a broadcast. Note that this postal model can be applied to any topology as long as it has sufficient connectivity.

Similar to the postal model, the *parameterized communication model* [22] considers the underlying network architecture to adjust routing algorithms in order to achieve optimality.

Message partition can be used to reduce the execution time of a broadcast in hypercubes. This is based on building up an edge-disjoint spanning tree. In this approach the message is partitioned into n segments, each transmitted along a different spanning tree.

Let $R(\{d_n, d_{n-1}, \ldots, d_2, d_1\}) = \{d_1, d_n, d_{n-1}, \ldots, d_2\}$ be a rotate right operation on coordinate sequence $\{d_n, d_{n-1}, \ldots, d_2, d_1\}$ which decides the formation of an n-level binomial tree. $R^i = R \cdot R^{i-1}$ represents i applications of R.

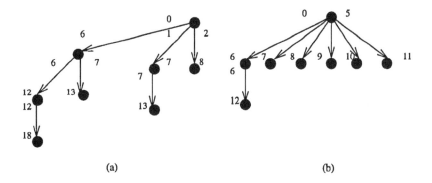

(a)   (b)

FIGURE 6.11
Comparison with $\lambda = 6$: (a) binomial tree and (b) optimal spanning tree.

At source node s:

> [select a $cs = \{d_n, d_{n-1}, \ldots, d_2, d_1\}$;
> $\forall_{1 \leq i \leq n} \parallel$ send $(m, R^i(cs))$ to $s^{(i)}$
>]

At the neighbor of s along dimension i:

> [**receive** $(m, R^i(cs))$ **from** $s \rightarrow$
> apply the conventional broadcasting algorithm
> using $R^i(cs)$ as the coordinate sequence.
>
>]

Suppose node 000 is the source in Q_3 and the coordinate sequence is $cs = \{2, 1, 3\}$. That is, the node set $* * *$, where $*$ is a don't care which can be either 0 or 1 is resolved by the sequence $2, 1, 3$. Then neighboring nodes of 000 are 001, 010 and 100 which have $\{3, 2, 1\}, \{1, 3, 2\}$, and $\{2, 1, 3\}$ as their coordinate sequence, respectively. Through one application of the conventional broadcast scheme on each neighbor of the source node, we have the broadcast tree shown in Figure 6.12 [25]. Table 6.4 shows the disjoint paths through which each node (except node 0) receives its message.

Among all-port and cut-through approaches, Ho and Kao [10] used the concept of dimension-simple path to recursively divide the network into subcubes of nearly equal size and each subcube has one node that has a copy of the message.

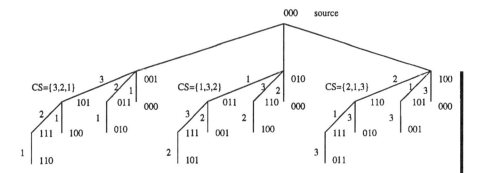

FIGURE 6.12
Edge-disjoint multiple binomial trees.

	Node	Paths via		
		Node 1	Node 2	Node 4
1		0	0-2-3	0-4-5
2		0-1-3	0	0-4-6
3		0-1	0-2	0-4-6-7
4		0-1-5	0-2-6	0
5		0-1	0-2-3-7	0-4
6		0-1-5-7	0-2	0-4
7		0-1-5	0-2-3	0-4-6

Table 6.4 Multiple paths to each node of a 3-cube.

6.5 Multicasting in Special-Purpose Networks

Multicast (one-to-many) communication refers to the delivery of the same message from a source to an arbitrary number of destination nodes. Both unicast, which involves a single destination, and broadcast, which involves all nodes in the network, are special cases of multicast. Multicast has several uses in the implementation of data parallel programming operations such as replication, barrier synchronization, and support of shared memory invalidation and updating in distributed shared memory systems [15].

6.5.1   General approaches

Two major routing parameters are *traffic* and *time*. Traffic is quantified in the number of communication links used to deliver the message to all its destinations. Time is the message transmission time. When two routing approaches have the same time steps, the one with smaller traffic steps should be selected. Traffic steps can be reduced by sharing links for different destinations. Normally, four approaches are used:

- *Multicast path problem*. Typically, a Hamiltonian path is constructed from the source. It is more suitable for the cut-through technique such as wormhole routing. An optimal multicast path is a shortest path that includes all the destinations.

- *Multicast cycle problem*. Similar to the multicast path problem. However, there is no need to send separate acknowledgment messages. The optimal multicast cycle is defined as one with the shortest length that includes all the destinations.

- *Steiner tree problem*. A subtree of a given topology that includes all the destinations. A minimum Steiner tree is the one with a minimal total length. Note that the length of each path to a destination may or may not be minimum.

- *Multicast tree problem*. A subtree of a given topology that includes all the destinations and the length of each path to a destination is minimum with respect to the given topology. An optimal multicast tree is the one with minimum traffic steps.

Unfortunately optimization problems for meshes and hypercubes are all NP-complete for all the above optimization problems. Heuristic multicast algorithms are normally used. In [3] sufficient conditions are provided for optimal multicast communicating in direct networks that employ a cut-through routing technique such as wormhole routing. We consider here two algorithms: one is path-based and the other is tree-based.

6.5.2   Path-based approaches

The basic path-based approach is based on first constructing a Hamiltonian cycle and the multicast set is forwarded based on this cycle. Short-cuts will be taken if one neighbor is closer to the next destination but still before that destination.

1. Construct a Hamiltonian cycle in a given mesh or hypercube.

2. Order all the nodes including destination nodes on the Hamiltonian cycle starting with the source node and following the cycle. This order breaks the Hamiltonian cycle into a Hamiltonian path.

3. For each intermediate node, if it is one of the destinations, a copy is kept and the address of the corresponding destination is removed. Forward the message together with the destination list to a neighbor that is ahead of the current node (in the order) and is closest to the next destination but is still before or at that destination.

When bidirectional links are used, only a Hamiltonian path rather than a Hamiltonian cycle is needed. The path defines a total order among nodes in the system. Each node (x, y) is assigned a number r in the total order [17]:

$$r(x, y) = \begin{cases} yn + x & \text{if } y \text{ is even} \\ yn + n - x - 1 & \text{if } y \text{ is odd} \end{cases}$$

The Hamiltonian path is defined as follows: Two nodes v and u are adjacent in the path iff $|r(v) - r(u)| = 1$. With this total order definition the mesh network can be partitioned into two subnetworks. One includes links from low-order nodes to high-order nodes (Figure 6.13 (b)); the other includes links from high-order nodes to low-order nodes Figure 6.13 (c).

In both subnetworks, in addition to the links in the Hamiltonian path, additional links (called short-cuts) are also included. Destinations are partitioned into two subsets based on their relative positions to the given source. One subset will be sent along the high-channel network and another one along the low-channel network. In order to route messages along shortest paths, we can define the following routing function. Suppose that the high-channel network is used. v and d, with $r(v) < r(d)$, are the intermediate node and destination node, respectively. If d is a neighbor of v, then forward message directly to d; otherwise, select a neighbor u of v such that:

$$r(u) = \max\{r(w) : r(w) < r(d) \text{ and } w \text{ is a neighbor of } v \}$$

The routing function for the low-channel network can be defined in a similar way.

Figure 6.13 (a) shows an example of a multicast in a 4×4 mesh. The Hamiltonian path connects nodes with an increasing order of their r values. Suppose that node 6 with address $(1, 1)$ is the source and nodes 0, 2, 10, 13 and 14 are destination nodes. Clearly, the low-channel network is used

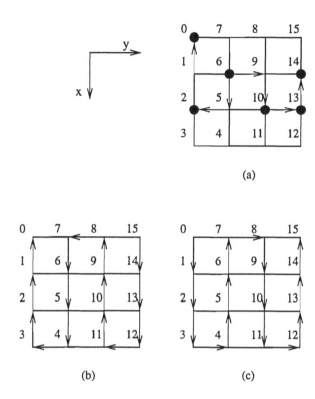

(a)

(b)   (c)

FIGURE 6.13
(a) A multicast in a 4×4 mesh. (b) The low-channel network. (c) The high-channel network.

to forward the message to nodes 0 and 2 using the following path based on the routing function:

$$\boxed{6} \to 5 \to \boxed{2} \to 1 \to \boxed{0}$$

Also, the high-channel network is used to forward message to nodes 10, 13, and 14.

$$\boxed{6} \to 9 \to \boxed{10} \to \boxed{13} \to \boxed{14}$$

6.5.3 Tree-based approaches

The greedy multicast algorithm by Lan [14] is suitable for hypercubes. In this algorithm each node, including the source, upon receiving a multi-cast message with a list of destination addresses, compares its own address with the destinations. A copy of the message is sent to the local processor if there is a match. If the multicast set is not empty, its current node will determine the neighbors to forward destinations in the list. The relative binary addresses of all the destinations are used to determine their preferred dimension sequences. Each of the n bit positions has a counter; the content in each counter represents the information of its corresponding dimension. The counter with the maximum number will be the winner and all the destinations that have 1 in this bit will be forwarded to the neighbor along that dimension. The same procedure is applied to the remaining destinations where the next preferred dimension is selected. This process terminates when the remaining multicast set is empty.

Figure 6.14 shows a multicast example in a 4-cube (destinations are represented as black nodes). Consider a 4-cube in which node 0010 intends to send a message to nodes in the multicast set $\{0000, 0001, 1001, 1100, 1110\}$. The actual addresses of all the destination nodes are first exclusive-ORed with the actual address of source 0010. The relative address of the multicast set becomes $\{0010, 0011, 1011, 1110, 1100\}$. The number of 1's in each column is added to produce the vector column-sum $(3, 2, 4, 2)$. The neighbor along the 2nd dimension has most preferred dimension. That is, node 0000 becomes the next forward node and the message sent to node 0000 contains the following subset $\{0000, 0001, 1001, 1100\}$. Only node $\{1110\}$ is left that can be forwarded either to the neighbor along dimension 3 as shown in Figure 6.14 or to the one along dimension 4. This process is repeated at each forward node. Each branch (of the multicast tree) continues until the remaining multicast set becomes empty. A multicast tree-based approach for 2-d meshes was reported in [17].

When cut-through networks are used, the recursive doubling approach can be used to construct heuristics. We use 2-d meshes under the one-port model as an example to illustrate the *U-mesh* algorithm proposed by McKinley et al. [18].

First, a lexicographical order ($<_l$) is defined on the node addresses in a 2-d mesh. That is, $(x_1, y_1) <_l (x_2, y_2)$ if $x_1 <_l x_2$ or $x_1 = x_2$ but $y_1 <_l y_2$. Suppose $P(n_1, n_2)$ is a shortest path between n_1 and n_2. It is easy to show that given $n_1 <_l n_2 <_l n_3 <_l n_4$, $P(n_1, n_2)$ and $P(n_3, n_4)$ are edge-disjoint. With the above property we can easily construct the following contention-free (within the same routing step) and minimum-step multicast algorithm. We assume that the source node is $(0, 0)$. Derive a list of nodes by rearranging destination nodes based on the lexicographical order and place the source node in front. Partition the list into two equal halves. The source sends the multicast message to the first node in the second sublist. Repeat the above splitting process until there is only one node in each sublist. If the source node is not $(0,0)$, one can always redefine the order so that the source node is the front one in the order.

Consider an example of a 4×4 mesh with node $(0,0)$ as the source and nodes $(1,0)$, $(1,1)$, $(1,2)$, $(1,3)$, $(2,0)$, $(2,1)$, and $(3,2)$ as destination nodes. The lexicographical order of destination and source nodes is $(0,0)$ $(1,0)$, $(1,1)$, $(1,2)$, $(1,3)$, $(2,0)$, $(2,1)$, $(3,2)$. In the first step the list is partitioned into two sublists $\{(0,0),(1,0),(1,1),(1,2)\}$ and $\{(1,3),(2,0),(2,1),(3,2)\}$. The source node sends the multicast message to the first node, $(1,3)$, in the second sublist. The process is repeated at each sublist. The following shows routing at each step together with each routing path. Each routing path is constructed by XY-routing.

- Step 1

  $\boxed{(0,0)} \to (1,0) \to (1,1) \to (1,2) \to \boxed{(1,3)}$

- Step 2

  $\boxed{(0,0)} \to (1,0) \to \boxed{(1,1)}$

  $\boxed{(1,3)} \to (2,3) \to (2,2) \to \boxed{(2,1)}$

- Step 3

  $\boxed{(0,0)} \to \boxed{(1,0)}$

  $\boxed{(1,3)} \to (2,3) \to (2,2) \to (2,1) \to \boxed{(2,0)}$

  $\boxed{(1,1)} \to \boxed{(1,2)}$

  $\boxed{(2,1)} \to (3,1) \to \boxed{(3,2)}$

References

[1] Badr, S. and P. Podar, "An optimal shortest-path routing policy for network computers with regular mesh-connected topologies", *IEEE Transactions on Computers*, **38**, 10, Oct. 1989, 1362-1371.

[2] Bar-Noy, A. and S. Kionis, "Designing broadcasting algorithms in the postal model for message-passing systems", *Proc. of the 1992 Symp. on Parallel Algorithms and Architecture*, 1992, 13-22.

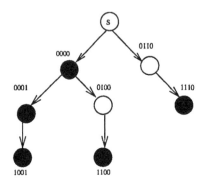

FIGURE 6.14
A tree-based multicast in a 4-cube.

[3] Bircher, B. D., A. -H. Esfahanian, and E. Torng, "Sufficient conditions for optimal multicast communication", *Proc. of the 1997 Int'l Conf. on Parallel Processing*, 1997, 390-393.

[4] Bolden, K. et al., " Myrinet - a gigabit per second local area network", *IEEE Micro*, Feb. 1995, 29-36.

[5] Cang, S. and J. Wu, "Minimizing Total Communication Distance of a Broadcast in Mesh Networks," *Proc. of the 12th Int'l Parallel Processing Symp. and the 9th Symp. on Parallel and Distributed Processing*, 1998, 10-17.

[6] Dijkstra, E. W., "A note on two problems in connection with graphs", *Numerische Mathematik*, 1, 1959, 269-271.

[7] Fleury, E. and P. Fraigniaud, "Deadlock avoidance in wormhole-routed networks", *Proc. of the ISCA 10th Int'l Conf. on Parallel and Distributed Computing Systems*, 1997, 378-384.

[8] Ford, L. R., Jr. and D. R. Fulkerson, *Flows in Networks*, Princeton University Press, 1962.

[9] Gaughan, P. T. and S. Yalamanchili, " Adaptive routing protocols for hypercube interconnection networks", *IEEE Computers*, 26, 5, May 1993, 12-24.

[10] Ho, C. -T and M. Kao, "Optimal broadcast in all-port wormhole routed hypercubes", *IEEE Transactions on Parallel and Distributed Systems*, 6, 2, Feb. 1995, 200-204.

[11] Johnsson, S. L. and C. - T. Ho, "Optimal broadcasting and personalized communication in hypercubes", *IEEE Transactions on Computers*, **38**, 9, Sept. 1989, 1249-1268.

[12] Kesaan, R., K. Bondalapati, and D. Panda, "Multicast on irregular switch-based networks with wormhole routing", *Proc. of the 3rd Int'l Symp. on High Performance Computer Architecture*, 1997, 48-57.

[13] Kim, J. H., Z. Liu, and A. A. Chien, "Compressionless routing: A framework for adaptive and fault-tolerant routing", *IEEE Transactions on Parallel and Distributed Systems*, **8**, 3, March 1997, 229-244.

[14] Lan, Y., A. H. Esfahanian, and L. M. Ni, "Multicast in hypercube multiprocessors", *Journal of Parallel and Distributed Computing*, **8**, 1990, 30-41.

[15] Li, K. and R. Schaefer, "A hypercube shared virtual memory", *Proc. of 1989 Int'l Conf. on Parallel Processing*, 1989, I 125-I 132.

[16] Libeskind-Hadas, R., D. Mazzoni, and R. Rajagopalan, "Optimal contention-free unicast-based multicasting in switch-based networks of workstations", *Proc. of the 12th Int'l Parallel Processing Symp. and the 9th Symp. on Parallel and Distributed Processing*, 1998, 358-364.

[17] Lin, X., P. K. McKinley, and A. H. Esfahanian, "Adaptive multicast wormhole routing in 2D mesh multicomputers", *Journal of Parallel and Distributed Computing*, **28**, 1995, 19-31.

[18] McKinley, P. K. et al., "Unicast-based multicast communication in wormhole-routed networks", *IEEE Transactions on Parallel and Distributed Systems*, **5**, 12, Dec. 1994, 1252-1265.

[19] McKinley, P. K. and D. F. Robinson, "Collective communication in wormhole-routed massively parallel computers", *IEEE Computers*, Dec. 1995, 39-50.

[20] Nelson, P. A. and L. Snyder, " Programming paradigms for nonshared memory parallel computers", in *The Characteristics of Parallel Algorithms*, L. H. Jamieson et al., eds., 1987.

[21] Ni, L. M. and P. K. McKinley, "A survey of routing techniques in wormhole networks", *IEEE Computers*, **26**, 2, Feb. 1993, 62-76.

[22] Nupairoj, N., L. M. Ni, J. -Y. L. Park, and H. -A. Choi, "Architecture-dependent tuning of the parameterized communication model for op-

timal multicasting", *Proc. of the 11th Int'l Parallel Processing Symp.*, 1997, 578-582.

[23] Panda, D. K., "Issues in designing efficient and practical algorithms for collective communication on wormhole-routed systems," *Proc. of the 1995 ICPP Workshop on Challenges for Parallel Processing*, 1995, 8-15.

[24] Pifarre, G. D., S. A. Felperin, L. Gravano, and J. L. C. Sanz, "Routing technique for massively parallel systems", *Proceedings of the IEEE*, **74**, 4, Apr. 1991, 488-503.

[25] Ramanathan, P. and K. G. Shin, "Reliable Broadcast in Hypercube Multicomputers", *IEEE Transactions on Computers*, **37**, 12, Dec. 1988, 1654-1657.

[26] Shin, K. G. and C -C. Chou, "A simple distributed loop-free routing strategy for computer communication networks", *IEEE Transactions on Parallel and Distributed Systems*, 4, 12, Dec. 1993, 1308-1319.

[27] Sullivan, H., T. Bashkow, and D. Klappholz, "A large scale, homogeneous, fully distributed parallel machine", *Proc. of 4th Annual Symp. on Computer Architecture*, 1977, 105-124.

[28] Tsai, Y. J. and P. K. McKinley, "An extended dominating node approach to collective communication in wormhole-routed 2D meshes", *Proc. of Scalable High-Performance Computing Conf.*, 1994, 199-206.

[29] Tasy, J. -J. and W. -T. Wang, "Nearly optimal algorithms for broadcast on d-dimensional all-port and wormhole-routed torus", *Proc. of the 12th Int'l Parallel Processing Symp. and the 9th Symp. on Parallel and Distributed Processing*, 1998, 2-9.

[30] Valiant, L., "General purpose parallel architectures", in *Handbook of Theoretical Computer Science*, J. van Leeuwen, ed., Amsterdam, The Netherlands: North-Holland, 1988.

[31] Warnakulasuriya, S. and T. M. Pinkston, "Characterization of deadlocks in interconnection networks," *Proc. of the 11th Int'l Parallel Processing Symp.*, 1997, 80-86.

[32] Wu, J., " An optimal routing policy for mesh-connected topologies", *Proc. of the 25th Int'l Conf. on Parallel Processing*, 1996, 267-270.

Problems

1. (a) Provide an addressing scheme for the following *extended mesh* (EM) with additional links.

   (b) Provide a general shortest routing algorithm for EMs.

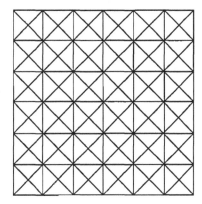

2. Suppose the postal model is used for broadcasting and $\lambda = 8$. What is the maximum number of nodes that can be reached in time unit 10. Derive the corresponding broadcast tree.

3. Suppose that the coordinate sequence is $cs = \{2, 1, 3\}$ at source node 0 of a 3-cube. Determine the edge-disjoint multiple binomial tree and multiple paths to each node of the 3-cube.

4. *Generalized hypercubes* (GHC) consist of $n_m \times n_{m-1} \times \ldots n_1$ nodes represented as $(i_m, i_{m-1}, \ldots, i_1)$, $0 \le i_k \le n_k - 1$. Two nodes $(i_m, i_{m-1}, \ldots, i_1)$ and $(j_m, j_{m-1}, \ldots j_1)$ in a GHC are connected iff there exists exactly one l $(1 < l < m)$ such that $i_k \ne j_k$ if $k \ne l$ and $i_k = j_k$ if $k = l$. The following is an example of a $4 \times 3 \times 2$ GHC.

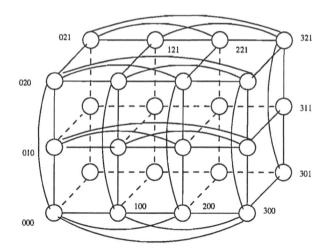

(a) Provide a general shortest-path routing algorithm for GHCs.

(b) Find the number of node-disjoint shortest paths between two nodes in an $n_m \times n_{m-1} \times \ldots \times n_1$ GHC.

5. Using Lan's greedy tree-based algorithm to derive a multicast tree for multicast set $\{0110, 0100, 1100, 0010, 1111\}$ in a 4-cube, assume that node 0000 is the source.

6. Suppose that a 6×6 mesh has been partitioned into two subnetworks (a low-channel network and a high-channel network). Determine the routing paths for the following multicastings:

  - $s = (4, 5)$ and $d = \{(1, 2), (2, 4), (3, 1), (5, 4), (6, 5)\}$
  - $s = (2, 4)$ and $d = \{(1, 1), (2, 3), (3, 3), (4, 4), (5, 5)\}$
  - $s = (3, 1)$ and $d = \{(2, 1), (3, 1), (4, 4), (5, 4), (6, 6)\}$

7. Suppose that U-mesh routing is used for the following multicasting: $s = (0, 0)$ and $d = \{(2, 0), (5, 3), (1, 6), (3, 5), (3, 3), (4, 2), (1, 5)\}$. Show all the routing paths to each destination and demonstrate that it is step-wise contention-free, i.e., there is no contention within each routing step.

Chapter 7

ADAPTIVE, DEADLOCK-FREE, AND FAULT-TOLERANT ROUTING

In network communication, deadlock can occur if messages are allowed to hold some resources while requesting others. In store-and-forward switching the resources are buffers and in wormhole-routing the resources are channels. In this chapter we focus on deadlock prevention and avoidance by restricting routing adaptivity while still maintaining fault tolerance capability. Virtual channels and virtual networks are commonly used to achieve deadlock-free, adaptive, and/or fault-tolerant routing.

7.1 Virtual Channels and Virtual Networks

We first examine a 3 × 3 mesh in Figure 7.1 and see how the freedom from deadlock is ensured using network partition. In this approach a given network is partitioned into several subnetworks. The routing message is routed through different subnetworks depending on locations of the source and destination nodes. In this example subnetwork in Figure 7.1 (b), called *positive network*, is used when the destination is at the righthand side of the source; otherwise, subnetwork in Figure 7.1 (c), called *negative network*, is applied. When the source and destination nodes are in the same column, either subnetwork can be used. Since there is no cycle in either of these two subnetworks, this routing process is deadlock-free.

What happens when the original network does not have double Y channels? One solution is to multiplex several *virtual channels* [13] on a single physical channel. Each virtual channel keeps its own buffer. This buffer

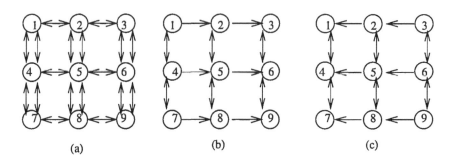

FIGURE 7.1
Adaptive double Y channel routing for a 3 × 3 mesh: (a) Double
Y channel mesh, (b) positive network, and (c) negative network.

is used to hold messages in case the same physical channel is currently
used by another virtual channel. Deadlock can be avoided if there is no
circular wait among virtual channels. Suppose the example of Figure 7.1
is changed to a single Y channel mesh. All the Y channels in (b) and (c)
are virtual channels. With two virtual channels sharing a single physical
channel, channel utilization can be increased. The virtual channel concept
provides the designer a network with replicated channels. However, routing
algorithms need to be carefully designed. For example, virtual channels can
be used in an ascending order of their labels to avoid circular dependency
among virtual channels.

An even higher level of virtualization is the concept of a *virtual network*
[33] where a given physical network is partitioned into several virtual networks. Note that each virtual network consists of a set of virtual channels.
The only restriction on the mapping is that nodes adjacent in the virtual
network are mapped to nodes adjacent in the physical network. Normally,
virtual channels within a virtual network are arranged in such a way that
no cycle exists among channels. Although an inter-virtual-network cycle
may still be possible, this can be avoided if virtual networks are used following a total or partial order. In the example in Figure 7.1 with single Y
channels, (b) and (c) can be considered as two virtual networks. Clearly
there is no cycle in each network. Because each routing process uses one
virtual network at most, no inter-virtual-network cycle will be generated.

Note that although virtual networks consist of virtual channels, virtual
networks and virtual channels are conceptually different. Normally, the
use of virtual channels is closely tied to the routing process including the

locations of source and destination. Virtual channels have to be carefully selected to ensure freedom from deadlock. Virtual networks are normally designed free of cycle. Therefore, a routing algorithm can be designed with no concern about deadlock unless there is an inter-virtual-network dependency.

Consider a unidirectional ring with four nodes. Deadlock may occur if several routing processes occur at the same time. Deadlock can be avoided by adding two virtual channels for each link as shown in Figure 7.2. Channels are split into high virtual channels, $C_{h0}, C_{h1}, C_{h2}, C_{h3}$, and low virtual channels, $C_{l0}, C_{l1}, C_{l2}, C_{l3}$. If the source address is larger than the destination address, any channel can be used to start with; however, once a high (or low) channel is selected, the remaining steps should use high (or low) channels exclusively. If the source address is smaller than the destination, high channels are used and high virtual channels are switched to low virtual channels after crossing node P_3. The corresponding channel dependency graph is shown in Figure 7.2 (b).

In the virtual network approach, the given ring is partitioned into two virtual rings as shown in Figure 7.2 (c). In this case there is a cycle within each virtual ring. An intra-virtual network cycle can be avoided by disallowing switching from C_{h0} to C_{h3} in vr_1 and from C_{l0} to C_{l3} in vr_0. Inter-virtual network cycle can be avoided if switching between rings is possible only from vr_1 to vr_0. Such a switch can be made at any step. For example, a routing from P_2 to P_0 can start from C_{h2}, and then switch at P_1 by using C_{l1}. If the destination address is larger than the source address, the switch of the virtual network has to be at node P_3 from vr_1 to vr_0, because both turns C_{h0} to C_{h3} and C_{l0} to C_{l3} are not allowed. Clearly, the routing process based on virtual networks is more adaptive than the one based on virtual channels. In order to ensure a switch from vr_1 to vr_0 generates a feasible routing path, if C_{li} is the switched channel in vr_0, then i must be no less than the remaining hop count.

Let us formalize the ring routing algorithm using one additional virtual channel for each unidirectional channel as shown in Figure 7.2 (b). This approach is called *double-ring routing*. Assume that n processes are used: $P_{n-1}, P_{n-2}, \dots P_1, P_0$. Channels are either high C_h or low C_l:

$P(n-1) ::=$
        $* [$ initiate a routing $\rightarrow$
                $[$ **send** (m, des) **to** $C_{h(n-1)}$
                $\square$ **send** (m, des) **to** $C_{l(n-1)}$
                $]$

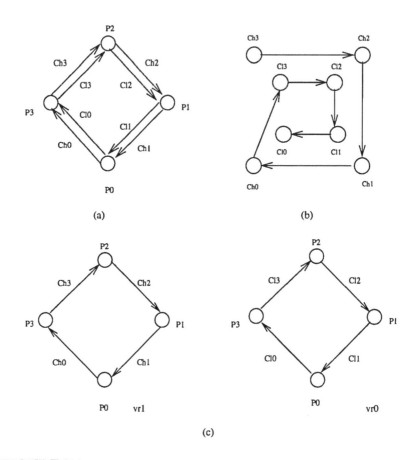

FIGURE 7.2
(a) A ring with two virtual channels, (b) channel dependency graph of (a), and (c) two virtual rings vr_1 and vr_0.

    □ **receive** (m, des) **from** C_{h0} →
        [$P_{n-1} = des$ → **send** (m) **to** local processor
        □ $P_{n-1} \neq des$ → **send** (m, des) **to** $C_{l(n-1)}$
        ]

    ]
$P(i : 0..n - 2) ::=$
    * [initiate a routing →
        [**true** → **send** (m, des) **to** C_{hi}
        □ $i > des$ →**send** (m, des) **to** C_{li}
        ]

□ **receive** (m, des) **from** $C_{h(i+1)}$ (or $C_{l(i+1)}$) $\rightarrow$
    [$P_i = des \rightarrow$ **send** (m) **to** local processor
    □ $P_i \neq des \rightarrow$ **send** (m, des) **to** C_{hi} (or C_{li})
    ]

]

Note that in the above algorithm when a process initiates a routing, either high or low level channels can be selected if $i > des$. If $i < des$, only high level channels are used.

7.2 Fully Adaptive and Deadlock-Free Routing

Adaptivity and deadlock-free are two contradicting goals. Deterministic and deadlock-free routing such as XY-routing for 2-d meshes and e-cube for n-cubes are simple but they are not adaptive. A deterministic routing may fail in a system with faulty components (links or nodes). For example, suppose an XY-routing process completed the routing along X dimension and is currently blocked by a fault along Y dimension. This message cannot move forward further.

On the other hand, adaptive routing without constraints is subject to deadlock. Therefore, the objective is to increase the degree of adaptivity without causing deadlock. Note that almost any fully adaptive routing can be made deadlock-free by including a sufficient number of virtual channels (or virtual networks). For example, a minimal and adaptive routing in n-cubes can be made deadlock-free if n virtual channels are included. Each routing step uses a higher labeled channel than the previous one. Because n steps are needed n virtual channels are sufficient to avoid a circular wait among virtual channels. However, there is overhead such as additional buffers when additional virtual channels are introduced. Therefore, we should also try to limit the number of virtual channels.

7.2.1 Virtual channel classes

As discussed earlier any given routing can be extended to ensure freedom from deadlock by using sufficient virtual channels. When a routing process starts, it uses virtual channel 1, vc_1. In the ith step virtual channel i, vc_i, of the corresponding link is used. Therefore, if the maximum length of a path in a given network, also called diameter, is D_{max}, a total of D_{max} virtual channels are needed.

In order to minimize the number of virtual channels we can partition a given network into several subsets of nodes such that no subset contains two adjacent nodes. For example, consider a 2-d mesh as a checkerboard with black and white squares (nodes). Black nodes form a subset and white nodes form another subset. Whenever a message is moved from a white node to a black node, the label of the corresponding virtual channel is increased by one. If the move is from a black node to a white node, the virtual channel label remains the same. Clearly, in a 2-d mesh the virtual channel label of a message changes at most half the number of total routing steps. In this way the total number of virtual channels is reduced by half.

We can generalize the above idea as follows: Partition the given network into k subsets, $S_1, S_2, ..., S_k$, such that no subset contains two adjacent nodes. When a message is moved from a node in subset S_i to a node in subset S_j and $i < j$, it is called a *positive move*; otherwise, it is called a *negative move*. Whenever a negative move occurs, the virtual channel label increases by one assuming that the virtual channel label starts from one. Therefore, the total number of virtual channels required is the maximum number of negative moves in a routing path. The challenge is to select an appropriate k and a k-subset partition such that the maximum number of negative moves in a routing process is minimized.

7.2.2   Escape channels

In some cases the concept of full adaptivity can be twisted ([4], [15], [43]). For example, a hybrid routing can be introduced using two routing processes: One is fully adaptive that uses virtual channels labeled as *non-waiting*, and the other is restrictive but deadlock-free routing (probably a deterministic routing such as XY-routing or e-cube routing) that uses virtual channels labeled as *waiting*. Initially, the fully adaptive routing is used until it is blocked; then the hybrid routing is switched to the restrictive routing. In the actual implementation virtual channels are divided into waiting and nonwaiting channels. A message that needs to traverse a busy waiting channel has to wait until that channel becomes available. Hence, a waiting channel is a channel that can block messages. A message that encounters a busy nonwaiting channel does not wait until that channel becomes available. Thus, a message considers nonwaiting channels first to reach its destination. If all nonwaiting channels are busy, the message considers waiting channels. Because a message only waits for waiting channels defined in the deadlock-free routing, the hybrid routing is also deadlock free. Obviously, a sensible partition of waiting and nonwaiting channels is the key for the efficiency of this hybrid approach.

In [16] the above approach is extended to allow a message to use nonwaiting (also called *regular*) channels after a waiting (also called *escape*) channel is used. This approach is called extension I. The increased flexibility in extension I also introduces new dependencies among the selected escape channels. An escape channel may *indirectly* depend on another escape channel via the use of one or more intermediate regular channels. As a result the cycle-free condition has to be extended to include all the indirect dependencies among escape channels. Unfortunately, the absence of cyclic dependencies is only a sufficient condition of freedom from deadlock; that is, for certain routing functions for a given wormhole network, extension I is still too weak to reach any conclusion. A cycle in the extended channel dependence graph may or may not correspond to a deadlock situation.

In [17] Duato further extended the above idea by using escape paths based on message destinations, i.e., different escape channels are used for different destinations. This approach is called extension II. A sufficient and necessary condition for deadlock-free is derived which has the same cycle-free condition; however, direct, indirect, direct cross (between escape channels used for different destinations), and indirect cross dependencies have to be included in forming an extended channel dependence graph.

Duato's extensions both can be used in deadlock avoidance ([16], [17]). In order to design a deadlock-free routing function, a routing subfunction, $R_1(x, y)$, a mapping from the current and destination nodes to the subset of the output channels of the current node, is first constructed. $R_1(x, y)$ is connected and cycle-free. Then $R_1(x, y)$ is expanded to $R(x, y)$ by adding more channels or splitting existing ones into virtual channels to increase the number of valid alternative paths without generating a cycle in the extended channel dependence graph of $R_1(x, y)$. This design procedure is also called *Duato's protocol*.

7.2.2.1 Dimension reversal routing

If minimal routing is not required, the number of virtual channels can be reduced. A general nonminimal deadlock-free routing for a k-ary n-cube (without wraparound connections) is as follows [14]: There are k virtual channels for each physical channel with one channel reserved as the escape channel for a dimension-ordered routing (which is deadlock-free). The message can be routed in any direction not necessarily along a minimal path. Each message is associated with a *dimension reversal* (DR) number that is the count of the number of times the message has been routed from a high-dimensional channel to a low-dimensional one. Whenever a routing message acquires a channel, it labels the channel with its current DR number. In order to avoid deadlock a message with DR of i cannot wait on a channel with a DR of j when $i \leq j$. When this situation occurs a virtual channel of the next level is used. We assume that each unvisited channel has a DR of 0. When the virtual channel number reaches k, the deterministic dimension-ordered routing is used.

7.3 Partially Adaptive and Deadlock-Free Routing

In this section we discuss three partially adaptive and deadlock-free routing algorithms.

7.3.1 Turn model

In many routing algorithms, routing adaptivity is traded for a small number of virtual channels. Such algorithms belong to partially adaptive routing. The *turn* model [22] for 2-d meshes provides a partially adaptive and deadlock-free routing. Figure 7.3 (a) shows an abstract cycle in a 2-d mesh. Figure 7.3 (b) shows four turns allowed in XY-routing. Clearly, it is too restrictive because a cycle can be avoided by removing one corner in each cycle. The basic concept behind the turn model is to prohibit minimum number of turns and then increase the adaptivity so that cycles are prevented. Figure 7.3 (c) shows a *positive-first routing* protocol where turns from the negative to positive directions, i.e., south to east and west to north, are disallowed. Figure 7.3 (d) shows a *negative-first routing* protocol where turns from the positive to negative directions, i.e., north to east and east to north, are disallowed.

Note that the turn model routing may or may not be adaptive depending on the locations of the source and destination nodes. Figure 7.4 shows two different locations of the source and destination nodes. If the destination is at the northeast or southwest side of the source, the positive-first routing is fully adaptive as shown in Figure 7.4 (a) where s and d represent source and destination, respectively; otherwise, it is deterministic as shown in Figure 7.4 (b). This uneven adaptivity may cause congestion or uneven

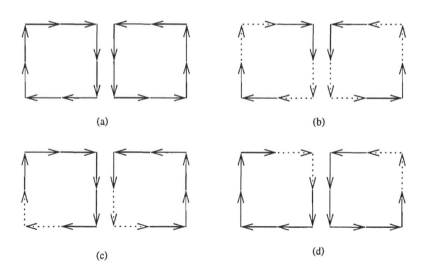

FIGURE 7.3
(a) Abstract cycles in 2-d meshes, (b) four turns (solid arrows) allowed in XY-routing, (c) six turns allowed in positive-first routing, and (d) six turns allowed in negative-first routing.

workload for certain cases. A balanced approach can be used where several different protocols, all based on the turn model with different regions of adaptivity, are combined using virtual channels. For example, if two virtual channels are allowed, we can design two turn models with complimentary adaptivities as used in [21]. The turn restriction can be further reduced as shown in [41]. An optimally adaptive, minimum distance circuit-switched routing is proposed in [34] for hypercubes. A routing algorithm is optimally adaptive if any further flexibility in communication will result in deadlock.

7.3.1.1 Planar-adaptive model

For general k-ary n-cubes, Chien and Kim [10] proposed a partially adaptive and deadlock-free routing. The basic idea is the following: Constrain the routing freedom to a few dimensions at a time and the hardware requirements (virtual channels) can be greatly reduced. For example, two dimensions are selected at a time and we have A_0, A_1, ... A_n planes with A_i spanning dimensions d_i and d_{i+1}. Figure 7.5 shows an example of three planes: A_0 (with dimensions d_0 and d_1), A_1 (with dimensions d_1 and d_2), and A_2 (with dimensions d_2 and d_3).

Within each A_i, three virtual channels are introduced with one along the

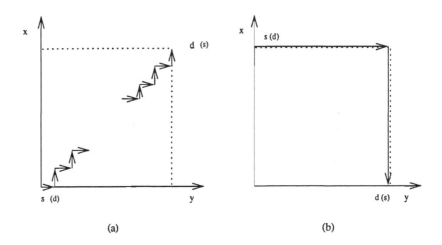

(a)   (b)

FIGURE 7.4
The adaptivity of positive-first routing: (a) fully adaptive and (b) deterministic.

ith dimension and two along the $(i+1)$th dimension. Let $d_{i,j}$ be the set of virtual channels j crossing dimension i of the network. A_i uses three virtual channels: $d_{i,2}$, $d_{i+1,0}$, and $d_{i+1,1}$. Since each virtual channel is bidirectional, we can partition $d_{i,2}$ into two unidirectional channels $d_{i,2}+$ and $d_{i,2}-$, then divide A_i into two subnetworks: the positive network consisting of $d_{i,2}+$ and $d_{i+1,0}$ as shown in Figure 7.1 (b) by treating X and Y as d_i and d_{i+1}, respectively, and the negative network consisting of $d_{i,2}-$ and $d_{i+1,1}$ as shown in Figure 7.1 (c).

A routing within A_i uses either the positive network or the negative network based on the locations of the source and destination nodes. The positive network is used if the destination id is larger than that of the source; otherwise, the negative network is used. Note that the other two virtual channels of d_i, $d_{i,0}$ and $d_{i,1}$ are used in plane A_{i-1}. That is, adjacent planes have one common dimension. Compared to fully adaptive routing the planar-adaptive approach sacrifices some routing freedom (adaptivity) to drastically reduce the number of virtual channels.

7.3.1.2   Other partially adaptive models

Li [25] proposed a relaxed version of e-cube routing. For any cycle in a hypercube we can always find two links along the lowest dimension, say dimension i, within the cycle such that one connects a node with 0 in the

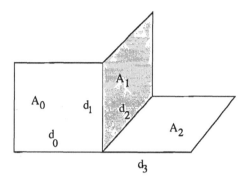

FIGURE 7.5
Allowed paths in planar-adaptive routing.

ith bit to another node with 1 in the ith bit (a positive link) and another link connects a node with 1 in the ith bit to another node with 0 in the ith bit (a negative link). To break the cycle we only need to disallow a transition from a positive link of a higher dimension to a negative link along dimension i unless it follows dimension ordering in e-cube routing. If e-cube routing follows the increasing order of dimensions, a transition from channel c_1 along dimension $dim(c_1)$ to channel c_2 along dimension $dim(c_2)$ is allowed iff one of the following is true:

1. $dim(c_1) < dim(c_2)$, or

2. c_2 is positive

We assume that dimensions are labeled from right to left; that is, the rightmost bit is in dimension 1. Following the above rules, transition: $(10010, 00010) \rightarrow (00010, 00000)$ is not allowed and transitions: $(10010, 10110) \rightarrow (10110, 11110)$ and $(10010, 10110) \rightarrow (10110, 00110)$ are allowed based on rules 1 and 2.

A similar model based on the *extended turn model* can be used in n-cubes. Assume $s = s_n s_{n-1} ... s_1$ and $d = d_n d_{n-1} ... d_1$ are source and destination nodes. Let S be the set of dimensions in which s and d differ. S is partitioned into S_1 (positive transition set) and S_2 (negative transition set), where $i \in S_1$ if $s_i = 0$ and $d_i = 1$ and $i \in S_2$ if $s_i = 1$ and $d_i = 0$. The routing is divided into two phases. In the first phase the message is routed through the dimensions in S_1 in any order and in the second phase the message is routed through the dimension in S_2 in any order. For example, if $s = 0101$ and $d = 1010$, then $S_1 = \{2, 4\}$ and $S_2 = \{1, 3\}$. The following four routing paths are legal:

$$0101 \to 1101 \to 1111 \to 1011 \to 1010$$

$$0101 \to 0111 \to 1111 \to 1011 \to 1010$$

$$0101 \to 1101 \to 1111 \to 1110 \to 1010$$

$$0101 \to 0111 \to 1111 \to 1110 \to 1010$$

In an n-cube any cycle has at least one transition from positive to negative and one transition from negative to positive. By disallowing one such transition no deadlock will occur. In the above model, only transitions from positive to negative are allowed. To evaluate routing adaptivity, we denote S as the set of dimensions that defer in s and d and it is partitioned into S_1 and S_2 as discussed earlier. In a fully adaptive routing algorithm there are $|S|!$ different routing options, while using the extended turn model there are $|S_1|!|S_2|!$ options. When $S = 0101$ and $d = 1010$, since $|S| = 4$, $|S_1| = 2$ and $|S_2| = 2$ there are $|S|! = 4! = 24$ routing options using a fully adaptive routing and $|S_1|!|S_2|! = 2!2! = 4$ options using the extended turn model.

The *origin-based routing* [20] is an extension of XY-routing in 2-d meshes. An origin node o is a priori selected (see Figure 7.6). The routing is divided into two phases. Phase 1 is from source s to origin node o and phase 2 is from origin node o to destination node d. The network is partitioned into two subnetworks. The IN network consists of all the unidirectional channels that are directed toward origin node o while the OUT network consists of all the unidirectional channels that are directed away from origin node o. The first phase of the routing process uses the IN network and the OUT network is used in the second phase. Figure 7.6 shows only the IN network. The OUT network can be derived from Figure 7.6 by inverting the direction of each link. In order to decide the turning point between these two phases for source s and destination d, an *outbox* is constructed (see Figure 7.6) which is a rectangle with origin node o and destination node d as two opposite corner nodes. Actually, the outbox is a submesh comprised of all the nodes on a shortest path between destination node d and origin node o. Formally, the origin-based routing forwards a routing message towards destination node d using the IN network; once it reaches the boundary of the outbox it switches to the OUT network.

source

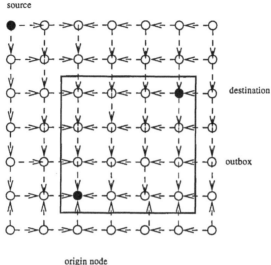

origin node

FIGURE 7.6
An example of origin-based routing in a 2-d mesh.

7.4 Fault-Tolerant Unicasting: General Approaches

As the number of processors in a distributed system increases the probability of processor failure also increases. Therefore, it is important that routing algorithms remain feasible in the presence of faults. We still try to maintain a certain degree of adaptiveness and ensure freedom from deadlock.

Many studies have been conducted which achieve fault tolerance by adding (or deleting) nodes and/or links. However, adding and deleting nodes and/or links require modifications of network topologies that may be expensive and difficult. We focus here on achieving fault tolerance using the inherent redundancy present in the network without adding space nodes and/or links. Several decisions need to be made before the design of routing algorithms:

1. A minimal path or a nonminimal path.

2. Types of faults: link faults, node faults, or the combination of link and node faults.

3. Limited number of faulty components or unlimited number of faulty components.

4. Knowledge of fault distribution: local, global, and limited global.

5. Redundant or non-redundant.

6. Backtracking or progressive.

The minimal routing path requires optimal routing in the presence of faults. This requirement is relaxed in nonminimal routing where a nonminimal path is acceptable.

Link and node faults are different. Typically, when a node fails, all its adjacent links are treated as faulty. However, the reverse situation does not hold, i.e., if one or more adjacent links of a node are faulty, this node can still be healthy unless it is isolated.

The number of faulty components (links or nodes) plays an important role in designing a fault-tolerant routing algorithm. Usually, it is relatively easy to design a routing algorithm that can tolerate a limited (or constant) number of faults.

Knowledge of fault distribution determines the effectiveness of a routing algorithm. Typically, local-information-based routing cannot achieve optimality because of its limited view of the system. Optimality is possible if global information is provided, although a separate process is needed to collect global information in a timely manner. Limited global information is a balance between local and global information.

Fault-tolerant routing can be easily achieved using redundant routing. If k copies of a message are sent to a destination through node-disjoint paths, it can tolerate at least $k - 1$ faults. On the other hand, the traffic increases by $k - 1$ folds even when there is no fault in the system. The nonredundant approach sends only one copy of the message and tries to forward this message to the destination by going around faults.

Progressive protocols will wait, abort, or misroute, but prefer to move forward rather than back off and start over at a previous node. The progressive feature is important in wormhole routing where the routing message cannot go backward. There is an extension of wormhole routing called *pipelined circuit switching* [23] that allows backtrack. Backtracking protocols work under the assumption that it is better to search for other paths than to wait for one to become available.

A theory of fault-tolerant routing in wormhole networks is given in [18]. In this theory Duato analyzes the fault tolerance capability of wormhole networks by combining connectivity and deadlock freedom.

7.5 Fault-Tolerant Unicasting in 2-d Meshes and Tori

We classify here fault-tolerant routing algorithms based on the type of fault information used in a routing process. Routing based on local- and limited-global-information models is discussed first followed by routing based on other fault models.

7.5.1 Local-information-based routing

Many adaptive routing algorithms, such as the turn model, can tolerate a limited number of faults ($n-1$ faults in a k-ary n-cube). Redundant routing for 2-d meshes can tolerate at least three faults (links and/or nodes) if both the source and destination nodes have four neighbors.

In order to tolerate more faults the concept of fault region is normally used. A simple fault-tolerant and deadlock free routing is possible if the fault regions are convex shapes. The following rule transforms a concave region into a convex one by including some nonfaulty nodes in the region using the concept of safe/unsafe nodes:

1. All faulty nodes are unsafe. All nonfaulty nodes are initially safe.

2. If a nonfaulty node has two or more faulty or unsafe neighbors, its status is changed to unsafe.

Figure 7.7 shows an example of a faulty block where black nodes represent faulty nodes and gray nodes represent nonfaulty but unsafe nodes. It is easy to prove that the faulty blocks are disjointed and their distance is at least three. To reduce the number of nonfaulty nodes in a faulty block we can have the following extended definition of safe/unsafe nodes:

1. All faulty nodes are unsafe. All nonfaulty nodes are initially safe.

2. If a nonfaulty node has a faulty or unsafe neighbor in both dimensions, its status is changed to unsafe.

Figure 7.7 (b) shows the result of applying the extended safety node concept to the same example of Figure 7.7 (a). In this case, there are two disjoint faulty blocks. It can be proved that distance between two faulty blocks is at least two. However, the total number of nonfaulty nodes included in faulty blocks is less than the one based on the basic safe/unsafe definition.

A routing algorithm for a 2-d mesh or torus can be extended as follows:

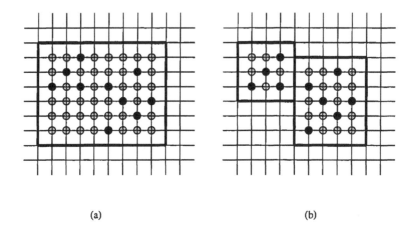

(a)   (b)

FIGURE 7.7
An example of faulty blocks based on two different definitions:
(a) Basic safe/unsafe definition and (b) extended safe/unsafe def-
inition.

1. If it is not blocked by a fault, route as in the fault-free case.

2. If it is blocked by a fault in dimension X (or Y), route in dimension Y (or X).

3. If it is blocked by a faulty block in dimension X and Y-distance has already been reduced to zero, misroute is necessary. Pick an arbitrary Y direction and begin misrouting. At the first opportunity route in dimension X toward the destination. Continue to route in dimension X only until it is possible to correct Y. That is, route along boundaries of the fault block.

A faulty block in dimension Y can be handled in a similar way. Figure 7.8 shows a routing example where the message is routed around a convex faulty region. Note that a message may get trapped in concave fault regions.

When a message goes around a convex faulty block, one dimension, X or Y, always monotonically increases or decreases. Note that a concave faulty block does not have such a feature. Therefore, each routing can stay on either the positive subnetwork or the negative subnetwork as we discussed in planar-adaptive routing. Therefore, the same routing algorithm in planar-adaptive routing can be used without introducing additional virtual channels. That is, three virtual channels are used for routing in n-d meshes ($n > 0$) to avoid deadlock. For n-d tori, two virtual channels are

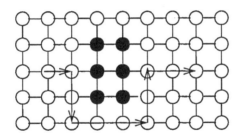

FIGURE 7.8
A message circumventing a convex faulty region (the gray node is the destination node).

required for each wraparound channel to break the cycles within the same dimension. Overall, six virtual channels are used for routing in n-d tori ($n > 0$). In 2-d meshes, two virtual channels are used and the network is partitioned into positive and negative subnetworks: 2 virtual channels are used. Similarly, four virtual channels are used in 2-d tori.

In the above calculation we assume that the basic safe/unsafe definition is used to construct disjoint faulty blocks, i.e., their distance is three and boundaries of faulty blocks, also called *faulty rings*, do not overlap. On the other hand, if the extended safe/unsafe definition is used, boundaries of faulty rings may overlap as shown in Figure 7.7 (b). Two virtual channels are no longer sufficient to remove cyclic dependencies between channels. A solution has been provided by Chalasani and Boppana [5] to use four virtual channels to create four disjoint acyclic virtual networks.

The above approach has been extended in [3] to be applied to both fully-adaptive and nonadaptive algorithms and handles faults on the network boundaries.

7.5.2   Limited-global-information-based routing

Wu [53] proposed an optimal fault-tolerant routing algorithm in 2-d meshes with block faults. First, he proved the following: Assume that node $(0,0)$ is the source node and node (i,j) is the destination node. If there is no faulty block that goes across X and Y axes, then there exists at least one minimal path from $(0,0)$, i.e., the length of this path is $|i| + |j|$. This result holds for any location of the destination node and any number and distribution of faulty blocks in a given 2-d mesh. The corresponding source is called *safe*[1]. The above result can be enhanced to allow block faults along both X and Y axes as long as their distance to the source node is longer than $|i|$ and $|j|$, respectively. The corresponding source node is called *extended safe*.

Two optimal and adaptively fault-tolerant routing algorithms are proposed: destination-directed routing and source-directed routing. For simplicity we assume that the source node is $(0,0)$ and the destination node is (i,j) with $i,j \geq 0$. That is, the routing is always northwest-bound.

In destination-directed routing, the concept of *region of minimal paths* (RMP) is introduced that includes all intermediate nodes of minimal paths for a given source and destination pair. To construct a RMP a west-bound line is initiated from destination node (i,j) until it reaches Y axis. When it hits a faulty block, it will go around the block first south-bound and then continue west-bound. Similarly, a south-bound line is constructed from destination (i,j) until it reaches X axis. When it hits a faulty block, it will go around the block first west-bound and then continue south-bound. It has been proved that the area enclosed by west-bound and south-bound lines and X and Y axes is the RMP. Figure 7.9 shows a sample RMP where the west-bound line is labeled as Path A and the south-bound line is labeled as Path B.

Destination-directed routing is applied only when the source node is extended safe.

- The source node sends a signal to the destination node following a path which may or may not be minimal.

- Upon receiving the signal, the destination node sends two signals: one west-bound and one south-bound. The west-bound signal establishes Path A of the RMP and the south-bound signal generates Path B of the RMP.

- Once the source node receives both returning signals from the destination node, it means that the RMP has been established. The source node then sends the routing message using any adaptive minimal routing.

- Once the boundary of Path A (or Path B) is met, the remaining routing should follow Path A (or Path B) to reach the destination node.

---

[1]The safe node concept here is different from the one used in faulty blocks.

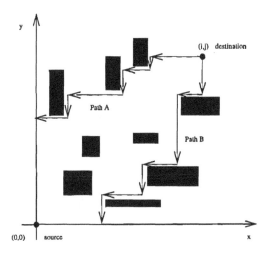

FIGURE 7.9
A sample region of minimal paths (RMP).

In order to support an optimal source-directed routing, faulty block information has to be distributed to certain nodes in the system. Figure 7.10 shows a faulty block with L_1, L_2, L_3, and L_4 being four parallel adjacent lines to the four lines of the faulty block. In this way the region ($x \geq 0$ and $y \geq 0$) is partitioned into eight subregions: R_1, R_2, R_3, R_4, R_5, R_6, R_7, and R_8 (see Figure 7.10). Points that are on one of these four lines can be associated with either of two adjacent regions. Clearly, points in regions R_1, R_2, R_3, R_7, and R_8 can be reached using any minimal routing algorithm. XY-routing (first X and then Y) can be used to reach any points in R_6. Similarly YX-routing (first Y and then X) can reach points at R_4. Either XY- or YX-routing can reach points at R_5.

In order to achieve optimal routing when the destination node is in either R_4 or R_6, certain nodes along lines L_1 (nodes that are west of (x,y)) and L_3 (nodes that are south of (x,y)) must have information about this faulty block. Such information can be encoded as the locations of relevant corners of this faulty block.

Specifically, we construct two conceptual paths for each faulty block:

Path 1: $(\infty, y') \rightarrow (x', y') \rightarrow (x', y) \rightarrow (x, y) \rightarrow (-\infty, y)$

Path 2: $(x', \infty) \rightarrow (x', y') \rightarrow (x, y') \rightarrow (x, y) \rightarrow (x, -\infty)$

Clearly, a routing message with a destination that is at the south or east side of path 1 should not pass path 1. Similarly, a message with a destination that is at the north or west side of path 2 should not pass path 2. Path information is stored at each node in the section between $(-\infty, y)$ and (x, y) for path 1 and at each node between $(x, -\infty)$ and (x, y) for path 2. In order to minimize path information only the location of each turn (corner of the faulty block) is essential. Therefore, (x', y) and (x', y') are needed for path 1 and (x, y') and (x', y') are essential for path 2.

Source-directed routing is the following: In a source-directed routing any adaptive minimal routing is used until one path (path 1 or path 2) of a faulty block is met.

- (L_1 of path 1 is met) If the destination node is at the south or east side of path 1, the routing message should stay on line L_1 until reaching the intersection of L_1 and L_4 of the faulty block; otherwise, it should cross line L_1.

- (L_2 of path 2 is met) If the destination node is at the north or west side of path 2, the routing message should stay on L_2 until reaching the intersection of L_2 and L_3 of the faulty block; otherwise, it should cross line L_2.

In the above approach two virtual channels are sufficient to avoid dead-lock. One simple solution is to use the positive network for northeast-bound and southeast-bound routing and use the negative network for the northwest-bound and southwest-bound routing. In [53] distribution of faulty block information in multiple-faulty-block cases is also discussed.

7.5.3   Routing based on other fault models

Although the rectangular faulty block model is simple, a faulty block may include many nonfaulty nodes which are disabled, i.e., they are not involved in the routing process. However, the convex nature of a rectangle facilitates simple and efficient ways to route messages around fault regions using a minimum number of virtual channels.

Several non-rectangular but convex faulty blocks have been introduced. Wu [54] enhanced the faulty block model to the *orthogonal convex polygon model*. Recall the standard definition of a convex polygon is a polygon P for which the line segment connecting any two points in P lies entirely within P. In an orthogonal convex polygon the line segment is restricted to either a horizontal or vertical line.

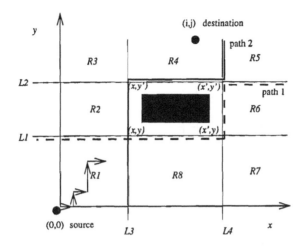

FIGURE 7.10
Minimal routing in a 2-d mesh with one faulty block (northeast-bound).

A process of converting a given rectangular faulty block into a set of disjoint orthogonal convex polygons was also introduced. This idea is motivated by the fact that certain nonfaulty nodes in the block can be activated by removing them from the block while still keeping the convex nature of the region. Other than the safe/unsafe concept used in the standard faulty block definition, Wu introduced the concept of disable/enable nodes and all faulty nodes are labeled as disable and all safe nodes are labeled as enable. A unsafe node is initially disable, but it can be changed to the enable status if it has two or more enable neighbors. Therefore, for a nonfaulty node there are three possible cases:

1. Safe and enable

2. Unsafe and enable

3. Unsafe and disable

Figure 7.11 shows the result of applying Wu's enable/disable rule to the faulty block of Figure 7.7. Clearly, the resultant region is an orthogonal convex polygon.

Among other fault models, Chalasani and Boppana [6] considered a faulty region in a general n-d mesh where any 2-d cross section of the fault region produces a single rectangular fault region. Chen and Wu [9] extended

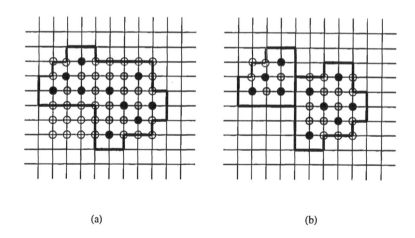

(a)   (b)

FIGURE 7.11
The result of applying the Wu's enable/disable rule: (a) basic safe/unsafe definition and (b) extended safe/unsafe definition.

faulty blocks to 3-d meshes called *faulty cubes*. Cunningham and Aversky provided another way of defining safe/unsafe nodes by considering many different fault locations. Suh et al. [44] studied routing in L-shape and U-shape concave regions; however, backtracking is required.

7.6 Fault-Tolerant Unicasting in Hypercubes

We group fault-tolerant unicasting algorithms for hypercubes based on the type of fault information used.

7.6.1 Local-information-based model

It has been proved [40] that for two arbitrary nodes u and w in an n-cube, such that $H(u, w) = k$, there are exactly n node-disjoint paths from u to w. These paths are composed of k disjoint paths of length k and $(n - k)$ disjoint paths of $k + 2$. If the limited number of faulty components L is less than n, the routing with multiple routes is straightforward. The message to be routed follows n node-disjoint paths and at least one is healthy. Therefore, the destination will be reached along that healthy path and the length of that path is at most $k + 2$.

Chen and Shin proposed the following four types of fault-tolerant routing algorithms [7]:

1. Faulty components are bounded by $n - 1$ and there is no guaranteed optimal path.

2. Faulty components are bounded by $n - 1$ and there is a guaranteed optimal path.

3. Faulty components are not bounded and there is no guaranteed optimal path.

4. Faulty components are not bounded and there is a guaranteed optimal path.

Cases 2 and 4 are desirable; however, there is excessive overhead in their corresponding algorithms. We consider a case 1 algorithm. To make the routing algorithm fault-tolerant a partial history of visited nodes is also kept in the message. The coordinate sequence $[d_1, d_2, \ldots, d_k]$ lists all the dimensions (called preferred dimensions) in which the current node and the destination node differ. For example, if 0010 and 0111 are the current node and the destination node, respectively, the corresponding coordinates sequence is $[1, 3]$.

The algorithm works as follows: In order to indicate the destination of a message, the coordinate sequence of a path is sent along with the message. Additionally, each message is accompanied with an n-bit vector *tag* to keep track of "spare dimensions" that are used to bypass faulty components. Note that spare dimensions are those dimensions not listed in the original coordinate sequence. All bits in the tag are reset to zero when the source node initiates a routing process. Therefore, such a message can be represented as $(k, [d_1, d_2, \ldots, d_k], message, tag)$ where k is the length of the remaining portion of the path and is updated as the message travels towards the destination. A message reaches its destination when k becomes zero.

When a node receives a message, the node checks the value of k to see if it is the destination of the message. If not, the node will try to send the message along one of those dimensions specified in the remaining coordinate sequence. Note that the coordinate sequence will also be updated as the message travels through the hypercube. Each node will attempt to route messages via shortest paths first. However, if all the links in those dimensions leading to shortest paths are faulty, the node will use a spare dimension to route the message via an alternate path. Recall that a tag keeps track of spare dimensions.

More formally, the routing algorithm [8] can be described as follows. Initially, the coordinate sequence includes all the preferred dimensions determined by exclusive-ORed the source and destination addresses. *tag* is initialized to 0 in all bits. Recall that $u^{(i)}$ represents the neighbor of u along dimension i.

$P(u) ::= [$ initiate-routing-process $\rightarrow$
$\qquad$ **send** $(k, [d_1, d_2, \ldots, d_k], m, 0)$ **to** $P(u)$
$\qquad \Box$ **receive** $(k, [d_1, d_2, \ldots, d_k], message, tag) \rightarrow$
$\qquad\qquad [\quad k = 0 \rightarrow$ save $(message)$
$\qquad\qquad \Box\, k \neq 0 \rightarrow$ intermediate-node
$\qquad\qquad]$
$\qquad]$

intermediate-node::=
$\quad [\quad$ The d_jth $(1 \leq j \leq k)$ link and neighbor are both healthy $\rightarrow$
$\qquad [\quad$ **send** $(k - 1, [d_1, \ldots, d_{j-1}, d_{j+1}, \ldots, d_k],$
$\qquad\quad message, tag)$ **to** $u^{(d_j)}$
$\qquad]$
$\quad \Box$ No link and neighbor are both healthy $\rightarrow$
$\qquad [\quad \forall_{1 \leq j \leq k} \parallel tag(d_j) := 1;$
$\qquad\quad tag(h) := 1,$ where $h = \min\{i : tag\,(i) = 0, 1 \leq i \leq n\};$
$\qquad\quad$ **send** $(k + 1, [d_1, d_2, \ldots, d_k, h], message, tag)$ **to** $u^{(h)}$
$\qquad]$
$\quad]$

Consider the faulty hypercube Q_4 in Figure 7.12. Suppose a message, m, is routed from $u = 0110$ to $w = 1001$. The original message in $u = 0110$ is $(4, [1, 2, 3, 4], m, 0000)$. Following the execution of the above algorithm node 0110 sends $(3, [2, 3, 4], m, 0000)$ to node $0110^1 = 0111$ which then sends $(2, [3, 4], m, 0000)$ to node 0101. Since the third dimensional link of 0101 is faulty, node 0101 will route $(1, [3], m, 0000)$ to 1101. However, since the third dimensional link of 1101 is faulty, node 1101 will use the first dimension (tag=0100,tag keeps track of preferred dimensions when a detour occurs), and send $(2, [3, 1], m, 0101)$ to 1100, which will, in turn, send $(1, [1], m, 0101)$ to 1000. Again, the first link of node 1000 is faulty. The second dimension (tag=0101 then) will be used and $(2, [1, 2], m, 0111)$ is routed to 1010. After this the message will reach the destination 1001 via 1011. The length of the resultant path is 8.

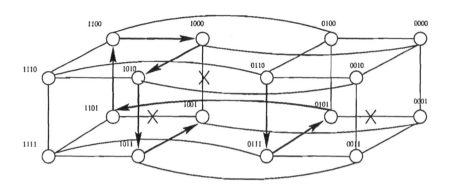

FIGURE 7.12
A faulty 4-cube.

Algorithms that guarantee a shortest path routing and tolerance of unbounded faulty components usually need to keep either the whole history of the routing path in the message transmitted or in network delay tables. Note that the above algorithm is limited to faulty hypercubes with fewer than n faulty links. A more complex algorithm [7] is required when there are more than $n - 1$ faulty links. A simplified version was presented in [26] where the routing process is progressive. To further reduce message overhead Gaughan and Yalamanchili [23] proposed to attach history information to links of a given network as the routing message passes through these links. As each candidate outgoing link is searched the history associated with the link remembers if this link has been searched or visited earlier. Tasi and Wang [46] proposed a fully adaptive, progressive, misrouting algorithm for faulty hypercubes, meshes, and tori.

7.6.2   Limited-global-information-based model: safety level

We consider here a reliable routing in hypercubes with node faults. This scheme is based on limited global information captioned by the *safety level* [49], [52] associated with each node. Basically, the safety level associated with a node is an approximated measure of the number of faulty nodes in the neighborhood.

Let $S(a) = k$ be the safety status of node a where k is referred to as the level of safety and a is called *k-safe*. A faulty node is 0-safe that corresponds to the lowest level of safety, while an n-safe node (also referred to as a *safe node*) corresponds to the highest level of safety. A node with k-safe status

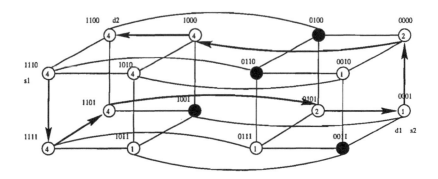

FIGURE 7.13
A fault-tolerant routing using safety levels.

is called *unsafe* if $k \neq n$.

Let $(S_0, S_1, S_2, \ldots, S_{n-1}), 0 \leq S_i \leq n$, be the non-descending safety status sequence of node a's neighboring nodes in an n-cube such that $0 \leq S_i \leq S_{i+1} \leq n - 1$. The safety status of node a is defined as follows: If $(S_0, S_1, S_2, \ldots, S_{n-1}) \geq (0, 1, 2, \ldots, n-1)[1]$ then $S(a) = n$ else if $(S_0, S_1, S_2, \ldots, S_{k-1}) \geq (0, 1, 2, \ldots, k-1) \wedge (S_k = k - 1)$ then $S(a) = k$. In the faulty hypercube shown in Figure 7.13 nodes 1000, 1010, 1100, 1101, 1110, and 1111 are safe. Faulty nodes 0011, 0100, 0110, and 1001 are 0-safe. Nodes 0001, 0010, 0111, and 1011 are 1-safe since each of them has two faulty neighbors. Nodes 0000 and 0101 are 2-safe.

The following algorithm determines the node status for each node. Each node $a(i)$ keeps a nondecreasing status sequence of neighboring nodes. Initially all nonfaulty nodes are n-safe. $n - 1$ iterations are needed to reach a stable state.

global-status::= $(n - 1)[P(0)\|P(1)\|P(2)...\|P(2^n - 1)]$

$P(i)$ ::= determine a nondecreasing status sequence $(S_0, S_1, S_2, \ldots, S_{n-1})$
    of neighboring nodes;
    $[\ (S_0, S_1, S_2, \ldots, S_{n-1}) \geq (0, 1, 2, \ldots, n-1)$
      $\rightarrow S(a(i)) = n$
    $\square\ (S_0, S_1, S_2, \ldots, S_{k-1}) \geq (0, 1, 2, \ldots, k-1) \wedge (S_{k-1} = k - 1)$
      $\rightarrow S(a(i)) = k$
    ]

The safety level has the following property: If the safety level of a node is k $(0 < k \leq n)$, there is at least one Hamming distance path from this node to any node within k-Hamming-distance. Actually, the safety level of a node not only indicates a routing capability but also provides routing information. When the safety level of the source is larger than the distance between the source and destination nodes, optimal routing is guaranteed. Actually, an optimal path is generated by selecting a preferred neighbor with the highest safety level at each routing step. A navigation vector, defined as a bitwise exclusive-OR of the current node and the destination node, is attached to the routing message.

Consider again the example in Figure 7.13. The number in each circle (node) represents the safety level of this node. In a unicast algorithm where $s_1 = 1110$ and $d_1 = 0001$ are the source and destination nodes, respectively, the navigation vector is $N_1 = s_1 \oplus d_1 = 1111$, and hence, $H(s_1, d_1) = 4$. Also, the safety level of source s_1 is 4. Therefore, the optimal algorithm is applied. Among preferred neighbors of the source, nodes $1010, 1100$, and 1111 have a safety level 4 and node 0110 has a safety level 0. A neighbor with the highest safety level, say 1111 along dimension 0, is selected. The navigation vector N is sent together with the message after resetting bit 0. At intermediate node 1111, based on navigation vector 1110, the preferred neighbor set is calculated as $\{0111, 1011, 1101\}$. Among preferred neighbors node 1101 has the highest safety level which is 4; therefore, 1101 is the next intermediate node with navigation vector 1100. At node 1101 preferred node 0101 with a safety level 2 is selected among two preferred neighbors (the other one is the faulty neighbor 1001). At node 0101 with navigation vector 0100 there is only one preferred neighbor which is 0001. Upon receiving the unicast message with a navigation vector 0000 node 1100 identifies itself as the destination node and terminates the unicast algorithm.

When the source node's safety level is lower than distance $|s \oplus d|$ between source s and destination d, as long as there is a preferred neighbor whose safety level is no lower than $|s \oplus d| - 1$, optimal routing is still possible by forwarding the message to that node. Otherwise, if there is a spare neighbor whose safety level is no lower than $|s \oplus d| + 1$, suboptimal routing is possible by forwarding the message to that node. The length of the resultant path is $|s \oplus d| + 2$.

Extensions of the safety level concept to include link faults and other cube-based networks can be found in [11] and [51].

7.6.3   Routing based on the extended safety level model: safety vector

The safety level concept has the following pitfall: The safety level k of a node only tells that there exists a Hamming distance path to any node within k-Hamming-distance. There is no information about the existence of a Hamming distance path to nodes that are more than k-Hamming-distance away.

The *safety vector* concept can effectively include faulty link information and provide more accurate information about the number and distribution of faults in the system. More specifically, $(a_1, a_2, ..., a_n)$ is the safety vector with a list of bits associated with node a in an n-cube. If $a_k = 1$, then there exists a Hamming distance path from node a to any node that is exactly k-Hamming-distance away.

Basically, the safety vector of a node can be easily calculated through $n-1$ rounds of information exchange among neighboring nodes. An optimal unicast algorithm between two nodes is guaranteed if the kth bit of the safety vector of the source node is set to one. The safety vector of a faulty node is $(0, 0, ..., 0)$. For a nonfaulty node a assume that $(a_1, a_2, ..., a_n)$ is a's safety vector and $(a_1^{(i)}, a_2^{(i)}, ..., a_n^{(i)})$ is the safety vector of a's neighbor along dimension i. If node a is an end node of a faulty link then node a's safety vector is $(0, 0, ..., 0)$ from the view of the other end node adjacent to the same faulty node, and

$$
a_1 = \begin{cases} 0 & \text{if } a \text{ is an end-node of a faulty link} \\ 1 & \text{otherwise} \end{cases}
$$

and

$$
a_k = \begin{cases} 0 & \text{if } \sum_{1 \le i \le n} a_{k-1}^{(i)} \le n - k \\ 1 & \text{otherwise} \end{cases}
$$

The calculation of safety vectors can be done in a similar way in calculating the safety level through message exchange and update among neighboring nodes. The routing algorithm is also similar to the one based on the safety level model. For details, refer to [51].

7.7 Fault-Tolerant Broadcasting

The objective of fault-tolerant broadcasting is to forward broadcast data to all nonfaulty nodes by going around faulty components. We use n-cubes to illustrate several approaches. For fault-tolerant broadcasting in tori and meshes the readers can refer to [2], [55].

7.7.1 General approaches

In general, fault-tolerant broadcasting can be classified based on (1) the way each destination receives the broadcast data, (2) the amount of information kept at each node, (3) the type of faulty components, and (4) the number of faulty components.

There are, in general, two ways that each destination receives the broadcast data:

- Each node may receive more than one copy. The corresponding algorithm is called *redundant broadcasting* [38]. Normally in redundant broadcasting the source node simultaneously sends copies of the broadcast data to its neighbors. This approach has a merit of simplicity and it does not require backtracking during the broadcast process. The flaw in this approach is the extra network traffic generated and extra copies of the broadcast data have to be discarded at the destination nodes. It is clear that redundant broadcasting is not necessary in the absence of faulty components.

- Each node can receive only one copy of the broadcast data. Therefore, broadcast algorithms should be designed such that the broadcast data are sent to each node once and only once. Algorithms of this type are called *nonredundant broadcast algorithms*.

In the broadcast process the amount of faulty component information kept at each node can be classified as local, limited global, and global. Local information contains only adjacent faulty components. Limited global information contains the distribution of faulty components in the neighborhood. Global information contains the distribution of all the faulty components. There are two types of faulty components: faulty links and faulty nodes. The number of faulty components can be either bounded or unbounded.

Among the approaches based on local network information, Al-Dhelaan and Bose [1] proposed a binomial-tree-based broadcasting for limited link and node faults. This approach was enhanced by Wu and Fernandez [47] and it guarantees time-step optimal. Li and Wu [29] proposed a general broadcast scheme with local network information that can tolerate any number of faults. However, backtracking is required and network information (faulty component information) has to be incorporated as a queue into the broadcast data. Broadcast schemes based on global information normally use routing tables [35] to keep global information. Taking advantage of the hypercube topology, Raghavendra [37] studied a broadcast approach based on the concept of free-dimension that also uses global information.

The fault-tolerant broadcasting based on local information normally requires routing history as part of the broadcast data in order to reach each node once and only once. Fault-tolerant broadcasting based on global information, although it has a merit of simplicity, requires a process which collects global information. The broadcasting based on limited global information is a compromise of the above two schemes. This broadcast scheme is relatively simple and no backtracking is required as in approaches using local information. On the other hand, collecting limited global information is much less expansive than the approaches using global information. The challenge is to identify the right type of limited global information based on which cost-effective broadcasting can be derived.

7.7.2 Broadcasting using global information

Wu [47] proposed an efficient broadcasting using global information. The type of faults under consideration is link faults and the number of faults is limited to $n - 1$ in an n-cube.

In the proposed method the source node knows the global network information which means that this node knows the distribution of faulty components. Therefore, the broadcast structure can be decided at the source node. The proposed method consists of two steps. In the first step a *coordinate sequence* is determined at the source node. This sequence decides on the structure of an extended binomial tree. The second step is the broadcast process in which each node, upon receiving the broadcast data and the coordinate sequence determined at the source node, continues the broadcast process determined by the coordinate sequence. This scheme can tolerate at least $n - 1$ link faults. However, when there are more than $n - 1$ faults in an n-cube, this scheme still may work but a *feasibility checking* process is required to determine the applicability of the scheme. It has been shown that a spanning binomial tree is guaranteed to be found if there exists such a tree originated from the given source node. In this sense the corresponding broadcast method is optimal. When there does not exist such a binomial tree originated from a given source node, e.g., any node with adjacent faulty links, an extended binomial tree structure is used and the length of the path from the source node to a node is equal to their Hamming distance plus 2.

The basic fault-tolerant broadcast scheme consists of the following two steps: (1) Determination of a coordinate sequence at source node s (Algorithm 1). (2) Broadcasting based on the derived coordinate sequence (Algorithm 2).

Algorithm 1 {the splitting process}
/* at source node s in Q_n and $m = 1$ initially */

1. Randomly select a dimension i_m such that there are no faulty links in the i_mth dimension of Q_{n-m+1}, and Q_{n-m+1} is partitioned along the i_mth dimension into (Q_{n-m}, Q'_{n-m}). If such a dimension does not exist then return *infeasible*.

2. If all the faulty links in Q_{n-m+1} are in Q_{n-m} (or Q'_{n-m}), then stop and return $(T_{nonop}, i_m i_{m-1} \ldots i_1)$ (or $(T_{op}, i_m i_{m-1} \ldots i_1)$) where $i_m i_{m-1} \ldots i_1$ is a sequence of dimensions selected through repeated applications of step 1. Note that $i_m i_{m-1} \ldots i_1$ is in reverse order that these dimensions are selected. Otherwise, increment m by 1 and repeat steps 1 and 2 on Q_{n-m} until $n = m$.

Algorithm 2 /* fault-tolerant broadcasting */
/* $(Type, i_m i_{m-1} \ldots i_1)$ is determined using Algorithm 1 */

1. {optimal broadcasting} If $Type = T_{op}$, there is no faulty link in Q_{n-m}, then normal binomial-tree-based broadcasting is used in Q_{n-m} without any constraint and broadcasting outside Q_{n-m} is subject to $cs = i_m i_{m-1} \ldots i_1$.

2. {non-optimal broadcasting} If $Type = T_{nonop}$, there are no faulty links in Q'_{n-m}, then the following four steps are used.

   (a) s sends the broadcast data to its neighbor along the i_mth dimension denoted as $s^{(i_m)}$.

   (b) Normal binomial-tree-based broadcasting is applied in Q'_{n-m} with $s^{(i_m)}$ being the source node.

(c) Performs broadcasting in Q_{n-m} except s by sending the broadcast data from each node in Q'_{n-m} along the i_mth dimension to the corresponding node in Q_{n-m}.

(d) Performs normal binomial-tree-based broadcasting outside $Q_{n-m+1} = Q_{n-m} + Q'_{n-m}$ subject to $cs = i_{m-1}i_{m-2}\ldots i_1$.

7.7.3   Broadcasting using safety levels

We use safety levels as limited global information for optimal broadcasting. The broadcast algorithm is based on constructing an *injured spanning binomial tree* where all the faulty nodes are leaves of the tree.

The broadcast algorithm is based on the following property of safety levels: If a node is k-safe, then there exists an l-level injured spanning binomial tree with this node being the root in any l-subcube where l is no more than k. Therefore, if the source node is n-safe, there exists an n-level injured spanning binomial tree in an n-cube.

To implement a broadcast algorithm using safety level information, i.e., information regarding a neighbor's status, two sequences, namely, *descending status sequence* $(D_0, D_1, D_2, ..., D_{n-1})$ and corresponding *neighbor dimension sequence* $(d_0, d_1, d_2, ..., d_{n-1})$, should be kept at each node. Note that both sequences are available at each node after applying the *global-status* algorithm in Section 7.6.2. The coordinate sequence can be directly derived from the descending status sequence. An n-bit control word $LABEL$ is used to represent a subcube in the partition where each bit is a binary number with each 1 representing a $*$ in the subcube.

injured-hypercube-broadcasting ::=
{ $(d_0, d_1, ..., d_{n-1})$ and $(D_0, D_1, ..., D_{n-1})$ are descending
status and neighbor dimension sequences associated
with node a. Initially, $LABEL[j] = 1, 1 \le j \le n.$ }
[$j := 0$;
  (n) [$LABEL[d_j] \ne 0 \wedge D_j \ne 0 \rightarrow$
     [$LABEL[d_j] := 0; j = j + 1$;
       send the broadcast data and $LABEL$ to the
       neighbor along the d_jth dimension
     ]
  ]
]

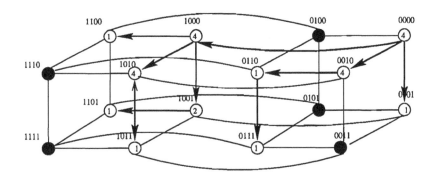

FIGURE 7.14
Broadcasting in a faulty 4-cube.

node	dss	nds	node	dss	nds
0000	(4,4,1,0)	(4,2,1,3)	0001	(4,2,0,0)	(1,4,3,2)
0010	(4,4,1,0)	(4,2,3,1)	0011	(4,1,1,1)	(1,4,3,2)
0100	(4,1,1,0)	(3,2,4,1)	0101	(1,1,1,0)	(4,3,2,1)
0110	(4,1,0,0)	(3,1,4,2)	0111	(1,0,0,0)	(1,4,3,2)
1000	(4,4,2,1)	(4,2,1,3)	1001	(4,1,1,1)	(1,4,3,2)
1010	(4,4,1,0)	(4,2,1,3)	1011	(4,2,0,0)	(1,2,4,3)
1100	(4,1,0,0)	(3,1,4,2)	1101	(2,1,1,0)	(3,1,4,2)
1110	(4,1,1,0)	(3,4,2,1)	1111	(1,1,1,0)	(4,3,2,1)

Table 7.1   The *dss* and *nds* for each node in the faulty Q_4 of Figure 7.14.

Table 7.1 shows the descending status sequence (*dss*) and the corresponding neighbor dimension sequence (*nds*) for each node in the Q_4 of Figure 7.14. Note that when two or more neighbors have the same safety status, there is more than one possible corresponding neighbor dimension sequence. Table 7.1 shows only one possible order for these cases. The resultant broadcast is shown in Figure 7.14.

7.8 Fault-Tolerant Multicasting

As discussed most multicast problems are NP-complete in meshes and hypercubes without faulty components. The problem becomes even harder in the presence of faults. Heuristic approaches are normally used. Again, we use n-cubes to illustrate different approaches. Also we only consider single multicast in the system, although there are some studies done on multiple multicasts [24].

7.8.1 General approach

It has been shown [31] that the problem of finding a time and traffic optimal solution for multicasting in hypercubes is NP-hard. A heuristic multicast algorithm proposed by Lan, Esfahanian, and Ni [28] achieves time optimality and traffic sub-optimality in a nonfaulty hypercube. This algorithm starts at the source node, and is executed at a set of intermediate nodes and each subset in the partition is sent to an appropriate neighbor. The partition is performed in such a way that destination nodes are sent to a few neighbors to achieve maximum sharing of common paths along shortest paths from the source node to each destination. To this end, an address summation of all the relative addresses of destination nodes with respect to this intermediate node is calculated. A destination is sent to a neighbor along dimension, say i, only if bit i in the address summation has the largest value among those bits that have value one in the relative address of this destination.

Several fault-tolerant multicast schemes have been proposed that can be classified by the amount of network information used at each node. In local-information-based multicasting [27] proposed by Lan each node knows only the status of its adjacent links and nodes. The simplicity is the main advantage of this scheme although an uncontrollable number of additional time steps may occur in the worst case. Time-optimal multicasting has been proposed in [27] that can be categorized as local-information-based multicasting. However, it is based on a restricted fault model – each node in the cube has at most one faulty neighbor.

The global-information-based multicasting [42] assumes that each node knows fault distribution in the network. This scheme guarantees time optimality. However, it requires a complex process to collect global information. The limited-global-information-based multicasting is a compromise of the above two schemes. It can obtain an optimal or suboptimal solution while maintaining a relatively inexpensive process that collects and maintains limited global information. Liang, Bhattacharya, and Tsai [30] proposed a multicast scheme where each node knows the status of all the links within two hops away (a particular format of limited global information). This scheme can tolerate up to $n - 1$ faulty links and the number of additional time steps required in the worst case is $2n$.

7.8.2 Path-based routing

In certain systems it is not efficient to replicate routing messages during a routing process where the tree-structure is used. Besides, the tree-like routing is subject to blocking if any of its branches is blocked. This problem becomes more serious for long messages. A solution is to prohibit branching during a routing process as is done in path-based routing.

In a path-based routing proposed by Lin et al. [32] the *dual-channel model* is used; that is, each channel is bidirectional. This scheme is based on finding a Hamiltonian path in the network. All the routing steps follow the selected Hamiltonian path (in two directions). Clearly, circular waiting is avoided and there is no starvation. Each (ordered) pair of source and destination appears in the path in one of the two directions. Note that the path-based routing is nonminimal and is suitable for wormhole-routed systems where distance between the source and destination nodes is negligible. In order to further reduce the length of a routing path, the message can be routed through disjoint paths as in the *multipath multicast routing* [32] in 2-d meshes. Tseng and Panda [45] generalized and improved Lin's approach to accommodate faults and networks that do not necessarily contain Hamiltonian paths. Robinson, McKinley, and Cheng [39] extended the path-based multicasting to torus networks.

When a system uses a half-duplex channel, the channel can send messages in both ways but only one direction at a time. The Hamiltonian path approach for bidirectional links is no longer feasible. Wu [48] extended the path-based scheme to a trail-based scheme. Basically, a *trail* $v_0 \rightarrow v_1 \rightarrow \ldots \rightarrow v_n$ in graph G is a *walk* in which all the edges are distinct. A walk in graph G is a finite sequence of edges. A *path* is a special trail in which all the nodes in the path are distinct. To ensure that each ordered pair of the source and destination nodes appears in a trail, each node should appear at least twice. By graph theory, any graph in which each node has an even node degree (≥ 4) has a trail on which each node appears at least twice. Also, any graph where there are more than three nodes that have a node degree less than 4 does not have such a trail. However, two appearances of each node is a necessary condition but not a sufficient condition. Consider a partial trail in the following where number i in each superscript of a node represents the ith appearance of this node.

$$v_i^1 \rightarrow v_i^2 \rightarrow v_j^1 \rightarrow v_j^2$$

Suppose both v_i and v_j appear only twice in the trail. Clearly, the pair (v_j, v_i) is not a feasible routing on this trail. Therefore, the necessary and sufficient condition is as follows: For any given node v_i there is at least one appearance of any other node to the left of the rightmost appearance of v_i and there is at least one appearance of any other node to the right of the leftmost appearance of v_i.

The path-based approach used in the double-ring routing in Section 7.1 meets the necessary and sufficient condition. Actually, any two consecutive Hamiltonian paths meet this condition. Note that two consecutive Hamiltonian paths require a stronger condition. However, if each node can appear no more than twice in a trail, then the condition for two consecutive Hamiltonian paths is a necessary and sufficient one. It is easy to see that there exist two consecutive Hamiltonian paths in any 2-d torus and any $k(\geq 4)$-cube. Figures 7.15 (a) and (b) show two edge-disjoint Hamiltonian circuits in a 4-cube. The general way to construct edge-disjoint Hamiltonian circuits in an n-cube, $n \geq 4$, is as follows:

1. Divide the given n-cube into two $(n-1)$-cubes along dimension n.

2. Construct two Hamiltonian circuits, one from each of the $(n-1)$-cubes.

3. Combine two edge-disjoint Hamiltonian circuits, one from each of two $(n-1)$-cubes, to form a Hamiltonian circuit in the n-cube. This can be done by removing one edge to break the loop in each circuit and adding two edges along dimension n to connect two broken circuits.

4. Combine the remaining two Hamiltonian circuits to form a Hamiltonian circuit in the n-cube.

5. Construct two edge-disjoint Hamiltonian circuits in the n-cube. Two consecutive Hamiltonian paths are derived by removing two adjacent edges, one from each of the two edge-disjoint Hamiltonian circuits in the n-cube.

Trailed-based routing has also been used in irregular networks using cut-through switches [36].

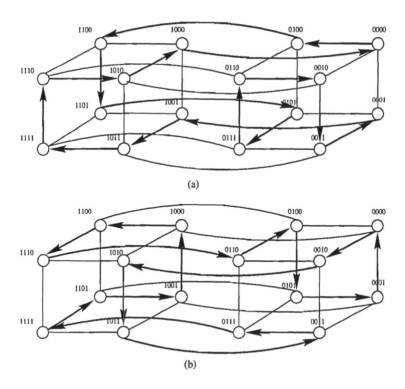

(a)

(b)

FIGURE 7.15
Two edge-disjoint Hamiltonian circuits in a 4-cube.

7.8.3 Multicasting in hypercubes used safety levels

The key issue in multicasting is that each intermediate node u (including source node s) forwards a set of destination nodes $\{u_1, u_2, ..., u_m\}$ to its appropriate neighboring nodes. We represent destination nodes in terms of their relative addresses with respect to node u, $R = \{r_i\}$, where $r_i = u \oplus u_i, 1 \leq i \leq m$. The *address summation, as* $= \sum_{r_i \in R} r_i$, represents the distribution of destination nodes along different dimensions. $|r_i| = \sum_{1 \leq j \leq n} r_i(j)$ represents the distance between nodes u and u_i. For example, if a set of destination nodes $\{u_1, u_2, u_3\} = \{0101, 1001, 0000\}$ and node $u = 1010$, then $R = \{r_1, r_2, r_3\} = \{1111, 0111, 1010\}$ with $|r_1| = 4, |r_2| = 3$, and $|r_3| = 2$ and $as = 2232$. In order to avoid recalculation of relative addresses we only calculate relative addresses at the source node. Whenever a destination node with relative address r is passed to the next node along dimension d, the dth bit of r is set to zero, i.e., the new relative address associated with this destination node will be $r^{(d)}$. In order to ensure time optimality we use the following simple strategy [28]. When the dth bit of r_i, the relative address of destination node u_i with respect to an intermediate node u, equals one, $r_i^{(d)}$ should be sent to u's neighbor, $u^{(d)}$, along dimension d.

When r_i of destination node u_i has more than one 1 value at different bits (dimensions), then relative address r_i can be forwarded along either of these dimensions. In this case a *conflict* arises. In order to resolve the conflict a priority order is determined among n dimensions. The formation of this priority order determines the result of a multicast. The priority order should be defined in such a way that it minimizes traffic by maximum sharing of common paths to destination nodes. The multicast message should not reach a *dead end* in a multicast. A dead end happens at an intermediate node when all the Hamming distance paths of a particular destination node are blocked by faulty neighbors. In this case a detour path or a backtrack process must be used to reach that destination. In order to avoid the dead end situation we should limit the number of destinations forwarded to neighbors that have faulty nodes nearby. Actually, this is the reason we use the safety level concept in the dimension priority decision.

Three approaches, safety-level-based multicasting (SLBM), modified safety-level-based multicasting (MSLBM), and address-sum-based multicasting (ASBM), are proposed in [50]. In the SLBM approach, the priority of a dimension is determined *a priori* based on the safety level of the neighbor along this dimension. The higher the safety level of the neighbor along a dimension the higher the priority order of this dimension. Two approaches can be used when there are two or more dimensions along which the corresponding neighbors have the same highest safety level. In the SLBM approach, a priority order among these dimensions is randomly selected. In the modified SLBM (MSLBM), the priority of a dimension is based on the corresponding bit value in the address summation of all destinations. Basically, if the neighbor along dimension d can carry maximum possible destination nodes, i.e., if $as(d)$ is the maximum value of all the bits in the address summation, then d has the highest priority. When there is more than one bit that has the same maximum value in the address summation, the selection is random. The next highest priority dimension is determined using the same approach but is based on the updated destination set, i.e., the one after removing those nodes to be forwarded to dimensions in higher priorities.

In the ASBM approach the dimension priority depends primarily on bit values in the address summation. A dimension has the highest priority if the corresponding neighbor can carry the maximum possible nodes. In order to ensure time optimality only those destination nodes that are no more than k-Hamming-distance away from the selected neighbor will be included, and k is the safety level of this neighbor. In this case the safety levels of all the neighbors and the relative distances of the destination nodes are used in the decision. A modified ASBM approach, following a similar approach as used in MSLBM, can be adopted when there is more than one neighbor that can carry the same maximum number of destination nodes. In this case the priority among these neighbors is based on their safety levels. In ASBM the priority among these nodes is randomly selected.

A multicast generated by SLBM, MSLBM, or ASBM is guaranteed to be time optimal if the source node is safe in any faulty n-cube. When the source node is unsafe and there are no more than $n - 1$ faulty nodes, the length of each path from the source to a destination is either the same or exactly two more than that of the corresponding Hamming distance path. A multicast generated by SLBM, MSLBM, or ASBM is guaranteed to be time optimal if the relative distance between the source and any destination is no more than the safety level of the source.

Figure 7.16 shows a Q_4 with four faulty nodes represented as black nodes: 1100, 0110, 0011, and 0001. Initially, all nonfaulty nodes are 4-safe, i.e., safe. After the first round of message exchange among neighboring nodes, the nodes (0010, 0111, 0100, and 1110) that have two or more faulty neighbors change their status from 4-safe to 1-safe. The status of all the other nodes remains unchanged. After the second round the status of nodes 0000 and 0101 change to 2-safe, since each of them has two 1-safe neighbors and one 2-safe neighbor. The safety level of every node remains stable after two rounds and the value associated with each node of Figure 7.16 represents the final safety level of the node. In Figure 7.16, suppose that the source node is the safe node 1000 and the multicast set is $u = \{u_1, u_2, u_3, u_4, u_5, u_6\} = \{0000, 0010, 0100, 0101, 0111, 1001\}$. The set of relative addresses between the source and destinations nodes is $R = \{r_1, r_2, r_3, r_4, r_5, r_6\} = \{1000, 1010, 1100, 1101, 1111, 0001\}$. Therefore, the address summation is $as = 5323$.

The SLBM approach uses only neighbors' safety levels in terms of the neighbor dimension sequence (ds) to determine the priority among the neighboring nodes. In this case dimension 2 has the highest priority, followed by dimension 1 and then dimension 4. Dimension 3 has the lowest priority. Since the 2nd bit value is one in r_2 and r_5, $r_2^{(2)}$ and $r_5^{(2)}$ together with the multicast message are passed to node 1010 (the neighbor of 1000 along dimension 2). In the subsequent discussion, we assume that the

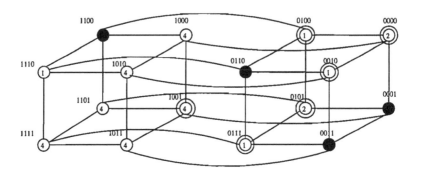

FIGURE 7.16
A faulty 4-cube with four faulty nodes.

multicast message is always attached with the relative address of each destination node forwarded from one node to another. Among the remaining nodes in R, r_4 and r_6 have value one in the 1st bit. Both $r_4^{(1)}$ and $r_6^{(1)}$ are passed to node 1001. Since the 4th bit value is one in the remaining r_1 and r_3, addresses $r_1^{(4)}$ and $r_3^{(4)}$ are passed to 1000's neighbor along dimension 4. No destination nodes are passed to the neighbor along dimension 3. The procedure is applied recursively to 1000's neighbors that receive destination nodes and a multicast tree is formed as shown in Figure 7.17 (a). The depth of this tree is the number of time steps used and the number of edges in the tree is the number of traffic steps used. In this case the time steps are 4 and the traffic steps are 10.

The MSLBM approach also uses the neighbor dimension sequence (ds) in determining the priority. However, when two or more neighbors have the same highest safety level, the address summation (as) on the remaining destination nodes is used to break the tie. In Figure 7.16, two neighbors of source node 1000 along dimensions 1 and 2 have the same safety level. Based on $as = 5323$ the neighbor along dimension 2 (node 1010) can carry 2 (the 2nd bit value of as) destination nodes and the neighbor along dimension 1 (node 1001) can carry 3 destination nodes. Therefore, node 1001 has a higher priority over node 1010. As a result, $r_4^{(1)}$, $r_5^{(1)}$, and $r_6^{(1)}$ are passed to 1001 and $r_2^{(2)}$ is passed to node 1010. Both $r_1^{(4)}$ and $r_3^{(4)}$ are passed to 1000's neighbor along dimension 4. Figure 7.17 (b) shows the resultant multicast tree with 4 time steps and 9 traffic steps.

In the ASBM approach the dimension priority is dependent on the address summation of destination nodes. That is, the dimension with the maximum bit value in the address summation has the highest priority. The

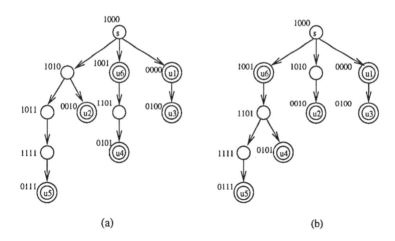

(a)   (b)

FIGURE 7.17
Two multicast trees generated using (a) SLBM and (b) MSLBM.

destination addresses with value one at this dimension will be sent to the corresponding neighbor. However, in order to avoid forwarding too many destinations to an unsafe or faulty neighbor, we forward destination addresses to a k-safe neighbor only when the corresponding destination nodes are at less than or equal to k-Hamming-distance away from this k-safe neighbor. When there are two or more neighbors that can carry the same maximum number of destination nodes, the selection is random although we can easily extend the ASBM algorithm in such a way that the selection among these neighbors is based on their safety levels. More detailed discussion on ASBM can be found in [50].

References

[1] Al-Dhelaan, A. and B. Bose, "Efficient fault-tolerant broadcasting algorithms for the hypercube", *Proc. of the 4th Conf. on Hypercube Concurrent Computers and Applications*, 1989, 123-128.

[2] Almohammad, B. and B. Bose, "Fault-tolerant broadcasting in

toroidal networks", in *Parallel and Distributed Processing*, J. Rolim, ed., LNCS 1388, 1998, 681-692.

[3] Boppana, R. V. and S. Chalasani, "Fault-Tolerant wormhole routing algorithms for mesh networks", *IEEE Transactions on Computers*, **44**, 7, July 1995, 848-863.

[4] Boura, Y. M. and C. R. Das, "Efficient fully adaptive wormhole routing in *n*-dimensional meshes", *Proc. of the 14th Int'l Conf. on Distributed Computing Systems*, 1994, 589-596.

[5] Chalasani, S. and R. V. Boppana, "Fault-tolerant wormhole routing in tori", *Proc. of the 8th Int'l Conf. on Supercomputing*, 1994, 146-155.

[6] Chalasani, S. and R. V. Boppana, "Communication in multicomputers with nonconvex faults", *Proc. of Euro-Par'95*, 1995, 673-684.

[7] Chen, M. S. and K. G. Shin, "Depth-first search approach for fault-tolerant routing in hypercube multicomputers", *IEEE Transactions on Parallel and Distributed Systems*, 1, 2, Apr. 1990, 152-159.

[8] Chen, M. S. and K. G. Shin, "Adaptive fault-tolerant routing in hypercube multicomputers", *IEEE Transactions on Computers*, **39**, 12, Dec. 1990, 1406-1416.

[9] Chen, X. and J. Wu, "Minimal routing in 3-D meshes using extended safety levels", Technical Report, TR-CSE-97-64, Florida Atlantic University, Nov. 1997.

[10] Chien, A. and J. Kim, "Planar-adaptive routing: low-cost adaptive networks for multicomputers", *Proc. of the 19th Int'l Symp. on Computer Architecture*, 1992, 268-277.

[11] Chiu, G. -M., "A fault-tolerant broadcasting algorithm for hypercubes", to appear in *Information Processing Letters*.

[12] Cunningham, C. M. and D. R. Aversky, " Fault-tolerant adaptive routing for two-dimensional meshes", *Proc. of 2nd Int'l Symp. on High Performance Computer Architecture*, 1995, 122-131.

[13] Dally, W. J. and C. L. Seitz, "The Torus routing chip", *Journal of Distributed Computing*, 1, 3, 1986, 71-83.

[14] Dally, W. J. and H. Aoki, "Deadlock-free adaptive routing in multicomputer networks using virtual channels", *IEEE Transactions on Parallel and Distributed Systems*, 4, 4, Apr. 1993, 466-475.

[15] Duato, J., "Deadlock-free adaptive routing algorithms for multicomputers: evaluation of a new algorithm", *Proc. of the 3rd IEEE Symp. on Parallel and Distributed Processing*, 1991, 840-847.

[16] Duato, J., " A new theory of deadlock-free adaptive routing in wormhole networks", *IEEE Transactions on Parallel and Distributed Systems*, 4, 12, Dec. 1993, 1,320-1,331.

[17] Duato, J., "A necessary and sufficient condition for deadlock-free adaptive routing in wormhole networks", *IEEE Transactions on Parallel and Distributed Systems*, 6, 10, Oct. 1995, 1,055-1,067.

[18] Duato, J., "A theory of fault-tolerant routing in wormhole networks", *IEEE Transactions on Parallel and Distributed Systems*, 8, 8, Aug. 1997, 790-802.

[19] Duato, J., S. S. Yalamanchili, L. Ni, *Interconnection Networks: An Engineering Approach*, The IEEE Computer Society Press, 1997.

[20] Liberskind-Hadas, R. and E. Brandt, "Origin-based fault-tolerant routing in the mesh", *Proc. of the 2nd Int'l Symp. on High Performance Computer Architecture*, 1995, 102-111.

[21] Glass, C. J. and L. M. Ni, " Maximally fully adaptive routing in 2D meshes", *Proc. of the 1992 Int'l Conf. on Parallel Processing*, 1992, I 101-I 104.

[22] Glass, C. J. and L. M. Ni, "The Turn model for adaptive routing", *Proc. of the 19th Int'l Symp. on Computer Architecture*, 1992, 278-287.

[23] Gaughan, P. T. and S. Yalamanchili, "A family of fault-tolerant routing protocols for direct multiprocessor networks", *IEEE Transactions on Parallel and Distributed Systems*, 6, 5, May 1995, 482-495.

[24] Kesavan, R. and D. K. Panda, "Minimizing node contention in multiple multicast on wormhole k-ary n-cube networks", *Proc. of the 1996 Int'l Conf. on Parallel Processing*, 1996, I 188-I 195.

[25] Li, Q., "Minimum deadlock-free message routing restrictions in binary hypercubes", *Journal of Parallel and Distributed Computing*, 15, 1992, 153-159.

[26] Lan, Y., "A fault-tolerant routing algorithm in hypercubes", *Proc. of the 1994 Int'l Conf. on Parallel Processing*, 1994, III 163-III 166.

[27] Lan, Y., "Fault-tolerant multi-destination routing in hypercube multicomputers", *Proc. of the 12th Int'l Conf. on Distributed Computing Systems*, 1992, 632-639.

[28] Lan, Y., A. H. Esfahanian, and L. M. Ni, "Multicast in hypercube multiprocessors", *Journal of Parallel and Distributed Computing*, 8, 1990, 30-41.

[29] Li, Z. and J. Wu. "A multidestination routing scheme for hypercube multiprocessors", *Proc. of the 1991 Int'l Conf. on Parallel Processing*, 1991, II 290-II 291.

[30] Liang, A. C., S. Bhattacharya, and W. T. Tsai. "Fault-tolerant multicasting in hypercubes", *Journal of Parallel and Distributed Computing*, 23, 3, Dec. 1994, 418-428.

[31] Lin, X. and L. M. Ni, "Multicast in multicomputer networks", *Proc. of the 1990 Int'l Conf. on Parallel Processing*, 3, 1990, 114-118.

[32] Lin, X. and L. M. Ni, "Deadlock-free message routing in multiprocessor interconnection networks", *Proc. of the 18th Int'l Symp. on Computer Architecture,* 1991, 116-125.

[33] Linder, D. H. and J. C. Harden, "An adaptive and fault tolerant wormhole routing strategy for k-ary n-cubes", *IEEE Transactions on Computers*, 40, 1, Jan. 1991, 2-12.

[34] Mahmood, A. D., J. Lynch, and R. B. Shaffer, "Optimally adaptive, minimum distance circuit-switched routing in hypercubes", *ACM Transactions on Computer Systems*, 15, 2, May 1997, 166-193.

[35] Perrcy, M. and P. Banerjee, "Distributed algorithms for shortest-path, deadlock-free routing and broadcasting in arbitrarily faulty hypercubes", *Proc. of the 20th Int'l Symp. on Fault-Tolerant Computing*, 1990, 218-225.

[36] Qiao, W. and L. M. Ni, "Adaptive routing in irregular networks using cut-through switches", *Proc. of the 1996 Int'l Conf. on Parallel Processing*, 1996, I 52-I 60.

[37] Raghavendra, C. S., P. J. Yang, and S. B. Tien, "Free dimensions – an effective approach to achieving fault tolerance in hypercubes", *Proc. of the 22nd Int'l Symp. on Fault-Tolerant Computing*, 1992, 170-177.

[38] Ramanathan, P. and K. G. Shin, "Reliable broadcast in hypercube multicomputers", *IEEE Transactions on Computers*, 37, 12, Dec. 1988, 1654-1657.

[39] Robinson, D. F., D. K. McKinley, and B. H. C. Cheng, "Path-based multicast communication in wormhole-routed unidirectional torus networks", *Journal of Parallel and Distributed Computing*, **15**, 2, 1997, 104-121.

[40] Saad, Y. and M. H. Schultz, "Topological properties of hypercubes", *IEEE Transactions on Computers*, **37**, 7, July 1988, 867-872.

[41] Schwiebert, L. and D. N. Jayasimha, "Optimally fully adaptive minimal wormhole routing for meshes", *Journal of Parallel and Distributed Computing*, **27**, May 1995, 56-70.

[42] Sheu, J. P. and M. Y. Su, "A multicast algorithm for hypercube multiprocessors", *Proc. of the 1992 Int'l Conf. on Parallel Processing*, 1992, III 18-III 22.

[43] Su, C. and K. G. Shin, "Adaptive deadlock-free routing in multicomputers using only one extra channel", *Proc. of the 22nd Int'l Conf. on Parallel Processing*, 1993, III 175-III 182.

[44] Suh, Y. -J. et al., " Software based fault-tolerant oblivious routing in pipeline networks", *Proc. of the 1995 Int'l Conf. on Parallel Processing*, 1995, I 101-I 105.

[45] Tseng, Y. -C. and D. K. Panda, "Trip-based multicasting in wormhole routed networks", *Proc. of the 7th Int'l Parallel Processing Symp.*, 1993, 276-283.

[46] Tasi, M. -J and S. -D. Wang, "A fault-tolerant adaptive routing algorithm for dynamically injured hypercubes, meshes, and tori", *IEEE Transactions on Parallel and Distributed Systems*, **9**, 2, Feb. 1998, 163-174.

[47] Wu, J. and E. B. Fernandez, "Broadcasting in faulty cube-connected-cycles with minimum recovery time", *Proc. of CONPAR92*, Springer Verlag, LNCS 634, Sept. 1992, 833-834.

[48] Wu, J., "A trail-based deadlock-free routing scheme in wormhole-routed networks", *Proc. of Southcon'95*, 1995, 285-288.

[49] Wu, J., " Safety levels – an efficient mechanism for achieving reliable broadcasting in hypercubes", *IEEE Transactions on Computers*, **44**, 5, May 1995, 702-706.

[50] Wu, J. and K. Yao, "Fault-tolerant multicasting in hypercubes using limited global information", *IEEE Transactions on Computers*, **44**, 9, 1995, 1162-1166.

[51] Wu, J., "Adaptive fault-tolerant routing in cube-based multicomputers using safety vector", *IEEE Transactions on Parallel and Distributed Systems*, **9**, 4, Apr. 1998, 321-333.

[52] Wu, J., "Reliable unicasting in faulty hypercubes using safety levels", *IEEE Transactions on Computers*, **46**, 2, Feb. 1997, 241-247.

[53] Wu, J., "Fault-tolerant adaptive and minimal routing in meshed-connected multicomputers using extended safety levels", *Proc. of the 18th Int'l Conf. on Distributed Computing Systems*, 1998, 428-435.

[54] Wu, J., "On constructing orthogonal convex polygons in 2-d meshes", Technical Report, TR-CSE-98-1, Florida Atlantic University, Jan. 1998.

[55] Zakrevski, L. and M. Karpovsky, "Fault-tolerant message routing for multiprocessors", in *Parallel and Distributed Processing*, J. Rolim, ed., LNCS 1388, Springer-Verlag, 1998, 714-730.

Problems

1. (a) Provide a shortest-path routing algorithm for the mesh interconnection network.

   (b) Provide a shortest-path routing algorithm for the mesh with up to one faulty link.

   (c) Provide a routing algorithm for the mesh with up to three faulty links. We assume each node knows local information in both (b) and (c).

2. Given a 4-cube with faulty nodes $\{0001, 0011, 1000, 1010, 1111\}$,

   - Determine the safety level of each node.
   - Prove that if the source node is safe, then there is a healthy Hamiltonian path from the source to any destination in any cube. (Hint: Use induction based on the distance between the source and destination nodes).
   - Show how to route a message from node 1110 to node 0000 using safety levels.
   - Provide a ring routing algorithm using two virtual networks.

3. Wu and Fernandez (1992) gave the following safe and unsafe node definition: A nonfaulty node is unsafe if and only if either of the following conditions is true: (a) There are two faulty neighbors, or (b) there are at least three unsafe or faulty neighbors. Consider a 4-cube with faulty nodes 0100, 0011, 0101, 1110, and 1111. Find out the safety status (safe or unsafe) of each node.

4. Determine two deadlock-free routing algorithms for the 3×4 torus network. Each link is bi-directional and no virtual channel can be used.

5. Determine a deadlock-free routing scheme in the following interconnection network.

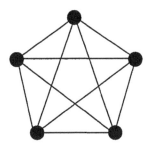

6. Consider the following turn models:

   - *West-first routing.* Route a message first west, if necessary, and then adaptively south, east, and north.

   - *North-last routing.* First adaptively route a message south, east, and west; route the message north last.

   - *Negative-first routing.* First adaptively route a message along the negative X or Y axis; that is, south or west, then adaptively route the message along the positive X or Y axis.

   Show all the turns allowed in each of the above three routings.

7. Show the corresponding routing paths using (1) positive-last, (2) west-first, (3) north-last, and (4) negative-first routing for the following unicasting:

(a) $s = (2, 1)$ and $d = (5, 9)$

(b) $s = (7, 1)$ and $d = (5, 3)$

(c) $s = (6, 4)$ and $d = (3, 1)$

(d) $s = (1, 7)$ and $d = (5, 2)$

8. In the origin-based routing given the locations of the source, destination, and origin nodes, find the total number of different paths. Explain how the location of the origin affects the number of different paths.

9. Given a 8×8 mesh with eight faulty nodes (2,4), (2, 6), (3, 5), (3,3), (3,7), (4,4), (4,6), (5,5):

   • Find all the faulty blocks based on two different definitions of safe/unsafe nodes.

   • Find orthogonal convex polygons that cover all these faulty nodes based on the concept of enable/disable nodes.

   • Find a set of disjoint orthogonal convex polygons that cover all these faulty nodes. In addition, the overall size of these orthogonal convex polygons is minimum.

10. Suppose that we use Li's extended e-cube routing algorithm to send a message from $s = 1011$ to $d = 0100$. Find all the legal shortest paths.

11. Consider a 2-d mesh with faulty blocks, assuming that node $(0, 0)$ is the source and node (i, j) is the destination. Prove that if there is no faulty block that goes across the X and Y axes, then there exists at least one minimal path from $(0, 0)$, i.e., the length of this path is $|i| + |j|$.

12. Construct an injured spanning binomial tree in the 4-cube of Figure 7.13:

   • Using node 1000 as the root node.

   • Using node 1111 as the root node.

13. Given a 4-cube with four faulty nodes 1111, 0101, 0100, 0011:

   • Calculate the safety level of each node.

   • Calculate the safety vector of each node.

14. Consider a multicasting with $s = 1001$, $d = \{1110, 0100, 1101\}$, and a set of faulty nodes $\{0000, 0101, 0111\}$ in a 4-cube.

   - Construct a multicast tree based on SLBM.
   - Construct a multicast tree based on MSLBM.
   - Compare these two multicast trees in terms of traffic steps used.

Chapter 8

RELIABILITY IN DISTRIBUTED SYSTEMS

An important objective in using distributed systems is to achieve high dependability that includes reliability, safety, and security. A fundamental issue is to detect and handle faults that may appear in a distributed system. In this chapter we study various methods of handling node, communication, Byzantine, and software faults in a distributed system.

8.1 Basic Models

The concept of dependability was initially proposed by Laprie [37] and extended in [21] and [38]. In general, the concept of dependability includes the following three components:

- *Reliability* which refers to the continuation of service in the presence of faults.

- *Safety* which refers to the non-occurrence of catastrophic failures.

- *Security* which refers to the avoidance, or tolerance, of deliberate attacks to the system.

Another concept related to safety is *fail-safe*. A fail-safe system produces a correct result or no result at all. A traffic control system is an example of a fail-safe system. We limit our attention here only to reliability aspects of dependability, specifically the detection and handling of faults. A *fault* is a physical defect, imperfection, or flaw that occurs within some hardware or software unit. An *error* is the manifestation of a fault. It is a deviation from accuracy or correctness. If the error results in the system performing one of its functions incorrectly, a system *failure* has occurred. A detailed explanation of these related concepts can be found in [37]. In this chapter, faults, errors, and failures are used interchangeably for some cases if they do not cause confusion. The general reliability problem posed by a distributed system is to ensure a globally consistent state of the system when faults occur. Four types of faults considered here are:

- node (hardware) faults

- program (software) faults

- communication faults

- timing faults

A more refined fault classification can be found in [25]. In general a communication subsystem includes both hardware (links) and software (protocols) parts. The communication faults considered here only include communication medium faults. In general, node, communication, and timing faults can be caused either by physical faults or by human faults (or design faults) while software faults are caused only by design faults.

Fault tolerance is based on *redundancy* which is simply the addition of information, resource, or time beyond what is needed for normal system operations. There are four types of redundancy:

- *Hardware redundancy*; for example, extra PEs, I/Os.

- *Software redundancy*; for example, extra versions of software modules.

- *Information redundancy*; for example, error detecting codes which use extra bits.

- *Time redundancy*; for example, additional time used to perform functions of a system.

Three basic fault handling methods are:

- *Active replication.* All replication modules are executed concurrently and their internal states are closely synchronized.

- *Passive replication.* Only one module is active but other modules' internal states are regularly updated by means of checkpoints from the active module.

- *Semi-active replication.* A hybrid of both active and passive replication. It has a relatively low recovery overhead.

Active replication uses the concept of fault masking to hide the occurrence of faults and prevent faults from resulting in errors. Passive replication, also called the dynamic method, achieves fault tolerance by detecting the existence of faults and performing certain actions to remove faulty components from the system. In this approach faults can be detected by periodic tests, self-checking circuits, and watchdog timers. *System-level fault diagnosis* [51], which studies ways to identify faulty components in a system, is a challenging problem, especially in a distributed system.

The detection of failures can also be classified into *external detection* and *internal detection.* External detection implies that responsibilities for detection of node failures are given to facilities external to the node. For example, a node B is tested by another node A. If node A is healthy, it is assumed node A is capable of detecting any deviation of node B from expected behavior. If node A is faulty, the diagnosis result can be random. Internal detection places failure detection mechanisms for a node within that node. Usually the testing component is considered as a *hardcore* which is assumed to be entirely reliable. A workable approach to fault detection may employ a combination of internal and external detections. Coding techniques can provide low-cost fault detection for buses, memories and registers.

We consider here only software-based fault handling. Two software models are generally used for this purpose:

- *Process-based model.* An application consists of a set of cooperating sequential processes: $[P_1 \parallel P_2 \parallel \ldots \parallel P_n]$.

- *Object-based model.* An application consists of a set of objects [40]; each object is an atomic action and encapsulation is achieved by accessing objects through a set of well defined interfaces.

Reliable systems based on object models have been addressed in [1], [60], and [61]. Process-based approaches can be found in [20] and [24]. The analogy between the process-based and object-based models has been discussed in [43].

The *hierarchical model* [11] is another popular abstract model where a system consists of a set of servers at different levels. If server A depends on server B, then the correctness of A's behavior depends on the correctness of B's behavior.

In the subsequent discussion we use the process-based model although most approaches discussed are general and can be applied to general models.

8.2   Building Blocks of Fault-Tolerant System Design

We now study three logical entities: stable storage, fail-stop processors, and atomic actions used as building blocks of many fault-tolerant systems.

8.2.1   Stable storage

Stable storage is a logical abstraction for a special storage that can survive system failure. That is, contents of stable storage are not destroyed or corrupted by a failure. The key issue in implementing a stable storage is to correctly execute two basic operations: *read* and *write*, through which a process can interact with storage media such as disks. The goal is to mask the undesirable events: For *read(address : a)* which returns (*status : good* or *bad, data : d*), the possible undesirable results are:

1. *a* is good, but read returns *bad*.

2. The same as above. Moreover, successive reads also return *bad*.

3. *a* is bad but read returns *good* or *a* is *good* but read returns different data d'.

For *write(address : a, data : d)*, the undesirable effects are:

1. *a* remains unchanged or changed to different data d'.

2. *a* becomes (*bad, d*).

In an ideal stable storage read always returns good data and write always succeeds. One simple approach [36], as used in one disk implementation, uses two operations *stableread(1)* and *stablewrite(1)*:

1. In *stableread(1)* a read operation is performed repeatedly until it returns a *good* status. It fails after a certain number of tries.

2. A *stablewrite(1)* performs a write operation followed by a read operation until *read* returns a *good* status and correct data.

However, *stableread(1)* and *stablewrite(1)* cannot cover decay events and crashes. A *decay event* does one of the following:

1. a goes from $(good, d)$ to (bad, d).

2. a goes from (bad, d) to $(good, d)$,

3. a changes from (s, d) to (s, d') with $d \neq d'$.

If a crash occurs when some operation is being performed on the disk, the result of the operation should be assumed to be unreliable. In order to get a better result each a is replicated and they are not decay-related. We then have *stableread(2)* and *stablewrite(2)*:

1. A *stableread(2)* performs a *stableread(1)* on one copy. If the result is bad, it does a *stableread(1)* to the other copy.

2. A *stablewrite(2)* does a *stablewrite(1)* to one of the copies. When this operation is successful, it performs a *stableread(1)* to the other copy.

If a crash occurs during a *stablewrite(2)*, a cleanup process is needed to copy a good copy to the bad copy or make both good copies consistent by copying one to the other.

The *disk shadowing* approach uses two disks which can also handle errors like disk failure. Another approach to approximate stable storage is through the use of *redundant arrays of inexpensive disks* (RAID) [46]. In this approach data are spread over multiple disks using bit-interleaving to provide high I/O performance. One or several check disks can be used to detect or mask faults. RAID offers significant advantages over conventional disks and can tolerate multiple failures [2].

8.2.2 Fail-stop processors

When a processor fails, most likely it does not perform any incorrect action and simply ceases to function. Such a processor is called a *fail-stop processor* [58]. More specifically, the effects of a fail-stop processor are: (1) The processor stops executing. (2) The volatile storage is lost but the stable storage is unaffected. (3) Any processor can detect the failure of a fail-stop processor.

If a processor does not behave like a fail-stop processor, we can force it through a careful design. One approach that uses reliable stable storage with one reliable storage processor (a processor that controls the storage medium) and $k+1$ processors is as follows [57]: Each of the $k+1$ processors runs the same program and accesses the same stable storage through the storage processor. A failure is detected if any of the requests is different, or any request does not arrive within a specified period. In either case, it is considered a failure and all the requests should be discarded. This approach generates a *k-fail-stop processor* as the system behaves like a fail-stop processor unless $k + 1$ or more components of the system fail [56].

8.2.3 Atomic actions

An *atomic action* is a set of operations which are executed indivisibly by hardware. That is, either operations are completed successfully and fully or the state of the system remains unchanged (operations are not executed at all). An action is atomic if during the execution of an action, the process performing is not aware of the existence of any outside activities and cannot observe any outside state change. Similarly, any outside processes cannot view any internal state change of an atomic action. This is so called the all-or-nothing property of atomic actions.

Atomic actions are needed in many applications including fault-tolerant ones. Their implementations also differ from case to case. We will discuss some of its applications in Chapter 11 where distributed database management systems are discussed.

8.3 Handling of Node Faults

Basic methods of handling node faults use either the software-based or the hardware-based approach. Since software and hardware are logically equivalent, we consider here only the software-based approach where a set of the same processes are replicated and assigned to different PEs.

The type of redundancy used depends on fault handling methods and the nature of faults which can be either *permanent* or *transient*. For permanent faults we use replacement through hardware redundancy and for transient faults we use retry through time redundancy. When the active replication approach is adopted, N-modular redundancy (NMR) is normally used. For example, in 3-modular redundancy (TMR) the same process is triplicated to perform a majority vote to determine the output. If one of the processors becomes faulty, the two remaining copies mask the result of the faulty processor when the majority vote is performed. However, it is relatively expensive to use the active replication in a distributed system. We will discuss an application of active replication in Chapter 11.

In passive replication either *forward recovery* or *backward recovery* can be used. In forward recovery it is assumed that the nature of the faults and damages in a system can be completely and accurately assessed. Therefore, it is possible to remove these faults and enable the system to move forward. Backward recovery applies to cases when it is not possible to foresee the nature of the faults and to remove them. System states have to be stored regularly so that when a failure causes an inconsistent state, the system can be restored to a previous fault-free state.

8.3.1 Backward recovery

Forward recovery is simpler than backward recovery but it is too restrictive. The generality enables backward recovery to provide a general recovery mechanism in distributed systems. In a backward recovery a process is restored to a prior state. The points in the execution of a process to which the process can later be restored are known as *checkpoints*. There are two ways of saving checkpoints of an active module that is a process or a processor [35].

1. Each checkpoint is multicast to all its backup passive modules.

2. Each checkpoint is stored in its local stable storage.

Checkpoints are normally stored in stable storage. Stable storage will not lose information because it guarantees the stability or permanence of the information stored in it.

Another approach [35] is based on *shadow pages*. Whenever a process needs to modify a page, this page is duplicated and maintained on stable storage. Only one of the copies undergoes all the modifications done by the process. The other copy is known as the shadow page. If the process fails, the modified copy is discarded and the system is restored based on the shadow page. If the process is successful, each shadow page is replaced by the corresponding modified page.

In order to guard against failure occurrences when the old checkpoint is replaced by the new one, it is required that the checkpoint process be atomic; that is, either the new checkpoint is placed or the prior checkpoint is retained. The approach used in *Sequoia* [6] provides an atomic checkpoint process by tolerating a single failure of processors at any point. Assume that states are initially in cache and should be copied to memory (a stable

Condition	Failure	Action
$T_{a1} = T_{a2} = T_{b1} = T_{b2}$	None	None
$T_{a1} > T_{a2} = T_{b1} = T_{b2}$	Flush bank A	Copy bank B to bank A
$T_{a1} = T_{a2} > T_{b1} = T_{b2}$	In between	Copy bank A to bank B
$T_{a1} = T_{a2} = T_{b1} > T_{b2}$	Flush bank B	Copy bank A to bank B

Table 8.1   Failure conditions [7] (©1993 IEEE).

storage). Two memory banks are used: one for the old checkpoint and the other for the new checkpoint. The role of these two banks alternates in the subsequent operations. A fixed timestamp is written to the memory bank before the flush (T_{a1} for bank A or T_{b1} for bank B) and after the flush (T_{a2} or T_{b2}). The cache is written sequentially into two banks in six steps. Since the four timestamps are sequentially written, a failure can be described by the timestamps that are different (see Table 8.1).

Clearly, when all four timestamps are equal, the checkpointing process completes successfully. If T_{a1} is the only written timestamp, then the failure occurred during the flush to bank A; that is, the new checkpoint (in bank A) is incomplete. In this case the old checkpoint (bank B) must be copied to bank A and the recovery process will roll back to the old checkpoint.

When processor faults are permanent, replacements of these faulty processors are required. Usually there is a set of backup PEs, called a *backup group*, in passive replication schemes [69] with at least one backup PE for each active module. An *n-backup* group intends to maintain at all times n backup PEs in the group. If it is found that the number of PEs in a group is not enough, this group will try to recruit another member. In the approach using a stable storage each passive module unit gets checkpoints from the stable storage after the crash of an active module.

When processor faults are transient, no replacement of processors is required. During the system recovery each process needs to be restored to its most recent checkpoint and data modified by a process need to be restored to a proper state. Note that this process still runs on the same processor.

Since most distributed algorithms are non-deterministic in the active duplication, all the copies of a process must resolve non-determinism in an identical manner. For a detailed discussion on this issue see [43].

8.3.2 Roll-forward recovery

The *roll-forward recovery* approach ([41], [50]) is an example of the semi-active replication where a failure is detected by a comparison mismatch between two active modules or by a TMR (triple-modular redundancy) voting among three active modules [23] triggering a validation step. However, all the participating processors continue execution and a spare is used to determine which of the divergent processors is correct.

One forward recovery strategy is lookahead execution with rollback. Initially copies of a process (task) are executed at different processors. At the checkpoint the results of these versions are voted (or compared). If the voting is successful, we obtain a correct result that is saved in stable storage. Based on this result, copies of the next task are executed. If, on the other hand, the voting fails, we execute copies of the next task based on each of the results of the previous task. Simultaneously a rollback execution of the previous task is implemented, i.e., the previous task is re-executed on spare processors in order to obtain a correct result. Then we keep the results of the next task which were based on the correct versions of the previous task and discard the others. In this way we avoid wasting time for rollback execution. Although rollback execution cannot be avoided if all the versions fail (all the results are incorrect) or the re-execution of the previous task does not get a correct result, rollback time is saved by taking advantage of existing correct results without restarting from the beginning.

Figure 8.1 (a) shows the roll-forward recovery scheme proposed by Pradhan and Vaidya [50] where I_i, I_{i+1}, and I_{i+2} are checkpoint intervals. Two processes X and Y execute the same version of a process and their results are compared right before each checkpoint. S represents the spare processor which performs validation for two intervals I_i and I_{i+1}. We have the following four situations [50].

- *No concurrent retry.* Both X and Y execute correctly in interval I_i.

- *Concurrent retry without rollback.* This situation occurs when a single processor (either X or Y) fails and there is no fault within two consecutive checkpoint intervals. That is, a fault occurs in I_i and during two validation intervals (I_{i+1} and I_{i+2}) there is no fault.

- *Rollback after one interval of concurrent retry.* In this case the concurrent retry does not succeed and the system is rolled back to the beginning of interval I_i. This corresponds to the case when two processes in I_i fail in the same checkpoint interval I_i (although I_i of S really occurs after I_i of X and Y). Note that in this case both X and

Y rollback by two intervals, and it occurs after the spare has completed one validation interval. If we use $(X_{I_i}, Y_{I_i}, S_{I_i})$ to represent the status of X, Y, and S during interval I_i with 0 for faulty, 1 for healthy, and d for don't care (i.e., either faulty or healthy), we have three cases: (1, 0, 0), (0, 1, 0), (0, 0, d).

- *Rollback after two intervals of concurrent retry.* In this case one additional fault occurs in checkpoint interval I_{i+1} and the system is rolled back to the beginning of interval I_{i+1}. This situation corresponds to scenarios described as follows: If we use $(X_{I_i}, Y_{I_i}, S_{I_i}, X_{I_{i+1}}, Y_{I_{i+1}}, S_{I_{i+1}})$ to represent the status of X, Y, and S during intervals I_i and I_{i+1}, we have the following four cases: $(1,0,1, d,d, 0)$, $(1,0,1,0, d,d)$, $(0,1,1, d,d,0)$, and $(0, 1, 1,d, 0, d)$. Note that X and Y rollback by two intervals to I_{i+1} after the spare has completed two validation intervals.

In the approach proposed by Long, Fuchs, and Abraham [41] (see Figure 8.1 (b)) the diverged processors after I_i are themselves duplexed during interval I_{i+1} of both X and Y to ensure both processors continue to be duplexed. At the end of validation step I_i of S, duplexed copies are compared to ensure no faults occur during interval I_{i+1} of both X and Y. In Pradhan and Vaidya's approach [50] a third processor performs the validation step. Each of the two processors X and Y may diverge during the validation step since neither computation is duplexed. Therefore, the spare processor which itself can be faulty at interval I_i (but the comparison is done by a hardcore component assumed to be error-free) has to perform a second validation (I_{i+1} of S). This validation checks the correctness of interval I_{i+1} of the correct processor, X or Y, after interval I_i. Three processors are used for a period of two validation intervals in Pradhan and Vaidya's approach [50] compared to five processors used for a period of one validation interval used in Long, Fuchs, and Abraham's approach [41].

Huang, Wu, and Fernandez [23] extended the forward recovery checkpointing using voting among n versions instead of comparison between two versions. In general, an (n, m)-pattern represents n-version for regular execution and m-version for validation. Long, Fuchs, and Abraham's approach corresponds to a (2,1)-pattern. A reliability optimization problem was also studied in [23]. Here, we use Long, Fuchs, and Abraham's approach to illustrate the optimization problem. When a computation is duplexed, how do we assign processors (new and used ones) to different duplex groups? In this case there are three new processors and two used processors (ones that have been used in previous intervals). Under the assumption that processor

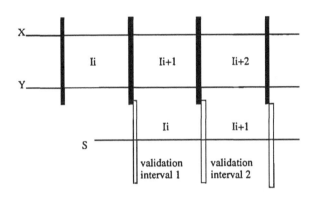

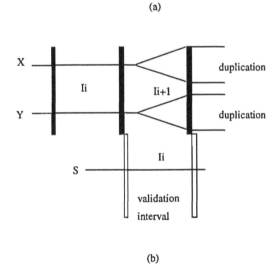

(b)

FIGURE 8.1
Two roll-forward recovery schemes (a) with two validation intervals and (b) with one validation interval.

failure rate increases monotonically with respect to time, it has been proved that the best processor assignment, in terms of achieving highest system reliability (with hardware faults only), is to assign all the used processors to a single duplex group.

8.4 Issues in Backward Recovery

We consider two special issues in backward recovery: One is the storage of checkpoints and the other is the checkpointing method itself.

8.4.1 Storage of checkpoints

Normally checkpoints should be saved in stable storage. Because there are many ways to implement stable storage, the storage of checkpoints differs from application to application. Bowen and Pradhan [8] considered two efficient ways of storing and retrieving *checkpoint data*. In [8] checkpoint data contain checkpoints and *active data* include regular data.

A *leveled* scheme is used that contains a single mapping for the memory hierarchy: register and cache (level 1), memory (level 2), and disk (level 3). This requires the upper levels of memory to hold the modified data while the changes are not yet reflected at the lower levels. Clearly, active data cannot be put into a lower level than the one where checkpoint data are stored. Possible assignments include:

1. Store active data at level 1 (register and cache) and checkpoint data at level 2 (memory) and level 3 (disk).

2. Store active data at level 1 and level 2 and checkpoint data at level 3.

In the *cache-based checkpoints* [8] active data are stored at CPU registers and cache and checkpoint data are stored in main memory. Checkpoint and rollback requirements are the following:

Checkpoint:

- Save the local state (CPU registers) to a special memory save area.

- Flush the modified cache lines to main memory.

Rollback:

- Load the CPU registers from the special memory save area.

- Invalidate all modified lines in the cache.

One important issue is the frequency of flushing the modified cache lines to keep cache and memory consistent. In a *write-through* cache this flushing is done instantly when the cache copy is modified. In a *write-back* cache this update is done when the cache is copied back because of cache miss. The write-back offers a quick recovery since memory will not need to be undone in the event of a processor failure. The presence of caches may cause different copies of the same piece of data resulting in cache and memory incoherence. The incoherence problem can be handled by either *invalidate* (the other copies) or *write-update* (by updating the other copies). Details of these two approaches are beyond the scope of this book.

The above cache-based checkpoint approach cannot control checkpoint frequency, because checkpoint frequency depends on the size of cache and cache hit ratio. In a *dual* scheme there is a mapping of two pieces of data called active and checkpoint to the same level in the memory hierarchy. These two copies are also called twin pages and they switch roles when a new checkpoint is made. That is, active data become checkpoint data and checkpoint data become active data. Possible assignments include:

1. Store both active and checkpoint data at one single level such as level 2 or level 3.

2. Store both active and checkpoint data at several adjacent levels such as from level 1 to level 3 or from level 2 to level 3.

8.4.2 Checkpointing methods

Suppose that each process periodically checkpoints its state on stable storage and processes establish checkpoints independently. A global state is defined as a collection of local states (checkpoints), one from each local process. Two undesirable situations can occur:

- *Lost message.* The state of process P_i indicates that it has sent a message m to process P_j. P_j has no record of receiving this message.

- *Orphan message.* The state of process P_j is such that it has received a message m from the process P_i but the state of the process P_i is such that it has never sent the message m to P_j.

A lost message may or may not correspond to a real loss of message m (because of failure of communication links). The message may still be in transit. The cause can be the improper setting of checkpoints of P_i and P_j in a global state formation. Another case occurs when P_j crashes after it has received message m but before the next checkpoint (see Figure 8.2 (a) by ignoring the receiver log). An orphan message can be caused by a failure. For example, P_i fails after sending message m and is rolled back to its prior checkpoint. In this case the receipt of m is recorded in P_j but the sending of m is not recorded in P_i (Figure 8.2 (b) by ignoring the sender log). In order to avoid an orphan message, P_j rolls back to a prior checkpoint to erase its memory of the orphan message. However, it may happen that, between its prior checkpoint and the current one (also called the latest checkpoint), P_j sends P_i another message n which is now an orphan (assume that P_i received n before the current checkpoint shown in Figure 8.2). Therefore, P_i needs to rollback further. This effect, where rolling back one process causes one or more other processes to roll back, is known as the *domino effect* (see Figure 8.3). It is clear that there is a need for coordination among the processes either at the time of establishing checkpoints or at the beginning of a recovery.

A strongly consistent set of checkpoints consists of a set of local checkpoints such that there is no orphan or lost message. A consistent set of checkpoints consists of a set of local checkpoints such that there is no orphan message. Obviously a strongly consistent set of checkpoints consists of a set of local checkpoints such that no information flow takes place between any pair of processes during the interval spanned by the checkpoints. If every process takes a checkpoint after sending a message, the set of the most recent checkpoints is always consistent, because the latest checkpoint at each process corresponds to a state where all the messages recorded as receive have already been recorded elsewhere as send. Therefore, rolling back a process to its latest checkpoint will not cause any orphan message. However, it is normally not strongly consistent.

Checkpointing can be either synchronous, asynchronous, or a combination of both. Another choice is whether or not to log messages that a processor sends or receives.

Synchronous checkpointing

The processes involved coordinate their local checkpointing actions to ensure all recent checkpoints be consistent. It is difficult to enforce all processes to take checkpoints at the same time. Two phases, *tentative* and *permanent* checkpoints, are used in [33]. Tentative checkpoints can

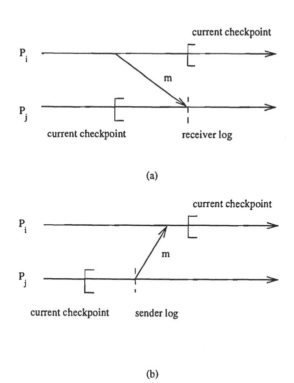

FIGURE 8.2
(a) An example of a lost message. (b) An example of an orphan message.

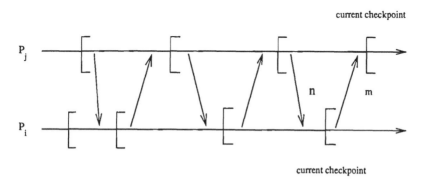

FIGURE 8.3
An example of domino effect.

either be made permanent checkpoints or undone in the second phase while permanent checkpoints cannot be undone.

There are several issues in synchronous checkpointing. Only the most recent consistent set of checkpoints needs to be maintained. It is required to keep a minimum number of processes in a consistent set. There is no need to include two independent processes in the set. More specifically, a processor P_i needs to take a checkpoint only if there is another process P_j that has taken a checkpoint that includes the receipt of a message from P_i and P_i has not recorded the sending of this message. In this way no orphan message will be generated and resultant checkpoints are consistent, but may or may not be strongly consistent.

Asynchronous checkpointing

Each process takes its checkpoints independently without any coordination. Finding the most recent consistent set of checkpoints depends on the way orphan messages are detected. The existence of orphan messages is discovered by comparing the number of messages sent and received. A consistent set of local states is identified when the number of messages received agrees with the number of messages sent for any pair of processes.

More formally, an *interval dependence graph* defines dependence relationships between intervals of different processes (or processors). An interval is the time between receiving two consecutive messages. The interval dependence graph can be easily captured by the vector clock associated with each process. A set of checkpoints (with vector clock LC_i at process i) are consistent iff there do not exist i and j such that $LC_i \leq LC_j$. Note that condition $LC_i \leq LC_j$ corresponds to an orphan message between P_i and P_j.

Hybrid checkpointing

This approach makes better use of both synchronous and asynchronous approaches. Synchronous checkpoints are established in a longer period while asynchronous checkpoints are used in a shorter period. That is, within a synchronous period there are several asynchronous periods. Therefore, we have a controlled rollback without introducing too much overhead in establishing checkpoints.

A similar approach called *quasi-synchronous checkpointing* [44] preserves process autonomy by allowing processes to take checkpoints asynchronously and uses communication-induced checkpoint coordination for the progression of the recovery line which helps to bound rollback propagation during a recovery.

Logging messages

In order to minimize the amount of computation undone during a roll back, all incoming and outcoming messages can be logged. The former is called a *receiver log* and the latter a *sender log*.

Receiver logs at P_j help to reduce rollback at P_j by replaying incoming messages after a checkpoint is restored to a consistent state where no orphan messages are received but all required messages have been sent. In Figure 8.2 (a) the set of current checkpoints of P_i and P_j will be consistent if a receiver log of message m is taken at P_j. Once the current checkpoint of P_j is restored after a failure, the incoming message m can be replayed from the log at P_j.

Sender logs at P_i can provide rollback-free recovery as long as other processors do not fail at the same time. In Figure 8.2 (b) if P_i fails after sending message m, once the current checkpoint of P_i is restored it remembers that it sent message m based on the sender log. Therefore, there is no need to send again. If receiver P_j fails and there is no receiver log, it can still recover and obtain the message from the sender log.

Normally all message-logging-based recovery methods require the process under consideration be deterministic; otherwise, the messages in a log may not be consistent with the one after re-running the process. A more efficient logging called *adaptive logging* can be found in [10].

Checkpointing has been used to tolerate fault, to balance system workload, and to do many other functions [64]. Another major concern in checkpointing is to minimize the cost of checkpointing. The cost of checkpointing includes the interval between two consecutive checkpoints and the amount of data to be saved. The cost of checkpointing can be reduced either by latency hiding techniques or by memory exclusion techniques.

Several efficient implementation techniques [15], [49] have been proposed to minimize the overhead of checkpointing to a few percent of the execution time. A portable checkpointing scheme has been reported in [54] where checkpointing and recovery can be performed on different processor architectures and operating system configurations.

8.5 Handling of Byzantine Faults

In the fail-stop model we assume that a processor stops functioning and never resumes its operation. In other cases a fault may act maliciously. For example, a faulty processor may send different messages to different processors to confuse them. This type of fault is called a *Byzantine fault*. One important application is the *agreement protocol* in which a set of processes needs to agree on a common decision where processes in the system under consideration exhibit Byzantine faults. Again, we assume that each process runs on a distinct processor and we use the terms process and processor interchangeably.

8.5.1   Agreement protocols in synchronous systems

Consider the following simple decentralized decision algorithm:

- Each participant sends its local decision (a Boolean value) to all the other participants.

- A decision is made by each participant based on its local value and the values received from all the other participants (usually the decision is a *majority voting*).

Figure 8.4 shows an example with four participants who can send their local decisions directly to others. If the only failed node P_1 is fail-stop, all the healthy nodes (P_2, P_3 and P_4) can still reach a correct consensus T through a majority voting at their respective sites (Figure 8.4 (a)) assuming that P_2 and P_4 pick T and P_3 selects F. Symbol - represents an arbitrary decision. If the failed node P_1 acts maliciously and sends different values (as its local value) to different healthy nodes, the healthy nodes may not reach a consensus as shown in Figure 8.4 (b). Note that we only show that this particular protocol does not work; later we will demonstrate that there is no protocol to ensure a consensus among the healthy processes in a 3-process system with one process acting maliciously.

The study of the effect of malicious faults was first discussed in [47] and later formalized by [34] as the *Byzantine generals problem*. Several divisions of the Byzantine army camp outside an enemy camp with each division commanded by its own general. Generals from different divisions communicate only through messengers and some of the generals may be traitors. After observing the enemy camp the generals must decide on a common battle plan and an algorithm must be designed to meet the following two requirements:

1. All loyal generals decide on the same plan of action, and

2. A small number of traitors cannot cause the loyal generals to adopt a wrong plan.

		receiver			
		P_1^*	P_2	P_3	P_4
sender	P_1^*	–	–	–	–
	P_2	T	T	T	T
	P_3	F	F	F	F
	P_4	T	T	T	T
decision		–	T	T	T

(a)

		receiver			
		P_1^*	P_2	P_3	P_4
sender	P_1^*	T	F	F	T
	P_2	T	T	T	T
	P_3	F	F	F	F
	P_4	T	T	T	T
decision		–	T	F	T

(b)

FIGURE 8.4
Two results under different fault assumptions: (a) fail-stop fauls
and (b) Byzantine faults.

More formally, an agreement protocol is correct if the following conditions
are met:

- *Consistency.* All (correct) processes agree on the same value and all
  decisions are final.

- *Validity.* The value agreed upon by the processes must have been
  some (correct) process' input.

- *Termination.* Each process decides on a value within a finite number
  of steps.

8.5.2 Agreement with one sender

Let us start with a simpler requirement: Every nonfaulty process in the
system uses the same value from process P_i for decision making. In this way
the general problem of consensus is reduced to an agreement by processes
in a system on the value for a particular process, say P_0. More formally:

- All nonfaulty processes use the same value v_0 for process P_0.

- If the sending process P_0 is nonfaulty, then every nonfaulty process uses the value P_0 sends.

This requirement is called *interactive consistency*. The difficulty in achieving the above requirement is that information sent by a process to another cannot be trusted. Therefore, to agree on a value sent by a process, besides getting the value from that process, the values received by other processes are also needed to verify the original value. However, those forwarding processes may also be faulty. Their messages also need to be verified. In [47] it has been proved that consensus can be reached in the presence of k faulty nodes only if the total number of the processes is at least $3k + 1$. We assume that each nonfaulty process executes the protocol correctly; a faulty process can behave in any manner. Also, each message sent by a process is delivered correctly to the receiver by the message system; that is, the communication is reliable. The message receiver knows which process has sent the message. The absence of a message can be detected typically through a timeout. A default value is used at the receiver in this case.

The protocol works in $k + 1$ rounds of message exchange between processes. In the first round the sender (initiator) sends its message to $n - 1$ processes. Since each receiver cannot trust the value it receives, it has to collect values received by other receivers. That is, each receiver P_i acts as a sender and forwards the message (received at round 1) to all the other processes except the original sender and itself, i.e., $n - 2$ copies are sent. However, each message in round 2 still cannot be trusted like the ones in round 1. Therefore, round 3 is needed. A majority of the values (one from process P_i in round 2 and $n - 3$ messages from other processes in round 3) is taken to determine the value sent by process P_i in round 2. At the kth round each receiver sends the value of this round only to those receivers who have not been the transmitters of this particular message. Therefore, each message is attached with a list S of transmitters.

This recursive process continues until reaching the $(k + 1)$th round. An intuitive explanation is that there are at most k faults, i.e., up to k messages at different rounds cannot be trusted. The reason for $3k+1$ processes is that in the last round the number of processes involved is $(3k + 1) - k = 2k + 1$. In the worst case when all the faulty processes are still in this group, a majority of processes are fault-free.

The interactive consistency algorithm IC [34] is as follows:

IC(l), where $l < k$ and initially $l = 0$ and $S = \{\}$.

1. The sender sends its value with transmitter list S to all the other processes, $(n - 1 - l)$ in total.

2. Let v_i be the value process P_i received from the sender or a default value is used if no value is received. Process P_i acts as the sender in $IC(l + 1 \neq k)$ to send value v_i together with transmitter list $S \cup \{P_i\}$ to each of the other $n - 2 - l$ processes not in the transmitter list. If $l + 1 = k$, $IC(k)$ is called.

3. For each process P_i, let v_j be the value received by process P_j (but forwarded from P_j to P_i). Node P_i uses the value $majority(v_j)$ where $j \notin S$.

$IC(k)$

1. The transmitter sends its value to all the other $n - 1$ processes.

2. Each process uses the value it receives from the sender or uses the default value if it receives no value.

Consider an example of seven processes P_i, $0 \leq i \leq 6$. Assume that $k = 2$ (up to two faults) and $n = 7$ in this case. P_0 is the sender. Let m be the original message and m_i the message received by P_i (from P_0) at round 1. However, each m_i cannot be trusted and it needs to be verified against m_j ($i \neq j$). For example, to verify m_1, P_1 collects six messages $m_{21}, m_{31}, m_{41}, m_{51}, m_{61}$, where m_{21} means that a copy of m_2 is forwarded from P_2 to P_1. However, each m_{i1} still cannot be trusted and needs to be compared against the ones sent from P_i to P_j, $j \neq 1$. For example, m_{21} needs to be compared with m_{231} (and m_2 sent from P_2 to P_3 and then forwarded to P_1), m_{241}, m_{251}, and m_{261}. The recursion ends here and the updated m_{21} (called m'_{21}) is set to be $majority(m_{21}, m_{231}, m_{241}, m_{251}, m_{261})$. Similarly, m_{31} (called m'_{31}) can be updated in the same way, i.e., by $majority(m_{31}, m_{321}, m_{341}, m_{351}, m_{361})$, and the same process for the others. Then the recursion goes back to round 1; m_1 is updated (called m'_1) to $majority(m_1, m'_{21}, m'_{31}, m'_{41}, m'_{51}, m'_{61})$.

In the above algorithm the total number of message exchanges is $(n - 1)(n - 2)...(n - k - 1)$ which has a complexity of $O(n^k)$, since k can be $(n-1)/3$. However, it is possible to trade the number of rounds for message complexity as discussed in [13]. Garay and Moses [5] proposed the first polynomial Byzantine agreement protocol for $n > 3k$ processors in $k + 1$ rounds.

8.5.3 Agreement with many senders

The *interactive consistency* [34] for one sender can be easily extended to many senders by a simple replication of the protocol for each sender. It has been shown that the problem is solvable for and only for $n \geq 3k+1$ where k is the number of traitors and n is the total number of generals. Algorithms to solve this problem need at least k rounds of information exchange [12].

The following algorithm [34] shows how to tolerate one fault through two rounds of information exchange with $n = 4$ and $k = 1$:

1. Each process (on its own PE) sends its local value to the other three processes.

2. Each process sends the information it has obtained in the first round to all the other processes.

3. Each process applies a decision process (majority voting) to its private value and the values received in the above two steps.

In Table 8.2 [66] v_i is the private value of process P_i and v_i^k (with superscript k) represents different types of faulty value. Symbol - represents an empty value. Without loss of generality, P_1 is assumed to be a traitor who acts in a malicious way by sending different values to other P_i's. The result vector for each general is derived by applying a majority voting to each column of the four vectors received in these two rounds. The result vectors for P_2, P_3 and P_4 are the same which is (v_1^8, v_2, v_3, v_4) and each element except the one from v_1 corresponds to the original message. Note that v_1^8 is derived by a majority vote on v_1^1, v_1^2, and v_1^3. Therefore, all the loyal generals can reach the same decision by applying any deterministic function such as majority, mean, etc.

Note that the above interactive consistency algorithm is slightly different from the one presented in the previous section. Here a value received in round k is transmitted to all the other nodes rather than those nodes that have not been the transmitters. Also, the original value v_i does not participate in the final majority voting at each P_i. One can easily show that the algorithm in the previous section also works for this example.

Fisher, Lynch, and Merritt [18] gave a simple proof that, with three processes and at most one possible faulty process, the other two processes cannot agree on their decisions. Figure 8.5 shows three cases. In scenario 1, P_1 is faulty and P_2 and P_3 start with the same input value 0. By the validity condition the algorithm should ensure that P_2 and P_3 both decide on value 0. In case 2, P_2 is faulty, P_1 starts with 1, and P_3 starts with 0.

$P1^*$	$P2$	$P3$	$P4$
first round:			
$(-, v_2, v_3, v_4)$	$(v_1^2, -, v_3, v_4)$	$(v_1^1, v_2, -, v_4)$	$(v_1^3, v_2, v_3, -)$
second round:			
$(v_1^2, -, v_3, v_4)$	$(v_1^1, v_2, -, v_4)$	$(v_1^2, -, v_3, v_4)$	$(v_1^2, -, v_3, v_4)$
$(v_1^1, v_2, -, v_4)$	$(v_1^3, v_2, v_3, -)$	$(v_1^3, v_2, v_3, -)$	$(v_1^1, v_2, -, v_4)$
$(v_1^3, v_2, v_3, -)$	$(-, v_2^4, v_3^4, v_4^4)$	$(-, v_2^5, v_3^5, v_4^5)$	$(-, v_2^6, v_3^6, v_4^6)$
result vectors:			
$(v_1^7, v_2^7, v_3^7, v_4^7)$	(v_1^8, v_2, v_3, v_4)	(v_1^8, v_2, v_3, v_4)	(v_1^8, v_2, v_3, v_4)

Table 8.2 An algorithm for reaching agreement.

If P_2 sends the same message to P_3 as it did in case 1, P_3 will see the same situation as in case 1. Therefore, the algorithm must decide on value 0. In case 3, P_3 is faulty and both P_1 and P_2 start with 1. If P_3 sends the same messages to P_1 as it has done in case 2, then P_1 sees the same situation as in case 2. Again, the algorithm must decide on value 0. However, the two nonfaulty processors both have an input value of 1 so the decision of 0 violates the validity condition. This proves that consensus is impossible.

8.5.4 Agreement under different models

The agreement problem discussed in the above subsection assumes that the system is synchronous. A system is synchronous if all processors proceed at predictable speeds. Formally, processors are synchronous iff there exists a constant $s \geq 1$ such that for every $s+1$ steps taken by any processor, every other processor will have taken at least one step; otherwise, the system is asynchronous. Fisher, Lynch, and Paterson [17] showed that agreement cannot be achieved in an asynchronous distributed system. Since then many researches have been conducted on the problem under various failure and synchrony assumptions.

Turek and Shasha [62] considered the following parameters (represented by a Boolean variable) for the agreement problem.

- The system can be either synchronous ($A = 1$) or asynchronous ($A = 0$).

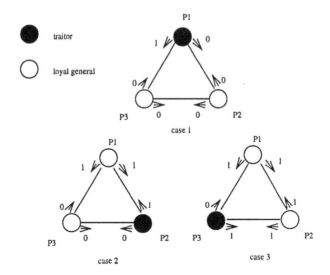

FIGURE 8.5
Cases leading to failure of the Byzantine agreement.

- Communication delay can be either bounded ($B = 1$) or unbounded ($B = 0$).

- Messages can be either ordered ($C = 1$) or unordered ($C = 0$).

- The transmission mechanism can be either point-to-point ($D = 0$) or broadcast ($D = 1$).

A *Karnaugh map* (*K*-map) can be constructed for the agreement problem (see Table 8.3). Minimizing the above Boolean function we have the following expression for the conditions under which consensus is possible:

$$AB + AC + CD = True$$

The three product terms correspond to the following three cases:

1. ($AB = 1$): Processors are synchronous and communication delay is bounded.

2. ($AC = 1$): Processors are synchronous and messages are ordered.

3. ($CD = 1$): Messages are ordered and the transmission mechanism is broadcast.

AB CD	00	01	11	10
00	0	0	1	0
01	0	0	1	0
11	1	1	1	1
10	0	0	1	1

Table 8.3 Conditions under which consensus is possible.

In all the other cases consensus is impossible. For example, consensus is impossible if $\bar{A}\bar{B}C\bar{D} = 1$, i.e., the system is asynchronous, communication is unbounded, messages are ordered, and the transmission mechanism is point-to-point.

In order to see why consensus is impossible for the above system, we consider a practical example of dating through e-mail. Suppose John in Boca Raton wants to invite Mary in Miami to a concert in Fort Lauderdale at 6:00 p.m. that night. He sent an email message at 8:00 a.m. that morning. Upon receiving John's invitation at 8:15 a.m., Mary hesitated for about two hours and then sent an acknowledgment to accept at 10:15 a.m. Once John received Mary's acknowledgment at 11:00 a.m., he may wonder "if Mary doesn't know that I received her acknowledgment, she will think that I won't wait for her because I won't risk wasting time to drive from Boca Raton to Fort Lauderdale. I'd better send an acknowledgment to her acknowledgment." If this continues, we can see that no agreement can be reached between Mary and John.

This problem can be solved if both John and Mary know the network is reliable and delay is bounded and Mary responds to the invitation within a certain time limit. The simplest solution is that John invites Mary by calling her directly since the telephone line is more reliable and with limited communication delay.

This problem can be made simpler if John just tries to let Mary know his intent through his first message. The agreement problem can be much more difficult if Mary changes her mind later and refuses to send a message.

Agreement on a shared memory can be handled by treating it as a distributed environment with broadcasting capability without ordered messages. For example, once two processors have written their messages to the shared memory there is no way for a third processor to determine which processor wrote its message first.

Several different varieties of the Byzantine generals problem have been proposed:

1. Boolean values or arbitrary real values for the decisions [14].

2. Unauthenticated or authenticated messages [34].

3. Synchronous or asynchronous [9], [14], [17].

4. Completely connected network or partially connected network [12], [34].

5. Deterministic or randomized [48], [53].

6. Byzantine faults or fail-stop faults [17].

7. Non-totally decentralized control system and, in particular, hierarchical control systems [66].

There are several other related agreement problems [42]:

- *K-agreement problem.* Instead of requiring that all participants decide exactly on the same value, decisions are limited to a small number k of distinct values.

- *Approximate agreement problem.* Instead of requiring that all participants decide exactly on the value, they agree to within a small real-valued tolerance.

Study of agreement problems has not only theoretical importance but also practical use. On the theoretical side it helps in the understanding of many basic distributed algorithms, especially spread of a wave of information. On the practical side results obtained can be used to solve the clock synchronization problem in a faulty environment and the commitment problem in distributed database systems.

See [62] for a survey on the general agreement problems in distributed systems. In the next subsection, we show one extension in which messages are authenticated.

8.5.5   Agreement with authenticated messages

In the regular agreement model a faulty receiver may forward a different value of a message. The problem becomes easier if receivers cannot tamper with the original message. This is done by adding a *digital signature* to its message. However, a faulty receiver may still send one node with the original message and send another node with a tampered message (it will be discarded at the corresponding receiver). The faulty sender may send different messages to different receivers. Each of these messages cannot be further changed without being discarded at the receivers. The key in this agreement is to collect a sufficient number of versions of the message sent from the sender.

We consider agreement with one sender in a system with k faults. Again we assume that the network itself is completely connected and reliable. Each message m is associated with a list S of transmitters (also called signatures). Each process P_i has a set V_i ({} initially) which holds incoming messages.

$P(0)::=$ **send** (signed message, $\{0\}$) **to all**
$P(i) ::= [$ **receive** (m, S) and m is not tampered $\rightarrow$
$\qquad\qquad V_i = V_i \cup m; S = S \cup \{i\};$
$\qquad\qquad |S| \leq k \rightarrow$ **send** $(m, S \cup \{i\})$ **to all**
$\qquad\qquad\qquad\qquad$ the processes not in S

$\quad]$

Note that in the above algorithm P_0 (the sender) is excluded in the process set. The final result is derived by applying a deterministic function to elements in V_i. Because V_i's at different healthy processes are the same, their final results are also the same. Note that V_i's are sets; any redundant element will be deleted. In the above algorithm condition $|S| > k$ at exit ensures that the message has been passed around more than k times to different processes. At least one of the intermediate nodes (forwarding processes) is non-faulty, i.e., a nonfaulty process must have sent the same message to all those that had not yet received it. The deterministic function can be mean, average, or max. Note that if the sender is healthy, V_i has only one value.

The above algorithm does not reduce message complexity compared to a regular agreement with one sender. However, condition $n \geq 3k + 1$ is changed to a much weaker $n \geq k + 2$. That is, the above algorithm works for any system using authenticated messages as long as there are more receivers (at least $k + 1$) than faults (k).

8.6   Handling of Communication Faults

In Chapter 7 we discussed many reliable routing algorithms that identify
a routing path by avoiding faults. Here we consider another way to achieve
reliable communication with both positive and negative acknowledgments.
This approach is done by fault detection followed by a recovery process.

The simplest way to handle communication faults is to use a timeout
mechanism with acknowledgments. In this approach a message is sent
through a selected path. If the sender does not receive an acknowledgment signal from the receiver, the sender will resend the message either
through the same path if it is suspected to be a transient fault or through
another node-disjoint path if it is suspected to be a permanent fault.

The timeout approach can be summarized and expressed in the following
algorithm in an environment with permanent faults:

$$success :=F; \ i := 1;$$
$$* [\ \neg \ success \land i < \text{number-of-node-disjoint-path} \rightarrow$$
$$[\ \text{setup} \ (t);$$
$$\text{send message } m \text{ to receiver along the } i\text{th path};$$
$$[\ \textbf{receive } ack \textbf{ from } \text{receiver} \rightarrow success := \text{T}$$
$$\Box \ \textbf{timeout} \ (t) \rightarrow i := i+1$$
$$]$$
$$]$$
$$]$$

In the above algorithm communication completes successfully if *success*
is T; otherwise, communication fails. Another approach is to send the
message along all the node-disjoint paths simultaneously. There may or
may not be an acknowledge signal sent from the receiver depending on the
requirement. A similar timeout mechanism is used in the receiver.

$$\text{sender} ::= \forall_i \ || \ \text{send message } m \text{ to receiver along the } i\text{th path}$$
$$\text{receiver} ::= * [\ \textbf{receive } \text{message } m \textbf{ from } \text{the } i\text{th path} \rightarrow$$
$$[\ \text{store message } m \text{ together with } id = i;$$
$$\text{first-time } (m) \rightarrow \text{setup } (t)$$
$$]$$
$$\Box \ \textbf{timeout} \ (t) \rightarrow$$
$$\text{decision-on (all the messages received)}$$
$$]$$

If the message will not be corrupted in transmission, the receiver can accept the first arrived message without delaying its decision (and all the subsequent messages will be discarded).

For collective communication where there is more than one destination, reliable communication is more complicated. We use broadcasting as an example. Basically, a reliable broadcasting has the following property: The broadcast message must be received by all the nodes that are healthy. Again, we use the acknowledgment protocol to implement a reliable broadcast process. Assume that a spanning tree with the source node as the root is generated. $Succ(p)$ represents the successor of node p in the spanning tree.

The algorithm works as follows: Starting from the root node the message is forwarded along the spanning tree. At intermediate node i, upon receiving a message, forwards it to all its successors $Succ(i)$ and each sends an acknowledgment back to node i. If node i does not receive an acknowledgment from one of the successors, say j, then node i takes over the responsibility of node j and forwards the message to the nodes in $Succ(i)$. Note that redundant copies may be sent (this happens when node j forwards the message to its successor before crushing), but duplicates can be detected by each receiver.

We consider an efficient reliable broadcast process called *Trans protocol* [45] that uses a combination of positive and negative acknowledgments. Assume that an application has many broadcast messages initiated from different processes in the system. By combining acknowledgment to a previous broadcast with the next broadcast, explicit acknowledgments can be reduced. The basic idea can be illustrated in the following example with three nodes:

- Node P broadcasts message m_1,

- Node Q receives message m_1 and piggybacks a positive acknowledgment on the next broadcast initiated from Q, say m_2.

- When node R receives m_2, if it has received m_1, R realizes that it does not need to send an acknowledgment since Q has acknowledged it. If R has not received m_1, it knows about this loss by the acknowledgment on m_2, and requests retransmission by sending a negative acknowledgment in the next message R broadcasts. (Note that a positive acknowledgment to m_2 will be sent at the same time.).

Let us consider an example to illustrate the above protocol. We use A, B, C, D to represent messages, a, b, c, d acknowledgments for the messages, and $\bar{a}, \bar{b}, \bar{c}, \bar{d}$ negative acknowledgments. Consider the following message sequence:

$$A, Ba, Cb, Db, Ec, F\bar{c}d, Cb, G\bar{d}ef$$

Message A is sent first, acknowledged by the sender of B, which is in turn acknowledged by the senders of C and D. Note that both senders of C and D realize they do not need to send an acknowledgment for A because the sender of B has acknowledged it. The sender of E acknowledges C and the sender of F acknowledges the receipt of D but a negative acknowledgment of C. Some node (not necessarily the original sender) retransmits C. The sender of G acknowledges both e and f but a negative acknowledgment of d (after receiving F).

There are two other types of collective communications: atomic and causality. *Atomic broadcast* requires not only that a broadcast message reaches all the nodes but also different messages sent by different nodes be delivered to all the processes in the same order. *Causal broadcast* requires both reliable and atomic. Besides, causality requires that the messages be delivered in an order that is consistent with the causality between them. The above protocol can be extended to perform atomic broadcast. This is done by constructing the sequence of messages from both positive and negative acknowledgments [45]. Causal broadcast and multicast are typically implemented with a timestamp associated with each message [7].

The handling of communication and node faults can be combined to form a more powerful model. Figure 8.6 (a) shows a model of sender and receiver. A combined active fault handling model for both communication and node is shown in Figure 8.6 (b) where all the resources have a four-fold replication. Each sender sends a copy of the message to each receiver (four in all). Each receiver exchanges messages received with each of the other three receivers.

A passive reliable sender and receiver model is shown in Figure 8.7 where each message is multicast to three processes (including the receiver) and the sender and the receiver each has a backup. In order to enforce *data consistency* at different processes the multicast must be atomic. That is, the message should be sent to all the destinations successfully or no destination receives the message.

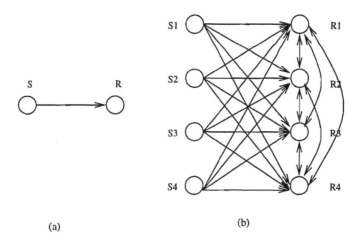

(a)

(b)

FIGURE 8.6
(a) A sender and receiver model with sender S and receiver R.
(b) An active reliable sender and receiver model.

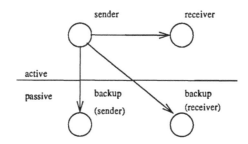

FIGURE 8.7
A passive reliable sender and receiver model.

8.7   Handling of Software Faults

Software fault tolerance is also achieved by means of redundancy: active redundancy (n-version programming) or passive redundancy (recovery blocks):

- *N-version programming* [4]. Several independently-developed software versions are executed concurrently at different PEs; a final decision algorithm (e.g., majority voting) outputs the current result.

- *Recovery blocks* [55]. Several independently-developed software versions are executed sequentially at the same PE (can be on different PEs). Before execution of the first (primary) version the state of the computation is saved in a *recovery point*. At the completion of the block an acceptance test is applied. If this test fails, the recovery point is used to restart the failed computation and an alternative version is then executed. This continues until the acceptance test succeeds or the computation fails.

Both n-version programming and recovery blocks are only for sequential applications. The distributed execution of recovery blocks has been studied by [31] where the primary and alternate versions run at the same time on different processors and their roles can be switched. More specifically, the primary version is executed on the primary node and the alternate version is executed on a backup node. Both nodes receive the input data simultaneously (from the previous computation) and execute their versions concurrently. The results of each version are checked at its local node. If the primary version passes the test, it will forward its results to the next computation; otherwise, the alternative version will be informed (the failure of the primary version) and it will send out its results provided these results have passed the test. There is a watchdog at the backup node and it will take the rule of the primary node if it does not generate results within the time limit. In the subsequent discussion we concentrate only on software fault tolerance schemes for a set of communicating sequential processes. The *conversation* [55] is one of the most promising methods for designing reliable concurrent software.

The conversation is a language construct that is a concurrent generalization of the recovery block [22] used in sequential software and defined as an atomic action [40] for a set of communicating processes. The reason for the use of conversations is to prevent the domino effect [55]. A conversation

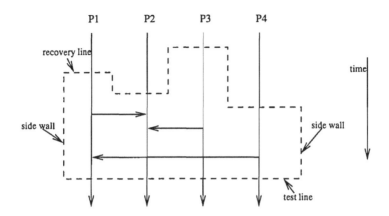

FIGURE 8.8
The boundaries of a conversation.

involves two or more processes and constitutes an atomic action enclosed by a set of boundaries. The boundaries of a conversation consist of a recovery line, a test line and two side walls (Figure 8.8). A *recovery line* is a set of recovery points that are established before any process communication. A *test line* is the correlated set of the acceptance tests of the interacting processes. Two *side walls* prevent the processes within a conversation from interacting with processes outside the conversation. A conversation is successful only if all its processes pass their acceptance tests at the test line. If any of the acceptance tests fail, all the processes within the conversation go back to the recovery line (recovery to the previous state by replacing necessary variables with the ones saved in the recovery points) and retry using their alternate try blocks.

There are several modifications in the concept of conversation such as *colloquy* [19] which is an extension of the conversation, and the *consensus recovery block* [59] which combines the ideas of n-version programming [4] and conversation. A system structure for conversations in real-time applications is discussed in [3].

Fault tolerant software approaches require the users to write versions which should be as different as possible to avoid *correlated faults*, where all or most versions fail with the same input value. These approaches are: (1) different programming teams [32], (2) different problem specifications [27], (3) different programming languages [52], and (4) different programming paradigms [16]. Systematic studies on software design diversity are discussed in [28].

Another important aspect in the design of conversations is to define their boundaries. This is an example of implementing an atomic action. The key is to ensure that internal changes are not visible from the outside, and vice versa. Generally these boundaries can be determined *a priori* or dynamically. Dynamic boundary decision methods [30] suffer from the problem of recovery points overhead, especially in a system with many interprocess communications. These methods define the boundaries atomically regardless of the function. Therefore, they cannot define conversations based on the criticality of each function in the system. The main drawback is, although they can dynamically define boundaries, new versions must be defined statically. Therefore the *a priori* method is preferable.

Tyrrell [63] used Petri nets to identify the states of a system where one statement in application programs corresponds to one transition in a Petri net; the conversation boundary is then decided from the state reachability tree of the system. There are several problems with this method: (1) There are no systematic ways of identifying the states. This can result in a too large Petri net graph which is a serious problem, especially in a complex system. (2) Since the state reachability tree only provides one of the interleaving views of the system, some information is lost; the consequence is that some possible conversation boundaries cannot be determined. (3) The Petri net graph of the system is derived from an algorithm implemented in the Occam language (derived from CSP). It is better to decide conversation boundaries before implementation.

In [65] Wu and Fernandez studied a systematic way of identifying the state to alleviate the first problem. In this method Petri net transitions are defined only for input and output statements in application programs. This method not only reduces the size of the Petri net but also reduces the number of steps needed to derive conversation boundaries from the application program. The last two problems have been addressed in [67] in which Wu and Fernandez proposed a novel boundary decision method: The problem specification is described by a high level modified Petri net. This specification can be easily transformed into a state model called an *action-ordered tree*. The conversation boundaries are then determined from this tree. It is proved that the method proposed is complete in the sense that all the possible boundaries can be determined and has the merit of simplicity. Studies have already been done on the unification of software and hardware faults. See [39] and [68] for details.

Several implementations of the conversation structure have been proposed using monitors [29] and CSP-like structures [26].

References

[1] Allchin, J. E., "An architecture for reliable decentralized systems", Ph.D. dissertation, School of Info. and Computer Science, Georgia Inst. of Tech., Sept. 1983.

[2] Alvarez, G. A., W. A. Burkhard, and F. Cristian, "Tolerating multiple failures in RAID architectures with optimal storage and uniform declustering", *Proc. of the 24th Annual Int'l Symp. on Computer Architecture*, 1997, 62-72.

[3] Anderson, T. and J. C. Knight, "A framework for software fault tolerance in real-time systems", *IEEE Transactions on Software Engineering*, **9**, 3, May 1983, 355-364.

[4] Avizienis, A., "The N-version approach to fault-tolerant software", *IEEE Transactions on Software Engineering*, **13**, 12, Dec. 1985, 1491-1510.

[5] Bernstein, P. A., "Sequoia: A fault-tolerant tightly coupled multiprocessor for transaction processing", *Computer*, **21**, 2, Feb. 1988, 37-45.

[6] Birman, K. P. and T. A. Joseph, "Reliable communication in the presence of failure", *ACM Transactions on Computer Systems*, **5**, 1, Feb. 1987, 47-76.

[7] Bowen, N. S. and D. K. Pradhan, "Processor- and memory-based checkpoint and rollback recovery", *IEEE Computers*, **26**, 2, Feb. 1993, 22-30.

[8] Bracha, G. and S. Toueg, "Asynchronous consensus and broadcast protocols", *Journal of the ACM*, **32**, 4, Oct. 1985, 824-840.

[9] Chow, R. and T. Johnson, *Distributed Operating Systems and Algorithms*, Addison-Wesley Publishing Company, 1997.

[10] Cristian, F., "Understanding fault-tolerant distributed systems", *Communications of the ACM*, **34**, 2, Feb. 1991, 57-78.

[11] Dolev, D. N., "The Byzantine generals strike again", *Journal of Algorithms*, **3**, 1, Jan. 1982, 14-30.

[12] Dolev, D. N. and H. Strong, "Authenticated algorithms for Byzantine agreement", *SIAM Journal of Computing*, **12**, 4, Nov. 1983, 656-666.

[13] Dolev, D. N., A. Lynch, S. S. Printer, E. W. Stork, and W. E. Weihl, "Reaching approximate agreement in the presence of faults", *Journal of the ACM*, **33**, 3, July 1986, 499-516.

[14] Elnozahy, E. N., D. B. Johnson, and W. Zwaenepoel, "The performance of consistent checkpointing", *IEEE Symp. on Reliable and Distributed Systems*, 1992, 39-47.

[15] Fernandez, E. B. and M. H. Fernandez, "Fault-tolerant parallel algorithms", *Proc. of IEEE Southeastcon '91*, 1991, 466-469.

[16] Fisher, M. J., N. A. Lynch, and M. S. Paterson, "Impossibility of distributed consensus with one faulty process", *Journal of the ACM*, **32**, 2, Apr. 1985, 374-382.

[17] Fisher, M. J., N. A. Lynch, and M. Merritt, "Easy impossibility proofs for distributed consensus problems", *Distributed Computing*, **1**, Jan. 1986, 26-39.

[18] Garay, J. A. and Y. Moses, "Fully polynomial Byzantine agreement for $n > 3t$ processors in $t + 1$ rounds", *SIAM Journal on Computing*, **27**, 1, Feb. 1998, 247-290.

[19] Gregory, S. T. and J. C. Knight, "A new linguistic approach to backward error recovery", *Proc. of 13th Int'l Symp. on Fault-Tolerant Computing*, 1985, 404-409.

[20] Gregory, S. T. and J. C. Knight, "Concurrent system recovery", in *Dependability of Resilient Computers*, T. Anderson, ed., BSP Professional books, 1989, 167-190.

[21] Heimann, D. I., N. Mittal, and K. S. Trivedi, "Availability and reliability modeling for computer systems", in *Advances in Computers*, **31**, M.C. Yovits, ed., Academic Press, Inc., 1990, 176-235.

[22] Horning, J. J., H. C. Lauer, P. M. Melliar-Smith, and B. Randall, "A program structure for error detection and recovery", *Proc. of Conf. on Operating Systems: Theoretical and Practical Aspects*, IRIA, 1974, 177-193.

[23] Huang, K., J. Wu, and E. B. Fernandez, "A generalized forward recovery checkpointing scheme", in *Parallel and Distributed Processing*, J. Rolim, ed., LNCS 1388, Springer-Verlag, 1998, 623-643.

[24] Jalote, P., "Fault tolerant processes", *Distributed Computing*, **3**, 1989, 187-195.

[25] Jalote, P., *Fault Tolerance in Distributed Systems*, Prentice Hall, Inc., 1994.

[26] Jalote, P. and R. H. Campbell, "Atomic actions for fault-tolerance using CSP", *IEEE Transactions on Software Engineering*, **12**, 1, Jan. 1986, 59-68.

[27] Kelly, J. P. J. and A. Avizienis, "A specification-oriented multi-version software experiment", *Proc. of the 13th Int'l Symp. on Fault-Tolerant Computing*, 1983, 120-126.

[28] Kelly, J. P. J., "Software design diversity", in *Dependability of Resilient Computers*, T. Anderson, ed., BSP Professional Books, 1989.

[29] Kim, K. H., "Approaches to mechanization of the conversation scheme based on monitors", *IEEE Transactions on Software Engineering*, **8**, 5, May 1993, 189-197.

[30] Kim, K. H., J. H. You, and A. Abouelnaga, "A scheme for coordinated execution of independently designed recoverable distributed process", *Proc. of the 16th Int'l Symp. on Fault-Tolerant Computing*, 1986, 130-135.

[31] Kim, K. H. and H. O. Welch, "Distributed execution of recovery blocks: an approach for uniform treatment of hardware and software faults in real-time applications", *IEEE Transactions on Computers*, **38**, 5, May 1989, 626-636.

[32] Knight, J. C. and N. G. Levenson, "An experimental evaluation of the assumption of independence in multiversion programming", *IEEE Transactions on Software Engineering*, **12**, 1, Jan. 1986, 96-109.

[33] Koo, R. and S. Toueg, "Checkpointing and rollback recovery for distributed systems", *IEEE Transactions on Software Engineering*, **13**, 1, Jan. 1987, 23-31.

[34] Lamport, L., R. Shostak, and M. Pease, "The Byzantine generals problem", *ACM Transactions Program Language System*, **4**, 2, 1982, 382-401.

[35] Lampson, B. W. and H. E. Sturgis, "Crash recovery in a distributed storage system", unpublished report, Computer Science Laboratory, Xerox Palo Alto Research Center, Palo Alto, Ca, 1976.

[36] Lampson, B. W., "Atomic transactions", in *Distributed Systems – Architecture and Implementations,* B. W. Lampson, M. Paul, and H. J. Sieger, ed., Springer-Verlag, 1981, 246-265.

[37] Laprie, J. C., "Dependable computing and fault tolerance: concepts and terminology", *Proc. of the 15th Int'l Symp. on Fault-Tolerant Computing,* 1985, 2-11.

[38] Laprie, J. C., "Dependability: a unifying concept for reliable computing and fault tolerance", in *Dependability of Resilient Computers,* T. Anderson, ed., BSP Professional Books, 1989, 1-28.

[39] Laprie, J. C., J. Arlat, C. Beounes, and K. Kanoun, "Definition and analysis of hardware and software fault-tolerant architectures", *IEEE Computers,* **23**, 7, July 1990, 39-51.

[40] Lomet, D. B., "Process structuring, synchronization, and recovery using atomic actions", *Proc. of ACM Conf. on Language Design for Reliable Software, SIGPLAN Notices,* **12**, 3, 1977, 128-137.

[41] Long, J., W. K. Fuchs, and J. A. Abraham, "Forward recovery using checkpointing in parallel systems", *Proc. of Int'l Conf. on Parallel Processing,* 1992, I 272-I 275.

[42] Lynch, N. A., *Distributed Algorithms,* Morgan Kaufmann Publishing, Inc., 1996.

[43] Mancini, L. V. and S. K. Shrivastava, "Replication within atomic actions and conversations: a case study in fault-tolerance duality", *Proc. of the 19th Int'l Symp. on Fault-Tolerant Computing,* 1989, 454-461.

[44] Manivannnan, D. and M. Singhal, "A low-overhead recovery technique using quasi-synchronous checkpointing", *Proc. of the 1996 IEEE 16th Int'l Conf. on Distributed Computing Systems,* 1996, 100-107.

[45] Melliar-Smith, P. M., L. E. Moser, and V. Agrawala, "Broadcast protocols for distributed systems", *IEEE Transactions on Parallel and Distributed Systems,* **1**, 1, Jan. 1990, 17-25.

[46] Patterson, D. A., G. Gibson, and R. H. Katz, "A case for redundant arrays of inexpensive disks (RAID)", *Proc. of ACM SIGMOD,* 1988, 109-116.

[47] Pease, M., R. Shostak, and L. Lamport, " Reaching agreement in the presence of faults", *Journal of the ACM,* **14**, 1, Jan. 1988, 30-37.

[48] Perry, K. J., "Randomized Byzantine agreement", *IEEE Transactions on Software Engineering*, **11**, 6, June 1985, 539-546.

[49] Plank, J. S., M. Beck, G. Kingsley, and K. Li, "Libckpt: Transparent checkpointing under Unix", *Proc. of USENIX Winter 1995 Technical Conf.*, 1995, 213-223.

[50] Pradhan, D. K. and N. H. Vaidya, "Roll-forward checkpointing scheme: concurrent retry with nondedicated spares", *Proc. of Workshop Fault-Tolerant Parallel and Distributed Systems*, 1992, 166-174.

[51] Preparata, F. P., G. Metze, and R. T. Chien, "On the connection assignment problem of diagnosable systems", *IEEE Transactions on Computers*, **16**, 6, Dec. 1967, 848-854.

[52] Purtilo, J. M. and P. Jalote, "A system for supporting multi-language versions for software fault-tolerance", *Proc. of the 19th Int'l Symp. on Fault-Tolerant Computing*, 1989, 268-274.

[53] Rabin, M., "Randomized Byzantine generals", *Proc. of the 24th Symp. on Foundations of Computer Science*, 1983, 403-409.

[54] Ramkumar, B. and V. Strumpen, "Portable checkpointing for heterogeneous architectures", *Proc. of the 27th Int'l Symp. on Fault-Tolerant Computing*, 1997, 58-67.

[55] Randell, B., "System structure for software fault tolerance", *IEEE Transactions on Software Engineering*, **1**, 2, June 1975, 221-232.

[56] Schneider, F. B., "Byzantine generals in action: implementing fail-stop processors", *ACM Transactions on Computer Systems*, **2**, 2, May 1984, 145-154.

[57] Schneider, F. B., D. Gries, and R. D. Schlichting, "Fault-tolerant broadcasts", *Science of Computer Programming*, 4, 1984, 1-15.

[58] Schlichting, R. D. and F. B. Schneider, "Fail stop processors: An approach to designing fault-tolerant computing systems", *ACM Transactions on Computer Systems*, **1**, 3, Aug. 1983, 222-238.

[59] Scott, R. K. et al., "The consensus recovery block", *Proc. of the Total Sys. Reliability Symp.*, 1983, 74-85.

[60] Shrivastava, S. K., "Structuring distributed systems for recoverability and crash resistance", *IEEE Transactions on Software Engineering*, **7**, 7, July 1981, 436-447.

[61] Svobodova, L., "Resilient distributed computing", *IEEE Transactions on Software Engineering*, **10**, 5, May 1984, 257-268.

[62] Turek, J. and D. Shasha, "The many faces of consensus in distributed systems", *IEEE Computers*, June 1992, 8-17.

[63] Tyrrell, A. H. and D. J. Holding, "Design of reliable software in distributed systems using the conversation scheme", *IEEE Transactions on Software Engineering*, **12**, 9, Sept. 1986, 921-928.

[64] Wang, Y. -M, Y. Huang, K. -P. Vo, P. Y. Chuang, and C. Kintala, "Checkpointing and its applications", *Prof. of the 25th Int'l Symp. on Fault-Tolerant Computing*, 1995, 22-30.

[65] Wu, J. and E. B. Fernandez, "A simplification of a conversation design scheme using Petri nets", *IEEE Transactions on Software Engineering*, **15**, 5, May 1989, 658-660.

[66] Wu, J. and E. B. Fernandez, "The design of decentralized control algorithms in distributed systems", *Proc. of ISMM Int'l Conf. on Intelligent Distributed Processes*, 1989, 84-97.

[67] Wu, J. and E. B. Fernandez, "Using Petri nets for fault-tolerance in concurrent software", *IEEE Transactions on Parallel and Distributed Systems*, **5**, 10, Oct. 1994, 1106-1112.

[68] Wu, J., Y. Wang, and E. B. Fernandez, "A uniform approach to software and hardware fault tolerance", *Journal of System and Software*, **26**, 2, Aug. 1994, 117-128.

[69] Zhang, C. and C. Q. Yang, "Analytical analysis of reliability for executing remote programs on idling workstations", *Proc. of IEEE 9th Annual Int'l Phoenix Conf. on Comp. and Comm.*, 1990, 10-16.

Problems

1. Use a practical example to illustrate the differences among faults, errors, and failures.

2. Describe the differences between a fault-tolerant system and a fail-safe system. Provide an example for each of these two systems.

3. Show that *stablesend*(1) and *stablewrite*(1) cannot cover decay events and crashes while *tablesend*(2) and *stablewrite*(2) can.

4. Verify that cases (1, 0, 0), (0, 1, 0), (0, 0, d), where each element represents the state of X, Y, and S in interval I_i, correspond to rollback after one interval of concurrent retry in Pradhan and Vaidya's approach for roll-forward recovery.

5. Discuss the differences between logs and checkpoints. What are the pros and cons of logging messages?

6. Consider a distributed system with at most k fail-stop processors and at most 1 fail-insane processor which exhibits Byzantine type of faults.

   (a) At least how many processors are required to ensure that all healthy processors decide upon the same plan of action?

   (b) Assume the maximum network delay is δ. The processor response time can be neglected. Design an agreement protocol among healthy processors.

   (c) Assume a database is replicated among all the healthy processors in the system. Modify the mutual consistency algorithm using the given network delay δ. Discuss different types of modifications.

7. Consider the consensus problem in a non-totally decentralized control system where the system is partitioned into a set of units. A centralized control method (majority voting) is used for the PEs within each unit and a decentralized method is used to get a global decision among these units. The whole decision process consists of three stages:

   (a) Local decision: Each local supervisor does a one-round majority voting on the values collected from its local PEs.

   (b) Global decision: A decentralized decision algorithm (for the Byzantine generals problem) is applied at the local supervise level.

   (c) Value dispatching: Each local supervisor dispatches its final value to its local PEs.

   Assume there are n_1 units with n_2 PEs including the local supervisor in each unit. Let m be the number of Byzantine faults (a Byzantine fault can be a local supervisor or a PE) in the system.

(i) Determine the following three cases by defining m in terms of n_1 and n_2:

- There exists an agreement algorithm among all the healthy nodes.
- There does not exist such an algorithm.
- There may or may not exist such an algorithm depending on the distribution of Byzantine faults.

Justify your results.

(ii) Discuss the selection of n_1 and n_2 when the total number of PEs in the system is given.

8. Demonstrate that the algorithm in Section 8.5.2 works for the case when $n = 4$ and $k = 1$ by constructing a table similar to Table 8.2.

9. Propose an extended N-version programming for a set of communicating processes. Discuss potential problems (if any) in such an extension. Compare your extended N-version programming with conversation which can be considered as an extended recovery block.

10. Explain the differences between a lost message and an orphan message. Why is an orphan message more severe than a lost message?

11. State the main advantages of hybrid checkpointing over synchronous checkpointing (or asynchronous checkpointing).

12. Illustrate the correctness of the agreement protocol for authenticated messages using a system of four processes with two faulty processes. You need to consider the following two cases:

(a) The sender is healthy and two receivers are faulty (the remaining receiver is healthy).

(b) The sender is faulty and one receiver is faulty (the remaining receivers are healthy).

Chapter 9

STATIC LOAD DISTRIBUTION

Distributed systems offer a tremendous processing capacity. However, in order to realize this capacity and take full advantage of it, good resource allocation schemes are needed. Load distribution is a resource management component of a distributed system that focuses on judiciously and transparently redistributing the load of the system among the processors such that overall performance of the system is maximized. Load distribution algorithms can be broadly characterized as *static* and *dynamic*. The former is discussed in this chapter and the latter is treated in the next chapter.

9.1 Classification of Load Distribution

General load distribution approaches can be classified as follows [4]:

- *Local vs. Global.*
  Local load distribution deals with assignment of processes to the time slots (units) of a single processor. Global load distribution first decides allocation of processes to processors and then performs a local schedule of these processes within each processor.

- *Static vs. Dynamic* (within the category of *Global*).
  In static load distribution, allocation of processes to processors is done at compilation time before processes are executed, while in dynamic load distribution no decision is made until processes execute in the system. The static approach is also called *(deterministic) scheduling* while the dynamic approach is called *load balancing*.

- *Optimal vs. Suboptimal* (within both *Static* and *Dynamic*).
  A load distribution approach is optimal if an optimal assignment can

be made based on criteria such as minimum execution time and maximum system throughput. In general, the load distribution problem is NP-complete. Suboptimal solutions are acceptable for some cases. Four types of algorithms (for both optimal and suboptimal) are used: *solution space enumeration and search, graph models, mathematical programming* (such as 0/1 programming) and *queuing models*.

- *Approximate vs. Heuristic* (within *Suboptimal*).
  In an approximate approach the load distribution algorithm searches only a subset of solution space and terminates when a "good" solution is found. In a heuristic approach the scheduling algorithm uses some special parameters that can approximately model the real system.

- *Centralized vs. Decentralized Control* (within *Dynamic*).
  In decentralized control the work involved in making decisions is distributed among different processors while such decisions are assigned to one processor in a centralized control.

- *Cooperative vs. Noncooperative* (within *Decentralized Control*).
  Dynamic load distribution mechanisms can be classified into ones that involve cooperation between distributed components (cooperative) and ones in which processors make decisions independently (noncooperative).

Figure 9.1 (a simplified one from [4]) shows the above taxonomy of load distribution algorithms. Another taxonomy of load distribution algorithms is discussed in [29] and covers some of the load distribution classifications that may not fit directly into the one above:

- *Single vs. Multiple Applications.*
  Most load distribution algorithms are targeted to a single application. Multiple applications can be converted into the case for one application. For example, when a graph model is used the multiple graphs for multiple applications can be considered as one graph. However, the distribution of processes in multiple applications is more complex than the one in one application. Average subgraph completion time is used for multiple applications and minimum completion time for a single application.

- *Nonpreemptive vs. Preemptive.*
  In a nonpreemptive load distribution algorithm, a task (process) cannot be interrupted once it has begun execution. In a preemptive load

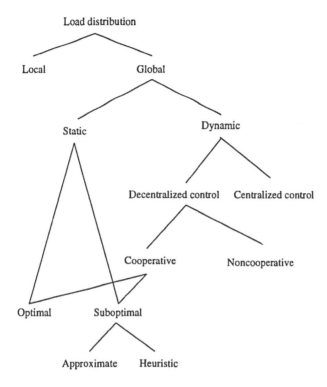

FIGURE 9.1
A taxonomy of load distribution algorithms.

distribution algorithm, a task can be interrupted and removed from the processor (it will be reassigned later).

- *Nonadaptive vs. Adaptive.*
  A nonadaptive load distribution algorithm uses only one load distribution policy (algorithm) and does not change its behavior according to the feedback from the system. An adaptive load distribution algorithm adjusts its load distribution policy (algorithm) based on the feedback. Typically, an adaptive load distribution algorithm is a collection of many load distribution algorithms. The selection among these algorithms depends on various parameters of the system.

Throughout the subsequent discussion we use the terms task and process interchangeably.

9.2   Static Load Distribution

In *static load distribution* algorithms, decisions of load distribution are made by using *a priori* knowledge of the system. Loads cannot be redistributed during the run time [24]. The objective is to schedule a set of tasks that have a minimum execution time on the target PEs. Static load distribution is also called the *scheduling problem*. In general, *processor interconnection, task partition* (grain-size decision) and *task allocation* [41] are three major decisions in the designing of a scheduling strategy. As mentioned earlier the general scheduling problem is NP-complete even under some simple assumptions on computation and communication costs. Therefore, most methods use mathematical tools such as graphs or heuristics ([9], [31], [36]) to obtain a suboptimal solution.

Normally both task and PE structures are represented by a graph model. We can use either a *task precedence graph* or a *task interaction graph* to model a set of tasks. In a task precedence graph also called a *direct acyclic graph* (DAG) (see Figure 9.2 (a)), each link defines the precedence order among tasks. Numbers associated with nodes and directed links are task execution time and the time needed for tasks to start their respective child tasks, respectively. In a task interaction graph (see Figure 9.2 (b)) each link defines task interactions between two tasks. Each link is associated with a pair of numbers that represent the communication costs when these two tasks are assigned to the same PE and when these two tasks are assigned to two different PEs.

9.2.1   Processor interconnections

As discussed in Chapter 1 the topology of an interconnection network can be either static or dynamic. Static networks are formed by point-to-point direct connections that do not change during process execution. Dynamic networks are implemented with switched channels that are dynamically configured to match the communication demand in user programs.

Sometimes the selection of a processor interconnection is tied up with the physical constraints of the processor used; for example, if we have a 16-node Transputer system, a special-purpose processor with four bidirectional links. Possible connections are:

Illiac mesh. A 4×4 Illiac mesh network is shown in Figure 9.3 (a). In general, an $n \times n$ Illiac mesh has a diameter of $n - 1$ that is only half the

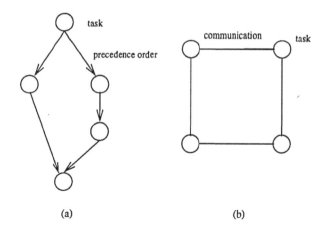

(a)   (b)

FIGURE 9.2
(a) Task precedence graph and (b) task interaction graph.

diameter for a regular mesh.

Torus. A 4 × 4 torus is shown in Figure 9.3 (b). It can be viewed as another variant of the mesh with a shorter diameter. This topology combines the ring and mesh and extends to higher dimensions. In general, an $n \times n$ binary torus has a node degree of 4 and a diameter of $2\lfloor n/2 \rfloor$. The torus is a symmetric topology. All added wraparound connections help to reduce the diameter by one-half than that of the mesh.

Hypercube. The n-cube consists of $N = 2^n$ nodes spanning along n dimensions with two nodes per dimension. A 4-cube (Figure 9.3 (c)) can be formed by interconnecting the corresponding nodes in two 3-cubes. The node degree of an n-cube is n as well as the network diameter.

WK network. WK is a hierarchical network. An n-level WK network consists of four $(n - 1)$-level WK networks with each treated as a virtual node. The basic unit is a 1-level WK network consisting of four nodes that are completely connected. Each node has one spare link to be used in constructing a WK network of the next level. Figure 9.3 (d) shows a 2-level WK network with 16 nodes (four 1-level WK networks).

9.2.2 Task partition

The granularity of a given task decomposition defined by the average size of the pieces of the decomposition can affect communication costs. An algorithm can be characterized by *fine-grain, medium-grain,* or *coarse-grain*

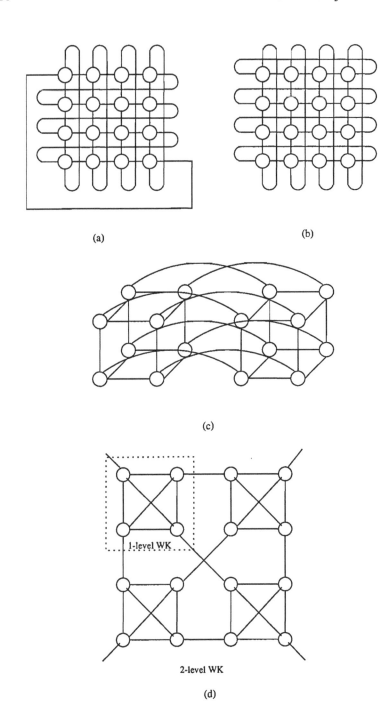

(a)

(b)

(c)

(d)

FIGURE 9.3
Different connections of a 16-node Transputer system: (a) Illiac
mesh, (b) torus, (c) hypercube, and (d) WK network.

granularity.

If the size of the data item (or grain size) is small, the granularity of this algorithm is fine-grain. If the size of the data item is large, the granularity of this algorithm is coarse-grain [23]. The algorithm whose granularity is between fine-grain and coarse-grain is medium-grain. If a grain is too large, parallelism is reduced because potentially parallel tasks are grouped into one task and are assigned to one processor. If a grain is too small, more overhead is generated in context switching and communication delay is increased.

One of the major goals of task partition is to eliminate as much as possible the overhead caused by interprocessor communication. Three general approaches can be used:

- *Horizontal or vertical partitioning.* The basic idea is to partition a given precedence graph horizontally or vertically. The concept of *critical path* (the longest path) is normally used for vertical partitioning [27]. The horizontal partition divides a given task graph into several horizontal layers and tasks are prioritized based on their layers.

- *Communication delay minimization partition.* The idea is to cluster nodes that communicate heavily. However, the concurrency of communicating tasks is lost if they are placed into the same processor. In [12] the partition algorithm tries to cluster tasks as long as the benefits of zeroing communication delays outweigh the serialization of parallel tasks. In [39] Stone showed how a partition problem can be transformed into a network flow problem that will be discussed in a later section.

- *Task duplication.* This is an alternative method of task partition [6], [22]. The idea is to eliminate communication costs by duplicating the tasks among the PEs. This approach preserves the original task parallelism; however, space requirement and synchronization overhead are increased. The use of task duplication to achieve fault tolerance is discussed in [5] and [42]. Task duplication can also be used to achieve fault-secure scheduling in which the final computation is guaranteed correct in the presence of processor faults. Detailed discussion can be found in [1], [40], [43] and will be discussed as the case study in this chapter.

Sometimes task partition is called *task clustering* to emphasize the grouping of a set of small tasks in a given graph model. Task partition treats a given graph as one unit and partitions it into groups (grains). Both task partition and task clustering generate a set of grains. Normally the number of grains is equal to the number of processors to simplify the task allocation process at the next stage.

9.2.3   Task allocation

Task allocation deals with assigning grains (as a result of task partition) to a parallel/distributed system under a given network interconnection.

If the number of nodes in a task graph and a processor graph is n each, there are $n!$ different ways of assigning the nodes of G_t (task graph) on the nodes of G_p (processor graph); we call each of these ways a mapping of G_t onto G_p. Some mappings are better than others in terms of total execution time. A typical set of assumptions for G_p are:

- There is no limitation of memory capacity.

- Each PE has the same capacity.

- The factor of network contention is neglected although the distance between two communicating (or precedence-related) tasks is still a factor for communication delay.

Note that task scheduling does not have to be done in two steps; namely, task partition and task allocation. The two-step approach is just to simplify the scheduling process that is normally NP-complete.

9.3   An Overview of Different Scheduling Models

As mentioned earlier most optimal scheduling problems are NP-complete. Most research efforts focus on the following approaches [38]:

- *Optimal scheduling* for special cases, i.e., models with special constraints.

- *Nonoptimal scheduling* that can be classified into *locally optimal solutions* and *suboptimal solutions.*

Optimal scheduling for special cases such as tree-structured DAGs and two-processor systems will be discussed in detail in a later section.

Locally optimal solutions use efficient search techniques to identify the (local) optimal schedule in the solution space of a problem. These solutions can be further classified into:

- *Solution space enumeration and search* [14]. A state space is first constructed where each state corresponds to a possible schedule. It then relies on various search techniques such as branch- and bound-search to find a solution in the space.

- *Mathematical programming* [35]. A given scheduling problem is converted to an integer, linear, or nonlinear programming problem. Three steps are used: (a) An objective function to be minimized is defined which is often the program execution time. (b) A set of constraints such as precedence relations and communication delays is also defined. (c) Solving the constrained optimization problem based on (a) and (b) using dynamic programming techniques.

- *Simulated annealing* [28]. Simulated annealing uses the properties of the physical annealing process to conduct a search for a local optimal scheduling solution. Normally such a process consists of (a) making small random changes to an initial (nonoptimal) schedule, (b) evaluating the new schedule, and (c) continuing this process until no improvement can be made, i.e., a local minimum solution is obtained.

- *Genetic algorithms* [17]. A genetic algorithm is a search algorithm based on the principles of evolution and natural genetics. It combines past results with new areas of the search space to generate future results. In [25] Kwok and Ahmad proposed a parallel genetic scheduling algorithm.

Like optimal solutions for special cases, locally optimal solutions are also extremely computation-intensive and time-consuming. Suboptimal solution methods rely on heuristic methods to obtain suboptimal solutions. Among them *list scheduling* is the most popular one. Two steps are used:

- Provide a priority list of tasks to be assigned to the PEs.

- Remove the top priority task from the list and allocate it to the appropriate PE.

List scheduling is very efficient for certain scheduling problems and optimal for two special cases to be discussed in a later section. Note that this approach cannot guarantee an optimal result. For some situations, it would be better to delay the assignment of the next ready process even when there is an idle processor. In order to evaluate the goodness of a heuristic approach, bounds on an optimal schedule are normally used. Several methods of estimating bounds can be found in [10].

In our discussion we classify scheduling methods based on two graph models used to represent given task graphs: task precedence graphs and task interaction graphs.

9.4   Task Scheduling Based on Task Precedence Graphs

We have a given set of processes $P = \{P_1, P_2, ...P_n\}$ that is to be executed by a set of identical processors. A partial order $<$ on P is also given. This partially ordered set $(P, <)$ is described by $G = (V, A)$ and is called *a task precedence graph* where V is a vertex set to represent the set of processes and A is an arc set to represent the precedence between processes. A link in A can be represented by (u, v) where u and v are two connecting processes (nodes) in V. In addition, two cost functions w are defined on each node and link. Specifically, $w(u) \in (0, \infty)$ is the cost of node u, where $u \in V$. $w(u, v) = (l, l')$ is the cost of link (u, v) where l' is the intraprocessor cost (if nodes u and v are assigned to the same processor) and l is the interprocessor cost (if nodes u and v are assigned to two different processors).

In the task precedence graph model the processor interconnection is not considered. It is assumed that communication delay is a fixed number for each processor pair. Actually it is encoded in l associated with each link. Normally intraprocessor communication cost l' (communication within a processor) is small compared to interprocessor communication cost l and can be neglected, i.e., $w(u, v) = l$.

The placement of processes on processors can be best described in a graphical model called the *Gantt chart*. A Gantt chart lists the processors vertically and the time horizontally (the time domain is partitioned into *time slots*). The blocks inside the chart represent the start time, duration, and ending time of each process in the given system. Both intraprocessor and interprocessor time delays can also be shown on the chart.

Figure 9.4 (a) shows a task precedence graph example with given interprocessor communication cost and task execution time. Figure 9.4 (b) shows a schedule of the application described in Figure 9.4 (a) to proces-

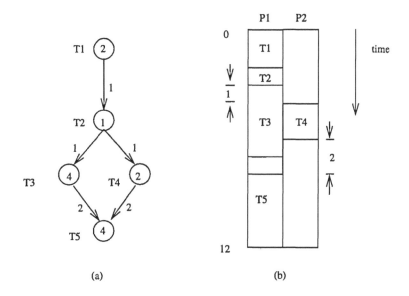

FIGURE 9.4
(a) A task precedence graph and (b) a schedule to two processors shown in a Gantt chart.

sors P_1 and P_2. The number inside each cycle represents the corresponding task execution time. The number associated with each link corresponds to the interprocessor communication time. The communication delay will occur if two connecting tasks are assigned to different processors. For example, $w(T_1) = 2$ and $w(T_1, T_2) = 1$, that is, the execution time of T_1 is 2 and interprocessor communication cost between T_1 and T_2 is 1 (there is no intraprocessor communication cost). In this example two interprocessor communications occur from T_2 to T_4 with one unit of communication delay and from T_4 to T_5 with two units of communication delay. The total execution time of this schedule is 12.

Communication delay greatly complicates the scheduling algorithm. Figure 9.5 (a) shows an example of three different schedules. If the communication delay d is more than the duration of task T_2 the schedule in Figure 9.5 (c) is better than the one in Figure 9.5 (d), i.e., it is better to assign all tasks to one processor if the communication delay is too large.

In general, we try to maximize the degree of parallelism and at the same time minimize the communication delay. However, most of the time these two conflict with one another. Therefore, a trade-off is needed. Sometimes one can get around this problem through *task duplication* to offset commu-

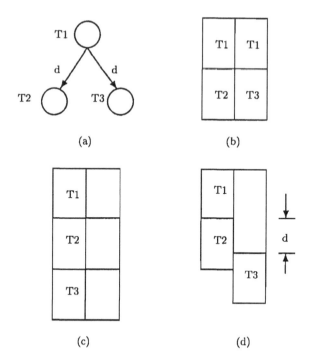

(a)

(b)

(c)

(d)

FIGURE 9.5
A task precedence graph (a) and three of its schedules (b), (c), and (d).

nication. Clearly, Figure 9.5 (b) has the best result since the interprocessor communication is avoided through task duplication.

As mentioned earlier the grain size problem in task partition, also called *clustering*, groups tasks in a given application into *clusters*. Typically, the number of clusters is the same as the number of processors. A clustering is called *nonlinear* if at least one cluster contains two independent tasks; otherwise, it is called *linear*. Figures 9.6 (a) and (b) show a linear and a nonlinear scheduling of three processes, respectively. A task precedence graph can be considered as a set of *fork* and *join* operations shown in Figures 9.7 (a) and (b). In order to define a good clustering policy, the concept of granularity of each fork (join) operation was introduced [12]. The grain of a fork x (join x) as shown in Figure 9.7 is the following:

$$g(x) = \min_{1 \le k \le n} \{c_k\} / \max_{1 \le k \le n} \{l_k\}$$

The grain of a given task precedence graph G is defined as:

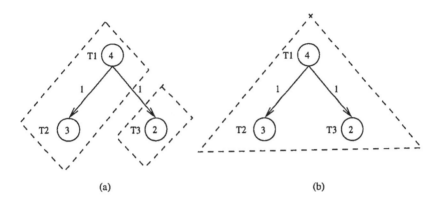

FIGURE 9.6
A task precedence graph with (a) linear clustering and (b) non-linear clustering.

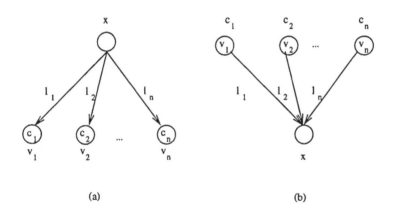

FIGURE 9.7
A fork operation (a) and a join operation (b).

$$g(G) = \min_{\forall x \in G} \{g(x)\}$$

A join or fork x (or graph G) is called coarse grain if $g(x) > 1$ ($g(G) > 1$); otherwise, it is called fine grain. In the example of Figure 9.6 it is a coarse grain fork since the minimum process cost is more than the maximum link cost ($g(x) = 2$). Gerasoulis and Yang [12] showed that when a given directed acyclic graph (task precedence graph) representing an application is coarse grain, that is, the communication cost along a link is less than the computation cost of the adjacent nodes connected by fork and/or join operations, any nonlinear clustering can be transformed into linear clustering with less or equal execution time. Note that the above conclusion implies that a linear clustering exists in a coarse grain application that outperforms any nonlinear clustering. However, for a fine grain application there may or may not exist a nonlinear cluster that outperforms any linear cluster.

In the example of Figure 9.6 if the linear clustering of Figure 9.6 (a) is used, its execution time is 7. The execution time for nonlinear clustering in Figure 9.6 (b) is 9. For the same example if we change both $w(T_1, T_3)$ and $w(T_1, T_2)$ to 4, the corresponding graph becomes a fine grain fork. In this case, nonlinear clustering with execution time 9 outperforms linear clustering with execution time 10.

9.5 Case Study: Two Optimal Scheduling Algorithms

As mentioned earlier most scheduling problems are NP-complete. In this subsection we consider two restricted scheduling problems that have polynomial-time complexity. In both cases it is assumed that communication costs are negligible and the execution time of each node in the precedence graph is uniform (one unit). Specific constraints are as follows:

1. The precedence graph is a tree in the first restricted scheduling problem.

2. There are only two processors available in the second restricted scheduling problem.

Both scheduling algorithms are highest-level-first approaches, i.e., nodes are selected based on their levels (priorities).

For case 1 the level of a node u is its distance to the root node plus one. Note that the higher the level the higher the priority of the corresponding node. When there are several nodes that have the same level, the one with all its predecessors executed will be the first selected. If there are several nodes that meet the above condition, the selection is random.

Figure 9.8 shows a tree-type precedence graph and the optimal schedule for this graph on three processors. Tasks T_1, T_2, T_3, and T_4 are at level 5. Tasks T_5, T_6, and T_7 are at level 4. Tasks T_8 and T_9 are at level 3. Tasks T_{10}, T_{11}, and T_{12} are at level 2. Task T_{13} is at level 1. The tasks at level 5 have the highest priority and the task at level 1 has the lowest priority.

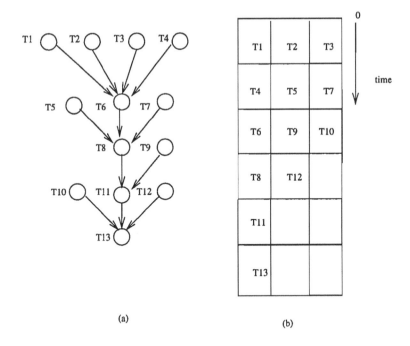

(a)

(b)

FIGURE 9.8
(a) A tree-structured task precedence graph and (b) a schedule
to three processors shown in a Gantt chart.

The tasks at the same level have the same priority. Assignment is based on priority starting from time slot one. However, tasks that have precedence relationships cannot be assigned to the same time slots. For example, T_6 must be assigned to a time slot after the one for T_4 in Figure 9.8.

In order to provide an efficient implementation a *ready* queue can be introduced. This queue includes all nodes of which all their predecessors have been executed. The selection of nodes in the ready queue is based on the priority of each task. In Figure 9.8, initially the ready queue is $\{T_1, T_2, T_3.T_4, T_5, T_7, T_9, T_{10}, T_{12}\}$ (for convenience, tasks in the ready queue are listed based on their priority orders). The first three tasks in the queue are assigned to time slot 1 and the ready queue becomes $\{T_4, T_5, T_7, T_9, T_{10}, T_{12}\}$. Once T_4, T_5, and T_7 are assigned to time slot 2, task T_6 is added to the ready queue: $\{T_6, T_9, T_{10}, T_{12}\}$. Again, the first three tasks in the queue are assigned to next time slot and the ready queue becomes $\{T_8, T_{12}\}$. Both T_8 and T_{12} are assigned to time slot 4 and task T_{11} is placed in the ready queue. T_{11} is assigned to time slot 5 and T_{13} is available for time slot 6. Note that the ready queue needs to be updated whenever a node is scheduled. In practice update can be delayed as long as there is at least one node left in the queue.

For case 2 with two processors the precedence graph can be arbitrary. The level is distinct for different nodes. Assuming there are k terminal nodes (nodes that do not have successors), label these nodes from 1 to k. Let S be the set of unassigned nodes with no unlabeled successors and one node will be selected to be assigned label i. Let $lex(u)$ be the ascending sequence of labels of all u's immediate successors. If $lex(u) < lex(u')$ (lexicographically as in a dictionary) for all u' ($u \neq u'$) in S, then u will be assigned i. Figure 9.9 shows a precedence graph with labels assigned to all the nodes following the above procedure. The label associated with each node is treated as its level. The optimal schedule in the Gantt chart is also shown in Figure 9.9 (b). The increasing priority order among tasks in this figure is: T_1, T_2, T_3, T_4, T_5, T_6, T_{11}, T_8, T_7, T_{10}, T_9. Note that the order for terminal tasks T_1, T_2, T_3 is randomly selected. In this example labels for T_1, T_2, and T_3 are 1, 2, 3, respectively. The immediate successors of T_4 are T_1 and T_2, hence $lex(T_4) = (1,2)$. Similarly $lex(T_5) = (1,3)$. Clearly $lex(T_4) < lex(T_5)$ (a smaller label corresponds to a lower order). Therefore, T_4 is assigned a label of 4 and T_5 a label of 5.

9.6   Task Scheduling Based on Task Interaction Graphs

In the second task model we use a task interaction graph and a set of processes to represent an application. Each edge (link) in a task interaction graph represents interaction between two communicating processes. An undirected graph $G_t(V_t, E_t)$ is used to denote this graph where V_t is a set of processes and E_t is a set of edges each of which is labeled with the communication cost (instead of precedence) between the corresponding pair of processes. Unlike the task precedence graph model the processor interconnection plays an important role in the scheduling using the task interaction graph model. Specifically, a processor graph $G_p(V_p, E_p)$ is used with vertex set V_p (each element is a processor) and edge set E_p (each element is a communication channel). Usually $|V_t| \leq |V_p|$ since we assume that a task partition has been performed. Now we make the assignment $M : V_t \rightarrow V_p$ and the following estimation of execution time. Recall that $w(u)$ and $w(u,v)$ represent costs of node u and link (u,v), respectively.

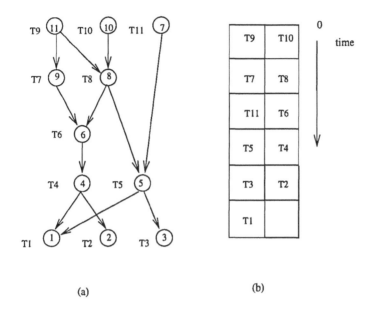

(a)   (b)

FIGURE 9.9
(a) A task graph (the number inside each node is the priority
number of the corresponding node) and (b) a schedule of this
graph to two processors shown in a Gantt chart.

The computation load of a processor $p \in V_p$:

$$Comp(p) = \sum_{u \in V_t} w(u)|M(u) = p$$

The communication load:

$$Comm(p) = \sum_{(u,v) \in E_t} w(u,v)|M(u) = p \neq M(v)$$

The total amount of computation and communication within an application:

$$Comp = \sum_{p \in V_p} Comp(p) = \sum_{p \in V_p} \sum_{u \in V_t} w(u)|M(u) = p$$

$$Comm = \frac{1}{2} \sum_{p \in V_p} Comm(p) = \frac{1}{2} \sum_{p \in V_p} \sum_{(u,v) \in E_t} w(u,v)|M(u) = p \neq M(v)$$

Note that the communication cost of a link is counted twice: one at each
of its connecting nodes. Therefore, a division by two is necessary when we

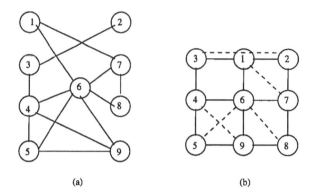

(a)   (b)

FIGURE 9.10
Mapping a task interaction graph (a) to a processor graph (b).

accumulate the communication cost at each processor. The total time for solving this application can be approximated as follows:

$$T = max\{\alpha Comp(p) + \beta Comm(p)\}, \text{where } p \in V_p$$

In the above approximation, α depends on the processing speed of each PE and β depends on the communication speed of each channel and the distance between two communicating processes. Note that if two processes u and v are adjacent in G_t, their images (mapping results of M) in G_p may or may not be adjacent. Ideally all communicating processes are assigned to adjacent processors to reduce interprocessor communications. Note that normally two processes should not be mapped to the same processor. These two processes should be clustered into one process during the task partition (clustering) phase. An approximate measure of the quality of a mapping is the number of edges of task graph G_t that are mapped onto edges of processor graph G_p. We call this number the *cardinality* of the mapping, that is, the number of communicating process pairs in G_t that are mapped to adjacent processors in G_p. Sometimes the cardinality of a mapping cannot exceed the number of links in G_t. If a mapping achieves this maximum, it is a perfect mapping.

For example, in Figure 9.10 a task graph (a) is mapped to a 9-processor graph (b) and the cardinality of the mapping is 8 out of 13 edges. Sometimes the cardinality of mapping may not accurately reflect the quality of a mapping. For example, it cannot distinguish the following two cases: (1) Two communicating processes are mapped to two processors that are

k-distance apart ($k > 2$) in the processor graph, and (2) two communicating processes are mapped to two processors that are 2-distance apart. The graph embedding techniques can be used here to distinguish the above two cases.

Suppose that the task interaction graph and the processor graph are viewed as graphs G_t and G_p, respectively. To obtain efficient emulation of G_p by G_t, i.e., embedding of G_t into G_p, various cost measurements of an embedding must be optimized.

- The *dilation* of an edge of G_t is defined as the length of the path in G_p onto which an edge of G_t is mapped. The dilation of the embedding is the maximum edge dilation of G_t.

- The *expansion* of the embedding is the ratio of the number of nodes in G_t to the number of nodes in G_p.

- The *congestion* of the embedding is the maximum number of paths containing an edge in G_p where every path represents an edge in G_t.

- The *load* of an embedding is the maximum number of processes of G_t assigned to any processor of G_t.

It is required that the load of an embedding be restricted to one, i.e., the mapping is one-to-one. Intuitively the dilation represents the maximum communication delay between communicating processes, the expansion is a measure of processor utilization, and the congestion measures the maximum congestion along a link.

Ideally we would like to find embeddings with minimal dilation, expansion, and congestion. In the example of Figure 9.10 the dilation is 2 because, in the worst case, two communicating processes (such as the process pair 1 and 7) are assigned to two processors that are 2-distance apart. The load is 1 since it is a one-to-one mapping. The congestion is 3. Congestion needs a more careful calculation since it depends on the routing path for each pair of communication processes. We should try to select routing paths such that the overall network congestion is minimized. In the example of Figure 9.10 (b), link (5,6) can be either mapped to (5,4) $\leftrightarrow$ (4,6) or (5,9) $\leftrightarrow$ (9,6). Similarly, link (4,9) can be mapped to either (4,6) $\leftrightarrow$ (6,9) or (4,5) $\leftrightarrow$ (5,9). In either case at least one link will be used twice assuming that each link is undirected, say (6,9). Note that processes 6 and 9 themselves are two communicating processes. Therefore, link (6,9) will be used three times. The expansion is clearly 1 since $|V_p| = |V_t|$.

In many practical applications statistical measurements can also be employed in the comparison such as variance V, standard variance σ (the square root of variance V), and maximum difference of computation and communication between any two processors, Max_{comp} and Max_{comm}. The mean of computation of processors and mean of communication of processors are denoted as $Mean_{comp}$ and $Mean_{comm}$, respectively.

$$Mean_{comp} = \frac{1}{|V_p|} \sum_{p \in V_p} Comp(p)$$

$$V_{comp} = \frac{1}{|V_p|} \sum_{p \in V_p} (Comp(p) - Mean_{comp})^2$$

$$\sigma_{comp} = \sqrt{V_{comp}}$$

$$Max_{comp} = max\{Comp(p) - Comp(q)\}, \quad p, \, q \in V_t$$

Similarly, we can define $Mean_{comm}$, σ_{comm}, V_{comm}, and Max_{comm}. Theoretically we should choose a schedule which has the smallest *Computation, Communication*, $Mean_{comp}$, $Mean_{comm}$, σ_{comp}, σ_{comm}, etc. However, in practice, no schedule can achieve the smallest values for all the measurements. Certain trade-offs are needed.

9.7   Case Study: Domain Partition

This section considers a domain partition problem as a special task interaction graph model. The application under consideration has a uniform distribution of workload in the entire domain. Each data element has four neighbors and all communications are among neighbors. That is, the task graph of the application is regular where each node has four neighbors. The neighborhood relationship can be easily derived from addresses of elements. For example, node (i, j) has four neighbors at $(i + 1, j)$, $(i, j + 1)$, $(i - 1, j)$ and $(i, j - 1)$. This plane-like task graph significantly reduces the complexity of the partition scheme. We also assume that the system under consideration uses the mesh topology. Therefore, we only need to focus on task partition (clustering) since task allocation becomes a trivial task.

With the assumption of uniform distribution of workload within the domain, we only need to balance workload assigned to each processor to minimize the amount of communication. We define the ratio between communication and computation in processor p as: $Comm(p)/Comp(p)$. Because the total amount of computation and the number of processors are given, $Comp(p)$ is a fixed value when the workload is balanced in the system. Therefore, minimizing the value of the ratio means minimizing the amount of communication. We need to decide the shape of each subarea such that its perimeter is minimum.

$$\min\{\frac{Comm(p)}{Comp(p)}\} = \frac{\sum_{(u,v)\in E_t} w(u,v)|M(u) = p \neq M(v)}{\sum_{u\in V_t} w(u)|M(u) = p} = \lambda \cdot R_{peri/surf}$$

In the above equation λ is the ratio of the amount of message exchange between two adjacent elements to the amount of computation of each data element and $R_{peri/surf}$ is the ratio of the perimeter of the subarea to the size of the subarea [3].

Obviously the ratio of communication to computation is positively correlated to $R_{peri/surf}$. We know that $R_{peri/surf}$ achieves minimum for a circle [3].

$$\min\{\frac{Comm(p)}{Comp(p)}\} = \lambda \cdot R_{peri/surf} = \lambda\frac{2\pi r}{\pi r^2} = \lambda\frac{2}{r}$$

where r is the radius of a circle. However, the neighborhood relationship cannot be easily determined when subareas are circles. Therefore, a circle is not a suitable shape for a subarea. A polygon can be used to approximate a circle. A rectangle is a good candidate to satisfy the requirement of low $R_{peri/surf}$ and suitable for the mesh topology. Assuming that *length* and *width* denote the long and short dimensions of a given rectangle, we have:

$$\min\{\frac{Comm(p)}{Comp(p)}\} = \lambda\frac{2(length + width)}{length \times width}$$

It is easy to see that $Comm(p)/Comp(p)$ reaches the minimum when $length = width$ given that $length \times width$ is a constant. This implies that the square shape will minimize the ratio $Comm(p)/Comp(p)$. Therefore, we should try to partition the task graph to a set of squares if it is possible. Wu et al. [44] proposed three partition methods for an irregular-shape task graph: *one-dimensional*, *two-dimensional*, and *hierarchical* partitions. In one-dimensional partition, a given domain is partitioned along a selected dimension, horizontal or vertical. Each subarea has at most two neighbors. As shown in Figure 9.11 the given irregular domain is partitioned into 16 subareas vertically. Although this partition can ensure that all the subareas have the same amount of workload, the communication cost is usually high, i.e., each subarea has a large perimeter.

In the two-dimensional partition, a given domain is partitioned along two dimensions. As shown in Figure 9.12 each subarea has at most four

FIGURE 9.11
The vertical partition of an irregular domain (16 subareas).

neighbors. All subareas are rectangles except for boundary subareas. The main flaw of this method is that it cannot balance the workload among the subareas. Compared to the one-dimensional partition, the two-dimensional partition reduces the overall communication cost.

Theoretically, in the hierarchical partition, a given task graph can be first partitioned into regular and irregular parts. Each regular part can then be partitioned into a set of subareas. Each irregular part will be further partitioned into regular and irregular parts. The above steps can be applied recursively. This method is more complex than the previous two methods but obtains better results. In [44] a simplified version resembling more a two-dimension partition than a hierarchical partition can ensure load balance among all the subareas with reasonable communication overhead. This simplified version was improved later in another study [45].

In many practical applications the cost (of the number of processors used) is also important; therefore, in many cases execution time is traded for cost.

A criterion related to cost can be defined as follows:

$$cost = total\ running\ time \times (number\ of\ processors\ used)^k$$

where k is a real number.

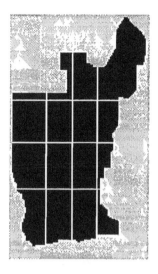

FIGURE 9.12
The two-dimensional partition of an irregular domain (16 subareas).

When too many processors are used in a distributed system, the maintenance problem occurs and the price paid to guarantee a high degree of reliability rises sharply. Therefore, after a certain point the larger the number of processors an algorithm uses to solve a problem, the more expensive (costly) the solution is. A detailed execution time and cost estimate based on the above model is shown in [44].

9.8 Scheduling Using Other Models and Objectives

There are many different models and objectives for a scheduling problem. For example, one may consider the factor of limitation of memory size or PEs with different capacities. Among different objectives one may consider timing constraints as in a real-time system. We consider here three scheduling algorithms based on different models and objectives.

9.8.1 Network flow techniques: task interaction graphs with different processor capacities

We consider an optimal scheduling of a given task interacting graph in a two-processor system in which each processor has different capacities for different tasks. We show a network flow problem and relate this to our scheduling problem.

Consider a task interaction graph. A *cutset* or *cut* of this graph is defined as a subset of the edges in this graph such that:

1. Removal of these edges disconnects the graph, and

2. no proper subset of these edges also satisfies property 1.

A *s-t cut* partitions the given graph into two components: G_1 and G_2, where $s \in G_1$ and $t \in G_2$. A *weighted graph* is one where there is a real number (representing cost) associated with each edge. The corresponding cut (and *s-t*) is called a *weighted cut* (and *weighted s-t cut*).

The *minimum weighted s-t cut* or *mincut* is a weighted *s-t* cut with minimum cut weight. Finding a mincut is equivalent to finding a maxflow. The Ford and Fulkerson's *maxflow-mincut* theorem [11] states that the minimum cut in a network must equal the maximum flow. The flow through the network obeys the following restrictions:

- The flow through an edge cannot exceed its capacity.

- The flow entering a node must equal the flow leaving the node for all nodes except the source (s) and the sink (t).

- s has no flow entering it and t has no flow leaving it. The flow leaving s must equal the flow entering t.

In order to find a minimum cut in a given network, a maxflow algorithm is first applied. The minimum weighted cutset can be found by searching outwards from s for unsaturated edges until no further progress is possible. An edge is saturated if it carries a flow equal to its capacity; otherwise, it is called unsaturated. Figure 9.13 shows the maximum flow of a given undirected weighted graph. The dashed line is the corresponding minimum weight cut. In this figure each edge is associated with two numbers: The first one indicates the weight on the edge and the second one is the actual flow through the edge.

More formally, let $c(u, v)$ denote the capacity of edge (u, v) and $f(u, v)$ the actual flow along (u, v). Clearly,

$$0 \leq f(u, v) \leq c(u, v)$$

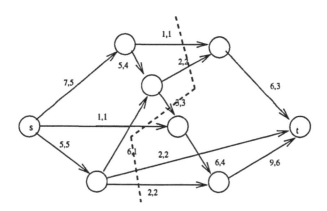

FIGURE 9.13
Maximum flow and the corresponding mincut.

The value of the flow $F(G)$ for a network $G = (V, E)$ is defined as the net flow leaving source s:

$$F(G) = \sum_u f(s, u) - \sum_u f(u, s)$$

Suppose G is partitioned into G_1 and G_2 based on a $s - t$ cut, then $F(G)$ is the flow from G_1 to G_2 minus the flow from G_2 to G_1.

$$F(G) = \sum_{u \in G_1, v \in G_2} f(u, v) - \sum_{u \in G_2, v \in G_1} f(u, v)$$

Clearly, the value of the flow from a network cannot exceed the capacity of any $s - t$ cut. In order to determine the maximum flow of a network, we consider a process that maximizes the flow in the network. A path P from source s to sink t is defined as a sequence of distinct vertices $P = (u_0, u_1, u_2, ...u_k)$, where $u_0 = s$ and $u_k = t$ such that P is a path in the underlying graph $G = (V, E)$. Clearly, for any two consecutive vertices u_i and u_{i+1} of P, either $(u_i, u_{i+1}) \in E$ or $(u_{i+1}, u_i) \in E$. The former case is called a *forward link* while the latter case is called a *reverse link*. For a given flow $F(G)$ an *augmenting path* of P is defined as follows: For each (u_i, u_{i+1}),

1. If (u_i, u_{i+1}) is a forward link, then:

$$\Delta_i = c(u_i, u_{i+1}) - f(u_i, u_{i+1}) > 0$$

2. If (u_i, u_{i+1}) is a reverse link, then:

$$\Delta_i = f(u_{i+1}, u_i) > 0$$

If P is an augmenting path, then we define Δ as follows:

$$\Delta = \min \Delta_i > 0$$

Each (u_i, u_{i+1}) of P for which $\Delta_i = \Delta$ is called a *bottleneck link* relative to $F(G)$ and P.

For a given G and $F(G)$ if an augmenting path P exists, we can construct a new flow $F'(G)$ such that the value of $F'(G)$ is equal to the value of $F(G)$ plus Δ. This can be done by changing the flow for each (u_i, u_{i+1}) of G as follows:

1. If (u_i, u_{i+1}) is a forward link then:

$$f(u_i, u_{i+1}) \leftarrow f(u_i, u_{i+1}) + \Delta$$

2. If (u_i, u_{i+1}) is a reverse link then:

$$f(u_i, u_{i+1}) \leftarrow f(u_i, u_{i+1}) - \Delta$$

Clearly these changes preserve the conservation of flow requirement. Moreover, the net flow from s is increased by the addition of Δ to the flow along (s, u_1). Figure 9.14 shows a network in which each link (u, v) is labeled with pair $(c(u, v), f(u, v))$. $P = \{s, u_1, u_3, u_2, t\}$ is an augmenting path with (s, u_1) and (u_2, t) being forward links and (u_1, u_3) and (u_3, u_2) being reverse links. Each link of the path except (u_3, t) is a bottleneck link and $\Delta = 1$. We can construct a new flow:

$$f(s, u_1) \leftarrow 2, f(u_1, u_3) \leftarrow 0, f(u_3, u_2) \leftarrow 0, f(u_2, t) \leftarrow 2$$

The idea of an augmenting path forms the basis of an algorithm by Ford and Fulkerson [11] to solve the maximum-flow problem. One can start with an arbitrary flow and increase its flow until there is no augmenting path in the resultant flow. It can be proved that a flow in which there is no augmenting path corresponds to a maximum flow. The challenge is to find a fast process to reach a flow with no augmenting path.

The best flow algorithms are given by Edmonds and Karp [8], Dinic [7], and Karzanov [21] that have complexities of $O(ne^2)$, $O(n^2e)$, and $O(n^3)$, respectively. n is the number of vertices and e the number of edges in the given graph.

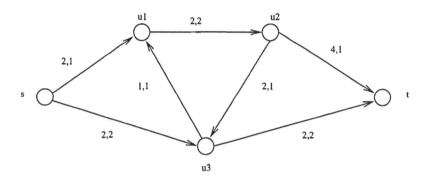

FIGURE 9.14
An augmenting path.

The application of the above flow algorithm is the assignment problem in distributed systems where each processor has different capacities [39]. Consider a two-processor system where each processor has different capacities for different tasks. Each task in a given task interaction graph is associated with two numbers: one for cost running on processor 1 and the other for cost running on processor 2.

Figure 9.15 shows such a task interaction graph. For example, for task T_2 (4,5) means that T_2 takes 4 units if it is assigned to processor 1 and 5 units if assigned to processor 2. In (3,-), - means an infinite number, that is, the corresponding task T_1 cannot be scheduled to processor 2. An assignment graph is constructed by including two additional nodes and $2n$ additional edges (n is the number of tasks in the given graph). Two additional nodes are source s and sink t. Among $2n$ additional edges n edges connect s to the n nodes in the given graph and the remaining n edges connect t to these n nodes. It is easy to see that (from Figure 9.16 that extends the graph in Figure 9.15) the weight of a cut in the assignment graph is equal to the total cost of the corresponding assignment, because any cut that disconnects s and t will cut exactly one of the two external edges incident on each task.

The above two-processor model can be extended to the m-processor model where each processor has different capacities. Stone's approach is static in the sense that once a task is assigned to a processor, it will remain there forever. Bokhari [2] proposed a dynamic approach for a system in which processor capacities vary over time.

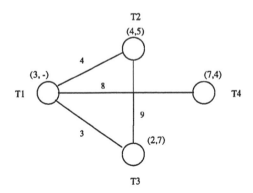

FIGURE 9.15
A task interaction graph.

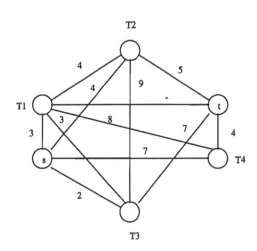

FIGURE 9.16
An assignment graph for the graph of Figure 9.15.

9.8.2 Rate monotonic priority and deadline driven schedules: periodic tasks with real-time constraints

Many scheduling problems have timing constraints which are typical in a real-time system. A real-time system has to be both fast and predictable. Predictability means that when a task is activated it should be possible to determine its completion time with certainty. For example, a typical question is: Will task T meet its timing requirements? Similar questions include: How may tasks will finish before their deadline? What will be the maximum utilization?

We consider two scheduling algorithms by Liu and Layland [33] for multiple periodic tasks in a single processor system. These two scheduling algorithms serve as base for many real-time scheduling approaches. It is assumed that all tasks have hard deadlines with a constant interval between requests. For example, task T_i has request period t_i and run time c_i. That is, task T_i appears once every t_i time units and has to be completed before its next request. All tasks are independent without communication.

Both rate monotonic and deadline driven algorithms are priority driven and preemptive with the first using a fixed priority assignment and the second using a dynamic priority. By dynamic priority we mean that its priority changes over time.

- *Rate monotonic scheduling.* Tasks with higher request rates will have higher priorities.

- *Deadline driven scheduling.* A task will be assigned the highest priority if the deadline of its current request is the nearest.

A given set of periodic tasks is schedulable if all its deadlines are met. It has been proved that for deadline driven scheduling a given set of tasks is schedulable if

$$\sum_{n}^{i=0} \frac{c_i}{t_i} \leq 1$$

That is, it is always schedulable as long as its overall utilization is under 1. For rate monotonic scheduling, however, a given set of tasks is schedulable if

$$\sum_{n}^{i=0} \frac{c_i}{t_i} \leq n(2^{\frac{1}{n}} - 1)$$

That is, for $n = 1$ the bound is 1, for $n = 2$ the bound is 0.828, for $n = 3$ the bound is 0.779, and so on. Note that when the above condition fails but the overall utilization is below 1, it may or may not be feasible. However, if there is a feasible scheduling based on a fixed priority, rate monotonic scheduling will always find one.

Consider two periodic tasks with the same initiate request time T_1: $c_1 = 3$, $t_1 = 5$ and T_2: $c_2 = 2$, $t_2 = 7$. The overall utilization is 0.887 which is more than the bound 0.828 for $n = 2$. It is easy to see that it is still schedulable using rate monotonic scheduling. For example, within 7 units two copies of T_1 can be scheduled at 0 and 5 and one copy of T_2 can be scheduled at 3. It can be verified that 7 copies of T_1 and 5 copies of T_2 can be scheduled within $5 \times 7 = 35$ units. Note that after 35 units the same request pattern occurs.

Consider two more periodic tasks with the same initiate request time T_1: $c_1 = 3$, $t_1 = 5$ and T_2: $c_2 = 3$, $t_2 = 8$ with an overall utilization of 0.975 (see Figure 9.17). Within the first 8 units two copies of T_1 can be scheduled at 0 and 5 since T_1 has a higher priority than T_2. The only available time slots are from 3 to 5 which are not enough for T_2 that has a deadline at 8. Therefore, this set of periodic tasks is not schedulable. Using deadline driven scheduling this set is schedulable. For example, within the first 10 units two copies of T_1 and one copy of T_2 can be scheduled. Specifically, the first of T_1 will be scheduled at time unit 0, since T_1 has a higher priority than T_2. T_2 will be scheduled at time unit 3. At time unit 5 another request of T_1 comes while T_2 is still running. The priority of T_2 is higher than T_1 since its deadline is at time unit 8 compared to the deadline of T_2 at unit 10. Again, it can be verified that 8 copies of T_1 and 5 copies of T_2 can be scheduled within the first $8 \times 5 = 40$ time units.

Checking the schedulability of a given task set T_i $(1 \leq i \leq n)$ can be tedious. In the worst case when $c_i's$ are relative prime, $c_1 \times c_2 \times ... \times c_n$ units of time have to be checked following the above approach. The schedulability test can be simplified using the fact that, for a set of independent periodic tasks, if each task meets its first deadline when all tasks are started at the same time (which corresponds to the worst case) then the deadlines for all tasks will always be met for any combination of starting times. To do so we use the concept of *scheduling points* for task T which are T's first deadline and the ends of periods of higher priority tasks prior to T's first deadline. All we need to check are scheduling points for the lowest priority task. If the task set is schedulable for one of its scheduling points, the task set is schedulable; otherwise, the task set is not schedulable.

Let us re-examine the example of T_1: $c_1 = 3$, $t_1 = 5$ and T_2: $c_2 = 3$, $t_2 = 8$ with an overall utilization of 0.975. The scheduling points for T_2 are 5 and 8; clearly, it is impossible to schedule one copy of T_1 and one copy of T_2 before point 5 and two copies of T_1 and one copy of T_2 before

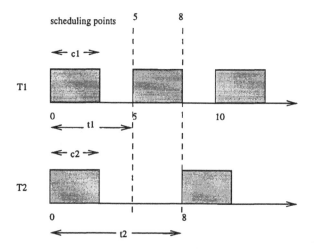

FIGURE 9.17
An example of periodic tasks that is not schedulable.

point 8. Therefore, this task set is not schedulable. Consider a task set of three tasks: $c_1 = 40$, $t_1 = 100$, $c_2 = 50$, $t_2 = 150$, and $c_3 = 80$, $t_3 = 350$. The overall utilization is $0.4 + 0.333 + 0.229 = 0.962$ (again more than the bound 0.779 for three tasks). The scheduling points for T_3 are 350 (for T_3), 300 (for T_1 and T_2), 200 (for T_1), 150 (for T_2), 100 (for T_1):

$$c_1 + c_2 + c_3 \leq t_1,$$

$$40 + 50 + 80 > 100;$$

$$2c_1 + c_2 + c_3 \leq t_2,$$

$$80 + 50 + 80 > 150;$$

$$2c_1 + 2c_2 + c_3 \leq 2t_2,$$

$$80 + 100 + 80 > 200;$$

$$3c_1 + 2c_2 + c_3 \leq 2t_3,$$

$$120 + 100 + 80 < 300;$$

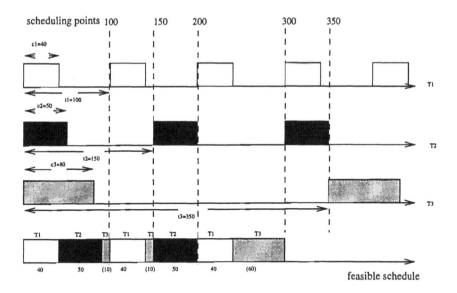

FIGURE 9.18
A schedulable periodic task.

$$4c_1 + 3c_2 + c_3 \leq t_1,$$

$$160 + 150 + 80 > 350.$$

Therefore, this set of tasks is schedulable at point 300 (see Figure 9.18).

Rate monotonic scheduling has been applied in many practical systems such as the 802.5 network and the FDDI access protocol. The rate monotonic scheduling has also been extended to periodic task with precedence constraints [18].

9.8.3   Fault secure schedule through task duplication: tree-structured task precedence graphs

The concept of fault security was first introduced in logic circuit design [20]. Banerjee and Abraham [1] applied this idea to scheduling. In their approach each node in the task graph is duplicated and results compared. The type of fault is restricted to a single hardware fault. Since many time slots of processors are idle as a result of conventional scheduling, they suggested to use these idle time slots for duplicates. Comparison of the results of the duplicates achieves the fault-secure property without affecting significantly the completion time of the task graph.

Gu, Rosenkrantz, and Ravi [15] further developed this approach by introducing the concept of *k-fault-secure scheduling*. In such a schedule for every fault pattern of at most size k, the output of a system is guaranteed to be either correct or tagged as incorrect. They considered schemes for special types of computation trees and showed that some well known parallel computation paradigms have binary trees as task graphs. In [43] Wu, Fernandez, and Dai studied the following two fault-secure scheduling problems where the computation graph under consideration is a complete binary tree with unit length tasks, unit length comparators, and negligible interprocessor communication costs.

1. Given the number of processors in the system the tasks are scheduled such that the total execution time is minimized and the resultant schedule is fault-secure. For convenience this number is restricted to 2^h, where h is a positive integer.

2. Given a deadline not smaller than the lower bound for conventional non-fault-tolerant scheduling, tasks are scheduled on a minimum number of processors such that they can still be completed within the given time limit and the resultant schedule is fault-secure.

Given a task precedence graph G which is a tree, a schedule σ maps nodes in G to time slots of processors. More specifically, $\sigma(N) = (P, i)$ where N represents a node in G, P is a processor, and i is a unit-time slot in the execution of tasks by P. Let $G(p)$ be a computation tree with depth p and the minimum total execution time of a schedule for $G(p)$ is p. To achieve the fault-secure property is to duplicate the execution of a task and then compare the results. The scheduling algorithm does this by duplicating each node and by carrying out binary equality tests on two versions. Fault detection occurs when some test reports "not equal". If any test reports a "not equal", we discard this output and the system is still safe. It has been shown [15] that to ensure 1-fault-security at least 2-version computation is necessary. However, depending on how the versions are arranged, a comparator that compares two versions of a node may or may not be necessary. Therefore, the key issue here is to arrange tests and duplicates.

Let us start with the test arrangement. Clearly two versions of a node should be assigned to two different processors to ensure a fault-secure computation. Suppose we want to test node N and its duplicate N'. We need

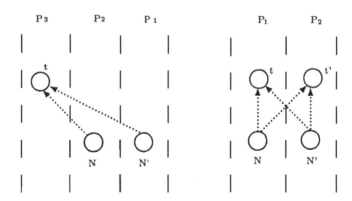

FIGURE 9.19
The assignment of the comparator (a) to a third processor (b) to one of two processors used.

to decide where to locate the comparator. It can be located at one of the two processors or at a third processor. When the comparator is located at a third processor, the 1-fault-secure property is straightforward. In Figure 9.19 (a), if one of the two processors (P_1 or P_2) on which two versions are assigned is faulty, the comparator (t) on P_3 (a healthy processor) will catch the error. If P_3 is faulty then the comparator can generate any decision (pass or fail); however both versions on the healthy processors produce correct results, the final outcome is still safe. If a comparator is located in one of the two processors on which the two versions are assigned, then 1-fault-security cannot be assured. Suppose the processor on which the comparator is assigned fails and the comparator passes the test, then the version on this faulty processor will be considered correct. In order to avoid this situation two versions of the comparator (t and t' in Figure 9.19 (b)) should be used and assigned to different processors. To choose between Figure 9.19 (a) or (b) one should note that the configuration in Figure 9.19 (a) saves one test; however, the test has to be run on a third processor.

Extending the idea used in Figure 9.19 by replacing each node by a subtree or a complete computation tree, we can derive the following scheme using only one or two comparators for the entire computation tree: Replace nodes N and N' in Figure 9.19 (a) by two versions of a complete computation tree G and each processor (except the third processor P_3) by a set of processors. We then derive two fault-secure schedules (one uses one comparator with one additional processor and the other uses two comparators but no additional processors) that use a minimum number of time slots and minimum possible time, i.e., the depth of the tree plus one. The basic fault-secure schedule uses the following steps:

1. The node set of $G(p)$ is partitioned into a set of precedence partitions $\{L_1, L_2, ..., L_p\}$ of levels, where L_i is the node set of nodes at level i.

2. The processor set is partitioned into two sets, P_{up} and P_{down}, of equal size.

3. The nodes in $G(p)$ are assigned level by level to entries of each time slot of P_{up} in a Gantt chart; that is, nodes in level i are assigned to time slot i (we assume that time slots start from 1).

4. The duplicated node set is also assigned in the same way into P_{down}.

5. When two comparators are used to check two versions of the root node, these two tests can be assigned to any two processors in P_{up} or P_{down} at time slot $p+1$ (the last time slot).

6. When one comparator is used, the test has to be assigned to a processor not in P_{up} or P_{down}.

Clearly, the minimum number of processors used is $|P_{up}| + |P_{down}| = 2 * max\{|L_i|\}$, where $1 \leq i \leq p$, and two comparators are used. One additional processor is required when one comparator is used.

In the computation tree shown in Figure 9.20 , $max\{L_1, L_2, L_3, L_4\} = 4$. Figure 9.21 shows a schedule produced by the above algorithm for the graph of Figure 9.20 where $P_{up} = \{P_1, P_2, P_3, P_4\}$ and $P_{down} = \{P_5, P_6, P_7, P_8\}$ and two comparators are used. Each number in the first line corresponds to time slot i. If N_j and N_j' are two versions of the same node, we use $t(N_j, N_j')$ to represent the equality test on N_j. If the test itself has two versions, we use $t(N_j, N_j')$ and $t'(N_j, N_j')$ to represent them. $N_k^*(N_i^*, N_j^*)$ represents the fact that the computation of N_k^* requires inputs from N_i^* and N_j^*.

Fault-secure scheduling with a fixed number of processors.

We now study bounds on time for a fault-secure schedule when the number of processors is fixed. We assume that the number of processors m is always a power of 2, say $m = 2^h$, where h is a positive integer. When $h > p$, there are enough processors to carry out the basic fault-secure scheduling and the processing time is bounded by $p+1$. When $h \leq p$, there are not enough processors to execute according to the basic scheduling algorithm

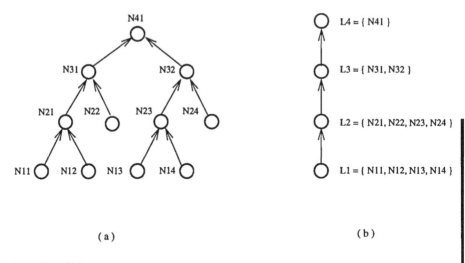

(a)   (b)

FIGURE 9.20
Example of a computation tree.

	1	2	3	4	5
P_1	N_{11}	$N_{21}(N_{11}, N_{12})$	$N_{31}(N_{21}, N_{22})$		
P_2	N_{12}	N_{22}	$N_{32}(N_{23}, N_{24})$		
P_3	N_{13}	$N_{23}(N_{13}, N_{14})$		$N_{41}(N_{31}, N_{32})$	
P_4	N_{14}	N_{24}			$t(N_{41}, N_{41}')$
P_5	N_{11}'	$N_{21}'(N_{11}', N_{12}')$	$N_{31}'(N_{21}', N_{22}')$		
P_6	N_{12}'	N_{22}'	$N_{32}'(N_{23}', N_{24}')$		
P_7	N_{13}'	$N_{23}'(N_{13}', N_{14}')$		$N_{41}'(N_{31}', N_{32}')$	
P_8	N_{14}'	N_{24}'			$t'(N_{41}', N_{41}')$

FIGURE 9.21
Fault-secure scheduling for the computation graph of Figure 9.20
by the basic fault-secure schedule.

and we need to develop other fault-secure scheduling algorithms. Since at least two processors are needed to perform a fault-secure computation, h is always greater than 0. For a non-fault-secure scheduling of an arbitrary computation tree G, Hu [19] found the following lower bound. Given m processors the minimum time T required to process a tree $G(p)$ of unit tasks is bounded as follows:

Let

$$q = \max_{1 \le x \le p} \{ \frac{1}{m} \sum_{j=1}^{x} |L_j| - x \}$$

then

$$T \ge p + \lceil q \rceil$$

Given $m = 2^h$ processors and a complete binary tree $G(p)$ with $h \le p$, then $T \ge 2^{p-h} + h - 1$. Given $m = 2^h$ processors and a complete binary tree $G(p)$ with $h \le p$, the minimum time T required for fault-secure scheduling is larger than or equal to $2^{p-h} + h$. Note that Hu's bound is for non-fault-secure schedules; that is, schedules where tasks are not duplicated. Therefore, if a fault-secure schedule matches this bound (with one more step), then this schedule is optimal. The following result shows another bound based on an ideal fault-secure scheduling that does not create any idle entries in a Gantt chart. Given $m = 2^h$ processors and a complete binary tree $G(p)$, let T be the total execution time of a fault-secure schedule. If $h \le p$, then

$$T \ge \begin{cases} 2^{p-h+1} & h = 1 \\ 2^{p-h+1} + 1 & h \ne 1 \end{cases}$$

Combining the above results we have the following bounds on time for a fault-secure computation. Given $m = 2^h$ processors and a complete binary computation tree $G(p)$, the minimum time T required to process a fault-secure computation of G on m processors is bounded as follows:

$$T = \begin{cases} p+1 & h \ge p \\ 2^{p-h} + h & 1 < h < p \wedge h + log(h-1) \ge p \\ 2^{p-h+1} + 1 & 1 < h < p \wedge h + log(h-1) < p \\ 2^p & 1 = h < p \end{cases}$$

When $h \ge p$ the basic fault-secure scheduling algorithm can be directly applied. When $1 = h < p$, i.e., there are two processors, we define a total order (or topological sorting order) of the computation tree based on the precedence order. Nodes in G are assigned to one processor based on this

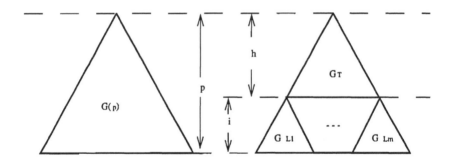

FIGURE 9.22
Partition of G_p into G_T and G_{L_j}.

total order and duplicates are assigned to the other processor. Since there are $2^p - 1$ nodes in G, 2^p time slots are needed that include the slot used for comparison. Obviously there are no idle entries in the resultant Gantt chart.

When $1 < h < p$, there are not enough processors available to execute the simple fault-secure scheduling. Assume a complete binary tree G_T of depth h is a subtree of the given computation tree G that shares the same root node with G (see Figure 9.22). Let $i = p - h$, i.e., i is the number of levels in G below subtree G_T. Nodes in the lower i levels consist of $m = 2^h$ independent complete binary trees G_{L_j} of depth i. The basic scheduling strategy is as follows: Each $G_{L_j}, 1 \leq j \leq m$, is first assigned to m distinct processors. In this case the first $2^{p-h} - 1$ time slots are used to process one version of all the G_{L_j} (see Figure 9.23). Then the simple fault-secure schedule is used to assign two versions of G_T using additional $h + 1$ time slots. The idle entries (the shadowed areas in Figure 9.23) generated in the scheduling of G_T are used to assign the duplicates and tests of nodes in G_{L_j}.

Depending on the values of p and h the idle entries may not be enough for the duplicates and the tests of nodes in G_{L_j}. Therefore, additional time slots may be needed. Let us first determine the point where there are just enough idle entries. We can achieve this objective in three steps. First, count the number of idle slots in the fault-secure schedule of the G_T part that may possibly be used in fault-secure computation for the nodes in G_{L_j}. Secondly, count the number of duplicates in G_{L_j} and tests of G_{L_j}. Third, arrange these computations and tests in the idle entries.

As a first step, we count the number of idle entries in the fault-secure

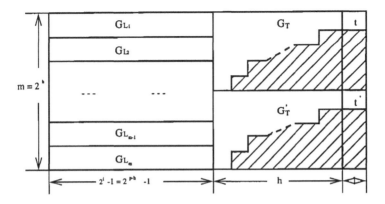

FIGURE 9.23
Fault-secure scheduling when $p > h$.

schedule of G_T. The total number of entries in the schedule for the G_T part is $m(h + 1) = 2^h(h + 1)$. $2(2^h - 1) - 2$ entries are used to include the two versions of G_T and two entries for the two tests, and hence, the total number of idle time slots in the schedule of G_T is

$$2^h(h + 1) - 2(2^h - 1) - 2 = 2^h(h - 1) \tag{9.1}$$

As a second step, we count the number of entries required for the duplicates and tests of G_{L_j} to provide the fault-secure property for the whole $G(p)$.

Since the output of one version of G_{L_j} is used as the input to both versions of G_T, at least one test is required for each subtree G_{L_j}. That is, 2^h entries are needed for the tests and obviously $2^h(2^i - 1)$ entries are used for the duplicates. Then, the total number of entries required for the duplicates and tests of G_{L_j} is

$$2^h + 2^h(2^i - 1) = 2^{h+i} \tag{9.2}$$

Equating expression (9.2) to (9.1), we get, $2^{h+i} = 2^h(h - 1)$, then $i = \log(h - 1)$.

When $i \leq \log(h - 1)$, no additional entries are used and the total time is

$$(2^i - 1) + h + 1 = 2^i + h = 2^{p-h} + h$$

which achieves the bound (when $i \leq log(h-1)$). When $i > log(h-1)$, the additional time needed can be calculated as follows:

$$\frac{2^{h+i} - 2^h(h-1)}{2^h} = 2^i - h + 1$$

By adding the time used to the above calculated additional time, we have,

$$(2^i + h) + (2^i - h + 1) = 2^i 2 + 1 = 2^{p-h+1} + 1$$

which achieves the bound (when $i \geq log(h-1)$).

Notice that the above derivation gives us only a necessary condition since we have not considered the precedence constraints of the computation G_{L_j}. The sufficiency condition is obvious. We assign duplicates level by level starting from nodes in level one and tests are assigned last after all the nodes in the corresponding subtree have been assigned. The idle entries to which duplicated tasks and tests are assigned are also arranged level by level starting from level $2^i + 1$. The only constraint that needs to be followed is that the two versions of each node and the test for these two versions should be assigned to three different processors. The enforcement of this constraint is straightforward. For a detailed discussion on this topic see [43].

Fault-secure scheduling under deadlines.

There are cases where we are allowed to exceed the minimum time $p+1$. We now consider how to determine the minimum number of processors $G(p)$ in a fault-secure computation under a given deadline $p+1+c$ where c is a nonnegative integer.

We generated in the last section a general fault-secure scheduling algorithm that produces fault-secure schedules with minimum total execution times for a given number of processors m ($m = 2^h$). Now the problem becomes: Given a $G(p)$ select a schedule that produces a fault-secure schedule of time $T \leq p+1+c$ and uses a minimum number of processors.

First let us consider the delays compared to the minimum execution time $p+1$ in the optimal results obtained in the last section,

- The delay is $D_1 = 0$ when $h \geq p$.

- The delay is $D_2 = h + 2^{p-h} - (p+1)$ when $(1 < h < p) \wedge (h + log(h-1) \geq p)$.

- The delay is $D_3 = 2^{p-h+1} + 1 - (p+1)$ when $(1 < h < p) \land (h + \log(h-1) \leq p)$.

- The delay is $D_4 = 2^p - (p+1) = 2^p - p - 1$ when $1 = h < p$.

We intend to determine $m = 2^h$ where h is a minimum positive integer such that D_i, $i \leq r \leq 4$, is less than or equal to a given c. More precisely,

- Let H_1 be the minimum h in a basic fault-secure schedule that satisfies

$$0 \leq c \land p \leq q$$

- Let H_2 be the minimum h in a fault-secure solution that satisfies

$$h + 2^{p-h} - (p+1) \leq c \land 1 < h < p \land p \leq h + \log(h-1)$$

- Let H_3 be the minimum h in a fault-secure solution that satisfies

$$2^{p-h+1} + 1 - (p+1) \leq c \land 1 < h < p \land h + \log(h-1) < p$$

- Let $H_4 = 1$ in a fault-secure solution that uses two processors and satisfies

$$2^p - p - 1 \leq c$$

Then the selection of h is as follows,

$$h = \min\{H_1, H_2, H_3, H_4\}$$

Notice that when $c = 0$, H_1 will give us the solution where $h = p$ and H_2 will give us the solution where $h = p - 1$. Taking the minimum, $h = p - 1$; i.e., $m = 2^{p-1}$ is the minimum number of processors to execute the fault-secure computation of $G(p)$ in $p+1$ time slots. For $c > 0$ the solution set H_1 is empty. When $c \geq 2^p - p - 1$, $H_4 = 1$ is selected.

Fault-tolerant scheduling by exploiting implicit redundancy has been studied under other models such as SPMD (single-program, multiple-data) [13] and MIMD [16].

9.9   Future Directions

Most of the existing heuristic-based scheduling algorithms perform comparably. It is unlikely that a better method can be found to achieve order-of-magnitude improvements in performance. Future research will probably focus on tools to support practical applications of theoretic scheduling algorithms [38]:

- *Development of a graph-generator tool.* The input to a graph generator will be a parallel program written in a high level language and its output will be a precedence graph or a task interaction graph.

- *Development of an execution-time-estimation tool.* It provides reasonably accurate estimates of the execution times of tasks and communication delays. This tool will probably be assisted by user estimates, simulation-based estimates, or profile-based estimates.

- *Development of a performance-profile tool.* This tool will read in the schedule of a parallel program on a given architecture and produce a graphical profile of the expected performance.

- *Development of a data-distribution tool.* Most existing scheduling methods are based on function distribution (scheduling) and ignore the data distribution issue. This tool will produce a more accurate result by considering various data distribution cases.

Another important area is benchmarking scheduling algorithms [26]. A set of benchmarks should have diverse structures without being biased towards a particular scheduling technique and still allow variations in important parameters. Samples of existing tools are: OREGAMI [32], Parafrase-2 [34], Parallax [30], PARSA [37], and PYRROS [46]. Most of them include a partitioner-tool, a scheduler-tool, and a performance-profiler-tool.

References

[1] Banerjee, P. and J. A. Abraham, "Fault-secure algorithms for multiple processor systems", *Proc. of the 11th Int'l Symp. on Computer*

Architecture, 1984, 279-287.

[2] Bokhari, S. H., "Dual processor scheduling with dynamic reassignment", *IEEE Transactions on Software Engineering*, **5**, 5, 1979, 341-349.

[3] Bokhari, S. H., *Assignment Problems in Parallel and Distributed Computing*, Kluwer Academic Publishers, 1987.

[4] Casavant, T. L. and J. G. Kuhl, "A taxonomy of scheduling in general-purpose distributed computing systems", in *Readings in Distributed Computing Systems*, T. L. Casavant and M. Singhal, ed., IEEE Computer Society Press, 1994.

[5] Chaudhary, V. and J. K. Agarwal, "A generalized scheme for mapping parallel algorithms", *IEEE Transactions on Parallel and Distributed Systems*, **4**, 3, March 1993, 328-346.

[6] Darbha, S. and D. P. Agrawal, "Optimal scheduling algorithm for distributed memory machines", *IEEE Transactions on Parallel and Distributed Systems*, **9**, 1, Jan. 1998, 87-95.

[7] Dinic, E. A., "Algorithm for the solution of a problem of maximum flow in a network with power estimation", *Soviet Mathematics: Doklady*, **11**, 5, 1970, 1277-1280.

[8] Edmonds, J. and R. M. Karp, "Theoretical improvements in algorithmic efficiency for network flow algorithms", *Journal of the ACM*, **19**, 2, Apr. 1972, 248-264.

[9] Efe, K., "Heuristic models of task assignment scheduling in distributed systems", *IEEE Computer*, **15**, 6, June 1982, 50-56.

[10] Fernandez, E. B. and B. Bussell, "Bounds on the number of processors and time for multiprocessor optimal schedules", *IEEE Transactions on Computers*, **22**, 8, Aug. 1973, 745-751.

[11] Ford, L. R. and D. R. Fulkerson, *Flows in Networks*, Princeton University Press, Princeton, New Jersey, 1962.

[12] Gerasoulis, A. and T. Yang, "On the granularity and clustering of directed acyclic task graphs", *IEEE Transactions on Parallel and Distributed Systems*, **4**, 6, 1993, 686-701.

[13] Gong, C., R. Melhem, and R. Gupta, "Loop transformations for fault detection in regular loops on massively parallel systems", *IEEE Trans-*

actions on Parallel and Distributed Systems, **7**, 12, Dec. 1996, 1238-1249.

[14] Greenblatt, B. and G. J. Linn, "Branch and bound style algorithms for scheduling communicating tasks in a distributed system", *Proc. of the IEEE Spring CompCon. Conf.,* 1987, 12-17.

[15] Gu, D., D. J. Rosenkrantz, and S. S. Ravi, "Construction and analysis of fault-secure multiprocessor schedules", *Proc. of the Int'l Symp. on Fault-Tolerant Computing Systems,* 1991, 120-127.

[16] Hashimoto, K., T. Tsuchiya, and T. Kikuno, "A new approach to realizing fault-tolerant multiprocessor scheduling by exploiting implicit redundancy", *Proc. of the 27th Int'l Symp. on Fault-Tolerant Computing,* 1997, 174-183.

[17] Holland, J. J., *Adaptation in Natural and Artificial Systems,* Univ. of Michigan Press, 1975.

[18] Hou, C. -J. and K. G. Shin, "Allocation of periodic task modules with precedence and deadline constraints in distributed real-time systems", *IEEE Transactions on Computers,* **46**, 12, Dec. 1997, 1338-1356.

[19] Hu, T. C., "Parallel sequencing and assembly line problems", *Operations Research,* **9**, Nov. 1961, 841-848.

[20] B. W. Johnson, *Design and Analysis of Fault-Tolerant Digital Systems,* Addison-Wesley Publishing Company, 1989.

[21] Karzanov, A. V., "Determining the maximal flow in a network by the method of preflows", *Soviet Mathematics: Doklady,* **15**, 2, 1974, 434-437.

[22] Kruatrachue, B. and T. Lewis, "Grain size determination for parallel processing", *IEEE Software,* **5**, 1, Jan. 1988, 23-32.

[23] Kumar, V., A. Grama, A. Gupta, and G. Karypis, *Introduction to Parallel Computing: Design and Analysis of Algorithms,* The Benjamin/Cummings Publishing Company, Inc., 1994.

[24] Kunz, T., "The influence of different workload descriptions on a heuristic load balancing scheme", *IEEE Transactions on Software Engineering,* **17**, 7, July 1991, 725-730.

[25] Kwok, Y. -K. and I. Ahmad, "Efficient scheduling of arbitrary task graphs to multiprocessors using a parallel genetic algorithm", *Journal of Parallel and Distributed Computing,* **47**, 1, 1997, 58-77.

[26] Kwok, Y. -K. and I. Ahmad, "Benchmarking the task graph scheduling algorithms", *Proc. of the 12th Int'l Parallel Processing Symp. and the 9th Symp. on Parallel and Distributed Processing*, 1998, 531-537.

[27] Lee, B., A. R. Hurson, and T. -Y. Feng, "A vertically layered allocation scheme for data flow system", *Journal of Parallel and Distributed System*, **11**, 3, 1991, 175-187.

[28] Lee, K. -G, "Efficient parallelization of simulated annealing using multiple Markov chains: an application to graph partition", *Proc. of the 1992 Int'l Conf. on Parallel Processing*, 1992, III 177-III 180.

[29] Lewis, T. G. and H. El-Rewini, *Introduction to Parallel Computing*, Prentice Hall, Inc., 1992.

[30] Lewis, T. G. and H. El-Rewini, "Parallax: A tool for parallel program scheduling", *IEEE Parallel and Distributed Technology*, **9**, 5, May 1993, 62-72.

[31] Lo, V. M., "Heuristic algorithms for task assignment in distributed systems", *IEEE Transactions on Computers*, **31**, 11, Nov. 1988, 1384-1397.

[32] Lo, V. M. et al., "OREGAMI: Tools for mapping parallel computations to parallel architectures", *International Journal of Parallel Programming*, **20**, 3, 1991, 237-270.

[33] Liu, C. L. and J. W. Layland, "Scheduling algorithms for multiprogramming in a hard real-time environment", *Journal of the ACM*, **20**, 1, 1972, 46-62.

[34] Polychronopoulos, C. D. et al., "Parafrase-2: An environment for parallelizing, partitioning, synchronizing, and scheduling programs on multiprocessors", *Proc. of the 1989 Int'l Conf. on Parallel Processing*, 1989, II 142-II 146.

[35] Prakash, S. and A. Parker, "SOS: synthesis of application-specific heterogeneous multiprocessor systems", *Journal of Parallel and Distributed Computing*, **16**, 4, Dec. 1992, 338-351.

[36] Salichs, M. A., "Task assignment across space and time in a distributed computer system", *IFAC Distributed Computer Control Systems*, 1983, 131-141.

[37] Shirazi, B. A. et al., "PARSA: A PARallel program Scheduling and Assessment tool", *Proc. of the 1994 Symp. on Assessment of Quality Software Development Tools*, 1994, 96-111.

[38] Shirazi, B. A., A. R. Hurson, and K. M. Kavi, *Scheduling and Load Balancing in Parallel and Distributed Systems*, IEEE Computer Society Press, 1995.

[39] Stone, H. S., "Multiprocessor scheduling with the aid of network flow algorithms", *IEEE Transactions on Software Engineering*, **3**, 1, Jan. 1977, 85-93.

[40] Vinnakota, B. and N. K. Jha, "Diagnosability and diagnosis of algorithm-based fault-tolerant systems", *IEEE Transactions on Computers*, **42**, 8, Aug. 1993, 925-937.

[41] Wu, J. and E. B. Fernandez, "A scheduling scheme for communicating tasks", *Proc. of the 22nd Southeastern Symp. on System Theory*, 1990, 91-97.

[42] Wu, J., "Fault-tolerant task scheduling", *International Journal of Mini and Microcomputers*, **13**, 3, 1991, 135-139.

[43] Wu, J., E. B. Fernandez, and D. Dai, "Optimal fault-secure scheduling", to appear in *The Computer Journal*.

[44] Wu, J., J. Pan, K. Gopu, F. Sklar, and Y. Wu, "Domain partition scheme for the Everglades Landscape Model (ELM)", *Proc. of the 4th Software Engineering Research Forum*, 1995, 53-59.

[45] Wu, J., H. Huang, C. Fitz, Y. Wu, and F. Sklar, "A new domain partition scheme for the Everglades Landscape Model (ELM)", to appear in *International Journal of Computers and Applications*.

[46] Yang, Y. and A. Gerasoulis, "PYRROS: static task scheduling and code generation for message passing multiprocessors", *Proc. of the 6th ACM Int'l Conf. on Supercomputing*, 1992, 428-437.

Problems

1. Compare the following pairs of related concepts:

   - Static load distribution vs. dynamic load distribution.

- Task precedence graph vs. task interaction graph.

2. Determine a schedule of the interaction graph in Figure 9.10 on a 3 × 3 mesh with a minimum cardinality.

3. Find an embedding of the interaction graph in Figure 9.10 on a 3 × 3 mesh with a minimum congestion. The dilation is limited to two and load to one.

4. Find an optimal schedule of the following tree-structured task precedence graph to two processors and three processors. Assume that the execution of each task is one unit.

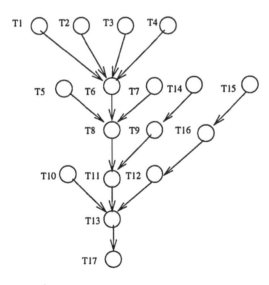

5. Find an optimal schedule of the following task precedence graph to two processors. Assume that the execution of each task is one unit.

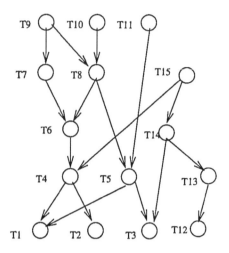

6. Consider the following two periodic tasks (with the same request time)

   - Task T_1: $c_1 = 4$, $t_1 = 9$
   - Task T_2: $c_2 = 6$, $t_2 = 14$

   (a) Determine the total utilization of these two tasks and compare it with Liu and Layland's least upper bound for the fixed priority schedule. What conclusion can you derive?

   (b) Show that these two tasks are schedulable using the rate-monotonic priority assignment. You are required to provide such a schedule.

   (c) Determine the schedulability of these two tasks if task T_2 has a higher priority than task T_1 in the fixed priority schedule.

   (d) Split task T_2 into two parts of 3 units computation each and show that these two tasks are schedulable using the rate-monotonic priority assignment.

   (e) Provide a schedule (from time unit 0 to time unit 30) based on deadline driven scheduling algorithm. Assume that the smallest preemptive element is one unit.

7. Use fault-secure scheduling to assign a 4-level complete binary tree to $m = 2^h = 8$ processors.

8. Repeat Problem 7 for (a) 16 processors, (b) 4 processors, and (c) 2 processors.

9. Use Stone's flow network approach to find an optimal schedule of the following graph to a two-processor system.

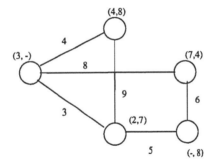

10. Prove Gerasoulis and Yang's result for the 2-processor scheduling problem (see Figure 9.6). Note that each communication cost and node cost should be represented by variables l and c, respectively.

11. Modify Gerasoulis and Yang's granularity definition $g(x)$ in a system where intraprocessor cost is nonzero. $g(x)$ should be defined in such a way that Gerasoulis and Yang's result is still valid.

Chapter 10

DYNAMIC LOAD
DISTRIBUTION

In a distributed system many algorithms contain nonuniform computation
and communication costs that cannot be easily determined *a priori*. In some
applications the workload evolves as the computation progresses meaning
that an initially good mapping can become bad. Dynamic load distribution
[10], [12], [24], [38], [46], [47] (also called *load balancing, load migration,* or
load sharing[1]) can be applied to restore balance. Dynamic load distribution algorithms use system state information (load information at nodes),
at least in part, to make load distribution decisions while static algorithms
make no use of this information. In this chapter basic dynamic load distribution approaches are discussed followed by an example of global dynamic
load distribution on hypercubes.

10.1 Dynamic Load Distribution

The limitation of static load distribution is that it assigns tasks to processors in a once-and-for-all manner and requires *a priori* knowledge of
program behavior. Most approaches ignore the effects of interference in a
system comprised of communicating processes and the effects of the evolving
process of computation. On the contrary, dynamic load balancing assumes
little or no compile-time knowledge about the runtime parameters such as
task execution times or communication delays. Dynamic load balancing
delays on the runtime redistribution of processes to achieve performance

---

[1]These items have subtle differences. In this text we use them interchangeably.

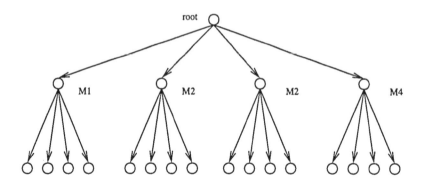

FIGURE 10.1
A state-space traversal example.

goals. Dynamic load balancing improves the system performance by providing a better dynamic utilization of all resources in the entire system.

Let us consider a *state-space traversal* example where a search tree, called a *game tree*, is generated while it is being searched. This approach is normally used in designing computer games such as checkers, chess, and go. In these games there are two players A and B. Each player takes a turn moving until one player wins (and the other loses) based on a predefined set of rules. In a game tree nodes correspond to board positions (or system states) and branches correspond to moves. Nodes on a path correspond to alternate moves between players.

Consider the example shown in Figure 10.1 where the root node corresponds to the current board position. Suppose player A needs to make a decision. There are four possible moves, M_i ($1 \le i \le 4$), for the next step. A good player normally calculates future steps by going deep into the search tree to evaluate the "goodness" of each (next) move. If there are four processors in a system, the static scheduling will assign one M_i to each distinct processor. However, certain branches may correspond to bad moves and these branches will be terminated in a few steps down the search tree. At this point the problem with static scheduling becomes apparent. The processor exploring the subtree rooted as a "bad" move expands considerably fewer nodes than other processors. Due to this imbalance in the workload, we may have a situation where one (or more) processor is idle while others are busy searching for a "good" move. A dynamical load balancing will re-schedule the load among processors. In this case the load balance algorithm transfers the load from the heavily loaded processors to the lightly loaded processors (including idle processors). Again, we use the terms task and process interchangeably.

10.1.1 Components of dynamic load distribution

Typically, a dynamic load distribution algorithm has six policies: initiation, transfer, selection, profitability, location, and information.

- *Initiation policy.* The responsibility of an initiation policy is to decide who should invoke load balancing activities. In a *sender-initiated* method the heavily loaded nodes initiate the load transfer process. In a *receiver-initiated* method the lightly loaded nodes start the load balancing process.

- *Transfer policy.* A transfer policy determines if a node is in a suitable state to participate in a load transfer. Most transfer policies are *threshold* policies [6]. Thresholds are expressed in units of load. When the workload of a node exceeds a threshold, workload in this node may need to be offloaded to another node in the network. If the load at a node falls below the threshold, the transfer policy decides that this node can be a receiver for a remote task.

- *Selection policy.* Source processors select the most suitable tasks for efficient and effective load balancing and send them to the appropriate destinations. The simplest approach is to select newly originated tasks that have caused the node to become a sender by increasing the load at the node beyond the threshold [6]. Such tasks are relatively inexpensive to transfer as the transfer is non-preemptive. Another approach is to preempt a running task; however, the cost resulting from the transfer of a running task may nullify the reduction in the response time realized by the transfer.

- *Profitability policy.* The imbalancing factor quantifies the degree of load imbalance within a given system. It is used as an estimate of potential profit obtainable through load balancing and weighed against the load balancing overhead to determine whether or not load balancing is profitable at that time. A decision on load balancing is made based on the value of $\phi(t)$ relative to the balancing overhead, $\psi(t)$, required to perform the load balancing, where $\phi(t)$ is the *load imbalance factor* to estimate the potential profit obtainable through load balancing at time t. This can be defined as a function of the difference between the maximum processor load before and after load balancing, L_{max} and L_{bal}, respectively.

$$\phi(t) = f(L_{max} - L_{bal})$$

In general, load balancing is profitable if the saving is greater than the overhead, i.e.,

$$\phi(t) > \psi(t)$$

There are three sources of balancing overhead: (1) The load information transferred among processors. (2) The decision-making process for the selection of a task (or several tasks) for task transfer. (3) The communication delays due to task migration itself.

- *Location policy.* Location policy is in charge of finding suitable nodes (locations) to share loads. A widely used method to find a suitable node is through *polling*. A node, usually the node that initiates the load balancing, polls another node to determine whether it is a suitable node for load sharing [3]. For a *local range approach* only nodes in the neighborhood are candidates for polling; on the contrary, any node in a system may be polled in a *global range approach*. Determining a node for polling from all candidates may be either random or based on the information collected during previous polls. An alternative to polling is to broadcast a query to determine if any node is available for load sharing.

- *Information policy.* Information policy is responsible for deciding when information on the states of other nodes in the system should be collected, where it should be collected, and what information should be collected. The more information collected at each node, the more efficient the corresponding load balancing process. However, the information collection process itself introduces overhead. Therefore, trade-offs are required.

10.1.2 Dynamic load distribution algorithms

In general, a dynamic load distribution algorithm must be general, adaptable, stable, scalable, fault-tolerant, and transparent to applications. Load balancing algorithms can be classified as follows [33] :

- *Global vs. local.* In a local load balancing algorithm, the workload is transferred among individual nodes in the neighborhood. In a global load balancing algorithm, rather than exchanging the load among nodes in the neighborhood, processors strive to calculate the load on the entire system and to adjust their own load relative to the global value.

- *Centralized vs. decentralized.* In a centralized algorithm, a central controller collects the system status information and makes the decision to balance the load. In a decentralized load balancing algorithm, the control mechanism is physically distributed to each node in the entire system. The semi-decentralized load balancing [14] is a trade-off between the centralized and decentralized algorithms.

- *Noncooperative vs. cooperative.* In a noncooperative approach, each node decides its own location and transfer policies without knowing the states of the other nodes in the system. Nodes coordinate with each other to make a load balancing decision in the cooperative approach.

- *Adaptive vs. nonadaptive.* In an adaptive approach [20], [45], load balancing policies are modified as the system state changes; these policies are unchanged in the nonadaptive approach.

10.2 Load Balancing Design Decisions

Several decisions in designing mechanisms for load balancing are considered in this section. A list of decisions follows:

1. *Static vs. dynamic algorithms.* Types of algorithms used.

2. *Various information policies.* Processor load information and task migration information.

3. *Centralized vs. decentralized algorithms.* Involvement of processors in assimilating load information.

4. *Migration initiation policy.* Processor initiating the load balancing process.

5. *Resource duplication.* Resources replicated and assigned to different processors.

6. *Classes of processes.* Types of processes in the system.

7. *Operating system vs. separate task initiated policy.* Load balancing done by an operating system or a dedicated process.

8. *Open loop vs. closed loop control.* Use of feedback to change parameters.

9. *Use of hardware vs. software.* System involvement in load balancing.

10.2.1 Static versus dynamic algorithms

When processes are well defined in terms of their execution time and resource requirements and their arrival rates are known beforehand, load balancing can be done with relative ease. The algorithms can be classified as static load distribution or scheduling algorithms discussed in Chapter 9.

For problems that deal with the unknown arrival rate of processes at processors, it is impossible to evolve a deterministic strategy to migrate processes to other processors. Some dynamic load distribution algorithms are non-preemptive (also called *load sharing*); that is, nodes can only distribute newly arrived tasks. Others are preemptive (also called *task migrations*) and can redistribute a running task. Non-preemptive approaches can be further classified into *at-most-once-schedule* and *multiple-schedule*. In at-most-once-schedule approaches once a task is scheduled to a processor, it cannot be redistributed even if it is still in a waiting queue. In multiple-schedule approaches a scheduled task can be redistributed as long as it is still in a waiting queue, i.e., it is not running. Normally the following steps are included in a task migration: (a) Suspend the migrating process on the source node, (b) transfer the process together with its current state to the destination node, and (c) resume the execution of the process in the destination node.

Two types of processes are defined, *generic* and *regular* [2]. A generic process can be individually allocated to any node. A regular process can only be assigned locally. That is, generic processes can be used for dynamic load sharing while regular processes cannot be shared or migrated.

10.2.2 Various information policies

Information policies decide the information needed for efficient load balancing. It is essential that an overloaded processor know the possible destinations. Moreover, the other processors in the system also need to know about the overloaded processors.

Periodic vs. aperiodic information

One way to collect system information is to query the status of the processors' load levels or broadcast these load levels. Broadcast or query can be done only when a critical situation like an overloaded or idle state is encountered. Alternatively, it can be done on a regular basis by all the processors. The former way is *aperiodic* while the latter is *periodic*.

A periodic method will result in more overhead if the load is not changing rapidly; however, it ensures that all the processors know about the level of load on the other processors with a sufficient degree of accuracy at any given time. The time period between two consecutive rounds of information exchanges is an important parameter. The period itself can be changed dynamically based on the performance of the system. On the other hand, an aperiodic exchange of information can save communication overhead but a processor that becomes overloaded or is idle has to spend time finding a suitable acceptor or donor of the workload.

Global vs. local information

Collecting global information may be too costly for a large system. An alternative is to collect local information within a certain range. Finding a *locally minimum* [22] loaded processor for load migration can be more suitable under certain circumstances than finding the global minimum. This will be true when the distance between the processors is large and the communication costs for large distances become prohibitive. Also, in cases where large files are to be sent to the destination processor as a part of load migration, it will be better to send the processes to a site closer to the sender even if there exists a processor that is more lightly loaded but further away. This strategy also allows a processor to keep less information on the system load.

Processor load information

Normally the workload of a processor is decided based on the CPU queue length, service rate, and number of processes. According to [1] the physical differences of processors like speed, size of main memory, paging activity and ratio of processing activities to input/output activities in the task are other factors to determine the workload.

In some situations when a process is executed repeatedly, the information from initial runs can be used to provide an estimate of the corresponding process load. History is a filter to keep track of process names and previous execution records to detect repeated processes. In [18] Kunz studied the influence of workload information on the effectiveness of a load balance scheme.

10.2.3   Centralized vs. decentralized algorithms

Centralized algorithms have a central processor that receives load information from other processors in the system.

In some centralized systems the central processor, after getting the complete picture of the load state of the system, sends the assimilated information to individual processors so that these processors know the system state when they need to migrate their processes or accept new processes. It is possible to design a system in a manner such that processors in need of new processes can request the central processor to suggest the target based on the information collected. In these systems the centralized processor need not send the global load state to the individual process. This is designed to reduce communication overhead. This technique is described in [2] and [47].

A single central processor also brings about a complete system failure in terms of load migration activity when the centralized processor fails. The similarity between the load balancing caused by newly arrived tasks and the load balancing caused by processor failure is discussed in [41].

Decentralized algorithms are implemented with each individual processor by sending the change in its load to all other processors or to its neighbors. The neighbors will, in turn, send the information to their neighbors. All the processors will have the global view after sufficient rounds of information exchange are done ([11], [22], [28], [35], [47]). Decentralized algorithms are more fault tolerant than centralized ones, but the burden of collecting the system state information is shifted from one dedicated processor to each individual processor. Thus, the overall time spent by a processor in collecting the system load information is likely to increase.

10.2.4   Migration initiation policy

There are two ways to initiate load balancing. When the overloaded processor is responsible for searching potential processors to accept its extra load, the algorithm is termed as *sender-initiated*. When the underloaded processor initiates a load balancing algorithm to obtain a task from an overloaded processor, the algorithm is called *receiver-initiated*. A combination of sender-initiated and receiver-initiated approach is called *symmetrically initiated*. A detailed discussion on migration initiation policy will be discussed in the next section.

10.2.5 Resource replication

When a task has to be migrated, the files and data involved must also be made available to the destination processor. If the files and data are large, the overhead involved in sending them to the destination processor will be substantial. In order to reduce migration overhead, migrating tasks can be replicated and assigned to different processors. [9] deals with replication of files among processors so this overhead can be minimized. This will entail more space usage among processes and also an extra mechanism to keep track of the most current version of the files.

10.2.6 Classes of processes

Distinction can be made regarding the type of processes. Processes belonging to a generic class like text processing, systems programs, simulation programs, interactive programs, etc., can be treated in a particular manner since they have similar characteristics. If the processes running on the system are very different from each other, they have to be treated on an individual basis. When there is more than one process class in a system, load balancing strategies can vary depending on the class of process under consideration. Load balancing strategies for multiple classes of processes are discussed in [17], [21], [26], and [27]. Most of the load balancing algorithms, however, consider a single task class in load balancing.

10.2.7 Operating system vs. separate task initiated policy

It is possible to incorporate load balancing strategies in the operating system itself so that load balancing becomes an integral part of the operating system. The other alternative is to have a separate load balancing process. [5] describes Charlotte, Sprite, and other operating systems that have load balancing strategies built into them. Sprite's migration mechanism provides a high degree of transparency for both migrated processes and users. Idle processors are identified and eviction is invoked automatically by demon processes.

10.2.8   Open loop vs. closed loop control

An open loop control algorithm does not take into account the results of past activities in making its decisions. A closed loop algorithm tries to prevent the algorithm from wandering away from the desired functionality by keeping tabs on its decisions and making changes in its parameters so that it progresses in the required manner. Closed loop algorithms [25] need to be designed carefully or they may become unstable and increase overhead. If the load between neighbors suddenly changes in such a way that a large amount of communication and migration activity occurs virtually disallowing any computation, the values of various thresholds should be adjusted so that less migration can occur.

10.2.9   Use of hardware vs. software

Load balancing can be done using software that tracks the processes at different processors. Hardware systems can also be employed for such an effort. The concept of semi-private memory as an architectural means of load balancing is introduced in [19]. A novel dynamic load balancing and user-allocation mechanism for an advanced session-based file-store architecture to improve overall system performance is discussed in [30]. Such an architecture comprises several LAN-based file servers working together to implement a global and distributed file store for a distributed system. The load balancing and user allocation algorithms are the responsibilities of a high-level coordinator that is either centralized or decentralized. The system mentioned in [23] has special-purpose low cost processors that handle overhead due to load balancing such as information gathering and task migration.

10.3   Migration Policies: Sender-initiated and Receiver-initiated

In the sender-initiated approach the sender may select its destination randomly or sequentially. Each processor keeps two thresholds: One for the overloaded situation (*high water mark* or HWM) and the other for the underloaded situation (*low water mark* or LWM). A simplified algorithm is shown below using DCDL where polling is random and limited by *Poll-Limit*. The CPU queue length is measured by *QueueLength*. A graphical

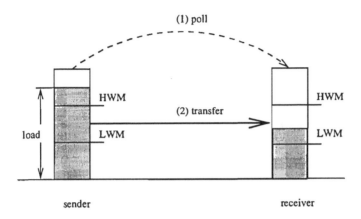

FIGURE 10.2
Sender-initiated load balancing.

description of the sender-initiated approach is shown in Figure 10.2.

```
/* a new task arrives */
queue_length ≥ HWM →
    * [  poll_set := φ;
         [ | poll_set | < poll_limit →
             [ select a new node u randomly;
               poll_set := poll_set ∪ node u;
               queue_length at u < HWM →
                   transfer a task to node u and stop
             ]
         ]
    ]
```

A *receiver-initiated* system makes the idle or underloaded processors so-
licit work from the overloaded processors. The research in [8], [22], [31], and
[47] treats this strategy in some detail. Whenever the load on a processor
becomes less than LWM, the processor sends requests to other processors.
If there are several overloaded processors, the receiver can accept as many
processes as will make its load level medium. A graphical description of
the receiver-initiated approach is shown in Figure 10.3.

```
/* a task departs */
queue_length < LWM →
```

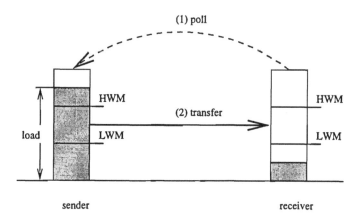

FIGURE 10.3
Receiver-initiated load balancing.

[*poll_limit*:=ϕ;
   * [| *poll_set* | < *poll_limit* →
          [select a new node *u* randomly;
             poll_set := *poll_set* ∪ node *u*;
             queue_length at *u* > HWM →
                 transfer a task from node *u* and **stop**
          ]
     ]
]

In the above algorithm it is assumed that the same algorithm will be applied after a predetermined period if it fails to find a suitable node for task transfer.

The results in [39] indicate that the load balancing decision considering the state of the destination performs better than the decisions that consider the state of the source. During the period of migrating the load, the receiver's load status can change abruptly after it is probed and found to be lightly loaded. In such cases a policy must be determined to see whether it will be mandatory for the receiver to process it, or the sender should try any other receiver. In some algorithms, once the receiver is drafted for load migration, the receiver stops accepting other senders' loads. In general, the sender-initiated algorithm outperforms the receiver-initiated algorithm in lightly loaded systems and vice versa in heavy loaded systems.

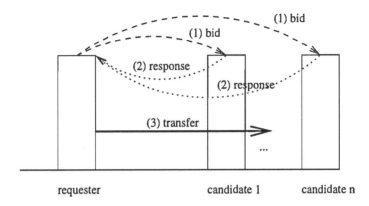

FIGURE 10.4
Bidding algorithm.

In the *bidding* algorithm a local site initiates bidding when it is over-loaded. At the local site requests for bids are sent to remote sites. When bids are received from remote sites, they are evaluated and the one that offers the lowest bid is selected [7]. A graphical description of the bidding algorithm is shown in Figure 10.4.

Another distributed and adaptive load-sharing scheme called *alternate* is proposed in [38]. This scheme alternates between sender-initiated and receiver-initiated, dynamically depending on the current system load with the goal of obtaining good performance at all load levels.

10.4 Parameters Used for Load Balancing

The formation and selection of a load balancing algorithm depend on a set of quantifiable components. These components are considered as parameters of the system in the following:

1. *System size.* Number of processors in the system.

2. *System load.* Load on processors.

3. *System traffic intensity.* Arrival rate of tasks at different processors.

4. *Migration threshold.* Load levels to trigger task migration.

5. *Task size.* Size of a task sufficient for migration effort.

6. *Overhead costs.* Costs incurred in communication and task placement.

7. *Response time.* Turnaround time for a task.

8. *Load balancing horizon.* Number of neighbors to be probed in determining task destination.

9. *Resource demands.* Demands on system resources by a task.

10.4.1 System size

The number of processors in the system is one of the parameters influencing load balancing decisions. More processors make it more probable for any overloaded processor to find an underloaded processor to migrate its tasks. This positive effect competes with the negative effect produced by the larger message passing overhead created by the large system size.

10.4.2 System load

Normally system load is measured by the CPU queue length as mentioned earlier. If the system is heavily loaded and more processes arrive at a processor, any migration of processes from a heavily loaded processor is likely to trigger a cascade of migrations away from other processors. This may lead to a phenomenon called *processor thrashing* that occurs when a task is migrated from a processor resulting in the destination processor remigrating the task. In such cases the incoming processes should not be migrated.

10.4.3 System traffic intensity

Processes arriving at processors can follow any random pattern. If processors can determine their traffic intensity and compare it with other processors, it is easier to estimate the instantaneous load level of the system. This enables the processors to make better decisions regarding task transfers.

10.4.4 Migration threshold

A threshold has to be determined heuristically either by experimentation or dynamic assessment of the characteristics of the system to decide an appropriate HWM (or LWM). If the processors are classified into lightly loaded, heavily loaded, and medium loaded as is done in several systems [22], [36], the exact number of processes in each of these categories needs to be determined. The load level used to trigger migration of processes in the system is a critical parameter because it may lead to system imbalance or thrashing if improperly chosen.

10.4.5 Task size

Normally it is inappropriate to migrate a task that is too small. Similarly very large processes or processes involving large amounts of data or file transfer are best handled by the local processor without migration. Thus, the optimum size of a task for migration becomes another important parameter. It is not easy to determine the size of a task; however, the size can be estimated based on the resources required, the task type (I/O-bound or CPU-bound), the memory requirement, and the number of data files needed. It is shown in [47] that large processes benefit substantially from load balancing while small processes do not as a result of the load balancing overhead.

10.4.6 Overhead costs

If the distance between the sender and receiver processors is long, the transfer and communication delay become more. If a processor is closer to the sender and has more load (but still is lightly loaded) than a processor which is farther from the sender, it will still be a better choice for migration if we take overhead costs into account. However, distance is not a major factor in a wormhole-routed system.

The factors that make up the overload costs are the measurement of the current load of a processor, messages to the decision making processor about load information, placement decisions to be made, and processes transferred between the processors. The number of probes made to select the most suitable destination to migrate a task has to be set up by the algorithm designer. This selection affects the performance of the system to a great extent. If a sufficient number of processors are not probed, only a suboptimal decision is reached. If more than necessary probes are done, the communication overhead will be high.

10.4.7   Response time

The turnaround time for a task is its response time. In order to estimate the load on a processor, we need to know the process response time. The response time is not evident unless data is collected after its previous run. The problems are the processes on which no information is available.

10.4.8   Load balancing horizon

The diameter of the neighbors to be considered in determining a possible destination for a task is called the *horizon* [16]. This parameter sets the number of neighbors to be probed in order to find a suitable destination processor to accept processes. In cases where the probing activity is expensive, a compromise has to be made between the loss of efficiency by not selecting the optimum site for a task migration and the cost incurred by probing. Thus, by selecting the horizon, the load can be balanced within the horizon of the processor, but, it is possible that, just beyond, there is a better candidate for migration that was not even considered.

10.4.9   Resource demands

The demands of a task on the resources of the system can influence its migration. Processes needing many resources for their completion will be constantly waiting for such resources to be available. This is likely to affect the system response time. In this sense the resource demands reflect the load on the processor.

10.5   Other Relevant Issues

As seen in the earlier sections several issues and parameters govern the designing of a load balancing system. Some discussion about the correlation between these two is defined as follows.

10.5.1   Code and data files

Load balancing operations are simpler in systems that have dedicated file servers. In order to balance loads, only the code lines are transferred to the destination processor. The required data files will be sent by the file server to the destination processor. When it is impossible to have a dedicated file server, as in the case of geographically distributed systems, an extra overhead of moving the required files is introduced. This makes the algorithm design more involved. The issue of sending executable code from one processor to another is addressed in [34].

10.5.2 System stability

When a processor is identified as a destination by several heavily loaded processors, the destination is likely to be overloaded. This condition will lead the destination to initiate another load balancing activity. A mechanism to stop further processes from arriving at overloaded processors is needed.

10.5.3 System architecture

Heterogeneity of architecture and configuration complicates the load balancing problem. Heterogeneity can arise due to the difference in the task arrival rate at processors of the same type. The system will also be heterogeneous if the processors have different task processing rates. Heterogeneity is treated in detail in [26], [32].

The way the system is connected also influences the load balancing algorithm. For example, the *dimension exchange* method is effective for cube-based systems or other high-dimensional systems but not for mesh-connected systems or other low-dimensional systems. For mesh-connected processors the average distance between different processors is larger and more processors will have to be traversed to send information to a given destination processor.

Although increasing the system size increases the possibility of finding an underloaded processor to accept more load, it is a potential problem for bus connected systems. Here, more processors mean more use of the bus and the bus becomes a bottleneck. The cost of transferring files for a bus-connected system is more than that of the hypercube or mesh configuration.

In a large and geographically distributed system the information maintained by different sites soon becomes obsolescent. Due to information lags dynamic state information is not available to various sites and decisions made using currently available information will be nonoptimal.

10.6   Sample Load Balancing Algorithms

In general, load balancing algorithms can be classified as *iterative* (also called *nearest neighbor*) and *direct* approaches. Nearest-neighbor methods rely on successive approximation through load exchanging among neighboring nodes to reach a global load distribution while direct methods determine senders and receivers first and then load exchanges follow. Note that in nearest-neighbor methods there is no need to identify senders and receivers; however, the challenge is to design a fast iterative scheme. In direct methods the main issue is to quickly pairwise potential senders and receivers.

We will focus on nearest-neighbor approaches and study three classes of deterministic methods: diffusion, dimension exchange, and gradient model. Another type of the nearest-neighbor approach is stochastic in nature; that is, stochastic approaches are used in an attempt to drive the system to equilibrium states with high probability. In these approaches randomized decisions are used in choosing, for example, a receiver in a sender-initiated scheme.

10.6.1   Direct algorithms

In direct algorithms the average system load is determined first. This is normally done by estimating the total system load through a global summation operation. Once the average system load is determined, it is broadcast to all the nodes in the system and each node determines its status: overloaded or underloaded based on the average load. We can call an overloaded node a *peg* and an underloaded node a *hole*.

Once all the nodes are identified as peg and hole, the next step is to fill holes with pegs preferably with minimum data movements. A good "filling" process with minimum data movements depends on given system parameters such as the underlying interconnection network. Nicol [29] designed an efficient algorithm of such a type for n-cubes.

10.6.2   Nearest neighbor algorithms: diffusion

In the diffusion model a time-based model is used where each node's update is synchronized by rounds. At round $t + 1$ each node u exchanges its load $L_u(t)$ with its neighbors' $L_v(t)$ where $v \in A(u)$ and $A(u)$ is the neighbor set of node u. $L_u(t+1)$ should also include new incoming load $\phi_u(t)$ between rounds t and $t+1$. Therefore, the diffusion method can be modeled using the linear system theory. More specifically the change of load in node u from time (round) t to $t+1$ is modeled as:

$$L_u(t+1) = L_u(t) + \sum_{v \in A(u)} \alpha_{u,v}(L_v(t) - L_u(t)) + \phi_u(t)$$

where $0 \leq \alpha_{u,v} \leq 1$ is called the diffusion parameter of nodes u and v which determines the amount of load exchanged between two neighboring nodes u and v.

10.6.3 Nearest neighbor algorithms: gradient

The basic idea of the gradient-based method is to maintain a contour of the gradients formed by the differences in load in the system. Load in high points (overloaded nodes) of the contour will flow to the lower regions (underloaded nodes) following the gradients. Normally the flow will migrate along the steepest gradient.

One of the major issues is to define a reasonable contour of gradients. The following is one model from [44]. The *propagated pressure* of a processor u, $p(u)$, is defined as

$$p(u) = \begin{cases} 0 & \text{if } u \text{ is lightly loaded} \\ 1 + \min\{p(v)|v \in A(u)\} & \text{otherwise} \end{cases}$$

Figure 10.5 shows a 4×4 mesh with the load associated with each node. Assume that a node is considered lightly loaded if its load is less than 3. In this case there are only two lightly loaded nodes. Intuitively the propagated pressure of a processor is the distance to a closest lightly loaded node.

10.6.4 Nearest neighbor algorithms: dimension exchange

The dimension exchange approach was initially proposed for n-cubes. In this approach, a sweep of dimensions (rounds) in the n-cube is applied. In the ith round neighboring nodes along the ith dimension compare and exchange their loads. It has been proved that after one sweep of dimensions, loads at all the nodes in an n-cube are balanced.

Recall that in an n-cube every node u has address $u_n u_{n-1} \ldots u_1$ with $u_i \in \{0,1\}$, $1 \leq i \leq n$, and u_i is called the ith bit (dimension) of the

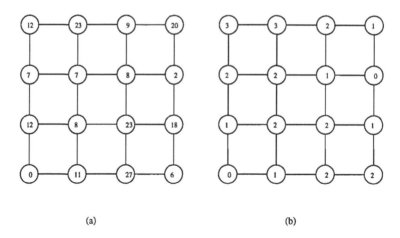

(a)   (b)

FIGURE 10.5
(a) A 4 × 4 mesh with loads. (b) The corresponding propagated pressure of each node (a node is lightly loaded if its load is less than 3).

address. By defining $u_i \in \{0, 1, *\}$ where $*$ represents 0 or 1 we can use $u_n u_{n-1} \ldots u_1$ to represent nodes as well as subcubes. For example, $0 * 1*$ a subcube (in 4-cube) that contains nodes 0010, 0011, 0110, and 0111. The notation $u^{(d)}$ represents the neighbor of node u along dimension d and $L(u)$ denotes the workload of node u. Node u is called an *even node* if its address has even number of 1's; otherwise, it is an *odd node*. For example, node 0000 in a 4-cube is an even node and node 0001 is an odd node.

In the dimension exchange (DE) algorithm each node balances its workload with its neighbor's following an arbitrarily selected dimension sequence. Absolute load balancing may not be possible between two neighbors when the sum of loads in two neighboring nodes is odd. To ensure randomness in load redistribution we let all the even (or odd) nodes carry the lighter load. Clearly this approach still ensures load balancing between these two nodes. An n-cube is load balanced if for every pair of neighboring nodes, u and $u^{(d)}$, $|L(u) - L(u^{(d)})| \leq 1$.

Algorithm A (the DE algorithm on a healthy hypercube)

1. Select a dimension d and balance every two neighboring nodes u and $u^{(d)}$ by performing one round of dimension exchange along dimension d. As a result the even node (say u) has load $\lfloor \frac{L(u)+L(u^{(d)})}{2} \rfloor$ and the odd node ($u^{(d)}$) has load $\lceil \frac{L(u)+L(u^{(d)})}{2} \rceil$.

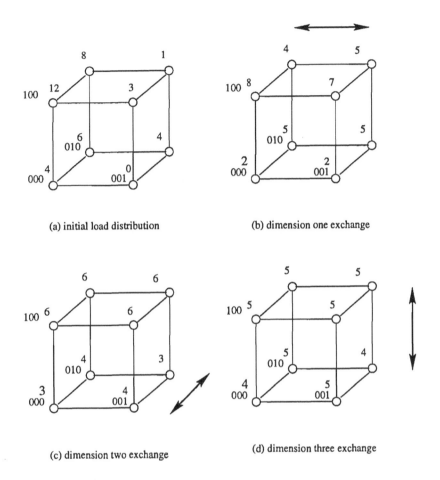

(a) initial load distribution

(b) dimension one exchange

(c) dimension two exchange

(d) dimension three exchange

FIGURE 10.6
Load balancing on a healthy 3-cube.

2. Repeat step 1 on the remaining $n-1$ dimensions following any sequence in the given n-cube.

Figure 10.6 shows how the workload at different nodes is balanced in a healthy 3-cube through three rounds of dimension exchange where the number associated with each node represents units of the workload. The effectiveness of the DE algorithm is proved theoretically [4] and through applications [40].

One way to extend the DE algorithm is by adding an *exchange parameter* (λ) to control the amount of load exchanged at each round. For example, suppose nodes u and v try to balance their loads. Their updated loads are the following:

$$L(u)' = (1 - \lambda)L(u) + \lambda L(v)$$

$$L(v)' = (1 - \lambda)L(v) + \lambda L(u)$$

Clearly when $\lambda = 0.5$ then it is a regular DE algorithm. In general, the optimal λ is not 0.5 for an arbitrary network. The selection of optimal λ's for the k-ary n-cube network and its variants are discussed in [43].

The DE algorithm can be applied in two different environments: (a) stand-alone processors and (b) processors with a host. In processors with a host there is a central controller in the host which collects information of faulty links and runs the DE algorithm. The DE algorithm can be initiated from a lightly loaded processor (receiver-initiated) by sending a special signal to the host or from a heavily loaded processor (sender-initiated). In stand-alone processors each processor is independent of others and tasks arrive directly at different processors. The initiator in either sender-initiated or receiver-initiated schemes decides the dimension sequence which is broadcast to each processor in the system.

In order to reduce the overall task migration time, the DE algorithm can be divided into two phases: (1) The DE algorithm is used to find the revised load "indices" that correspond to a balanced state, and (2) the actual load migrations take place based on the "indices" decided at step (1).

The dimension exchange approach can be extended to networks that are not constructed based on the dimension concept. Hosseini et al. [13] proposed an extended dimension exchange approach using the concept of edge-coloring. In the edge-coloring approach a minimum number of colors are used to color edges in a given undirected graph such that no two adjoining edges are of the same color. A dimension is defined as the collection of all edges of the same color and the number of rounds of message exchange equals the number of distinct colors.

In the example of Figure 10.7 three colors labeled as 1, 2, and 3 are used to color edges in the given graph. A dimension is then defined as the collection of all edges of the same color. The dimension-exchange algorithm consists of rounds. In this example, during round 1 nodes that are connected through edges with label 1 exchange their loads. That is, v_1 exchanges with v_2, v_3 with v_4, and v_5 with v_6. Similarly, during round 2 nodes that are connected through edges with label 2 exchange their loads. That is, v_1 exchanges with v_4, v_2 with v_5, and v_3 with v_6. In round 3 v_3 exchanges with v_5 and v_4 exchanges with v_6.

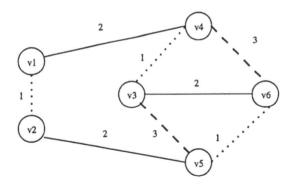

FIGURE 10.7
Extended dimension exchange model through edge-coloring.

Load balancing based on graph coloring has been extended to bus-oriented systems [15] where node coloring concept is used to group the processors.

10.7 Case Study: Load Balancing on Hypercube Multicomputers

In this section we study a global load balancing scheme on a faulty environment [41]. The approach is based on dimension exchange where each node exchanges its workload with its neighbors along a selected dimension in such a way that their workloads become equal. A global load balancing algorithm that can tolerate $n - 1$ faulty links is first presented for an n-cube. It is then extended to connected hypercubes with up to $2n - 3$ faulty links. Comparisons between the proposed scheme with the regular dimension-exchange-based scheme are also presented.

10.7.1 Dimension-exchange-based load balancing on faulty hypercubes

Clearly, the regular dimension-exchange-based load balancing algorithm (Algorithm A) cannot be directly applied to faulty hypercubes. Each faulty link disconnects a direct communication and disables load exchange between a pair of neighboring nodes. The following load balancing algorithm

(Algorithm B) is intended for faulty hypercubes that contain no more than $n-1$ faulty links. Given a faulty n-cube, Q_n, we divide this n-cube into two $(n-1)$-cubes, Q_{n-1} and Q'_{n-1}, along a fault-free dimension d, i.e., all the links along this dimension are healthy. We have the following two situations:

- If one of two $(n-1)$-cubes, say Q_{n-1}, is healthy, we first balance workloads between Q_{n-1} and Q'_{n-1} through one round of exchange along dimension d. Algorithm A is used to balance workloads in Q_{n-1}. Clearly, the workload at each node of Q_{n-1} then represents the load when the n-cube is globally balanced. We then balance workloads of Q'_{n-1} through Q_{n-1} using the following steps: (1) Through another round of message exchange along dimension d, each node u in Q_{n-1} knows the "excessive" (peg) or "insufficient" (hole) workload of neighbor $u^{(d)}$ (in Q'_{n-1}) along dimension d. A *virtual load* is defined at node u that is the current load of node u plus (minus) the excessive (insufficient) workload. However, only the excessive workload is shifted from $u^{(d)}$ to u at this stage. (2) Algorithm A is applied again to Q_{n-1} that balances the virtual load defined at each node in Q'_{n-1}. (3) Through the third round of message exchange along dimension d, holes in Q'_{n-1} are filled by shifting the insufficient amount of workloads from u to $u^{(d)}$.

- If neither of the two $(n-1)$-cubes is healthy, i.e., each of the two $(n-1)$-cubes contain no more than $n-2$ faulty links, the proposed scheme is recursively applied to each of these two $(n-1)$-cubes.

More specifically the above scheme is described in Algorithm B:

Algorithm B (load balancing on a faulty hypercube)

1. Determine a dimension d such that all the links along d are healthy.

2. Balance the workloads of all the neighboring nodes along dimension d through one round of dimension exchange.

3. Divide the given n-cube into two $(n-1)$-cubes along dimension d, Q_{n-1} and Q'_{n-1}.

4. If both of the $(n-1)$-cubes contain fewer than $n-1$ faulty links, recursively apply this algorithm to each $(n-1)$-cube that contains at least one faulty link, or apply the regular dimension-exchange based load balancing algorithm (Algorithm A) to each $(n-1)$-cube that is healthy, and then stop; otherwise go to step 5.

5. /* one of the $(n-1)$-cubes, say Q'_{n-1}, contains $n-1$ faulty links */
   Since there are at most $n-1$ faults in the n-cube, Q_{n-1} must be a healthy cube. Apply Algorithm A to Q_{n-1} to balance the workload at each node of Q_{n-1}.

6. /* all the nodes in Q_{n-1} are load balanced */
   For every pair of nodes u (in Q_{n-1}) and its neighbor $u^{(d)}$ along dimension d, let $ID_u = L(u^{(d)}) - L(u)$ be attached to u. If $ID_u > 0$ then ID_u units of load are shifted from node $u^{(d)}$ to node u. Define the *virtual load* of node u by $\hat{L}(u) = L(u) + ID_u = L(u^{(d)})$ (including the case when $ID_u \leq 0$).

7. Apply Algorithm A again on Q_{n-1} based on the virtual load defined in Step 6. Also the actual load changes with the change of the virtual load.

8. For each node u (in Q_{n-1}) such that $ID_u < 0$, shift ID_u units of load from node u to node $u^{(d)}$.

It is shown in [41] that a faulty n-cube with fewer than $n-1$ faulty links is load balanced after one application of Algorithm B. Clearly the selection of a dimension to partition a subcube is a major operation in Algorithm B. It is also shown in [41] that Algorithm B requires $O(mn)$ dimension selection operations where n is the dimension of the hypercube under consideration and m is the number of faulty links in the cube.

As an example we consider the load balancing problem on a faulty 4-cube with three faulty links: $(0000, 0100)$, $(0000, 0010)$, $(0100, 0101)$. Figures 10.8 and 10.9 show step by step the load balancing procedure defined in Algorithm B, where load balancing within Q_3 (Figure 10.8 (c)) is shown in Figure 10.6. In Figures 10.9 (a) and (b) two numbers are associated with each node: the one in parenthesis is the actual load and the other is the virtual load. When the actual load and the virtual load are the same, only one number is associated with the corresponding node.

Note that the proposed algorithm can be simplified without using the concept of virtual load: At step 6 of Algorithm B, workloads of two nodes in each pair (along a selected dimension) are exchanged and step 8 can then be deleted. More specifically,

6. /* all the nodes in Q_{n-1} are load balanced */
   For every pair of nodes u (in Q_{n-1}) and its neighbor $u^{(d)}$ along dimension d, let $ID_u = L(u^{(d)}) - L(u)$. If $ID_u > 0$ then ID_u units of load are shifted from node $u^{(d)}$ to node u; otherwise, ID_u units of load are shifted from node u to node $u^{(d)}$.

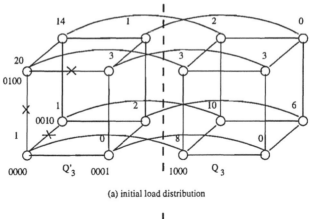

(a) initial load distribution

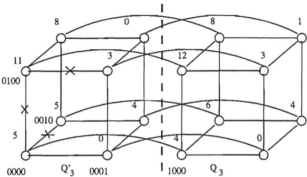

(b) dimension exchange along a fault free dimension (dimension 4)

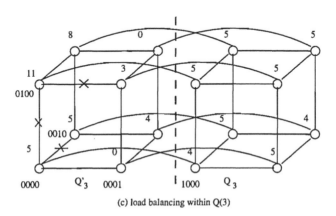

(c) load balancing within Q(3)

FIGURE 10.8
Load balancing in a faulty 4-cube with three faulty links.

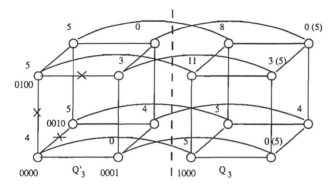

(a) calculating virtual loads (in Q(3)) through dimension exchange along dimension 4

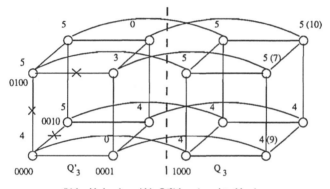

(b) load balancing within Q(3) based on virtual load

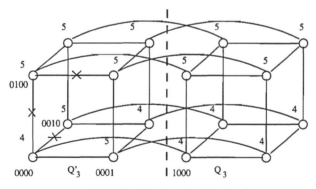

(c) final load balancing along dimension 4

FIGURE 10.9
Load balancing in a faulty 4-cube with three faulty links (continue).

The above approach has been extended to faulty hypercubes with more than $n - 1$ fault links but no more than $2n - 3$ faulty links. In a faulty hypercube (Q_n) with more than $n - 1$ faulty links we may not be able to find a fault-free dimension; however, we can always find a dimension d along which there is at most one faulty link (see Figure 10.10). We then divide the Q_n into two $(n - 1)$-cubes: Q_{n-1} and Q'_{n-1}. Since there are at most $2n - 3$ faulty links, one of the $(n - 1)$-cubes, say Q_{n-1}, is a connected cube and contains fewer than $n - 1$ faults. Now we can sketch our approach as follows: (1) Balance workloads between Q_{n-1} and Q'_{n-1} through dimension exchange along the selected dimension d. The workload of node $u^{(d)}$ (in Q'_{n-1}) that is adjacent to the faulty link along dimension d (if there is one) is shifted to one of the connected neighbors, say $u'^{(d)}$, before the dimension exchange. Similarly, the workload of the u is shifted to one of its connected neighbors (not necessary u'). (2) Balance workloads among nodes within Q_{n-1} using Algorithm B. (3) Define virtual workload for each node in Q_{n-1} through message exchange along dimension d. Virtual workload is also defined for node $u'^{(d)}$ in Q'_{n-1} based on the workload that has been shifted from node $u^{(d)}$ to node $u'^{(d)}$. The excessive workload at each node of Q'_{n-1} is shifted to the corresponding node in Q_{n-1} using Algorithm B. (4) Perform global load balancing through dimension exchange along dimension d. (5) Half of the load on $u^{(d)}$ is shifted to $u'^{(d)}$. For a detailed discussion on this algorithm the readers may refer to [41].

The condition for global load balancing using dimension exchange can be further tightened. In addition to the load balancing requirement another objective is to minimize the number of task-hops:

$$\sum_k e_k$$

where e_k is the number of tasks transmitted through the edge k. Obviously the regular dimension exchange algorithm does not meet this objective. In some cases an underloaded node may transfer some of its load to one of its neighbors (also an underloaded one) before receiving an additional load from other neighbors. In general, this problem can be converted to the maximum-flow minimum-cut problem. The traditional maximum-flow algorithm has a high complexity. Wu and Shu [42] proposed a parallel heuristic algorithm for n-cubes where all processors cooperate to collect load information and to exchange workload in parallel. With parallel scheduling it is possible to obtain high quality load balancing with a fully-balanced load and maximized locality. Communication costs can be reduced significantly

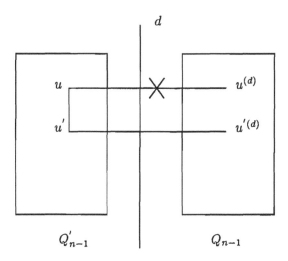

FIGURE 10.10
Partition a faulty *n*-cube along dimension *d* (using Algorithm B).

compared to the results obtained using the regular dimension exchange algorithm.

10.8   Future Directions

Most research and development in load balancing focus on the identification and evaluation of various policies for information distribution and task migration. In the future the main research emphasis will probably be to reduce overhead while keeping load balancing algorithms efficient. The type of information collection process is one of the keys. Effective load estimation is also important. Some possible research directions are the following:

- Combination of dynamic and static load distribution.

- Cost and effective load estimation.

- Scalable load balancing algorithms probably by a hierarchical system organization.

- A set of primitive supporting tools at the operating system level.

References

[1] Baumgartner, K. M. and B. W. Wah, "Gammon: a load balancing strategy in local computer systems with multi-access networks", *IEEE Transactions on Computers*, **38**, 8, Aug. 1989, 1098-1109.

[2] Bonomi, F. and A. Kumar, "Adaptive optimal load balancing in a non-homogeneous multi-server system with a central task scheduler", *IEEE Transactions on Computers*, **39**, 10, Oct. 1990, 1232-1250.

[3] Bryant, R. M. and R. A. Finkel, "A stable distributed scheduling algorithm", *Proc. of the 2nd Int'l Conf. on Distributed Computing Systems*, 1981, 314-323.

[4] Cybenko, G., "Dynamic load balancing for distributed memory multiprocessors", *Journal of Parallel and Distributed Computing*, **7**, 2, Oct. 1989, 279-301.

[5] Douglis, F. and J. Ousterhout, "Transparent process migration: Design alternatives and the Sprite implementation", *Software - Practice and Experience*, **21**, 8, Aug. 1991, 757-785.

[6] Eager, D. L., E. D. Lazowska, and J. Zahorjan, "A comparison of receiver-initiated and sender-initiated adaptive load sharing", *Performance Evaluation*, **1**, 3, 1986, 53-68.

[7] Ferguson, D., Y. Yemini, and C. Nikolaou, "Microeconomic algorithms for load balancing in distributed computer systems", *Proc. of the 8th Int'l Conf. on Distributed Computing Systems*, 1988, 491-499.

[8] Gulati, S., S. S. Iyengar, and J. Barhen, "Pebble-crunching model for fault-tolerant load balancing in hypercube ensembles", *Computer Journal*, **33**, 3, June 1990, 204-214.

[9] Hac, A., "A distributed algorithm for performance improvement through file replication, file migration and process migration", *IEEE Transactions on Software Engineering*, **15**, 11, Nov. 1989, 1459-1470.

[10] Hac, A., "Load balancing in distributed systems: A summary", *Performance Evaluation Review*, **16**, 2-4, Feb. 1989, 17-19.

[11] Hac, A. and X. Jin, "Decentralized algorithm for dynamic load balancing with file transfer", *Journal of Systems and Software*, **16**, 1, Sept. 1991, 37-52.

[12] Hanxleden, R. and L. R. Scott, "Load balancing on message passing architectures", *Journal of Parallel and Distributed Computing*, **13**, 3, Nov. 1991, 312-324.

[13] Hosseini, S. H., B. Litow, M. Malkawi, J. McPherson, and K. Vairavan, "Analysis of a graph coloring based distributed load balancing algorithm", *Journal of Parallel and Distributed Computing*, **10**, 2, Oct. 1990, 160-166.

[14] Ishfaq, A. and G. Arif, "Semi-distributed load balancing for massively parallel multicomputer systems", *IEEE Transactions on Software Engineering*, **17**, 10, Oct. 1991, 987-1004.

[15] Joshi, B. S., S. Hosseini, and K. Vairavan, "A load balancing algorithm for bus-oriented systems", *Proc. of the 8th IEEE Symp. on Parallel and Distributed Processing*, 1996, 370-374.

[16] Kale, L. V., "Comparing performance of two dynamic load distribution methods", *Proc. of 1988 Int'l Conf. on Parallel Processing*, 1988, I 8-I 12.

[17] Kim, C. and H. Kameda, "Optimal static load balancing of multiclass tasks in a distributed computer system", *Proc. of the 10th Int'l Conf. on Distributed Computing Systems*, 1990, 562-569.

[18] Kunz, T., "The influence of different workload descriptions on a heuristic load balancing scheme", *IEEE Transactions on Software Engineering*, **17**, 7, July 1991, 725-730.

[19] Lee, C. and L. Bic, "Load balancing using semi-private memory", *Proc. of the 10th Annual Int'l Phoenix Conf. on Computers and Communications*, 1991, 167-173.

[20] Leff, A. and P. S. Yu, "An adaptive strategy for load sharing in distributed database environments with information lags", *Journal of Parallel and Distributed Computing*, **13**, 1, Sept. 1991, 91-103.

[21] Li, J. and H. Kameda, "Load balancing problems for multiclass jobs in distributed/parallel computer systems", *IEEE Transactions on Computers*, **47**, 3, Mar. 1998, 322-332.

[22] Lin, F. C. H. and R. M. Keller, "The gradient model load balancing method", *IEEE Transactions on Software Engineering*, **13**, 1, Jan. 1987, 32-38.

[23] Lin, H. C. and C. S. Raghavendra, "A dynamic load balancing policy with a central task dispatcher (LBC)", *Proc. of the 11th Int'l Conf. on Distributed Computing Systems*, 1991, 264-271.

[24] Loui, M. C. and M. A. Sohoni, "Algorithm for load balancing in multiprocessor systems", *Information Processing Letters*, **35**, 5, Aug. 1990, 223-228.

[25] Lüling, R. and B. Monien, "Load balancing for distributed branch and bound algorithms", *Proc. of the 6th Int'l Conf. on Parallel Processing Symposium*, 1992, 543-548.

[26] Mirchandaney, R., D. Towsley, and J. A. Stankovic, "Adaptive load sharing in heterogeneous distributed systems", *Journal of Parallel and Distributed Computing*, **9**, 4, Aug. 1990, 331-346.

[27] Ni, L. N. and K. Hwang, "Optimal load balancing in a multiple processor system with many job classes", *IEEE Transactions on Software Engineering*, **11**, 5, May 1985, 491-496.

[28] Ni, L. N., C. W. Xu, and T. B. Gendreau, "A distributed drafting algorithm for load balancing", *IEEE Transactions on Software Engineering*, **11**, 10, Oct. 1985, 1153-1161.

[29] Nicol, D. M., "Communication load balancing in distributed systems", *Proc. of Scalable High Performance Computing Conf.*, 1992, 292-299.

[30] Santana, M. J. and E. J. Zaluska, "Load balancing in a session-based distributed file-store architecture", *Software - Practice and Experience*, **18**, 11, Nov. 1988, 1091-1107.

[31] Shamir, E. and E. Upfal, "Probabilistic approach to the load sharing problem in distributed systems", *Journal of Parallel and Distributed Computing*, **4**, 5, Oct. 1987, 521-531.

[32] Shenker, S. and A. Weinrib, "Optimal control of heterogeneous queuing systems: A paradigm for load-sharing and routing", *IEEE Transactions on Computers*, **38**, 12, Dec. 1989, 1724-1735.

[33] Singhal, M. and N. G. Shivaratri, *Advanced Concepts in Operating Systems: Distributed, Database, and Multiprocessors Operating Systems*, McGraw-Hill, Inc., 1994.

[34] Stamos, J. W. and D. K. Gifford, "Implementing remote evaluation", *IEEE Transactions on Software Engineering*, **16**, 7, July 1990, 710-722.

[35] Stankovic, J., "An application of Bayesian decision theory to decentralized control of scheduling", *IEEE Transactions on Computers*, **3**, 2, Feb. 1985, 117-130.

[36] Suen, T. T. Y. and J. S. K. Wong, "Efficient task migration algorithm for distributed systems", *IEEE Transactions on Parallel and Distributed Systems*, **3**, 4, July 1992, 488-499.

[37] Svensson, A., "History: An intelligent load sharing filter", *Proc. of the 10th Int'l Conf. on Distributed Computing Systems*, 1990, 546-553.

[38] Svensson, A., "Dynamic alternation between receiver-initiated and sender-initiated load sharing", *Proc. of Int'l Conf. on Databases, Parallel Architectures, and Their Applications*, 1990, 546-553.

[39] Wang, Y. T. and R. J. T. Morris, "Load sharing in distributed systems", *IEEE Transactions on Computers*, **34**, 3, Mar. 1985, 204-217.

[40] Willebeek-LeMair, M. H. and A. P. Reeves, "Strategies for dynamic load balancing on highly parallel computers", *IEEE Transactions on Parallel and Distributed Systems*, **4**, 9, Nov. 1993, 979-993.

[41] Wu, J., "Dimension-exchange-based global load balancing in faulty hypercubes", *Parallel Processing: Practice and Experience*, **9**, 1, Jan. 1997, 41-61.

[42] Wu, M. Y. and W. Shu, "A load-balancing algorithm for *n*-cubes", *Proc. of the 1996 Int'l Conf. on Parallel Processing*, 1996, III 148-III 155.

[43] Xu, C. -Z. and F. C. M. Lau, "The generalized dimension exchange method for load balancing in *k*-ary *n*-cubes and variants", *Journal of Parallel and Distributed Computing*, **24**, 1995, 72-85.

[44] Xu, C. -Z. and F. C. M. Lau, *Load Balancing in Parallel Computers: Theory and Practice*, Kluwer Academic Publisher, 1997.

[45] Xu, J. and K. Hwang, "Heuristic methods for dynamic load balancing in a message-passing multicomputer", *Journal of Parallel and Distributed Computing*, **1**, 1, May 1993, 1-13.

[46] Yamai, N., S. Shimojo, and H. Miyahara, "Load balancing algorithm on multiprocessor time-sharing systems", *Systems and Computers in Japan*, **21**, 8, Oct. 1990, 1-10.

[47] Zhou, S., "A trace driven simulation study of dynamic load balancing", *IEEE Transactions on Software Engineering*, **14**, 9, Sept. 1988, 1327-1341,

Problems

1. Show one or two applications such that

   - Static load distribution is not sufficient.
   - Dynamic load distribution is not necessary.
   - Both static and dynamic load distribution should be applied.

2. In a faulty 4-cube, links $0*11$, $*100$, and $00*1$ are faulty. The load distribution among the nodes (from node 0 to node 15) is: 4, 1, 6, 2, 7, 12, 8, 4, 23, 1, 5, 12, 2, 0, 12, and 2, respectively. Show how the extended dimension exchange method balances the loads in the system.

3. For the following 4×4 mesh find the corresponding propagated pressure of each node. Assume that a node is considered lightly loaded if its load is less than 2.

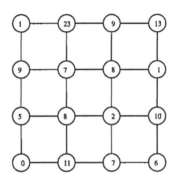

4. For the following graph find the minimum number of colors for the edge coloring process.

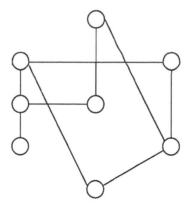

5. Apply the extended dimension exchange process to the colored graph derived from Problem 4. Show the load of each node after each round.

6. In the extended DE algorithm with exchange parameter λ, relate λ to the processing speed of each processor. Try to balance the workloads of nodes u (with processing speed s_u) and v (with processing speed s_v). How is parameter λ selected in this case?

Chapter 11

DISTRIBUTED DATA MANAGEMENT

A *database* is a collection of data objects organized especially for rapid search and retrieval. Distributed data management issues of special interest include: (1) synchronization of access to shared data while supporting a high degree of concurrency and (2) making data resilient to failures in the system.

11.1 Basic Concepts

In a database system a *data model* provides a way in which the stored data is organized for quick retrieval or other purposes. Over the years research in the area of database has resulted in many models such as the hierarchical, the network, the entity-relationship, the functional, the relational, and the object-oriented models. The relational model attained the most popularity for its simplicity, ease of use and manipulation via a *standard query language* (SQL).

A *database management system* (DBMS) is a software system that permits the management of the database. A database system is distributed if its data is dispersed among different physical locations. A data object can have multiple copies at different sites. A distributed database can be classified as follows according to the way data objects are dispersed and replicated:

- Unreplicated

- Fully replicated

- Partially replicated

Partially and fully replicated databases have overhead due to extra storage requirements and require complicated synchronization protocols to maintain mutual consistency. However, they have several desirable features [22]:

- *Improved responsiveness.* A request (of read and/or write) can be executed quickly without any communication if the local site has a copy of the data.

- *Enhanced reliability.* A site can access a data object even if some sites have failed or the network has been partitioned.

- *Reduced or no directory management.* The overhead of managing a directory and a resource locator service is absent or reduced.

- *Easier load balancing.* A computation can be readily transferred with or without reduced amount of moving data objects from site to site.

Another popular model for database is the object-based model. An *object* is any passive element of a computation (data, files, records in a database) whose state can only be modified or accessed by members of a well-defined set of *operations* or *functions*. The term *transaction* is used to describe a logically-related sequence of operations on one or more database objects. A transaction preserves the consistency of a database and terminates in finite time. A *query* is a *read-only transaction* and an *update* is a transaction that modifies at least one data object.

11.2   Serializability Theory

When several transactions access the same data object it should be assured that from the users' viewpoint they appear as indivisible operations on the database. This property is called *atomic execution* and is achieved by guaranteeing the following two properties [11]:

- A transaction is an "all or nothing" operation. Either all its actions are executed and the effects properly installed in the database, or all effects of the transaction are undone and the transaction is aborted.

- The concurrent execution of several transactions affects the database as if executed serially in some order. The interleaved order of the actions of a set of concurrent transactions is called a *schedule.*

Transactions: T_1 and T_2. Accounts: A (initial balance $20), B($10).

T_1		**begin**
	1	**read** A (obtaining $A\_balance$)
	2	**read** B (obtaining $B\_balance$)
	3	**write** $A_balance - 10 to A
	4	**write** $B_balance + 10 to B
		end

T_2		**begin**
	1	**read** B (obtaining $B\_balance$)
	2	**write** $B_balance -$5$ to B
		end

FIGURE 11.1
Concurrent transactions.

Without satisfying the atomic execution property, a *conflict* may arise when several transactions access the same data object. Two transactions conflict if and only if they operate on a common data object and at least one of the operations is a write. There are three types of conflict: *r-w* (read-write), *w-r* (write-read), and *w-w* (write-write). Conflicts may cause the following two anomalous situations:

- *Inconsistent retrieval.* Inconsistent retrieval occurs when a transaction reads some data objects of a database before another transaction has completed its modification of those data objects.

- *Inconsistent update.* Inconsistent update occurs when many transactions read and write onto a common set of data objects of a database leaving the database in an inconsistent state.

For the example in Figure 11.1, if transaction T_2 (which withdraws $5 from account B) is scheduled to run between the first and second write operations of T_1 (which transfers $10 from account A to account B) and assuming that initially the balances of accounts A and B are $20 and $10, respectively, then the sum of the account balance will be set at $30 ($A$: $10 and B: $20) instead of $25 ($A$: $10 and B: $15) which is an inconsistent state. The corresponding schedule is shown in Figure 11.2 (a). Note that in this implementation the $B\_balances$ of the two transactions correspond to two different variables.

One way to resolve conflicts is to execute the transactions serially one at a time in any order. This method ensures that a consistent state is trans-

Transaction (step)	Action
$T_1(1)$	**read** A (obtaining $A\_balance$)
$T_1(2)$	**read** B (obtaining $B\_balance$)
$T_1(3)$	**write** $A\_balance-\$10$ **to** A
$T_2(1)$	**read** B (obtaining $B\_balance$)
$T_2(1)$	**write** $B\_balance-\$5$ **to** B
$T_1(4)$	**write** $B\_balance+\$10$ **to** B
	(a)

Transaction (step)	Action
$T_1(1)$	**read** A (obtaining $A\_balance$)
$T_2(1)$	**read** B (obtaining $B\_balance$)
$T_2(1)$	**write** $B\_balance-\$5$ **to** B
$T_1(2)$	**read** B (obtaining $B\_balance$)
$T_1(3)$	**write** $A\_balance-\$10$ **to** A
$T_1(4)$	**write** $B\_balance+\$10$ **to** B
	(b)

FIGURE 11.2
A nonserializable schedule (a) and serializable schedule (b) for Figure 11.1.

formed into another consistent state. There are $n!$ possible *serial schedules* of n transactions. All of them generate the same consistent state from a common consistent state. A good concurrency control method (schedule) should allow an interleaved order of the actions of a set of concurrent transactions with the effect that such a schedule is the same as if the transactions had executed serially in some order. Such a schedule is called a *serializable schedule*. Figure 11.2 (b) shows a serializable schedule for the example in Figure 11.1.

We describe the theory of serializability in a more formal way. A *schedule* L (also called a *log*) captures the chronological order in which read and write actions of the transactions are executed under a concurrency control algorithm. We use $r_i[x]$ and $w_i[x]$ to represent read and write operation in transaction T_i of date object x. The following sequences show three transactions and three schedules over these transactions:

$$T_1 = w_1[x]w_1[y]r_1[z]$$

$$T_2 = r_2[z]r_2[y]w_2[x]$$

$$T_3 = w_3[z]r_3[z]w_3[x]$$

$$L_1 = w_1[x]r_2[z]r_2[y]w_2[x]w_1[y]r_1[z]w_3[z]r_3[z]w_3[x]$$

$$L_2 = w_1[x]w_1[y]r_1[z]r_2[z]r_2[y]w_2[x]w_3[z]r_3[z]w_3[x]$$

$$L_3 = w_1[x]w_1[y]r_1[z]r_2[z]w_3[z]r_2[y]r_3[z]w_2[x]w_3[x]$$

Schedule L_2 is a serial schedule since all three transactions are executed strictly serially. Two schedules are equivalent if all the transactions in both schedules see the same state of the database and leave the database in the same state after all the transactions are finished. More formally, if $w_i[x]$ and $r_i[x]$ are two operations in schedule L, we say $r_j[x]$ *reads from* $w_i[x]$ iff (a) $w_i[x] < r_j[x]$ and (b) there is no $w_k[x]$ such that $w_i[x] < w_k[x] < r_j[x]$. Two schedules over a transaction system are equivalent iff

1. Every read operation reads from the same write operation in both schedules.

2. Both schedules have the same final writes.

In schedules L_2 and L_3, $r_1[z]$ and $r_2[z]$ read from the initial z, $r_2[y]$ reads from $w_1[y]$, and $r_3[z]$ reads from $w_3[z]$. In addition, $w_3[x]$, $w_1[y]$, and $w_3[z]$ are final writers for data objects x, y, and z, respectively. Therefore, schedules L_2 and L_3 are equivalent.

When a non-serial schedule is equivalent to a serial schedule, it is called *serializable schedule*. The following result shows a way to check the serializability of a given schedule.

A *serialization graph* over a set of transactions $T = \{T_1, T_2, ..., T_n\}$ for a given schedule L is defined as follows: There is an edge from T_i to T_j provided for some x either $r_i[x] < w_j[x]$, $w_i[x] < r_j[x]$, or $w_i[x] < w_j[x]$. (Note that the order $<$ is based on the given L.) Then the given schedule L is serializable iff the corresponding serialization graph is acyclic. The serialization graph of L_1 is cyclic; therefore it is not serializable. Figure 11.3 shows the serialization graphs for L_1, L_2, and L_3.

In order to determine serialization graphs for schedules of Figure 11.1, we first perform the following conversion: $T_1(1) : r_1[A]$, $T_1(2) : r_1[B]$, $T_1(3) : w_1[A]$, $T_1(4) : w_1[B]$, $T_2(1) : r_2[B]$, and $T_2(2) : w_2[B]$. Then the schedule for Figure 11.2 (a) is:

$$r_1[A]r_1[B]w_1[A]r_2[B]w_2[B]w_1[B]$$

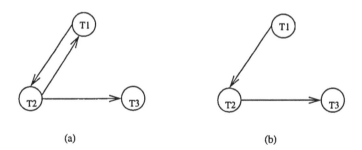

(a)   (b)

FIGURE 11.3
Serialization graphs for (a) L_1, (b) L_2 and L_3.

Clearly, there is an edge from T_1 to T_2 in the serialization graph since $r_1[B] < w_2[B]$. Also because $w_2[B] < w_1[B]$ there is an edge from T_2 to T_1. Therefore, this schedule corresponds to a non-serializable one. Similarly, the schedule for Figure 11.2 (b) is:

$$r_1[A]r_2[B]w_2[B]r_1[B]w_1[A]w_1[B]$$

The corresponding serialization graph is acyclic since there is only one edge (from T_2 to T_1) in the corresponding serialization graph.

11.3   Concurrency Control

One goal in distributed data management is to provide a systematic way to execute concurrent transactions in such a manner that their schedule is serializable. Either optimistic or pessimistic approaches can be used. *Optimistic approaches* assume that the conflicts between transactions are infrequent; no restrictions are placed on the way transactions should be executed. However, updates are needed to verify and ensure freedom from conflicts. In *pessimistic approaches* certain restrictions on transactions and their interactions will have to be imposed so that the serializability criterion is satisfied. We will consider two pessimistic approaches, lock-based and timestamp-based concurrency control, and one optimistic approach.

11.3.1   Lock-based concurrency control

One of the most popular concurrency control mechanisms is the *lock-based scheme* [7], [13] which inserts a set of lock and unlock statements in each transaction without providing explicit scheduling. In general, a locked object is not sharable except when all the operations are reads. A transaction must lock a data object before accessing it. In some applications two types of locks are used: *read locks* and *write locks*. Read locks are shared while write locks are exclusive. Hence, a transaction can lock a data object in two different modes: *exclusive* and *shared*. If a transaction has locked an object in the exclusive mode, no other transaction can lock it in any mode. If a transaction has locked an object in the shared mode, other transactions can lock it in the shared mode. Depending on how and when locks are placed on objects, locking schemes can be classified into *static locking* and *dynamic locking*.

In static locking a transaction acquires locks on all the data objects it needs before executing any action on the data objects. This approach is conceptually simple; however, it seriously limits concurrency since any two transactions that have a conflict must execute serially.

In dynamic locking a transaction acquires locks on different objects at different stages of executing a transaction. One dynamic locking scheme is *two-phase locking* where consistency is guaranteed if it is *well-formed* and *two-phase*. A transaction is well-formed if it

1. locks an object before accessing it,

2. does not lock an object that is already locked, and

3. before it completes, unlocks each object it has locked.

A schedule is *two-phase* if no object is unlocked before all needed objects are locked.

Figure 11.4 shows a well-formed, two-phase transaction based on this locking scheme. It has been proved that all legal schedules from two-phase locking are serializable. Two-phase locking has two phases: A *growing phase* during which a transaction requests locks and a *shrinking phase* which starts with the first unlock action and during which a transaction releases locks.

Two potential problems associated with the two-phase locking scheme are *deadlock* (in the growing phase) and *cascaded roll-back* (in the shrinking phase). Deadlocks may happen in the locking scheme where the locks are the competing resources. The deadlock prevention methods discussed in Chapter 4 can be applied. Cascaded roll-back occurs when a transaction

T_1: **begin**
     lock A
     read A (obtaining $A\_balance$)
     lock B
     read B (obtaining $B\_balance$)
     write $A\_balance-\$10$ **to** A
     unlock A
     write $B\_balance+\$10$ **to** B
     unlock B
     end

T_1: **begin**
     lock B
     read B (obtaining $B\_balance$)
     write $B\_balance-\$5$ **to** B
     unlock B
     end

FIGURE 11.4
Well-formed, two-phase transactions.

is rolled back because of a failure after it has released the locks on some data objects and other transactions have read those modified data objects. Therefore, any transactions that have read modified data objects should also be rolled-back. Although the cascaded roll-back problem can be solved by using the strict two-phase locking scheme where a transaction holds all its locks until it completes and releases them in a single atomic action, it reduces the degree of concurrency.

The locking scheme can also be implemented in a distributed replicated database. Three schemes can be applied:

- *Centralized locking algorithm* [8]. In this scheme transactions are processed in a distributed manner. However, the lock management is centralized. When a site receives its lock grant message, it executes a relevant transaction and then broadcasts an update message to all other sites that have copies of data objects updated by the transaction.

- *Primary-site locking algorithm* [24]. In this scheme both transactions and lock management are distributed. For each data object there is a single site designated as its primary site. All updates for a data object are first directed to its primary site. This approach has been adopted in the database system INGRES.

- *Decentralized locking.* The lock management duty is shared by all the sites. In this case the execution of a transaction involves the participation and coordination of many sites.

11.3.2 Timestamp-based concurrency control

In the timestamp-based approach [5] each transaction is assigned a timestamp and each site keeps track of the largest timestamp of any read and write processed thus far for each data object. These timestamps are denoted by $Time_r(x)$ and $Time_w(x)$, respectively. Let $read(x, ts)$ and $write(x, ts)$ denote a read and a write request with timestamp ts on a data object x. In an r-w conflict if the read operation has a smaller timestamp but arrives after the execution of the write operation, the corresponding transaction is aborted. Similarly in a w-r or w-w if the (first) write operation has a smaller timestamp but arrives after the execution of the read or (second) write operation, the corresponding transaction is aborted. More formally, a read (or write) request is handled in the following way:

- (Read) If $ts < Time_w(x)$ then the read request is rejected and the corresponding transaction is aborted; otherwise, it is executed and $Time_r(x)$ is set to $max\{Time_r(x), ts\}$.

- (Write) If $ts < Time_w(x)$ or $ts < Time_r(x)$, then the write request is rejected; otherwise, it is executed and $Time_w(x)$ is set to ts.

Suppose timestamps on x are $Time_r(x) = 4$ and $Time_w(x) = 6$ initially. We have the following sequence of read and write requests at data object x:

$$read(x, 5), write(x, 7), read(x, 9), read(x, 8), write(x, 8)$$

The first operation will be rejected (and the corresponding transaction is aborted), since $ts = 5 < Time_w(x) = 6$. The second operation is accepted and executed and $Time_w(x)$ is updated to 7. The third operation, $read(x, 9)$, is accepted and $Time_r(x)$ is updated to 9. The next read operation is also accepted since its timestamp is larger than $Time_w(x)$ but $Time_w(x)$ remains unchanged. The last operation, $write(x, 8)$, is rejected since $tc = 8 < Time_r(x) = 9$.

In order to reduce or eliminate aborts and restarts of transactions, we can use the following *conservative timestamp ordering* by executing the requests in strict timestamp order at all sites. In this approach each site keeps a write queue (W-queue) and a read queue (R-queue) in an order based on timestamps of requests. It is assumed that communication is order preserving. The algorithm is similar to Lamport's algorithm for mutual exclusion. A request (read or write) is executed only when it is ensured that there is no other request from another site which has a smaller (older) timestamp in the system.

- A read (x, ts) request is executed if all W-queues are nonempty and the first write on each queue has a timestamp greater than ts; otherwise, the read request is buffered in the R-queue.

- A write (x, ts) request is executed if all R-queues and W-queues are nonempty and the first read (write) on each R-queue (W-queue) has a timestamp greater than ts; otherwise, the write request is buffered in the W-queue.

When any read or write request is buffered or executed, buffered requests are tested to check if any of them can be executed based on the above two conditions.

11.3.3   Optimistic concurrency control

Both lock-based and timestamp-based concurrency control algorithms are pessimistic in nature. In other words, in a lock-based (or a timestamp-based) approach it is assumed that the conflicts between transactions are quite frequent. Optimistic algorithms [6], on the other hand, first tentatively perform updates locally and are made permanent and propagated only if there are no consistency conflicts. A timestamp-based optimistic algorithm is discussed in [18]. In this approach three phases are used: read, validation, and write. In the read phase, appropriate data objects are read and all the updates are made on temporary storage. In the validation phase, all the updates are checked to determine if any of them violate the consistency of the database. A conflict occurs if the write set of a transaction T is intersected by the read set of T. In this case T is restarted. If the check passes, then in the write phase all the updates of the transaction are made to the database.

Note that in a normal pessimistic concurrency control three phases are ordered differently as: validation, read, and write. No updates will occur if the validation process fails. Although optimistic concurrency control is conceptually simple, it has not been implemented in any commercial or prototype distributed DBMS. For a detailed discussion on concurrency control see [4], [17] and [19].

11.4 Replica and Consistency Management

Although data replication provides fast response and resiliency against failures, it introduces new problems of consistency and replica management [15]. The system must ensure that the concurrent execution of actions on replicated data is equivalent to a correct execution on non-replicated data. This property is also called the *one copy serializability* condition. Replica control algorithms ensure that the one copy serializability is met. Basically, replica control is also consistency control. It ensures that different copies of an object are mutually consistent so that the user gets the same view of the object. A node fault can be either fail-stop or Byzantine. A communication fault may lead to network partitioning, We discuss three approaches: primary site, active replica, and voting for connected networks. Approaches for partitioned networks are also included.

11.4.1 Primary site approach

We assume there are only node faults in the system and communication is reliable. The goal is to ensure that operations on each data object can still be performed even if up to k nodes in the system fail. In order to achieve this objective, the data is replicated on at least $k + 1$ nodes in the system. One node is designated as *primary* and the rest are *backups*. All requests are sent directly to the primary site.

- *Read request.* The primary site simply performs the operation and returns the results. No backup sites are involved. If the primary site fails, a new primary site is selected among the backups through an election process. Probably several new backups are selected to maintain at least $k + 1$ replications. Once the new primary site is elected the same procedure follows. If several backup sites fail but the primary site works, no modification is necessary. The primary site simply selects more backups to prepare for future failures.

- *Write request.* When the primary site receives a write request before performing the update, it sends the update request to at least k of its backups. This is to ensure that when the primary fails at least k other copies are in its backups. Once all backups have received the request the primary performs the operation and sends back the results. If several sites (primary and/or backups) fail, the same recovery process is used.

11.4.2   Active replicas

In the active replicas approach, all the replicas are simultaneously active. Instead of sending a request to a designated node such as the primary node in the primary site approach, a request is sent (broadcast) to all replicas. It is important that the agreement and order properties are satisfied. Agreement requires that all nonfaulty replicas receive every request and every nonfaulty replica processes the requests in the same order.

Maintaining mutual consistency at each particular time instance is rather difficult (actually impossible). It is aiming to achieve a weaker mutual consistency requirement: Each replica experiences the same sequence of modifications in such a way that when there are no more changes to be made, all replicas will have the same value.

The mutual consistency algorithm discussed below is very similar to Lamport's mutual exclusion algorithm based on timestamping. For each local update it is broadcast to all the other sites along with its time of update (timestamp). Each site i has a set of queues $Q_i[j]$ that hold the messages sent from site j. Since the messages in each queue are in the order in which they were sent, it is only necessary to examine the head of the queue to see the messages in order. A message at a site is considered to be *stable* if no request can come later to the state machine from any client that has a smaller timestamp [21]. Specifically, with logical clocks, a message m is stable at a site if the state machine has received a request with a larger timestamp than m from every site in the system. For a message to be stable, either more waiting time is needed for messages from other sites to arrive or forcing a reply message from other sites by sending query messages. It is easy to see that if there is a stable message, the message with the smallest timestamp must also be stable. Therefore, the selection process can start once a stable message is identified. There are three types of messages in this algorithm: $(modif, m, LC)$ where m is the modification and LC is time of modification, $(query, LC)$, a signal at time LC, and (ack, LC), an acknowledgment at time LC.

Initialization

> *clock*: $0, 1, \ldots, \infty$ (initially 0)
> $Q_i[j]$: array $[1, 2, \ldots, n]$ of message queues (initially empty)

site $(i) ::= *$ [modify the local copy $\rightarrow$
          send $(modif, m, clock)$ **to all**
          □ **receive** $(modif, m, LC)$ **from** site (j) $\rightarrow$
              add $(modif, m, LC)$ to $Q_i[j]$
          □ **receive** (ack, LC) **from** site (j) $\rightarrow$
              add (ack, LC) to $Q_i[j]$
          □ **receive** $(query, LC)$ **from** site (j) $\rightarrow$
              send $(ack, clock)$ **to** site (j)
          □ a modification message exists $\rightarrow$
              [a stable modification message exists
              $\rightarrow$ select a stable modification message
                  with the smallest timestamp
              □ there is no stable modification message
                  $\rightarrow$ [wait
                    □ **send** $(query, clock)$ **to** site (j),
                      where there is no message with a large
                      timestamp from site (j)
                  ]
              ]
          ]
      ]

Assume (LC, i) is the timestamp of a message from site i. The total order $\leq$ is defined as:

$$(LC_1, i) \leq (LC_2, j) \equiv (LC_1 < LC_2) \vee (LC_1 = LC_2 \wedge i < j)$$

11.4.3   Voting Protocol

A common approach to provide fault tolerance in distributed database systems is by replicating data at many sites. To enforce data consistency a common approach called single-write/multiple-read is used. This approach allows either "one writer and no readers" or "multiple readers and no writers" to access a data object simultaneously. The *quorum-voting* approach is an extension of single-write/multiple-read. A read is granted to a site if it acquires at least r votes (one vote for each copy of the data object at a distinct site) where r is the read quorum. A write is granted to a site if it gets at least w votes where w is the write quorum. Obviously in single-write/multiple-read, $r = 1$ and $w = v$, where v is the total number of votes. Note that we can assign different voting weights to different sites; therefore, v equals the number of sites only if each site gets one vote.

In order to avoid two writes updating the same data object at the same time, w should be more than the half of the total votes. To ensure that each read gets the latest copy of a data object, r should be large enough to include at least one latest copy of the date object (the latest copy can be identified by the timestamp associated with it). Therefore, the constraints on r and w can be summarized as

$$w > v/2$$

and

$$r + w > v$$

Note that the above two constraints allow more than one possible selection of w and r based on a given v. The performance and reliability characteristics of a system can be altered by judiciously assigning the number of votes to each replica and carefully selecting the values for r and w.

Consider a system with 7 nodes. One possible vote assignment is $w = 4$ and $r = 4$, i.e., for each write it should write to at least four copies. For each read at least four copies should be read; the one with the highest version number is the current version. Another possible solution is $w = 6$ and $r = 2$, i.e., at least six copies for each write and two copies for each read.

One potential problem of voting is that the number of nodes required in a quorum for performing an operation increases linearly with the number of replicas. One way to reduce a quorum is by organizing a hierarchical voting structure. Basically this structure forms a multi-level tree and a quorum is associated with each level. The physical copies of the object are stored only at the leaves of the tree. The same quorum requirement for read (r) and write (w) is applied to each level. A read (write) at level i depends on the corresponding groups at level $i + 1$ (we assume the leaves have the lowest levels and the root of the tree has the highest level which is 1). That is, a read (write) at level i is possible if all its children form a read (write) quorum at level $i + 1$.

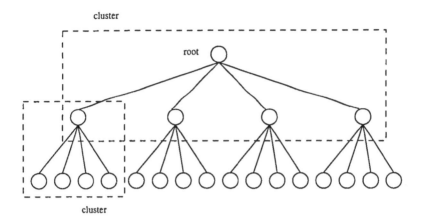

FIGURE 11.5
A 3-level tree in the hierarchical quorum voting.

Consider a 3-level tree (see Figure 11.5) in which each intermediate node has exactly four children. A total of 16 leaves are in the tree. A *cluster* in the tree consists of an interior node with all its children. In the given example a cluster consists of a non-leaf node with its four children. Assume that the read quorum is 2 and the write quorum is 3 for each cluster. For the root to obtain a read quorum it needs at least 2 reads at level 2; each of which in turn needs 2 reads at level 3. Hence, at least 4 reads at level 3 are needed. Similarly, for a write at the root it requires at least 3 writes at level 2; each of which in turn requires 3 writes at level 3. A total of 9 writes at level 3 are needed. Note that if 16 replicas are linearly organized, $w = 9$ and $r = 4$ do not satisfy the quorum requirement. However, in the hierarchical quorum voting the number of rounds for quorum collection is the depth of the tree whereas it requires only one round in the regular one-level majority voting.

11.4.4 Optimistic approaches for network partition: version vectors

Groups of nodes can become isolated in a partitionable network. The nodes in a group are able to communicate among themselves but not with nodes outside the group. Optimistic approaches place no restriction on transactions. If a network partitioning occurs, it is hoped that no conflict occurs. Detection of mutual inconsistency checks the consistency of copies of the same data object in disjoint subnetworks when these subnetworks are combined. One trivial method is to compare these copies element by element. The problem with this approach is the cost. The detection of mutual inconsistency among the copies of the object can be done by comparing the history associated with each copy where a history is a sequence of updates. In case of mutual inconsistency if there exists a history that covers all the other ones, that history is identified as the up-to-date copy and is broadcast to the other sites. A history H *covers* another history H' if H contains H' as its subsequence. The effect of this approach, however, depends on the relative size of the history compared with the size of the data object.

Another approach as has been used in the LOCUS operating system [20] uses *version vectors*. In this approach each file is associated with a vector of size n, $V = (v_1, v_2, ..., v_n)$, where n is the number of sites at which the file is stored. v_i is the version number (number of updates) performed at site i. If the network is completely connected, each update is performed at each copy of the file and each version is the same. However, if a partitioning occurs, vectors may diverge.

A vector V (of one copy of a file) *dominates* another vector V', if $v_i \leq v_i'$ for all i. That is, updates recorded in V' is a subset of the ones in V. Two vectors conflict with each other if neither dominates the other. Note that vector V is the same for copies of a file within a subnetwork. Therefore, the *dominate* operation compares histories at different subnetworks rather than different copies (as in the *cover* operation).

Figure 11.6 shows an example of a three-site network. Initially, three sites A, B, and C are all connected. B makes one update before the network is split into $\{A, C\}$ and $\{B\}$. Now A makes two updates and the corresponding vector becomes $< 2, 1, 0 >$. Node C then splits off node A and joins node B. Because the version vector of node C dominates the one of node B, the conflict is resolved by copying the file from node C to node B together with the version vector. During this grouping, node A makes one more update (and the associated vector becomes $< 3, 1, 0 >$). Node C makes one update and the associated vector becomes $< 2, 1, 1 >$. Now if these two groups join, version vectors conflicting with neither dominates the other one. The dynamic voting scheme discussed later prevents such a conflict by limiting certain updates to files: Only the site owning the majority of files that correspond to the latest update has the right to access files.

Maintaining mutual consistency is also important when a new site is created. It is required that each data object in the new site be an up-to-

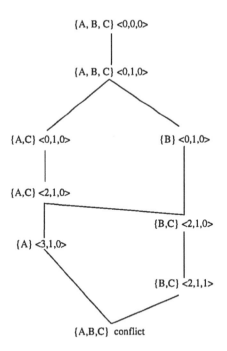

FIGURE 11.6
An example with version vectors.

date copy, but each data object is brought to this new site only when it is needed. A simple algorithm proposed by Attar et al. [1] is as follows:

1. Install a copy of a mutual consistency algorithm at new site S.

2. Signal the existence of S to all the other sites so that S is included at each site as one of the destinations to which the modification message is broadcast.

3. A data object is allowed to be read only if it has been modified by one of the other sites.

In the above approach the up-to-date copy of each data object is added to site S progressively at each update. Condition 3 indicates that no read is allowed unless there has been an update by one of the other sites. The logic behind this is quite simple: There is no copy of a data object at site S until an update is done by one of the other sites and the modification message is broadcast to all the sites including site S.

11.4.5   Pessimistic approach for network partition: dynamic voting

When a network partition occurs, it may happen that no site can obtain a read/write quorum. In other words, the system is completely unavailable. In the *majority-based dynamic voting* [16] the set of sites that form a majority of the latest version allows access to replicated data changes with the changing state of the system. Clearly dynamic voting allows operations to perform in groups that do not form a majority of the total sites as long as they include majority of the most recent update. To preserve consistency it has to ensure that no other group can perform any operation without including a node that has a latest version. In addition, no group of sites can form a majority of versions other than the latest one; otherwise, such a group will consider it has obtained a majority. After joining a group a site may want to catch up and update its state to the latest one. A site is allowed to update its state if and only if it belongs to a majority group.

In order to implement the above dynamic voting algorithm each copy is associated with a pair of (*version number, cardinality*) where version number k indicates the number of updates and the number of sites participated in the kth update is the cardinality. Consider a network with five sites and assume that it has completed the sixth update:

$$\{A : (6,5), B : (6,5), C : (6,5), D : (6,5), E : (6,5)\}$$

The network is partitioned into $\{A, B, C\}$ and $\{D, E\}$ and two updates are performed at subnetwork $\{A, B, C\}$ before forming another partition $\{A, D\}$ and $\{B, C, E\}$:

$$\{A : (8,3), D : (6,5)\} \quad \{B : (8,3), C : (8,3), E : (6,5)\}$$

Clearly, subnetwork $\{B, C, E\}$ forms the majority of the latest version (version 8); therefore, further updates are possible. Also site E can catch up but not D. Note that a catch-up is considered a new update even though there is no real change to the latest version. As a result version number and cardinality of each node (including the latest version) are updated. Subnetwork $\{B, C, E\}$ performs a catch-up once (and generates version 9) before A joins the subnetwork and another catch-up is performed:

$$\{D : (6,5)\}, \{A : (10,4), B : (10,4), C : (10,4), E : (10,4)\}$$

In the above example, if subnetwork $\{A, B, C, E\}$ is further partitioned into three subnetworks $\{A : (10, 4)\}$, $\{B : (10, 4), C : (10, 4)\}$, and $\{E : (10, 4)\}$, no partition forms a majority of the latest version. This problem can be solved by using *dynamic vote reassignment* [2] where the number of votes assigned to a site changes dynamically. The basic idea is to increase the vote (right) of each site in the majority partition. For example, in partition

$$\{D : (6, 5)\}, \{A : (10, 4)\}, \{B : (10, 4), C : (10, 4)\}, \{E : (10, 4)\}$$

each site has 1 vote. By increasing 0.5 votes to each B and C in the majority partition the total votes of B and C will be 3 at subnetwork $\{B, C\}$, and hence, subnetwork $\{B, C\}$ obtains a majority. Note that a further partition of B and C still results in a tie between B and C. A tie-breaker is needed to break a tie, e.g., assign 0.4 to B and 0.6 to C. Alternatively assign one node as a distinguished node and this approach is convenient to break a tie in an even split. A detailed discussion on weighted voting in a replicated database can be found in [12].

When a non-replicated database is partitioned, there are two major problems.

1. During a partition, transactions that access data in more than one subnetwork are unable to run.

2. A partition that occurs during the execution of a commit protocol (such as the two-phase commit protocol discussed later) can cause some nodes to commit and others to abort the same transaction.

One solution is to use commit and abort quorums. For example, in a system of four nodes the commit quorum is 3 and the abort quorum is 2. That is, a transaction can commit if three sites are ready and should abort if two sites are not ready. Note that many commit/abort quorums can be implemented via a vote assignment similar to a read/write quorum. Again, the commit quorum should overlap the abort quorum.

Another approach uses *compensating transactions* [9]. For example, consider a transaction that transfers funds from account A to account B. Suppose the transaction commits at A but is forced to abort at B. A compensating transaction run after the failure can examine the log records at A, determine the problem, and deposit the money back into account A.

In some cases we assign different votes to copies residing at different sites based on a priori knowledge, i.e., the reliability of each site. For example, if we have four sites A, B, C, D with one vote for each, the possible groups with a majority vote are:

$$\{\{A,B,C\},\{A,C,D\},\{A,B,D\},\{B,C,D\}\}$$

Note that another eligible group is $\{A,B,C,D\}$ but it can be derived from any other group. Therefore, we only include those *primitive groups* that cannot be derived from others. If B is given two votes and the rest one vote, the majority is still three votes. The primitive groups are:

$$\{\{A,B\},\{B,C\},\{B,D\},\{A,C,D\}\}$$

Note that it is difficult to determine a vote assignment to match a given set of primitive groups. Actually, if the number of nodes is more than five, there exist sets of primitive groups with no vote assignment corresponding to them [10]. Several heuristic vote assignment algorithms are proposed in [3].

A voting analysis on expressions using Boolean vectors is discussed in [25]. This approach applies to decision algorithms that use operations such as AND, OR, BMV (Boolean majority voting), MASK, etc. The objective is to show that, by using the concept of the weight of an operand, one can evaluate the structure of this algorithm with respect to the trustworthiness of its decisions or evaluate the effect of a given input operand.

Let every operand be associated with a pair (A, D) where A and D are nonnegative numbers. A is defined as the *approval weight* of the operand, its weight to approve the output of some algorithm. D is the *denial weight*, the weight to help decide that the output is wrong. For any operation, if the sum of approval weights of those operands with 1 is equal to or greater than 1, the resulting vector of the operation has a 1, similarly for the denial weight.

For the design of an algorithm of this type the definition of the weight of the operands should be based on the following criteria:

- The need to reflect exactly the intended weight of an operand in deciding the result based on its importance or criticality.

- Avoiding the vector sum of both the approval weights and the denial weights being individually less than 1.

- Avoiding the vector sum of both the approval weights and the denial weights being individually greater than or equal to 1.

For example, let a Boolean vector be $V = (v_1, v_2, ..., v_n)$. Let the corresponding weights for elements in this vector be (a_i, d_i). Then either $\sum_{i=1}^{n} a_i v_i$ is less than one or $\sum_{i=1}^{n} d_i v_i$ is less than one, but not both. For a logical AND operation every operand is associated with a pair $(1/m, 1)$. For a logical OR operation $(1, 1/m)$ is associated with each operand. m is the number of operands in the operation. For a BMV operation where every operand is associated with a pair $(2/(m + 2even(m)), 2/(m + 2odd(m)))$, where $odd(m)$ $(even(m))$ is a function with a value of 1 when m is odd (even) and 0 when m is even (odd). An evaluating algorithm for a sequence of operations and other details can be found in [25].

11.5 Distributed Reliability Protocols

In general, reliability techniques for distributed database systems consist of commit, termination, and recovery protocols. The primary requirement of commit protocols is to maintain the atomicity of distributed transactions. This means that even though the execution of the distributed transaction involves multiple sites, some of which may fail while executing, the effects of the transaction on the distributed database is all-or-nothing (or atomic commitment). For a single transaction there is a simple and elegant protocol that ensures the atomic commitment of the transaction. A transaction T starts by copying the relevant data from the database to volatile memory (a working space). When T, which executes on volatile memory, terminates normally, a two-step commit starts: The resulting values in volatile memory are copied to stable memory (the first step in Figure 11.7). These values are then copied to the database (the second step in Figure 11.7).

This commit protocol guarantees atomicity in the following ways: If no errors occur, the transaction (T) is executed as a whole; if an error occurs before the transaction results have been copied to stable memory (the first step), T is aborted. If an error occurs in the stage of writing the results to the database (the second step), this writing can be rewritten and will be valid because the transaction has already completed.

When a transaction involves several sub-transactions that are located at different sites, the commit protocol should ensure that the effects of local

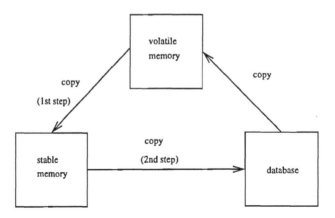

FIGURE 11.7
Two-phase commitment.

atomic commit actions (sub-transactions) are made permanent only after all the sites involved in the execution of the transaction agree to commit the transaction. Therefore, coordination among all the sub-transactions is necessary. Depending on the implementation of such a coordinator a *two-phase commit protocol* can have the following versions: centralized, hierarchical, linear, and fully distributed. Each site keeps two types of logs:

- *undo* log allows an uncommitted transaction to record in stable storage values it wrote. Should a system failure occur at this point, upon recovery stable storage will contain effects of the uncommitted transaction. These effects must be undone.

- *redo* log allows a transaction to commit before all the values written have been recorded in stable storage. If a system failure occurs at this point, on recovery stable storage will be missing some of the effects of the committed transaction. These must be redone by restarting to restore stable storage to its committed state.

Note that log data is redundant information collected for the sole purpose of recovery. Because volatile storage is lost in system failure, the log is kept in stable storage. If a data object is recorded in stable storage before the log entry for the data object is recorded in the stable log, the update cannot be undone if a crash occurs before the log is completed. The *write-ahead log* protocol should be used. Before recording uncommitted updates of data objects in stable storage, force the relevant undo entry to be written to the stable log, and before committing an update of a data object, the redo and undo log entries must be written on the stable log. In general, the *redo* and *undo* operations must be *idempotent*, i.e., repeatable any number of times since restart may be retried.

In the above approach it is required that all the committed transactions (before the failure) be redone even if they were done a long time ago. Clearly, this is not economic. In order to reduce the amount of *redo* that needs to be done during recovery, checkpoints can be used. Figure 11.8 shows an example of undo-redo log with checkpoints. In this example, during recovery after a crash, *undo* is applied for the entire transactions of T_1, T_4, and T_5, because all of them did not commit at the time of failure. *redo* is applied for T_2 and T_7 for actions after the latest checkpoint. *redo* is also used for the entire actions of T_3. Nothing needs to be done for T_6 since it completes before the last checkpoint.

The simplest and the most popular two-phase commit protocol is the centralized one [13]. In this protocol the node where the transaction is initiated is called *coordinator* and all the other nodes are called *participants*. This protocol is a centralized master-slave protocol. In the following, "prec" and "postc" stand for precondition and postcondition, respectively.

Phase 1
At the coordinator:

> /* prec: initiate state (q) */

1. The coordinator sends a *commit_request* message to every participant and waits for replies from all the participants.

> /* postc: waiting state (w) */

At participants:

> /*prec: initiate state (q)*/

1. On receiving the *commit_request* message, a participant takes the following actions. If the transaction executing at the participant is successful, it writes *undo* and *redo* log, and sends a *yes* message to the coordinator; otherwise, it sends a *no* message.

> /* postc: wait state (w) if *yes* or abort state (a) if *no* */

Phase 2
At the coordinator

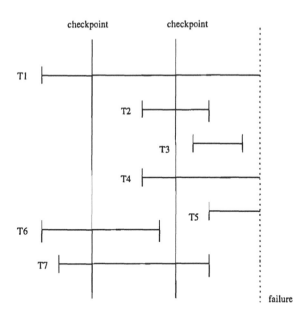

FIGURE 11.8
A recovery example.

/* prec: wait state (w) */

1. If all the participants reply *yes* then the coordinator writes a *commit* record into the log and then sends a *commit* message to all the participants. Otherwise, the coordinator sends an *abort* message to all the participants.

   /* postc: commit state (c) if *commit* or abort state (a) if *abort* */

2. If all the acknowledgments are received within a timeout period, the coordinator writes a *complete* record to the log; otherwise, it resends the commit/abort message to those participants from which no acknowledgments were received.

At the participants

/* prec: wait state (w) */

1. On receiving a *commit* message, a participant releases all the resources and locks held for executing the transaction and sends an acknowledgment.

location	time of failure	actions at coordi.	actions at parti.
coordi.	before *commit*	broadcasts *abort* on recovery	commited parti. undo the trans.
coordi.	before *complete* after *commit*	broadcasts *commit* on recovery	–
coordi.	after *complete*	–	–
parti.	in Phase 1	coordi. aborts the transaction	–
parti.	in Phase 2	–	commit/abort on recovery

Table 11.1   Site failures and recovery actions.

/* postc: commit state (c) */

/* prec: abort state (a) or wait state (w) */

2. On receiving an *abort* message, a participant undoes the transaction using the *undo* log record, releases all the resources and locks held by it, and sends an acknowledgment.

/* postc: abort state (a) */

This protocol can be modeled by a set of finite state machines with a set of states. The precondition and postcondition of each statement are listed in the protocol. The machine for the two-phase commit protocol is shown in Figure 11.9. Each machine has four states: initial (q), wait (w), abort (a), and commit (c). Each transition is represented by the conditions on the messages received that cause the state transition and the messages the machine sends.

When there are no failures or message losses, a transaction will commit if all participants agree to commit. Message losses can be handled by re-sending messages after the timeout. For site failures we consider the following cases as described in Table 11.1.

If the coordinator fails before recording the *commit*, upon recovery the coordinator broadcasts an *abort* message to all participants who agreed to commit undo the transaction using the *undo* log and abort. Other participants will abort the message. If the coordinator fails after *commit* but before *complete*, upon recovery the coordinator broadcasts a *commit* and waits for acknowledgment. No action is needed if the coordinator fails after the *complete*.

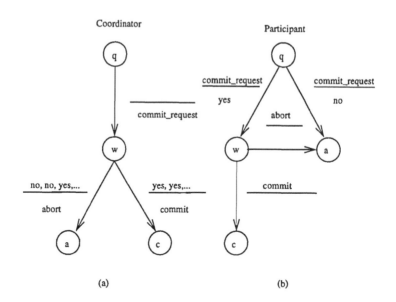

FIGURE 11.9
The finite state machine model for the two-phase commit protocol.

Note that in the above cases participants may have to wait until the coordinator recovers. If a participant has voted for *no*, it knows the final outcome; but if it has voted *yes*, it does not know the final decision. The participant can consult with other participants to decide what to do. This issue is part of *termination protocol*. If this participant finds another participant that has voted *no* or has received a final decision from the coordinator, it can tell the final decision. However, if all those participants that have voted *no* or have received the final decision have also failed, no conclusion can be derived.

If a participant fails and recovers later, it is desirable that it can decide the final state based on its local state (i.e., without consulting with others). This property is called *independent recovery*. If the participant fails in state *q* and it knows that the coordinator decides on aborting for receiving no signal, it can safely abort the transaction. If a participant fails in state *w* and if it voted *no* in state *q*, it knows the outcome to be abort; however, if it voted *yes*, then the final outcome can be either *commit* or *abort*. In this case the recovered participant has to contact the coordinator for the final result. A state that can be both a commit and an abort state is undesirable and should be eliminated.

Therefore, to avoid blocking we need to make sure that the *concurrent set* of each site does not contain both abort and commit states. The concurrency set of a site at a particular state is defined as the set of all the states of every site that may be concurrent with it. The *three-phase commit protocol* [23] is a nonblocking commit protocol that does not block in the event of site failures. This protocol is derived from the two-phase commit protocol by inserting a new state called *pending* between the wait state and commit state so that no state can be both in a commit and an abort state. However, the cost associated with a three-phase commit protocol is high. Some extensions have been proposed to reduce the cost for nonblocking in commitment [14].

The above centralized coordinator commit protocol can be easily modified into a *hierarchical commit protocol* by extending the communication structure into a tree of several levels. A single designated coordinator is at the root and messages flow along the links of the tree. The coordinator broadcasts to all its descendants by sending a message to its immediate descendants. Each descendant relays the message to nodes in its subtree. A leave node sends its response to its parent. An internal node in the tree collects responses from its descendants and, based on these responses, sends a single message to its immediate ancestor. A *linear commit protocol* is a special case of hierarchical commit protocol in which each node has at most one immediate parent and one immediate descendant. The centralized one is also a special case where there is only one level.

A heavily loaded coordinator may unnecessarily delay the termination of the protocol if it cannot process response messages as quickly as they arrive. Distributing the role of the coordinator is one way to eliminate this problem. The *decentralized two-phase commit protocol* [11] works as follows:

1. The originating site spawns the necessary sub-transactions as before. When a participant finishes its sub-transaction, it broadcasts its reply (*ok, nok*) not just to the originating site but to all the other participating sites.

2. Each site waits until it receives replies from all participants and then appropriately commits or aborts.

Note that if there are failures or timeouts, the participants cannot make unilateral decisions like the centralized coordinator. Instead, each participant must delay its decision until it gets all missing messages. If a message is missing, a participant can request it from any node that has already received it.

References

[1] Attar, R., P. A. Bernstein, and N. Goodman, "Site initialization, recovery and backup in distributed database systems", *IEEE Transactions on Software Engineering*, **10**, 6, Nov. 1984, 645-649.

[2] Barbara, D. and H. Garcia-Molina, "Optimizing the reliability provided by voting mechanisms", *Proc. of the 4th Int'l Conf. on Distributed Computing Systems*, 1984, 340-346.

[3] Barbara, D. and H. Garcia-Molina, "The reliability of voting mechanisms", *IEEE Transactions on Computers*, **36**, 10, Oct. 1987, 1197-1207.

[4] Barghouti, N. S. and G. E. Kaiser, "Concurrency control in advanced database applications", *ACM Computing Surveys*, **23**, 3, Sept. 1991, 271-317.

[5] Bernstein, P. A. and N. Goodman, "Timestamp based algorithms for concurrency control in distributed database systems", *Proc. of the 6th Int'l Conf. on Very Large Databases*, 1980, 126-136.

[6] Bernstein, P. A., V. Hadzilacos, and N. Goodman, *Concurrency Control and Recovery in Distributed Database Systems*, Addison-Wesley Publication Company, 1987.

[7] Eswaran, K. P. , J. N. Gray, A. Lorie, and I. L. Traiger, "The notion of consistency and predicate locks in a database system", *Communications of the ACM*, **19**, 11, Nov. 1976, 624-633.

[8] Garcia-Molina, H., "Performance comparison of two update algorithms for distributed databases, " *Proc. of the 3rd Berkeley Workshop on Distributed Data Management and Computer Networks*, 1978, 108-118.

[9] Garcia-Molina, H., "Using semantic knowledge for transaction processing in a distributed database", *ACM Transactions on Database Systems*, **8**, 6, June 1983, 186-213.

[10] Garcia-Molina, H. and D. Barbara, "How to assign votes in a distributed system", *Journal of the ACM*, **32**, 4, Oct. 1985, 841-860.

[11] Garcia-Molina, H. and R. K. Abbott, "Reliable distributed database management", *ACM Computing Surveys*, **75**, 5, May 1987, 601-620.

[12] Gifford, D. K., "Weighed voting for replicated data", *Proc. of the 7th ACM Symp. on Operating System Principles*, 1979, 150-162.

[13] Gray, J. N., "Notes on database operating systems", in *Operating Systems: An Advanced Course*, Springer-Verlag, 1979, 393-481.

[14] Guerraoui, R., M. Larrea, and A. Schiper, "Reducing the cost for non-blocking in atomic commitment", *Proc. of the 16th Int'l Conf. on Distributed Computing Systems*, 1996, 692-607.

[15] Herman, D. and Verjus, J. P., "An algorithm for maintaining for the consistency of multiple copies", *Proc. of the 1st Int'l Conf. on Distributed Computing*, 1979, 625-631.

[16] Jajodia, S. and D. Mutchler, "Integrating static and dynamic voting protocols to enhance file availability", *Proc. of the 4th Int'l Conf. on Data Engineering*, 1988, 144-153.

[17] Kohler, W. H., "A survey of techniques for synchronization and recovery in decentralized computer systems", *ACM Computing Surveys*, **13**, 2, June 1981, 149-183.

[18] Kung, H. T. and J. T. Robinson, "On optimistic methods for concurrency control", *ACM Transactions on Database Systems*, **6**, 2, June 1981, 213-226.

[19] Özsu, M. T. and P. Valduriez, *Principles of Distributed Database Systems*, Prentice-Hall, Inc., 1991.

[20] Parker, D. S. Jr. et al., "Detection of mutual inconsistency in distributed systems", *IEEE Transactions on Software Engineering*, **9**, 3, May 1983, 240-247.

[21] Schneider, F. B., "Implementing fault-tolerant services using the state machine approach: A tutorial", *ACM Computing Surveys*, **22**, 4, Dec. 1990, 299-319.

[22] Singhal, M. and N. G. Shivaratri, *Advanced Concepts in Operating Systems: Distributed, Database, and Multiprocessor Operating Systems*, McGraw-Hill, Inc., 1994.

[23] Skeen, D., "Nonblocking commit protocols", *Proc. of the ACM SIGMOD Int'l Conf. on Management of Data*, 1981, 133-142.

[24] Stonebraker, M., "Concurrency control and consistency of multiple copies of data in distributed INGRES", *IEEE Transactions on Software Engineering*, **3**, 3, May 1979, 188-194.

[25] Wu, J. and E. B. Fernandez, "A weighted tree model for algorithms with boolean vector operations", *Proc. of the 20th Southeastern Symp. on System Theory*, 1988, 150-154.

Problems

1. For the following two transactions:

   T1 **begin**
          1 **read** A (obtaining $A\_balance$)
          2 **write** $A\_balance-\$10$ to A
          3 **read** B (obtaining $B\_balance$)
          4 **write** $A\_balance+\$10$ to B
      end

   T2 **begin**
          1 **read** A (obtaining $A\_balance$)
          2 **write** $A\_balance+\$5$ to A
      end

   (a) Provide all the interleaved executions (or schedules).

   (b) Find all the serializable schedules among the schedules obtained in (a).

2. Point out serializable schedules in the following

   $$L_1 = w_2(y)w_1(y)r_3(y)r_1(y)w_2(x)r_3(x)r_3(z)r_2(z)$$

   $$L_2 = r_3(z)r_3(x)w_2(x)r_2(z)w_1(y)r_3(y)w_2(y)r_1(y)$$

   $$L_3 = r_3(z)w_2(y)w_2(x)r_1(y)r_3(y)r_2(z)r_3(x)w_1(y)$$

   $$L_4 = r_2(z)w_2(y)w_2(x)w_1(y)r_1(y)r_3(y)r_3(z)r_3(x)$$

3. Initially timestamps on x are $Time_r(x) = 3$ and $Time_w(x) = 2$. We have the following sequence of read and write requests at data object x:

$$write(x, 2), read(x, 1), read(x, 4), write(x, 3), write(x, 5), read(x, 6)$$

Show the result of timestamp-based concurrency control on each read and write request and the value of $Time_w(x)$ and $Time_r(x)$ after executing each request.

4. Discuss the pros and cons of implementing a distributed database using (1) the unreplicated approach, (2) the fully replicated approach, and (3) the partially replicated approach.

5. Show that if there is at most one conflict between any two transactions, any interleaved execution will be serializable. Provide a counter example in which there are two conflicts.

6. Show that being only well-formed does not guarantee serializability.

7. Consider two concurrent transactions T_1 and T_2 which write the same data object x and perform concurrency control using two-phase locking. Show that if T_1 wrote x before T_2, then the lock-point of T_1 must precede the lock-point of T_2. (The lock-point of a transaction is the stage at which it has acquired all needed locks.)

8. Consider a system with 10 sites. Determine all the possible read and write quorum pairs. Provide some guidelines on the selection of read and write quorum among all the possible ones.

9. Consider a system with 31 nodes. Organize them in a two-level hierarchy and specify the hierarchical voting parameters for it.

10. The two extremes of voting occur when $r = 1$ and when $r = n/2$, where n is the total number of votes. What are the differences in terms of performance for these two cases?

11. Consider the following execution of six transactions. What actions are needed during recovery for each of the transactions?

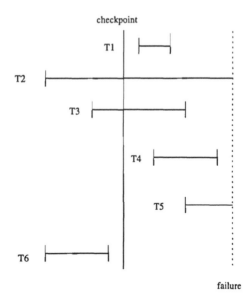

12. The dynamic voting algorithm is applied to a network of five sites. The network is partitioned into $\{A, B, C\}$ and $\{D, E\}$ after six updates. Two updates have been performed at $\{A, B, C\}$ before another partition occurs:

$$\{A : (8,3), D : (6,5)\} \quad \{B : (8,3), C : (8,3), E : (6,5)\}$$

Clearly, $\{B, C, E\}$ forms a majority of the latest version (version 8); therefore, further updates are possible. Site E can catch up and get a copy of version 8. Can D catch up at $\{A, D\}$? Why? If your answer is negative, provide a list of potential problems if D is allowed to catch up.

13. What is the use of the *undo* and *redo* log?

14. Garcia-Molina proposed the following *write-ahead* log protocol:

   - Before over-writing an object in stable storage with uncommitted updates, a transaction should first write its undo for this update.

   - Before committing an update to an object in stable storage, the transaction must write the undo and redo log.

   Why is this write-ahead log protocol important?

15. Modify the two-phase commit protocol to commit a transaction if a quorum of the participants vote *yes*.

16. Skeen proposed the three-phase commit protocol as shown in the following finite state machine. Show recovery actions for each case of site failure. You are required to provide the location and time of each failure and the corresponding actions at the coordinator and each participant.

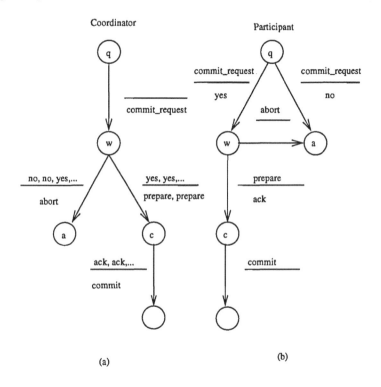

(a)   (b)

17. A voting method called *voting-with-witness* replaces some of the replicas by *witnesses*. Witnesses are copies that contain only the version number but no data. The witnesses are assigned votes and will cast them when they receive voting requests. Although the witnesses do not maintain data, they can testify to the validity of the value provided by some other replica. How should a witness react when it receives a read quorum request? What about a write quorum request? Discuss pros and cons of this method.

Chapter 12

DISTRIBUTED SYSTEM APPLICATIONS

In this chapter we discuss applications of distributed systems in operating systems, file systems, shared memory systems, database systems, and heterogeneous computing systems. Future directions for distributed system design are also included.

12.1 Distributed Operating Systems

There are a number of advantageous features which motivate research in the areas of network operating systems (NOSs) and distributed operating systems (DOSs). Some of these are resource sharing, performance, reliability and availability, scalability, price advantage, and transparency.

A *network operating system* allows users at independent processors to communicate via a shared file system but otherwise leave each user as the master of his/her own processor. This system has the following characteristics that distinguish it from a *distributed operating system* [55]: (1) Each computer has its own operating system. (2) Each user requires some kind of "remote login" to access different processors. (3) Users are aware of where files are kept and must move files between processors (not for systems with a shared file system). (4) The system provides little or no fault tolerance.

A distributed operating system is one that looks to its user like an ordinary centralized operating system but runs on multiple, independent PEs. Distributed operating systems turn the entire collection of hardware and software into a single integrated system, like a traditional time sharing system. Let us consider the mechanisms used for file transfer from one processor to another to see the difference between network and distributed operating systems. In a network operating system each site maintains its own local file system. If a user at one site wants to access a file at another site, the file must be copied explicitly from one site to another through the file transfer protocol (FTP) provided by the Internet. In a distributed operating system the user can access remote files without knowing the physical locations of these files. The following two approaches can be used:

- *Data migration.* The needed file is automatically transferred to the local site without the explicit involvement of the user. One approach is to transfer the entire file as is done in the Andrew file system [22]. Another approach is to transfer only portions of the file that are necessary for the immediate task. Other portions are transferred later as needed. Sun's Network File System (NFS) [43] uses the latter approach.

- *Computation migration.* In this approach computation, rather than data (file), is transferred across the system. This can be done using either *remote procedure call* or *message passing* to invoke a predefined procedure at the remote site. The procedure executes appropriately and returns needed results to the local site.

The key difference between a network operating system and a distributed operating system is the concept of transparency. Although a network operating system can offer a certain degree of transparency, a distributed operating system provides more varieties of transparency at different levels [56]:

- *Access transparency.* The user cannot recognize whether a resource is local or remote.

- *Concurrency transparency.* Multiple users can share resources automatically without knowing the existence of others.

- *Failure transparency.* The nature of a failure and its handling is transparent to the user.

- *Location transparency.* Users cannot recognize where resources such as CPUs, memories, and files are located.

- *Migration transparency.* Resources can be moved from one location to another without changing their name; therefore, the user is not aware of such a migration.

- *Parallel transparency.* Various process activities can happen simultaneously without the user's knowledge.

- *Performance transparency.* Processes can be executed on an arbitrary processor(s) without each user noticing and without a noticeable difference in performance.

- *Replication transparency.* The system can make additional copies of files and databases on its own. At the user level the user only sees one copy.

Tanenbaum and Renesse [55] listed five key issues that distributed systems' designers are faced with:

1. *Communication primitives.* Techniques used in shared memory such as semaphores and monitors are generally not applicable. Instead, message passing is used that can be either a client-server model that uses two primitives: message passing (send and receive) or remote procedure call.

2. *Naming and protection.* Naming can be seen as a problem with the mapping between two domains such as mapping of virtual addresses into physical addresses in a virtual memory system.

3. *Resource management.* Processor allocation, scheduling, and load balancing are the three main components of resource management. The key is to obtain an accurate global state information in a cost-effective way.

4. *Fault tolerance.* One of the key advantages of distributed systems is there are enough resources to achieve fault tolerance.

5. *Services.* A distributed operating system should provide the following services: file, print, process, terminal, mail, boot, and gateway.

The communication and fault tolerance issues were treated in earlier chapters. Part of resource management was discussed in Chapters 8 and 9, and the other part will be treated in the section on distributed shared memory. Naming and protection are part of distributed file systems. We focus on the type of services [55] in the subsequent discussion.

12.1.1   Server structure

A *service* is a software entity running on one or more PEs and providing
a particular type of function to clients. A *server* is the service software
running on a single processor. A *client* is a process that can invoke a
service using a set of operations. The simplest way to implement a service
is to have one server that has a single, sequential thread of control that
looks like this:

$$* [\text{ get-request; carry-out-request; send-out-reply }]$$

One simple variation is to maintain a table to keep track of the status
of multiple partially completed requests. This approach has better performance but bad structure. In order to get both good performance and clean
structure, the server can be structured as a collection of mini-processes
(also called *threads*) sharing the same code and global address but each
with its own stack for local variables. One way to assign each task a job
is through a dispatcher whose tasks are to accept new requests and assign
them. Another way is to have each task capable of accepting new requests
for work.

12.1.2   Eight types of services

- *File service*
  There are three components of a traditional file service : *disk, flat file*,
  and *directory*. The disk service provides reading and writing raw disk
  blocks. The flat file service deals with providing its clients with an
  abstraction consisting of files. The directory service provides a mechanism for naming and protecting files. One important issue is the
  way the three components of a traditional file service are integrated.
  Garbage collection is another important design issue. Detailed discussion on file service is discussed in the section on distributed file
  systems.

- *Print service*
  Print service provides service to clients so they can print data on one
  of the available printers. In some cases the whole file is sent to the
  print server and the server must buffer it. In other cases only the file
  name and its capability (which defines access right for each user) are
  sent and the server reads the file block by block as needed.

- *Process service*

  Process service creates new processes as needed and maintains them. A process is a program whose execution has started but is not yet completed. A process can be in three basic states: running, ready, or blocked. A data structure called a *process control block* (PCB) is used to store information about a process such as id, process state, etc. Typical operations on processes are create, kill, suspend, schedule, change-priority, etc.

- *Terminal service*

  There are several ways to organize a terminal service. The simplest way is to hardwire each terminal to the processor its users normally log on to. If the system consists of a pool of processors that are dynamically allocated as needed, it is better to connect all the terminals to one or more terminal servers that serve as concentrators. The terminal service is also used to support multiple windows per terminal with each window acting as a *virtual terminal*.

- *Mail service*

  Mail service provides a demon process (if system is on or off) and supports a machine-independent mail service.

- *Time service*

  Time service provides two types of service: It provides clients the time when asked and it broadcasts the correct time periodically to keep all the clocks on the other processors synchronized.

- *Boot service*

  The boot service has two functions: Bringing up the system from scratch when the power is turned on and helping important services that survive crashes.

- *Gateway service*

  Gateway service is required when systems at different (remote) sites communicate with each other. It converts message and protocol from format to those demanded by the wide area network carrier.

12.1.3   Microkernel-based systems

One approach to distributed operating system design which is becoming popular is to build a set of independent system servers using primitive, generic services of a microkernel. A microkernel provides essential services such as process scheduling, interprocess communication, memory management, low-level network communication, and interrupt dispatching. These essential services form a foundation for less essential system services and applications. It appears as a layer between the hardware layer and a layer consisting of system components called subsystems.

A microkernel operating system provides a structure defined to cope with the increased complexity of operating system development for distributed systems. It offers the following advantages compared to the traditional monolithic operating systems [19]:

- A clear microkernel interface enforces a more modular system structure.

- The operating system is more flexible and tailorable.

- The size of a microkernel is small and all the code runs in a common, shared address space.

- Easier to provide real-time support for mission critical applications.

The challenge to the microkernel-based operating system designer is to make the application under these emulated environments run as efficiently as it runs under its native operating system. Commercial and research prototypes of distributed operating systems include: Amoeba [34], Chorus [42], Clouds [15], DCE (distributed computing environment) [4], Galaxy [47], Mach [40], Saguaro [1], V-system [14], and Wiselow [3]. Among them Amoeba, Chorus, and Mach are microkernel-based systems. Several commercial systems also use microkernel such as Puma on the Intel Paragon and AIX on the IBM SP-2.

12.2   Distributed File Systems

A *file* is an unstructured sequence of data and usually is an uninterpreted sequence of bytes. A *file system* is a subsystem of an operating system whose purpose is to provide long-term storage and sharing of information. Satyanarayanan [33] listed four key issues in designing a file system.

- *Naming.* How does the user name files? Is the name space flat or hierarchically organized?

- *Programming interface.* How do applications access the file system?

- *Physical storage.* How is the file system abstraction mapped onto physical storage media? Is the programming interface independent of storage media?

- *Integrity.* How are files kept consistent across power, hardware, media, and software failures?

Sinha [48] listed the following ten desirable properties of a file system: transparency, user mobility, performance, simplicity and ease of use, scalability, high availability, high reliability, data integrity, security, and heterogeneity.

A distributed file system is merely a distributed implementation of the multi-user, single-site file system abstraction. The challenge is to realize this abstraction in an efficient and robust manner. Again, the multiplicity of servers and storage devices should be transparent to clients. A client interface for a file service is formed by a set of file operations such as creating a file, deleting a file, reading from a file, and writing to a file.

Two important goals of a distributed file system are network transparency and high availability. Two important services presented in a distributed file system are the name server and cache manager. Cache managers can reside at both clients and file servers.

12.2.1   File accessing models

A file accessing model consists of two components: accessing remote files and unit of file transfer. A user requests access to a remote file through remote services. Requests for accesses to remote files are delivered to the server. The server performs the accesses and the results are returned to the user (client). One of the most commonly used forms of remote service is the remote procedure call. In order to ensure good performance of the remote service, we can use a form of caching. If the needed data are not already cached at the local site, a copy of the data is brought from the server to the user. When the caching approach is used for remote access, the unit of file transfer needs to be determined. The unit can be the whole file, a block, a record, or a byte.

12.2.2   File sharing semantics

File sharing semantics define when modifications of a *mutable file* made by a user are observable by other users. A file is mutable if an update overwrites its old contents. A file is *immutable* if it cannot be modified once it has been created except to be deleted. An immutable file system needs to keep a history of immutable versions for each file. In practice the space usage can be reduced by keeping only the difference between the old and new versions.

There are at least three file-sharing semantics [31]:

- *Unix semantics.* In this semantic a write to an open file by a user immediately becomes visible to other users who have this file open.

- *Session semantics.* A session consists of an open file operation, a series of read/write operations, and a close file operation. In this semantic all updates within a session are visible to other remote processes only after the close of this session. However, multiple clients are allowed to perform both read and write accesses concurrently on the same file. These clients may generate different versions of a file but only one version is kept (normally the one which closes its session).

- *Transaction semantics.* A transaction resembles a session. However, a transaction ensures the all-or-nothing property. If two or more transactions start up at the same time, the system ensures that the final result is the same as if they were all running in some sequential order.

12.2.3   Merge of file systems

The first issue faced is to merge several file systems. Three approaches can be used:

- The first approach is not to merge them at all.

- The second approach is to have *adjoining file systems*. In this approach, a virtual super-directory above the root directories of all the connected processors is used. All path names are processor dependent. The Newcastle Connection [10] uses this approach.

- The third approach is the way merger is done in distributed operating systems. There is a single global file system visible from all the processors. LOCUS [57] is an example using this approach.

In the Unix system a name space is *mounted* at an internal node or a leaf node of a name space tree. A node onto which a name space is mounted is called a *mount point.*

12.2.4 Protection

Each file in the file system has a small table associated with it (called an *i*-node in Unix) telling who the owner is and where the disk blocks are located. Each user has a User IDentifier (UID) to access his/her files. To access a remote file there are four approaches:

- All remote users wanting access to the files on processor *A* should first log onto *A* using a user name that is local to *A*.

- Any user can access files on any processor without having to log in but the remote user has the UID corresponding to a guest or some other publicly known login name.

- The operating system provides a mapping between UIDs so that a user with UID *a* on his/her local processor can access a remote processor on which his/her UID is *b*.

- In a distributed system there should be a unique UID for every user and this UID should be valid on all processors without any mapping.

12.2.5 Naming and name service

Naming is a problem of mapping between two domains. For example, the directory system in Unix provides a mapping between ASCII path names and *i*-node numbers. The mapping of virtual addresses onto physical addresses in a virtual memory system is another example. There are three ways to organize a name server:

- A centralized system maintains a table or database providing the necessary name-to-object mappings.

- Partition the system into domains each with its own name server. A global naming tree is constructed. When a name, say *a/b/c*, is looked up by the local name server, it may well yield a pointer to another domain (name server) to which the rest of the name (*b/c*) is sent for further processing.

- Each processor manages its own names. To look up a name, one broadcasts it on the network. At each processor the incoming request is passed to the local name server which replies only if it finds a match.

A naming service in a distributed file system should provide the following:

- *Location transparency* where the name of a file does not reveal any hint as to its physical storage location.

- *Location independence* where the name of a file needs not be changed when the file's physical storage location changes.

12.2.6   Encryption

Encryption is an indispensable part for enforcing security in a distributed system. It is primarily of value in preventing unauthorized release and modification of data. The key to this mechanism is a handshake type of protocol in which each party challenges each other to prove its identity. Currently, most systems use one of two distinct methods:

- An authentication server that is physically secure maintains a list of user passwords.

- The public key scheme as used in Sun's Network File System (NFS) maintains a publicly readable database of authentication keys that are encrypted with user passwords.

The latter approach has the attractive feature that physical security of the authentication server is unnecessary.

12.2.7   Caching

Caching is usually used in a distributed file system to reduce delays in the accessing of data. The concept of caching is to retain recently accessed disk blocks in the cache so that repeated accesses to the same information can be handled locally without additional network traffic.

One issue is the *cache consistency problem.* If the client site determines that its cached data are out of date, an up-to-date copy of the data needs to be cached. Two approaches can be used:

- *Client-initiated approach.* The client initiates a validity check by contacting the server and checks that the local data are consistent with the master copy.

- *Server-initiated approach.* The server records for each client the files it caches. When the server detects a potential inconsistency, it must react.

When the file server maintains the current state information for a file that has been opened for use by a client, it becomes *stateful*. A *stateless*

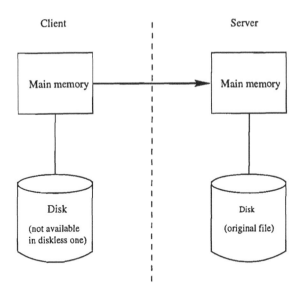

FIGURE 12.1
Possible cache locations in a file system.

server does not maintain any client state information. One problem with the stateful server is that state information may be lost in the event of a failure.

Another issue is that the data cached by a client should be in the main memory, in a local disk at the client, or in the main memory at the server (see Figure 12.1). Note that the original file is kept on the disk of the server. The advantages of using cache in the main memory at the server are the following: (1) It is easy to implement and is transparent to the clients. (2) It is easy to enforce the consistency between the original file and the cached one. However, this scheme does not eliminate the network access. The advantages of using the cache in the main memory at the client are the following: (1) It can be applied in diskless workstations. (2) It provides fast accessing of data. The disadvantage is that it competes with the virtual memory system for physical memory space. Another pitfall is that large files cannot be cached completely in the local main memory. Also, a disk is normally more reliable than main memory. Caching in the local disk eliminates the network access. However, it does not work if the client is a diskless workstation. A disk access is still required even when there is a cache hit.

The third issue is the *writing policy* that decides when a modified cache block at a client should be transferred to the server. The most expensive one is *write-through*. An alternate one is *delayed writing policy*. For example, updates at the server are delayed until the file is closed at the client. Commercial and research prototypes of distributed file systems include: Andrew [22], Coda [44], Locus [39], Sprite [35], Sun's Network File System (NFS) [43], and Unix United (also called Newcastle Connection) [10]. See [31] for a survey of distributed file systems.

12.3   Distributed Shared Memory

Two types of parallel/distributed systems have been popular: tightly coupled systems and loosely coupled systems. A tightly coupled system is more straightforward to program because it is a natural extension of a single-processor system. Loosely coupled systems include both networks of workstations and multicomputers without shared memory.

There has been much research into message passing in loosely coupled systems. A shared memory approach can simplify programming. Therefore, a shared memory abstraction is sometimes implemented on a loosely coupled system. Such a shared memory abstraction is called *distributed shared memory* (DSM) [27]. The advantages offered by DSM include simpler abstraction, flexible communication environment, and ease of process migration.

DSM research issues are similar to those of research in multiprocessor caches, networked file systems, and management systems for distributed or replicated databases. Many algorithms in these domains can be transferred to DSM systems or vice versa. However, their details and implementations can vary significantly because of differences in the cost parameters and in the ways they are used. Figure 12.2 shows a general structure of distributed shared memory where shared memory represents the logical view from the user and local memory refers to the physical view. The unit of sharing represents the size of units that can be moved between different local memory.

Nitzberg and Lo [37] listed the following design choices for DSM:

1. *Structure and Granularity*
   Granularity refers to the size of the unit of sharing which can be a byte, word, or page. A method of structuring the shared memory is

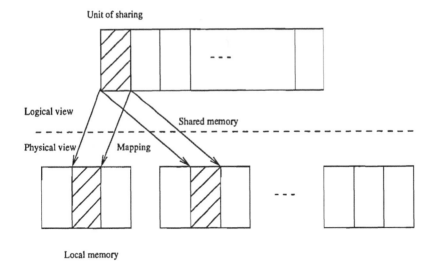

FIGURE 12.2
Distributed shared memory

by data type which can be objects or tuple space as used in Linda [12]. Ivy [27] is a page-based system where the unit of sharing is a page.

2. *Coherence semantics*

   The most commonly used semantics for memory coherence is strict consistency in which a read operation returns the most recently written value. In general, it is hard to enforce strict consistency semantics. Various relaxed coherence semantics are commonly used.

3. *Scalability*

   DSM systems scale better than tightly coupled shared memory systems. However, care should be taken to avoid (or reduce) central bottlenecks; for example, a bus is used as a communication medium to perform global operations.

4. *Heterogeneity*

   The processors in DSM may not have the same representation for basic operation types. However, we should avoid situations when the overhead of conversion outweighs the benefits.

5. *Data location and access*

To support data sharing DSM should be able to locate and retrieve the data accessed by a user process.

6. *Replacement strategy*

   If the local memory is full, a cache miss implies not only a fetch of the accessed data block from a remote site but also a replacement.

Two important design issues we consider are memory coherence algorithms and data location and access. Three different ways of implementing DSM systems are hardware, operating system, and compiler approaches [56].

12.3.1   Memory coherence problem

A memory is coherent if the value returned by a read operation is always the same as the value written by the most recent write operation to the same address. Two basic operations in a DSM are:

$$\text{data} := \textbf{read}(\text{address})$$
$$\textbf{write}(\text{data, address})$$

We discuss here two ways to classify various coherence algorithms: one by Stumm and Zhou [52] and the other by Li and Hudak [28]. There are many other consistency models which vary from application to application. The above model is called a *strict consistency model*. All the other models are based on relaxing this model but a set of applications under consideration should still function correctly. A relaxation will improve the performance of some applications because better concurrency can be achieved. However, a weak consistency model may not be able to support correct execution of other applications. A detailed discussion on the models of coherence semantics can be found in [56].

12.3.2   Stumm and Zhou's Classification

Stumm and Zhou categorized algorithms by whether they *migrate* and/or *replicate* data. Therefore, there are four types of algorithms.

Central-server algorithm (nonmigrating and nonreplicated).

This algorithm uses a central server that is responsible for servicing all accesses to shared data and maintains the only copy of the shared data. Both read and write operations involve the sending of a request message to the server using the following steps:

1. (Client) Sends a data request to the central server.

2. (Central server) Receives the request, performs data access and sends a response.

3. (Client) Receives the response.

The central server may become a bottleneck. To alleviate this problem several servers can be used. In that case clients must multicast their requests to all servers.

Migration algorithm (migrating and non-replicated).

In this algorithm the data is always migrated to the site where it is accessed. This is a "single-read/single-write" protocol consisting of the following steps:

1. (Client) If the needed data object is not local, determines the location and then sends a request.

2. (Remote host) Receives the request and then sends the object.

3. (Client) Receives the response and then accesses the data object (read and/or write).

The migration algorithm works well in applications with high locality reference and can be integrated with the virtual memory system of the host operating system if the size of the data object is chosen equal to the size of a virtual memory page. However, thrashing may occur in some cases.

Read-replication algorithm (migrating and replicated).

This is a "multiple-read/single-write" protocol in which replication reduces the average cost of read operations. However, some of the write operations may become more expensive. The algorithm for a write operation works as follows:

1. (Client) If the needed data object is not local, determines the location and sends a request.

2. (Remote host) Receives the request and then sends the object.

3. (Client) Receives the object and then multicasts either invalidates or updates to all sites that have a copy of the data object.

4. (Remote host) Receives an invalidation signal and then invalidates its local copy, or receives an update signal and then updates the local copy.

5. (Client) Accesses the data object (write).

The algorithm for a read operation is as follows:

1. (Client) If the needed data object is not local, determines a location that has a copy and sends a request.

2. (Remote host) Receives the request and then sends the object.

3. (Client) Accesses the data object (read).

Full-replication algorithm (non-migrating and replicated).

This is a "multiple-read/ multiple-write" protocol. One way to keep the replicated data consistent is to globally sequence the write operations using a *global sequencer* (all the timestamps are given by this sequencer). In this way each site performs the same sequence of write updates. Two algorithms are discussed here: One assumes that the client is responsible to broadcast the update (after receiving a sequence number) and the other assumes that the sequencer is in charge of assigning sequence numbers to a write request and broadcasts the request together with the assigned number.

Full-replication algorithm 1:

1. (Client) If it is a write, sends the data object to the sequencer.

2. (Sequencer) Receives the data object and adds a sequence number. Sends the client a signal with the sequence number and multicasts the data object together with the sequence number to all the other sites.

3. (Client) Receives the acknowledgment and updates local memory based on the sequence number of each data object.

   (Other sites) Receive the data object and update local memory based on the sequence number of each data object.

Full-replication algorithm 2:

1. (Client) If it is a write, sends a signal to the sequencer.

2. (Sequencer) Receives the signal and adds a sequence number. Sends the client a signal with the sequence number.

3. (Client) Receives the sequence number, multicasts the data object together with the sequence number and updates the local memory based on the sequence number of each data object.

4. (Other sites) Receive data and update local memory based on the sequence number of each data object.

Both algorithms use a single global gap-free sequencer; therefore, if a gap in the sequence numbers is detected, either a modification was missed or a modification was received out of order, in this case a retransmission of the modification message is requested.

12.3.3 Li and Hudak's Classification

Among four algorithms classified by Stumm and Zhou, the read-replication algorithm is commonly used in DSM systems. In the read-replication algorithm coherence is enforced by either *invalidation* or *write-through* (or write-broadcast). Write-through is too costly in a large system. Although the theoretical analysis on *snoopy cache* coherence suggests that combining the invalidation approach with the write-through approach may be a better solution, it is still an open problem whether this approach can be applied to DSM systems. Li and Hudak [28] proposed three ways of implementing a invalidation-based read-replication algorithm: centralized manager, a fixed distributed manager, and a dynamic distributed manager.

Centralized manager algorithm.

A centralized manager algorithm is similar to a monitor consisting of a data structure and certain procedures that provide mutually exclusive access to the data structure. The centralized manager resides on a single processor and maintains a table that has one entry for each page. Each entry has three fields:

- The *owner* field points to the most recent processor to have write access.

- The *copy set* field lists all processors that have copies of the page.

- The *lock* field is used for synchronizing requests.

Each processor also has a page table that has two fields: access and *lock*. The access field keeps information on the accessibility of pages on the local processor. Each processor knows the centralized manager and can send a request if the data object is not locally available. When there is more than one process on a processor waiting for the same page, the locking mechanism prevents the processor from sending more than one request.

In this algorithm a page does not have a fixed owner and there is only one manager that knows who the owner is. The owner of a page sends a copy to the processor requesting a read copy. As long as a read copy exists, the page is not writable without an *invalidation* operation. The successful writer to a page always has ownership of the page.

Distributed manager algorithms.

There are two types of distributed manager algorithms: the fixed and the broadcast. In the fixed algorithm every processor is given a predetermined subset of the pages to manage. Normally, an appropriate hashing function is used to map pages to processors. In the broadcast algorithm a faulting processor broadcasts into the network to find the true owner of a page. Performance is poor because all processors have to process each broadcast request, slowing down the computation on all processors.

Dynamic distributed manager algorithms.

The heart of a dynamic distributed manager algorithm is to keep track of the ownership of all pages in each processor's local pagetable. In a pagetable the *owner* field of the centralized manager is replaced with another field, *probowner*, whose value can be either the true owner or the probable owner of the page. The *probowner* field forms a chain from node to node that eventually leads to the real owner. When a message is received the owner of a page can be deduced and the *probowner* field is updated. The average length of a probable owner chain is the key to the performance of this algorithm. Simulation results show this number is between 2 and 3 in many applications.

When a node reads a page that is not cached in local memory, the memory management hardware generates a read fault. The read fault handler recognizes the page as a DSM page. A read request is sent along the probable owner chain. When the request reaches the owner, the owner returns a read-only copy of the page and records the identity of the requesting node in the copyset. When the requester receives the page, it updates its probowner field to be the node that returned the page.

Before a node writes to a page it must first become the page owner and invalidate all copies of the page. A write fault is generated if the page is not present in local memory or is present in the read-only mode. If it is not already the page owner, the node sends a write request to the probable owner. Each node that forwards the write request updates its probowner field to be the requester and the requester now becomes the new owner. Any requests for the page that arrive at the new owner before it actually receives ownership are queued and serviced after the transfer of ownership is completed. The owner returns a copy of the page and the copyset of the page. The requester is now the new page owner. The previous owner invalidates its copy of the page and updates its probowner field to be the new owner. If the copyset is not empty, the owner has read-only access to the page. The owner must ensure that it has the only copy of the page before writing to it. The owner sends an invalidate message to each node in the copyset to enforce sequential consistency. When a node receives an invalidate message, it invalidates the page, updates the probowner field, and returns an acknowledgment to the owner. When all invalidate messages have been acknowledged the owner can write to the page.

One direction of research on DSM is to achieve reliable DSMs [9], [59], [60]. Reliable DSMs are especially important in systems with a large number of processors where the probability of processor failure cannot be neglected. Several research protocols have been developed, including Alewife [26], Dash [30], Ivy [28], Linda [11], Midway [5], Mirage [17], and Munin [13].

12.4   Distributed Database Systems

A distributed database is a collection of multiple, logically interrelated databases distributed over a computer network. A distributed database includes a distributed database management system (distributed DBMS) that permits the management of the distributed database and makes the system transparent to the user.

Traditionally database systems are implemented on top of general-purpose operating systems. However, such an operating system may support with high overhead features to maintain generality. These features may not be required in a database system. Some services provided by a general purpose operating system are inadequate for supporting database systems. For example, operating systems support an abstraction of files that are an uninterpreted byte sequence. A database system requires an object with rich and complex structures (especially in object-oriented database systems). Therefore, to achieve high performance a new operating system should be developed that efficiently supports only the features needed by database systems. Differences between distributed file systems and distributed database systems [33] are the following:

- A file system views the data object in a file as an uninterpreted byte sequence. A database encapsulates substantial information on the types and logical relationships of data objects stored in it.

- They differ in the naming scheme used. A file system provides access to a file by name. A database, on the other hand, allows association access.

- Distributed databases are particularly difficult on a large scale whereas distributed file systems spanning tens of nodes are commonplace.

Possible design alternatives along three dimensions are as follows [38]:

- *Autonomy* deals with control distribution. Three types of autonomy are tight integration, semi autonomy, and full autonomy.

- *Distribution* deals with data objects. Data objects can be replicated or non-replicated. In both cases data objects can be stored at one site or be physically distributed over multiple sites.

- *Heterogeneity* deals with various forms in a distributed database system including hardware, data models, query language, and interfaces.

The alternative system architectures based on the above taxonomy are shown in Figure 12.3 [38]. Among these alternatives two are basic regarding the way data objects are placed: *partitioned* and *replicated*. The two fundamental design issues are *fragmentation*, the separation of the database into partitions called *fragments*, and *distribution*, the optimum distribution of fragments.

The main advantages of a distributed DBMS over a centralized DBMS system are:

1. *Transparency.* A distributed DBMS offers several forms of transparency (i.e., distribution, replication, and fragmentation).

2. *Reliability.* A distributed DBMS eliminates single point of failure. Data replication increases database availability.

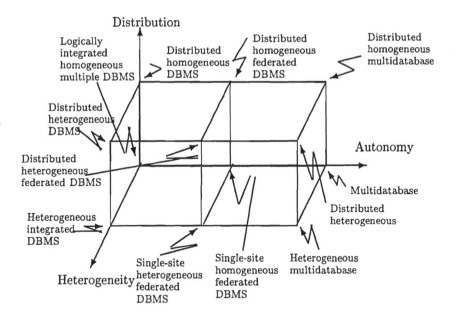

FIGURE 12.3
Alternative architectures [38] (©1991 IEEE).

3. *Performance.* A distributed DBMS alleviates contention for CPU and I/O services. They also support interquery and intraquery parallelism.

4. *Expandability.* In a distributed DBMS it is much easier to accommodate increasing database size. Major system overhauls are seldom necessary; expansion can usually be handled by adding processing and storage power to the network.

5. *Shareability.* If the information system is not distributed, it is usually impossible for organizations that have geographically distributed operations to share data and resources. A distributed DBMS therefore makes this sharing feasible.

The distribution of database causes the following problems:

1. *Distribution of control.* Distribution creates problems of synchronization and coordination.

2. *Security and integrity.* Security means preventing/detecting/deterring

the improper disclosure of information while integrity means preventing/detecting/deterring the improper modification of information.

3. *Complexity and cost.* A distributed DBMS is inherently more complex than the centralized DBMS. The additional hardware (including communication subsystems) also increases hardware costs. Furthermore, added complexity also increases software costs.

The complexity of a distributed DBMS is reflected in multilevel control due to the presence of global and local DBMSs. The global DBMS can be either centralized or decentralized. In centralized control all global processing is controlled by a central computer. In decentralized control each node keeps a copy of the distributed DBMS. The complexity of a distributed DBMS also makes *semantic integrity* difficult. By semantic integrity we imply the preservation of a meaningful database against erroneous updates. *Interprocess integrity*, also known as concurrency or internal consistency, implies the protection of the database against errors caused by the simultaneous update of related data by two or more users. *Internodal integrity* refers to the protection of the system against the potential inconsistency caused by the update of replicated data. Security can easily be controlled in a central location. The handling of security related issues in a distributed DBMS is much more involved. For example, in a distributed DBMS a network is involved which is a medium that has its own security requirements.

Commercial systems normally use either *time-multiplexity* or *data-multiplexity* approaches to improve performance. In time-multiplexity the DBMS accepts only read-only access during regular operating hours while updates are batched. The database is then closed to query activity during off-hours when the batched updates run sequentially. In data-multiplexity two copies of the database are used: one for ad hoc querying (called the query database) and the other for updates by application programs (called the production database). At regular intervals the production database is copied to the query database.

There are several open research problems related to the distributed DBMS design.

1. *Network scaling problem.* Problems remain on the scalability of some protocols and algorithms as systems become geographically distributed or as the number of system components increases.

2. *Distributed query processing.* Problems include correct transformation of the input query to efficient low-level execution and optimal query processing.

3. *Integration with distributed operating systems.* There is a mismatch between the requirements of the DBMS and the functions of current operating systems.

4. *Heterogeneity.* A distributed DBMS is likely to have many different representations for similar data objects. However, an end user desires an integrated presentation of global information.

5. *Concurrency control.* The traditional concept of a transaction as short-lived and atomic is no longer suited to the distributed DBMS environment.

6. *Security.* Problems include unsecured communication links and varying levels of security at different nodes.

The next-generation database systems may need a data model more powerful than the relational model. Two possible candidates are:

- An *object-oriented DBMS* that combines object-oriented programming and database technologies to provide greater modeling power and flexibility to programmers of data-intensive applications.

- A *knowledge-base DBMS* that makes the database management more intelligent by managing knowledge in addition to data objects.

One branch of knowledge base management systems is *data mining* (also called knowledge discovery in databases, or KDD) techniques to recognize patterns in data and predict patterns from the data. The US Department of the Treasury has fielded a data-mining application that sifts through all large cash transactions to detect potential money laundering. This application runs on a six-processor SUN server [20].

A taxonomy based on the solutions according to the way global system integrates the local DBMS is studied in [7] where distributed databases rank first in the order followed by multidatabases, federated databases, and interoperable systems. Several research prototypes and commercial products of distributed DBMS are: ADDS (Amocha Distributed Database Systems) [6], Ingres [51], JDDBS (Japanese Distributed Database Systems) [54], Mermaid [8], Orion [25], and System R [32].

12.5   Heterogeneous Processing

Heterogeneous processing [18] is defined as the tuned use of diverse processing hardware to meet distinct computational needs in which codes or code portions are executed at different PEs to maximize overall performance.

A computation type is referred to as the *execution mode*. Possible execution modes are: scalar, vector, dataflow, systolic, etc. An application has a homogeneous workload if it contains one type of computation (execution mode); otherwise, it has a heterogeneous workload. An application with a heterogeneous workload can be effectively executed in a heterogeneous system that supports more than one execution mode by providing different computation models.

Two popular models of heterogeneous system construction are:

- *Mixed-machine systems.* Different execution modes by interconnecting several different machine models (mixed-machine systems).

- *Mixed-mode systems.* Different execution modes by reconfigurable parallel architecture obtained by interconnecting the same processors.

Mixed-machine systems exhibit spatial heterogeneity while mixed-mode systems exhibit temporal heterogeneity. Ekmecic et al. proposed [16] a classification based on execution modes/machine models:

- Single Execution Mode/Single Machine Model (SESM)

- Single Execution Mode/Multiple Machine Models (SEMM)

- Multiple Execution Modes/Single Machine Model (MESM)

- Multiple Execution Modes/Multiple Machine Models (MEMM)

SESMs are uniprocessor systems and SEMMs are networks of different processors. Both support one type of computation. MESM and MEMM are mixed-machine systems and mixed-mode systems, respectively.

Heterogeneous applications can be divided into three phases:

- *Parallelism detection*
  This phase is responsible for identifying parallelism within each task. It is conceptually the same as in conventional parallel distributed computing.

- *Parallelism characterization*
  This phase estimates computation parameters for each task of an application.

- *Resource allocation*
  This phase determines the place and moment for execution of each task. This phase is similar to scheduling problems with one extra dimension of complexity. Each processor has different computation power in terms of memory capacity and processing speed.

The objective of heterogeneous processing can be expressed as an optimization problem that minimizes

$$\sum t_{i,j}$$

such that

$$\sum c_j \leq C$$

where $t_{i,j}$ equals the time for processor i on code segment j, c_j equals the cost for processor j, and C equals the specified overall cost constraint.

The heterogeneous system also brings some problems, especially the following conversion problems:

- *Data structure conversion.* Since data structures and models are different in a heterogeneous system, it is necessary to convert the data into some common form before the processing can begin.

- *Command conversion.* In a heterogeneous system such as heterogeneous database, the global transaction language for one system is likely to be different from one system to another system. It becomes necessary to provide a translation mechanism between different systems. In addition, each system may have its own model of privacy/integrity that must be converted into a globally recognized form.

Several open problems are:

- Fast communication media and powerful protocols especially for MESM systems.

- Efficient and fast conversion of incompatible data formats between different processors.

- Proper programming environments and system software support.

The heterogeneity has been used in many fields such as programming environments, mapping, and scheduling. Applications of heterogeneous computing include, but are not limited to, image processing [58], climate modeling [41], and multimedia applications [24]. There are still no widely used commercial heterogeneous systems. There are several dedicated systems and/or prototypes used in scientific environments. PASM (Partitionable SIMD/MIMD from Purdue University) [46] and TRAC (Texas Reconfigurable Array Computers) [45] are two representative MESM systems while Nectar (from Carnegie Mellon University) [2] and PVM (Parallel Virtual Machine) [53] are two sample MEMM systems.

12.6   Future Directions of Distributed Systems

Distributed system design began in the 1970s with a few simple experimental systems. Since then great progress has been made in this field. For example, a study in [21] estimated that 28.8 million people in the U.S. who are 16 years and older have access to the Internet, 16.4 million use the Internet, 11.5 million use the Web, and 15.1 million have used the Web to purchase items. Today the Internet reaches millions of people in almost a hundred countries on all continents of the world. Real applications already run on both centralized and network systems. The move to another platform as provided by a distributed system is inevitable and should be legitimized. The advantages of distributed systems have been put forward for this purpose [23]. These include location transparency of resources, scalability and customization of system platforms, fault tolerance and sharing of resources and suitability for distributed applications.

Recently *virtual distributed partnerships* have been established in the U.S. For example, NSF's Partnerships for Advance Computational Infrastructure (PACI) [49] has a detailed plan for creating a National Technology Grid to provide desktop access to various computational science and engineering problem solving environments. The PACI program currently supports two centers at University of Illinois at Urbana-Champaign and University of California in San Diego.

Researchers and system builders still face several open design issues. The first issue is to predict the behavior of a distributed system. This requirement is especially important for real-time constraints. Consider the problem of predicting a distributed system behavior while it is executing. Such a system will be made up of a large number of components, operating asynchronously from one another. Moreover, few distributed systems operate in steady state: Load fluctuations are common as new tasks arrive and active tasks terminate. These aspects make it nearly impossible to make accurate detailed statements.

The second issue is the scaling and administration of a distributed system. A system is said to be scalable if it can handle the addition of users and resources without suffering a noticeable loss of performance or increase in administrative complexity. Scaling affects the following design issues [36]: naming, authentication, authorization, accounting, communicating, the use of remote resources, and the users' ability to easily interact with the system. Each component of the scale introduces its own problems. Although some suggestions have been provided [29] to design scalable systems, more insight is needed.

The third issue is the security and authentication in a distributed system. As the size of a distributed system grows, such as the Internet, security becomes increasingly important and increasingly difficult to implement. The bigger the system the more vulnerable it is to attack. Authentication is the system verification of a user's identity. Typically techniques are password-based, host-based, or encryption-based. Many systems leave authorization to the individual server. Few systems provide accounting in a distributed manner.

The fourth issue is the tools and environment support for a distributed system. This includes tools for specifying, analyzing, transforming, debugging, creating, and verifying distributed software. Advances in theory, practical tools, methods, and languages are essential to build an efficient and user-friendly distributed system.

Finally, an integration of various techniques to design a distributed system with significantly improved fault tolerance, resource sharing, and performance is required. Such a system provides a seamless access from users at different geographical locations and functions as a single, coherent, virtual machine allowing user access to network-wide resources.

References

[1] Andrews, G. R. et al., "The design of the Saguaro distributed operating system", *IEEE Transactions on Software Engineering*, **13**, 1, Jan. 1987, 104-118.

[2] Arnould, E. A. et al., "The design of Nectar: A network backplane for heterogeneous multicomputers", *Proc. of ASPLOS III*, 1989, 205-216.

[3] Austin, P., K. Murray, and A. Wellings, "The design of an operating system for a scalable parallel computing engine", *Software: Practice and Experience*, **21**, 10, Oct. 1991, 989-1013.

[4] Bershad, B. N., M. J. Zerkanskas, and W. A. Sawdon, "The Midway distributed shared memory system", *Proc. of IEEE COMPCON Conf.*, 1993, 528-537.

[5] Bever, M. et al., "Distributed systems, OSF DCE, and beyond", in *DCE - the OSF Distributed Computing Environment*, A. Schill, ed., Springer-Verlag, 1993, 1-20.

[6] Breitart, Y. and L. Tieman, "ADDS: heterogeneous distributed database system", in *Distributed Data Sharing Systems*, E. A. Schreiber and W. Litwin, ed., Amsterdam: North-Holland, 1985, 7-24.

[7] Bright, M. W., A. R. Hurson, and S. H. Pakzad, "A taxonomy and current issues in multidatabase systems", *IEEE Computers*, Mar. 1992, 50-60.

[8] Brill, D., M. Templeton, and C. Yu, "Distributed query processing strategies in Mermaid: A frontend to data management systems", *Proceedings of the IEEE*, 1984, 211-218.

[9] Brown, L. and J. Wu, "Snooping fault-tolerant distributed shared memories", *Proc. of the 14th Int'l Conf. on Distributed Computing Systems*, 1994, 218-226.

[10] Brownbridge, D. R., L. F., Marshall, and B. Randell, "The Newcastle connection or Unixes of the world unite!", *Software: Practice and Experience*, **12**, 12, Dec. 1982, 1147-1162.

[11] Carriero, N. and D. Gelernter, "Linda in context", *Communications of the ACM*, **32**, April 1989, 444-458.

[12] Carriero, N. and D. Gelernter, *How to Write Parallel Programs: A First Course*, MIT Press, 1990.

[13] Carter, J. B., J. K. Bennett, and W. Zwaenepoel, "Implementation and performance of Munin", *Proc. of the 13th Symp. on Operating Systems Principles*, 1991, 152-164.

[14] Cheriton, D. R., "The V distributed system", *Communications of the ACM*, **31**, 3, 1988, 314-333.

[15] Dasgupta, P. et al., "The design and implementation of the Clouds distributed operating system", *USENIX Computing Systems Journal*, **3**, 1, 1990.

[16] Ekmecic, I., T. Tartalja, and V. Milutinovic, "EM^3: A contribution to taxonomy of heterogeneous computing systems", *IEEE Computers*, **28**, Dec. 1995, 68-70.

[17] Fleisch, B. D. and G. J. Popek, "Mirage: A coherent distributed shared memory design", *Proc. of the 12th ACM Symp. on Operating Systems Principles*, 1989, 211-223.

[18] Freund, R. F. and H. J. Siegel, "Heterogeneous processing", *IEEE Computers*, June 1993, 13-17.

[19] Gien, M., "Microkernel architecture: Key to modern operating system design", *Unix Review*, **8**, 11, Nov. 1990, 10.

[20] Hedberg, S. R., "Parallelism speeds data mining", *IEEE Parallel and Distributed Technology*, Winter 1995, 3-6.

[21] Hoffman, D. L., W. D. Kalsbeek, and T. P. Novak, "Internet and Web Use in the U.S.", *Communications of the ACM*, **39**, 12, 1997, 36-46.

[22] Howard, J. H., M. L. Kazar, S. G. Menees, D. A. Nichols, M. Satyanarayanan, and R. N. Sidebotham, "Scale and performance in a distributed file system", *ACM Transactions on Computer Systems*, **6**, 1, Feb. 1985, 55-81.

[23] Johansen, D., and R. van Renesse, "Distributed systems in prospective", in *Distributed Open Systems*, F. M. T. Brazier and D. Johansen, ed., IEEE Computer Society Press, 1994, 175-179.

[24] Khokhar, A. A. and A. Ghafoor, "A heterogeneous processing (HP) framework for multimedia query processing", *Proc. of the Workshop on Heterogeneous Computing*, 1994, 51-57.

[25] Kim, W. et al., "Architecture of the Orion next-generation database system", *IEEE Transactions on Knowledge and Data Engineering*, **2**, 1, Jan. 1990, 109-124.

[26] Kranz, D., "Integrating message passing and shared memory: Early experiences", *Proc. of the 15th Symp. on Principles and Practice of Parallel Programming*, 1993, 54-63.

[27] Li, K., *Shared Virtual Memory on Loosely Coupled Multiprocessors*, Ph.D. dissertation, Yale University, Department of Computer Science, Sept. 1986.

[28] Li, K. and P. Hudak, "Memory coherence in shared virtual memory systems", *ACM Transactions on Computer Systems*, **7**, 4, Nov. 1989, 321-359.

[29] Lampson, B. W., "Hints for computer system design", *Proc. of the 9th ACM Symp. on Operating Systems Principles*, 1983, 51-81.

[30] Lenoski, D. et al., "The directory-based cache coherence protocol for the dash multiprocessor", *Proc. of the 17th Int'l Symp. Computer Architecture*, 1990, 148-159.

[31] Levy, E. and A. Silberschatz, "Distributed file systems: Concepts and examples", *ACM Computing Surveys*, **22**, 4, Dec. 1990, 322-374.

[32] Lindsay, B. G., "A retrospective of R*: A distributed database management system", *Proceedings of the IEEE*, **75**, 5, May 1987, 668-673.

[33] Satyanarayanan, M., "Distributed file systems", in *Distributed Systems*, S. Mullender, ed., Addison-Wesley Publishing Company, 1989, 149-188.

[34] Mullender, S. J. et al., "Amoeba: A distributed operating system for the 1990s", *IEEE Computers*, May 1990, 44-53.

[35] Nelson, M., B. Welch, and J. K. Ousterhout, "Caching in the Sprite network file system", *ACM Transactions on Computer Systems*, **6**, 1, Feb. 1988, 134-154.

[36] Newman, B. C., "Scale in distributed systems", in *Readings in Distributed Computing Systems*, T. L. Casavant and M. Singhal, eds., IEEE Computer Society Press, 1994, 463-489.

[37] Nitzberg, B. and V. Lo, "Distributed shared memory: A survey of issues and algorithms", *IEEE Computers*, August 1991, 52-60.

[38] Özsu, M. T. and P. Valduriez, "Distributed Data Management: Unsloved Problems and New Issues", in *Readings in Distributed Computing Systems*, T. L. Casavant and M. Singhal, eds., IEEE Computer Society Press, 1994, 512-544.

[39] Popek, G. and B. Walker, *The LOCUS Distributed System Architecture.*, MIT Press, 1985.

[40] Rashid, R. F., "From RIG to accent to Mach: The evolution of a network operating system", *Proc. of Fall Joint Computer Conf., AFIPS*, 1986, 1128-1133.

[41] Rinaldo, F. J. and M. R. Fausey, "Event reconstruction in high energy physics", *IEEE Computers*, **26**, 6, June 1993, 68-77.

[42] Rozier, M. et al., "Chorus distributed operating systems", *ACM Computing Surveys*, **1**, Oct. 1988, 305-379.

[43] Sandberg, R., D. Goldberg, S. Kleinman, D. Walsh, and B. Lyone, "Design and implementation of the Sun network file system", *Proc. of USENIX 1985 Summer Conf.*, June 1985, 119-130.

[44] Satyanarayanan, M. et al., "Coda: A highly available file system for a distributed workstation environment", *IEEE Transactions on Computers*, **39**, 4, Apr. 1990, 447-459.

[45] Sejnowski, M. C. et al., "An overview of the Texas reconfigurable array computer", *Proc. of 1980 AFIPS National Computing Conf.*, 1980, 631-641.

[46] Siegel, H. J. et al., "An overview of the PASM parallel processing system", *Computer Architecture, Tutorial*, D. D. Gajski et al., eds., IEEE Computer Press, May 1986, 387-407.

[47] Sinha, P. et al., "The Galaxy distributed operating system", *IEEE Computer*, Aug. 1991, 34-41.

[48] Sinha, P. K., *Distributed Operating Systems: Concepts and Design*, IEEE Computer Society Press, 1997.

[49] Smar, L., "Toward the 21st Century", *Communications of the ACM*, **40**, 11, Nov. 1997, 29-32.

[50] Stankovic, J. A. and K. Ramamritham, "What is predictability for real-time systems – An editorial", *Real-Time System Journal*, **2**, Dec. 1990, 247-254.

[51] Stonebraker, M. et al., "Performance enhancements to a relational database system", *ACM Transactions Database Systems*, **8**, 2, June 1983, 167-185.

[52] Stumm, M. and S. Zhou, "Algorithm implementing distributed shared memory", *IEEE Computer*, May 1990, 54-64.

[53] Sunderam, V. S., "PVM: A framework for parallel distributed computing", *Concurrency: Practice and Experience*, **2**, 4, Dec. 1990, 315-339.

[54] Takizawa, M., "Heterogeneous distributed database system: JD-DBS", *Data Engineering*, **6**, 1, 1983, 58-62.

[55] Tanenbaum, A. S. and R. van Renesse, "Distributed operating systems", *ACM Computing Surveys*, **17**, 4, Dec. 1985, 419-470.

[56] Tanenbaum, A. S., *Distributed Operating Systems*, Prentice Hall, Inc., 1995.

[57] Walker, B., G. J. Popek, R. English, C. Kline, and G. Theil, " The LOCUS distributed operating system", *Proc. of the 9th Symp. on Operating Systems Principles*, 1983, 49-70.

[58] Weems, C. C., "Image understanding: A driving application for research in heterogeneous parallel processing", *Proc. of the Workshop on Heterogeneous Computing*, 1993, 119-126.

[59] Wu, K. -L. and W. K. Fuchs, "Recoverable distributed shared virtual reality memory", *IEEE Transactions on Computers*, **39**, 4, Apr. 1990, 460-469.

[60] Zhou, S., M. Stumm, K. Li, and D. Wortman, "Heterogeneous distributed shared memory", *IEEE Transactions on Parallel Distributed Systems*, **3**, 5, Sept. 1992, 540-554.

Problems

1. Differentiate the following types of operating systems:

   - time sharing
   - network

- distributed

Point out the type of transparency each system can offer.

2. What are the major differences between the microkernel-based system and the conventional monolithic system? What are the potential advantages of a microkernel-based system?

3. Discuss the advantages and disadvantages of three file-sharing semantics: Unix semantics, session semantics, and transaction semantics.

4. Discuss the advantages and disadvantages of three cache location policies: main memory of the client, disk of the client, and main memory at the server.

5. Discuss the pros and cons of using large page size and small page size in a page-based DSM system such as Ivy.

6. Discuss the relative advantages and disadvantages of the four algorithms based on Stumm and Zhou's classification: central-server algorithm, migration algorithm, real-replication algorithm, and full replication algorithm.

7. Explain the difference between security and integrity. Give two cases of security violation and one example of integrity violation.

8. What are the major differences between a distributed DBMS and a distributed file system? A distributed DBMS cannot scale as well as a distributed file system. Why?

9. In heterogeneous processing, what are the major differences between the mixed-machine system and the mixed-mode system? Propose a set of rules to determine a particular model for a given application.

Appendix

A list of common symbols in DCDL

□	Alternate
*	Repetition
‖	Parallel
→	Condition
;	Sequence
send	Output
:=	Assignment
receive	Input
::	Definition
[	Begin
]	End
∀	For all (universal quantifier)
∃	There exist (existential quantifier)
=	Equal
≠	Unequal
∨	OR
∧	AND
¬	NOT

Index

Ada, 45, 56
ANSI, 33
applet, 20
application
  bulk mode, 20
  burst mode, 20
ATM, 3
atomic action, 264
atomic instruction
  Compare-and-Swap, 103
  Fetch-and-Add, 103
  Test-and-Set, 103

batch processing, 1
Bernstein's conditions, 43
bidding, 123
BSP, 45

C, 33
  C++, 33
  HPC++, 33
  MPC++, 33
cache, 271, 430
  invalidate, 271, 437
  snoopy, 437
  write-back, 271
  write-through, 271, 431
  write-update, 271
causal relation

causal path, 86
  zigzag path, 85
causally related, 77
CDC, 54
checkpoint, 86
  interval, 86
clock, 68
  implementation
    matrix, 89
    scalar, 87
    vector, 89
  logical, 68, 87
  physical, 68, 92
CLU, 56
command
  alternative, 40
  fork, 37
  guarded, 35
  join, 37
  parallel, 35
  parbegin/parend, 38
  repetitive, 40, 48
  sequential, 35
communication, 31, 173, 176
  all-to-all, 176
  broadcast, 173, 190
    atomic, 288
    binomial tree, 194, 238
    causal, 288